Parental Control of Television Broadcasting

LEA's Communication Series

Jennings Bryant/Dolf Zillmann, General Editors

Selected titles include:

Price • The V-Chip Debate: Content Filtering from Television to the Internet

Livingstone/Bovill • Children and Their Changing Media Environment: A European Comparative Study

Harris • A Cognitive Psychology of Mass Communication, Third Edition

Bryant/Bryant • Television and the American Family, Second Edition

For a complete list of titles in LEA's Communication Series, please contact Lawrence Erlbaum Associates, Publishers.

PARENTAL CONTROL OF TELEVISION BROADCASTING

Edited by

Monroe E. Price
Cardozo School of Law, Yeshiva University

Stefaan G. Verhulst
Oxford University

LAWRENCE ERLBAUM ASSOCIATES, PUBLISHERS

2002   Mahwah, New Jersey   London

The final camera-ready copy for this volume was prepared by the editors

Lawrence Erlbaum Associates, Inc., Publishers
10 Industrial Avenue
Mahwah, NJ 07430

Cover design by Kathryn Houghtaling Lacey

Library of Congress Cataloging-In-Publication Data

Parental control of television broadcasting / edited by Monroe E. Price, Stefaan G. Verhulst.
p.   cm. — (LEA's communication series)
Includes bibliographical references and index.
ISBN: 0-8058-2978-4 (cloth: alk. paper)—0-8058-3902-X (pbk.: alk. paper)
1. Television and family. 2. Television and children. 3. Television programs–Rating.
4. Television–Censorship. I. Price, Monroe Edwin, 1938– II. Verhulst, Stefaan (Stefaan G.)

Books published by Lawrence Erlbaum Associates are printed on acid-free paper, and their bindings are chosen for strength and durability.

Printed in the United States of America
10 9 8 7 6 5 4 3 2 1

Contents

Preface and Acknowledgments   vii

Introduction and Summary Finding   xi
    General Conclusions   xiii
    Problems With the V-chip Model   xiv
    Looking to a Digital Future   xvi
    Positive Approaches to Parental Choice   xvii
    Recommendations for the Transition   xviii
    Encouraging Pluralism in Approaches
       to Enhancing Parental Choice   xx
    Placing a Premium on Programme Information   xxi
    Broadcaster Responsibility and Regulatory Monitoring   xxiii
    Media Education and Literacy Campaigns   xxiv

1   Technical Devices and Rating Systems   1
    Background   1
    Factors in the European Environment Affecting Choice
       of Technical Device   4
    Technical Devices in the Analogue Setting
       and Standard Rating Schemes   8
    Shifting the Paradigm: Technical Devices and Plural Ratings   13
    Technical Devices in the Digital Setting   25
    Technical Devices, Ratings, and Watersheds   35
    The Costs of a Negative Approach and the Benefits
       of a Positive Approach to Child Protection   38

2   Rating Systems: Comparative Country Analysis
    and Recommendations   43
        General Framework and Conclusions   44
        Typology of Rating Systems   45
        Comparative Country and Media Analysis   57
        Conclusions   91

3   Family Viewing Alternatives: Economic Justifications
    Social Efficiency and Educational Support   107
        Economic Efficiency and Regulatory Interventions   108
        Social Efficiency   110
        Media Education and Literacy   119

Annex 1: Comparative Analysis of Rating Systems   133
        Cinema Rating Systems   133
        Video Rating Systems   167
        TV Rating Systems   182
        Internet Rating Systems   218
        Horizontal Treatment of Media   236

Annex 2: Methodology   239
        Template: Parental Control of Film, Broadcasting,
            Audiovisual, and Online Services
            in the European Union   239
        Country Reports: List of Experts   253
        Questionnaire for Broadcasters   257
        Contact List   264

References   283
        General   283
        Media and Children: Theories   286
        Websites   288
        International Instruments   289
        European Union (Chronological Order)   290
        Council of Europe (Chronological Order)   291
        National References   292
        Glossary of Acronyms   304

Author Index   307
Subject Index   309

Preface and Acknowledgments

BACKGROUND

The protection of minors from harmful content is a matter of strong public interest. Children, and not only the very young, are more vulnerable to influence than adults and, in the modern world, do not always have the guidance of their parents. Traditionally, to deal with this and related questions, societies relied on a practice of public responsibility by licensed broadcasters, or, in some contexts, a public service monopoly, especially in television. Broadcasting regulation supported parental supervision through the establishment of guidelines governing the portrayal of harmful content, the development of a specific programme schedule or watershed policy, and the classification and consequent announcement (acoustic or visual) of programmes.

At the European level, these principles are enshrined in Article 22 of the *Television Without Frontiers Directive*, as amended in 1997. These approaches, originally established for terrestrially based mass audience channels, became much more difficult to maintain as the sources of television programming multiplied and new technologies made the prospect of regulation far more unmanageable. New mechanisms and paradigms appropriate for a multichannel and digital environment need to be considered.

Worldwide, in the late 1990s, there was a search for alternatives, often for technical devices that would empower parents to make decisions more easily about television within their households. A shift from the state to the home of the instruments of control and responsibility was considered possible. In Canada, the United States, and elsewhere, the device known as the V-chip was adopted as a technique of choice. The question was whether European law should adopt a similar approach. To determine policy in the European Union, in 1997, the European Parliament enacted Article 22b.2 of the amended *Television Without Frontiers Directive* to carry out an investigation of the possible advantages and drawbacks of further and new measures for facilitating parental or guardian control over the programmes that minors might watch. According to the *Directive*, this survey was to consider, *inter alia*, the desirability of requiring new televisions to be equipped with a technical device enabling parents or guardians to filter out certain programmes, establishing appropriate rating systems, and encouraging family viewing policies and other educational and awareness measures. At the same time, the study would take into account experience gained in this field in Europe and elsewhere and the views of interested parties such as broadcasters, producers, educationalists, media specialists, and relevant associations.

The European Commission asked the Programme in Comparative Media Law and Policy (PCMLP) at the University of Oxford to conduct the study. The final text, conclusions, recommendations, and background materials are found in this book. The results were adopted by the European Commission on 19 July 1999 in its consequent *Communication on the Study on Parental Control of Television Broadcasting to the Council, European Parliament, and Economic and Social Committee* (COM/99/371 FINAL). The staff of the Programme looked across media, national boundaries, and technologies to consider possible directions for public policy. The study sought to differentiate between those technical devices that were designed, first, for analogue broadcasting and those that were more suitable in a digital age. It looked at approaches that required government or universal rating and labeling systems and those that appeared to allow greater diversity in ratings approaches. It examined modes that might lead to greater or less harmonization across national boundaries.

The Commission's *Communication* indicated that the study would be an important component in the evaluation of the application of the amended *Television Without Frontiers Directive*. The study came to serve another function. The Commission, preparing for a digital world, used the findings of the study in its discussions with the Digital Video Broadcasting Group (DVB), a global consortium with a membership of over 220 broadcasters, manufacturers, network operators, and regulatory bodies in more than 30 countries worldwide now. This gave the study a global impact. The discussions with the DVB focused on the technical and commercial feasibility of implementing the concepts contained in the study, notably the operational requirements of technical devices to facilitate parent or guardian control over the programmes that minors watch.

Finally, the study formed the basis of discussions between the Commission and relevant bodies (boards of film classification, broadcasters, Internet operators, the video industry, Member States, viewers, and users) with the purpose of promoting the development of descriptive rating systems adapted to the digital environment in Europe.

In these ways, the study was used to identify how and to what extent educational and awareness measures should be taken for future television viewing. We are delighted that the efforts of the Programme's staff can now reach a larger audience through publication of the study. The global debates on the relationship of broadcasting to values, on the role of the state against the role of the household, and on the impact of new technologies on culture, practice, and identity all require the best possible grounding in review and analysis of ongoing practices.

STRUCTURE AND METHODOLOGY

Article 22 of the *Directive* determined the structure of the study and formed its the terms of reference. These included:

- An analysis of the technical devices available to assist in parental control of television broadcasting services. As a result, the study describes different devices, their cost, availability, and the infrastructure needed to introduce them.
- A corresponding analysis of potential ratings or labeling systems to work in conjunction with or in the place of technical devices. The study provides a comparative analysis of rating systems used in film, video, and online services.
- An overview and assessment of the educational and awareness measures in the field of protection of minors and harmful content. The study provides a review of available considerations in this field of viewer literacy.

In addition to these three main strands of analysis, discussed in the executive summary, the study provides for background information and analysis in the following areas:

- An overview of the main media theories focusing on the effect and impact of specific types of content on children and their behaviour;
- An assessment of the economic impact and social efficacy of different protective measures;
- A comparison of the regulatory contexts and rating systems for film, video, television, and online services concerning the protection of minors from harmful content. This comparison comports with the so-called 'horizontal treatment' of the protection issue, contributing to the establishment of shared definitions and applications for classification systems for programmes and content in each of the four media sectors concerned.

Several methods were used. First, the conceptual framework of the study was based on research linking the creation, implementation, and perception of parental control mechanism with larger theoretical constructs about the use of all the relevant (electronic) media by children, as well as with market tendencies and international policy and legal issues. It was crucial to illuminate this wider context in order to evaluate a variety of parental control mechanisms. Review of the existing academic and market research literature and statistical data, interviews with the main scholars and actors involved, legal analysis, and economic modeling underpins the current structure. The Programme commissioned country reports in all European Member States to assess the regulatory frameworks, technological capabilities, cultural contexts, and relevant policy concerns. A template (see annex 2) was developed and used by all country experts seeking information in a standard and thus comparable form. A mail survey was used in order to map the views and opinions of different stakeholders. A questionnaire was sent to a selective sample of (500) broadcasters, Internet service providers, content providers, interest groups (including educationalists), and associations (domestic and European) in all European Member States so that the experience gained could be taken into account.

The study as presented here is essentially as it was submitted to the Commission. An additional annex providing background theories and research, not reproduced here, is available directly from the Programme. The study was prepared and written by the Programme's able staff under the direction of Joseph Perkovich, then director of research at the Programme. A cross-disciplinary and multi-national group assisted Mr. Perkovich. These included a core team of researchers including Frederic Pinard, Claire Roberts, and Sylvia Geissbauer. In addition to coordination responsibilities, Mr. Perkovich had substantial responsibility for chapter 1. Mr. Pinard was responsible for the comparative analysis and chapter 2 and Ms. Roberts was responsible for the study of media effects. Statistical support and coordination of the country reports could not have taken place without Ms. Geissbauer. The economic analysis was based on the contributions of Professor Pietro Vagliasindi's work. Many others provided advice and support. The co-directors played a conceptual, editorial, and supervisory role.

An army of country experts formed the backbone of the comparative analysis (the studies of France and the United Kingdom were conducted at the Programme by Frederic Pinard and Stefaan Verhulst). They included: Dr. Albrecht Haller (Austria), Mr. Serge Robillard (Belgium and Luxembourg), Dr. Brigitte Tufte and Dr. Thomas Tufte (Denmark), Dr. Ann Mustonen (Finland), Dr. Runar Woldt and Ms. Emmanuelle Machet (Germany), Dr. Petros Isoifides (Greece), Dr. Marie McGonagle (Ireland), Ms. Cristina Cabella (Italy), Prof. Jo Groebel (Netherlands), Dr. Helena Sousa and Dr. Manuel Pinto (Portugal), Dr. Alberto Perez Gomez (Spain), and Dr. Jonas Wall (Sweden). We would also like to thank David Hughes of the European Commission for his helpful direction and advice as well those experts who took part in the seminar on the interim results of the study that took place in Oxford. Finally, Nancy Beatty Edlin and Bethany Davis Noll at the Programme and Linda Bathgate and Eileen Engel at Lawrence Erlbaum Associates helped see that the study reached a larger audience.

—Monroe E. Price and Stefaan G. Verhulst
   Co-Directors, Programme in Comparative Media Law and Policy

Introduction and Summary Findings

The Directorate General X of the European Commission has requested a study of the techniques and technologies available to facilitate parental choice, addressing specifically the television environment. This is prompted by the interest, at European level, in parental choice devices of the kind that have been adopted elsewhere in the world, especially the United States and Canada. This study only encompasses choice mechanisms to protect children from harmful content; it does not consider approaches to illegal content. As several European Union documents have outlined, it is necessary to differentiate between these categories of content.[1] They represent different issues of principle, and call for very different legal and technological responses. Furthermore, as the study also shows, what is considered harmful depends on cultural differences and can be distinct according to different age groups. All this has to be taken into account in defining appropriate approaches to protect children against undesired material whilst ensuring freedom of expression.

A significant public interest lies in protecting children from viewing excessive television violence and other programming that may produce harmful effects. Children are presumed, quite justifiably, to be different from adults, to be more vulnerable, less able to apply critical judgemental standards, and more at risk.[2] Ordinarily, society depends on parental supervision to protect children, but

---

[1] Compare the European Commission, Illegal and harmful content on the Internet, 16 October 1996, with the Green Paper on the protection of minors and human dignity, 1996.

[2] The study reviews the existing research on children and media in the accompanying annex. It reveals two main schools of thought. The first contends that media violence has a direct and harmful influence on children. The second argues that this influence is subject to the context in which violent content is depicted. Underlying both positions is an understanding that environmental factors are an important element in the degree to which children are influenced by violence.

there are elements of the current system that have limited the scope of such supervision. The era in which the family as a single unit watches programming together is ending, and this process will be accentuated in a multichannel, multi-set digital era. This decline has occurred as the vast outpouring of transnational channels has made it more difficult for regulatory authorities to monitor the way companies comply with programming standards based on cultural sensitivities. New forms of technology have also increasingly upset established patterns of parental choice.

In this context, new ways of enhancing parental choice and of governing, based on a partnership between industry, social groups, and government, to accomplish that goal are necessary. Europe-wide action that is cost-effective, administratively viable, capable of general adoption, and empowers parents is imperative. This study ranks and recommends approaches that can be taken at the European level to fulfill these needs.

The very definition of enhanced parental choice is complicated. Partly, it is a matter of ensuring that parents or guardians have adequate information, in a manner efficient to obtain and use, to exercise the authority that is vested in them. However, the key element for most policy discussions is how to empower parents when they cannot be with their children. The goal, for the purposes of this study, is to increase the power and capacity of a parent (or guardian) to control what is on the television set when the parent is not present or able to monitor the content consumed. That is why the international community emphasizes blocking technologies or other techniques to make proxy decisions on programming.

Fears exist that these blocking technologies would become 'upstream censoring' techniques, violating freedom of expression rights as safeguarded in the relevant International Treaties and constitutions of the Member States. Nonetheless, in the specific case of parental choice it must be noted that this argument is not so relevant; the decision to not receive the information is decided directly by the potential end user and not by an intermediary. This is not to say, however, that blocking regimes may not adversely affect the likelihood of financing for some programming based on concerns that some types of content are more susceptible to being blocked from potential audiences.

Others argue that the right of children to receive information may be curtailed by the introduction of these mechanisms. It is therefore clear that, as with all other public policy decisions in the field of communications, a balance has to be found between rights and responsibilities of the media industry, as well as between the empowerment of parents to protect their children and the protection of children as individuals with the right to receive information and entertainment.

Finally, the contributions of existing measures, such as watersheds, icons, and acoustical warnings, to the project of enhancing parental choice must be examined. Technical devices too may have drawbacks, which require the continuation of social safety net measures that protect children in those instances where parents cannot or will not exercise sufficient responsibility to protect their children. As a number of commentaries have noted, broadcaster responsibility cannot be abandoned because of the possibility, in a relatively weak and inconclusive form, of mechanisms that improve the capacity for parental supervision.

GENERAL CONCLUSIONS

1. In the current analogue system, the United States and Canadian approach is not technically feasible for Europe. Moreover, analogue technologies available in Europe are cumbersome, unlikely to become fully operational in all regions within a reasonable period, subject to circumvention, and likely to be rendered obsolete by emerging technologies.

2. At present, technical measures alone cannot achieve compliance with Article 22 of the *Television Without Frontiers Directive*, which calls for measures that 'ensure that minors in the area of transmission would not normally hear or see broadcasts' that would be 'likely to impair their physical, mental, or moral development'.

3. Rather than focus on the V-chip, as it is being implemented in the United States and Canada, regulatory approaches in Europe should be directed at the opportunities and challenges of the digital environment. Digital technology allows for the operation of technical devices that offer a much higher level of protection.

4. Nonetheless, during a transition period, there are specific efforts in the current, predominantly analogue setting that may be advanced to provide useful, albeit imperfect, technical devices. The use of electronic programme guides (EPGs) and the proliferation of an open technical standard for receiving analogue EPG signals by new analogue sets and set-top boxes should be strongly encouraged.

5. Our recommendations for parental choice schemes in a digital age favour a model in which: a monopoly rating source is less dominant, pluralism in rating agencies and techniques is fostered, and *parental selection* of desirable programme content criteria mobilises available analogue and digital technologies.

6. Descriptive ratings, as a rule, should be preferred over evaluative ratings.[3] Descriptive ratings delegate to parents, guardians, and minors a greater ability to assess programmes for themselves. Descriptive ratings are also better equipped to overcome cultural differences.

---

[3] 'Descriptive ratings' refers to a set of indicators that permit viewers to make their own assessment of the suitability of the work while 'evaluative ratings' refers to a judgement released by an intermediate entity, classically based on an age level suitability hierarchy.

7. No foreseeable rating or labelling system is a total substitute for broadcaster responsibility. Broadcaster responsibility standards must be sustained at present levels.

8. Consistent with both transitional and long-range approaches, more emphasis must be placed on media literacy education and critical approaches to television viewing by parents and children alike.

PROBLEMS WITH THE V-CHIP MODEL

Our study of the United States and Canadian approach demonstrates major technological differences between analogue broadcasting transmission in Europe and in North America. These differences make adaptation of the specific V-chip technology adopted there all but impossible in Europe.[4]

Technical devices that empower parents have two primary qualities: they depend on a stream of information about given programmes, which accompanies it to the receiver, and on the ability of the parent to control in advance which programmes are to be blocked or watched.

The North American scheme depends on the availability of line 21, field 2 of the Vertical Blanking Interval (VBI), a space that has long been reserved there for closed captioning and is thus available for the transmission of programme-related labelling information. No Member State has a similar requirement and, in fact, the Vertical Blanking Interval capacity to transmit such data is not available in any Member State.

While use of the Teletext band and the possibilities provided by set-top box gateways may provide workable European alternatives to the North American approach, the majority of alternative technological methods for use in the European analogue environment have substantial design flaws and may require years to introduce them widely. These limitations preclude a decreased reliance on other techniques such as content regulation and watersheds.

Furthermore, the United States approach and its Canadian counterpart presuppose a dominant labelling scheme, with relatively uniform icons, so as to simplify the process for the parent. While there is much to be said for this uniform scheme, it is inconsistent with the varied practices of Member States and reduces the opportunity for cultural differences and for pluralistic approaches to the way in which media are used in the shaping of society.

One of the problems of the V-chip design is that it is not impregnable to tampering. A United Kingdom Joint Working Party concluded, 'in order to make the blocking kit comprehensible to adults, researchers have repeatedly produced sys-

---

[4] In chapter 2, however, the study identifies a number of technical devices with some promise in an analogue system.

tems that children can understand and outwit within a very short time'. Another technical difficulty is the dependence on an uncertain software package in which problems will be solved; but solutions will probably yield additional problems. As the Working Party pointed out, 'at one point in the Canadian trials, the V-chip blocked out national hockey games and left some inappropriate films unscrambled' (Violence and the Viewer 1998: 25).

Industry and government are actively encouraging the introduction of digital terrestrial, satellite, and cable television (High Level Group on Audiovisual Policy 1998). The pace of this development will render a focus on analogue technology not entirely practical. Even in the United States and Canada, which is more suited to the technology, digital broadcasting will take many years to become standard. American research has shown that while nearly two thirds of parents say they would use the V-chip to block inappropriate programmes, the take up of new television sets containing the device is much lower. In Europe, households replace their television sets on an average of once every 10 years and older sets are typically transferred to other rooms or passed down to children for use in their bedrooms. As the above-mentioned study in the United Kingdom put it:

> More than 60 percent of 10- to 16-year-olds now have televisions in their bedrooms. Children whose viewing is unsupervised, or whose families cannot afford the latest technology, will be put at risk if, with the excuse of the V-chip behind them, broadcasters are encouraged to relax the standards on which we currently rely. The V-chip would therefore be an inadequate 'quick-fix' solution that would not protect the most vulnerable viewers. (Violence and the Viewer 1998: 25)

However, the same rationale applies for the introduction of digital television sets. As a result the study recommends no relaxation of broadcaster accountability and standards within an analogue setting.

If the transition from black and white television to colour sets is any indication, the analogue legacy may last a generation. This legacy thus requires the facilitation of analogue-compatible technical and rating systems in Europe during the digital transition. While the limitations of VBI-based devices particularly and video band devices generally render V-chip type systems ill advised in the European technical context, Teletext-based devices may provide a workable modality for analogue televisions. The use of analogue televisions will continue for many years as legacy sets remain in households and new analogue models introduce technologies such as NexTView EPGs to European homes.

Further, the pervasiveness of set-top boxes as a necessary intermediary for signal reception may enable the use of analogue devices during the transition period to digital. Satellite, cable, and subscription services have used set-top boxes for years, and the highly successful EPGs, both in North America and

Europe, have used these interfaces to store parallel databases of programming related information. The market penetration of these set-top interfaces is not likely to abate, thereby providing a strong opportunity for deploying effective blocking and filtering technologies within this modality. The primary shortcoming of this strategy lies in the fact that set-top boxes, by and large, are proprietary systems that receive nonstandardised signals. Thus, to effectively deploy, via set-top boxes and new analogue sets, analogue-based technical and rating systems at the European level the standardisation of signals dedicated to programming related information is essential.

The V-chip experiences provide valuable lessons. North American labelling schemes are the product of a system of self-regulation, but the nature of the specific self-regulatory approaches, particularly in the United States, could lead to outcomes inconsistent with European objectives. In Canada, the V-chip system evolved from a multiyear process involving the regulatory body and a consortium of organisations. In the United States, the process was coordinated, if not dominated, by the Motion Picture Association of America. Greater cynicism and lower performance may have resulted from the United States approach, however, it cannot yet be concluded whether or not the differences in processes led to meaningfully different outcomes. Furthermore, factors such as differences in media literacy support make drawing a conclusion difficult.

The technical inapplicability and the institutional shortcomings of the North American system, coupled with the increasing move to digital broadcasting, cause us to reject the V-chip as a meaningful option for Europe. However, elements of the North American experience, including the further development of labelling systems and coordinated icons, provide useful models. These analogue models can be improved for the European context and integrated into the improved technical and programming information capacities to be found in the digital future.

LOOKING TO A DIGITAL FUTURE

Given the current focus in Europe (and elsewhere) on the introduction of digital television, the study recommends that the Commission and the Parliament encourage parental choice mechanisms for the digital age. Digital television, however delivered, offers greater flexibility in the design of parental empowering techniques. In this context, more room for third party or multiple rating systems is possible. In the context of an enormous increase in volume of material produced, having government (or major industry) representatives define what should be the subject of ratings or labelling and how they should be delivered has raised significant concerns.

The nature of the regulatory or governmental function shifts in a digital era. While a major question in the analogue system is determining whether there is any usable technical device, as the study shows in chapter 2, the actual technical issues of providing information and linking it to a filtering or blocking mechanism at the receiver end is less complex, mechanically, when the switch to digital occurs. The problem is not technique, but structure. For example, a supplier of programming that provides a set-top box may serve not only as the gatekeeper for programming, but for rating information as well. If the goal is to allow many rating systems to have access to the consumer, then the regulator will have to ensure that a nondiscriminatory flow of alternative programme descriptions and alternative and pluralistic ways of filtering and screening are encouraged. The analogue rating schemes, especially the United States and the Canadian V-chip model, virtually demand a monopoly provider. Digital approaches, on the other hand, offering the possibility of pluralistic ratings, undermine this monopoly.

Several types of rating providers may emerge. They may act in a competitive or complementary fashion. Broadcasters are likely to retain the rating function but it is also possible that, at the beginning of the chain, content producers will rate their content themselves on the grounds of criteria designed by one or several neutral bodies. This last response would overcome the problem of programming volume but would also require a possibly undesirable level of producer control. From this milieu may arise third party rating providers clearly identified as dedicated to specific values or a specific type of programme. In this context, a premium should be placed on providing viewers with the most useful information to make content-based selections using their personal discretion. This would require the creation of sufficiently sophisticated information about the content. This information could be realised by the content producers or the third party rating providers. A certain categorisation of the programmes must also be organised in order for the viewer to preselect programmes and then digest the information provided. Broadcasters, as some already do, may perform this task.

POSITIVE APPROACHES TO PARENTAL CHOICE

A second difference will be the shift from a combination of ratings and blocking mechanisms to inclusive or 'whitelist' electronic programme guides. In a pluralistic setting, some entities rating and recommending programs will approve a list of offerings rather than go through the far more cumbersome process of rating them. Content screening organisations will download the unique programme identifiers of screened programs to those consumers who have selected them as screening provider.

The consumer's screener choice would result in only those selected programmes making their way to the monitor. The emergence of screening entities specialised in children's programming delivery is foreseeable in this approach. In order to avoid any untoward remunerative influences, such a system would require screening entities to be financially and administratively independent from the content creation industry as well as from content providers.

Thus, it is not only the technical nature of filtering mechanisms that will change with the shift from analogue to digital, but, very likely, the entire model of parental choice itself. Parents will, if they so desire, subscribe to competing content screening organisations, which may for instance be religion or value-based, or appeal to linguistic or national identities. These screening organisations will perform both search and find functions (locating all programming that is in the French language for example), while at the same time filtering out programmes inconsistent with the parent's goals as reflected in the choice of rating or filtering service. In these early days of digital, patterns are already emerging of the kind of content screening organisations that will appear. A limitation for would-be filterers, however, is their ability to catalogue and categorise the millions of hours of material that will eventually exist for television, and their ability to gain a sufficient market share to underwrite the costs of rating this material. As demonstrated by the Internet, where a premium is placed on data about data, or 'metadata', economic incentives arise to support the ability of metadata providers to gain access to this information. Similarly, in an EPG-based interface where programming is sifted through and selected by navigating information about programme content, content producers are presented with a tremendous inducement to make their programming widely available to information providers.

RECOMMENDATIONS
FOR THE TRANSITION

This study recommends that no technical device be immediately mandated for analogue broadcasting, but rather recommends that emphasis be placed on other means to facilitate the transition to a digital future. In the absence of widely available technologies for parental choice, steps need to be taken to minimise harm to minors.

1. The primary responsibility for minimising harm to minors should continue to be placed on the broadcaster; positive programming and the use of watersheds should continue.

2. Informational rating systems, with an emphasis on on-screen icons, acoustic, or text warnings should be encouraged.

3. European coordination of on-screen icons should be facilitated to increase the acceptance of trans-frontier distribution of European works, and to enhance the protection of children. There are many impediments to implementing harmonised icons, and the efforts towards coordinated on-screen icons should proceed with a recognition of this. Many of these impediments are legitimate manifestations of cultural and state-based differences, the protection of which is ensured by the E. C. Treaty of Amsterdam.[5]

4. Standardisation of both analogue and digital transmission signals for programming related information should be a target. This standardisation policy should have two foci. The first focus should be new analogue sets and set-top box gateways. The NexTView standard endorsed by the European Association of Consumer Electronics Manufacturers (EACEM) appears poised as the standard for EPG signals in analogue sets for Europe. Such technology should, if necessary, be encouraged to extend to proprietary set-top boxes as well. Proliferation of an EPG signalling standard will enable the voluntary use of the filtering and blocking capacities, promote the growth of multiple programme screening services, and foster the acclimation of European households to multiple rating and information provision. The second focus should be the digital application programme interface (API). European regulatory authorities (namely, the Digital Audio-Visual Council [DAVIC] and the Digital Video Broadcasting Project [DVB]) should closely monitor the progress of industry groups and their constituent companies in achieving API interoperability. It is critical that the standard not impose onerous licensing royalties on the industry and that it strikes the difficult balance between technical robustness and modest memory requirements. If the industry-led effort to interoperability shows signs of floundering, the European Commission should be prepared to intervene.

5. A coordinated information campaign should be engaged, dealing with parental education and the development of proper attitudes toward the use of television by minors. This campaign should be fashioned after public campaigns in the tobacco and liquor areas. Licence requirements within Member States may be appropriately linked to participation in this campaign.

6. For the transition to the digital era, partnerships must be enhanced. These partnerships should be undertaken to advance common descriptive criteria, transmission standards, and media literacy. Government, industry, and citizen groups should contribute to the development of common descriptive criteria.

---

[5] The treaty establishing the European Community states, 'The Community shall contribute to the flowering of the cultures of the Member States, while respecting their national and regional diversity ...The Community shall take cultural aspects into account in its action under other provisions of this Treaty, in particular in order to respect and to promote the diversity of its cultures' (Title XII, Culture, Article 151, par. 1, 4).

Industry and government should collaborate between and among themselves to establish the needed technical transmission standards. Industry, citizen groups, schools, and advocacy groups should work to ensure the attainment of media literacy goals.

A European platform should be erected to coordinate the gathering of these key actors in order to maintain a constant dialogue, share experiences and practices, and plan for the future.

ENCOURAGING PLURALISM IN APPROACHES TO ENHANCING PARENTAL CHOICE

One of the advantages of the digital environment will be the opportunity for multiple approaches to enhancing parental choice, allowing greater sensitivity to differences among populations of Member States, cultural values, and determinations of appropriate concerns for screening and filtering. While the actual adoption of these mechanisms is still to come, the study recommends certain principles that could guide the Commission and media authorities in Europe through the process.

The study recommends, for the longer term, the following guidelines for a digital parental choice regime with elements applicable to the analogue transition:

1. To the extent possible, evaluative judgements should be based on transparent criteria evenly applied so that viewers may surmise the bases for determinations of a given age suitability. In addition, evaluative judgements should be developed through a partnership of stakeholders. In some instances, a Member State may establish criteria which it applies itself, or which are applied by third parties. This may act as a *referent* for viewers to gauge other ratings and information.

2. The principle of transparency and consistency within rating schemes does not mean that all groups must apply the same criteria. In fact, competition among third party rating providers will be based precisely on differences in criteria and the corresponding fidelity in applying particular criteria.

3. Where there is dependence on self-rating by producers or third party ratings, supervisory or quality control measures should be established, either at the industry level or with the participation of the state. Such entities, like the United States oversight panel, might have a mixed membership of public interest, industry, and state representatives and may be guided by a code of practice developed by the relevant stakeholders.

4. No limit should be placed on the nature of specific third party rating, whitelisting, or similar parental choice initiatives (other than consumer protection measures). Rating services may be evaluative, descriptive, more clearly based on objective criteria, or based solely on the reputation of the third party filtering entity. Where, however, it is the government that provides the rating service, or the rating is more clearly a monopoly controlled by the industry itself, the consideration of transparency and objectivity becomes more vital.

5. Especially where prescreened programme packages are assembled by third parties, the criteria for assisting parental choice will be quite extensive. Third parties will screen for religious and cultural preferences, varying philosophies of child-rearing, language training, and criteria far removed from the current emphasis on violence and sexually explicit images. While niche filtering can be viewed as quasi-censorial, the interest in encouraging pluralistic third party and multiple rating approaches in a digital environment should take precedence.

6. In a world in which third party preferential package approaches dominate, however, creating a common public sphere and understanding a wide variety of differing values may rise in importance. One possibility is to suggest that some programmes, such as public service television or election coverage, be technically immune from screening devices. The study suggests this for future consideration, and as a matter for consensus among rating entities.

7. One consequence of an approach which recognises multiple ratings of the same product by competing rating services is that there is no 'correct' or even 'best' rating for a programme. Even different broadcasters may rate the same programme differently where the evaluative rating is tied to the broadcaster's own reputation and function in the programming spectrum.

8. The multiplicity of rating providers or screening entities will also create the need for informing viewers in order for them to identify such entities properly. This task may be performed by a single body, popularly identified as an authority in the field of broadcasting activities in a given country and capable of providing viewers with the information necessary to assess the correspondence of the orientation of particular rating bodies to their own requirements and values.

PLACING A PREMIUM
ON PROGRAMME INFORMATION

Complex rating and labelling requirements are associated with considerations of information flow. The study makes these additional recommendations on access to information and transmission of information because the success of any parental choice scheme depends on the creation of information about a programme and the transmission of that information to the parent. Rules or practices on access to information about programmes must be encouraged or developed; furthermore, additional requirements on which participants must carry what information in what form must be established.

1. In order to facilitate the proliferation of third party providers, efforts to minimize structural and legal barriers on market entry should be made. The centralisation of certain programming information functions such as the assigning of unique program identifiers should receive serious consideration. Similarly, both analogue and digital protocols in the basic architecture for affixing ratings and providing programming information should be designated (as it is on the Internet within the Platform for Internet Content Selection--PICS). This should be obtained either by industry standardisation or legislative intervention.

2. In a system that encourages third party ratings, those third parties must have access to unique programme identifiers. If a Muslim third party entity seeks to establish, in a digital environment, a package of programming that it deems appropriate, and its threshold for violence or indecency is higher than that of the programmer or the broadcaster then it needs to have access to that information. The standard description labelling disclosures alone may not provide, in advance, sufficient information for this judgement. The third party entity will include or exclude, based on experience, negotiation, and on the unique program identifier. If however, it is to be effective in sending a packet of electronic information to its subscribers, it must have an accurate set of such identifiers available.

3. If a Member State requires programmers or broadcasters to self-rate, then any programme transmitted by the programmer should have the rating imbedded in the transmission of the programme according to the established technical standards.

4. Broadcasters and Teletext and EPG service providers should be very strongly encouraged to carry third party ratings. Nonetheless, a decision by a broadcaster to carry or transmit the rating of one organisation or third party entity should not oblige it to carry the ratings of other third party services. In such an environment, it is quite reasonable to anticipate the rapid rise of an array of providers dedicated to different kinds of children's programming.

5. Where there is, under the law of a Member State, a governmental rating agency, the broadcaster or transmitter of information must carry that rating imbedded in the electronic transmission of the programme. At bottom, such ratings shall offer a *referent* to viewers.

6. The study recommends the permanent provision of information concerning rating providers. This information should be provided at Member State level and should be generated by a designated body popularly recognised as an authority in media activities.

7. Newspapers should have access to industry self-rating information and a compulsory licence to publish it. Newspapers should be encouraged to contribute to media literacy and, in a variety of ways, to encourage parental understanding of video offerings and their responsibility. Newspapers should not be required to publish such ratings, with the possible exception of providing the aforementioned *referent* rating. Newspapers can become third party rating providers and determine what programmes they wish to rate and what rating or descriptive information to provide.

BROADCASTER RESPONSIBILITY AND REGULATORY MONITORING

It should be explicit that any model for enhancing parental authority is not a wholesale substitute for broadcaster responsibility and government supervision. It also need not become a substitute for parental responsibilities. No broadcaster or channel ought to be able to characterise a wholly inappropriate programme as acceptable merely because of the particular nature of the channel or service on which it appears.

Watershed rules should apply as long as people watch channels according to a schedule determined by the broadcaster. Current patterns of television watching will persist, patterns in which there is substantial allegiance to branded channels and time schedules. At some point, in a digital era, this form of television watching may change. However, the possibility of this change (particularly because it is not known how rapid habits will change), is not a reason to abandon or weaken the watershed responsibility.

No matter how imperfect they are, the very existence of parental choice mechanisms will, in part, result in efforts to undermine broadcaster responsibility and the government's role in broadcasting. These demands should be resisted until there is sufficient confidence that parental authority and other associated techniques have made a major difference in the viewing habits of children.

An important question is whether the regime of parental choice ought to affect regulatory patterns for subscription television programming differently than patterns for free-to-air television. Satellite or cable channels of a specialised nature should be held to slightly less rigorous requirements.[6] The selection of such channels demonstrates, to a small degree, parental choice. While this selection does not preclude parents and children from being unintentionally exposed

---

[6] For example, the deep penetration of cable among the Benelux countries precipitates the distinction between satellite or cable services in general and specialised satellite or cable channels. Where, for geographical or cultural reasons, satellite or cable services are the predominant source of basic television, the construction of parental choice is less compelling.

to unsavoury material, the choice to introduce a given channel to one's home does create circumstances slightly different from merely turning the channels haphazardly among terrestrial offerings.

Also, as some of the study's country reports demonstrate, satellite services are packaged with greater capacity for continued parental choice options and with technical devices that facilitate that choice. For satellite services, in particular, watershed requirements may be altered or shifted because of the presence of the increased parental choice options that are inherent in the technical devices that accompany such services.

Industry-based research on parental choices in the satellite and emerging terrestrial digital services should be maintained on a Europe-wide basis to provide a framework for future discussions of watershed and other parental choice policies. The availability of parental choice technical devices over cable is far more varied than over satellite signal distribution. Member States should encourage cable systems to upgrade their technologies to enhance their capacity for parental choice, and should provide incentives by promising adjustment of watershed times and other similar requirements where appropriate.

MEDIA EDUCATION AND LITERACY CAMPAIGNS

In this study of Member State practices and practices elsewhere, one issue stands out above all others: no parental choice system, however user-friendly, however ample in information and easy to control, can work independently of a considered, well-funded education or literacy campaign. This will be true in the transition analogue period and in a digital era. Such a campaign must include an on-screen campaign, a campaign directed at children and parents as well as a general campaign involving society at large.

1. The study recommends that, as part of self-regulation, broadcasters agree to continuous on-screen efforts to provide general awareness of ratings and parental choice mechanisms. Such a campaign would differ from Member State to Member State. It would be directed at children, to help them understand and to reinforce parental choices. It would also reinforce the legitimacy of self-regulation and the importance of engaging in parental choice activity for parents. The culture of self-rating and pluralism in rating underscores the need for increased media literacy and the need for media labelling nongovernment groups to play a greater role in the process of literacy training.

2. The study recommends that there be a general awareness effort concerning parental choice mechanisms. Partly, this may be accomplished by the involvement of multiple rating efforts mirroring civic organisations. Also, individuals

should be informed about modes of parental choice through their social lives: religious organisations, schools, ethnic, and cultural entities. All groups that have a stake in building and reinforcing loyalties and see assisting members to shape identities as part of their role should participate on this plane.

3. The study recommends that schools incorporate in their curricula critical viewing skills to enable children more effectively to understand the relationship of television to their lives and to encourage greater self-control over television viewing. Such curricula should also emphasise the importance of familial decision-making in television choices and should be worked out by a partnership of all involved.

1

Technical Devices
and Rating Systems

Often, rating and labelling discussions are divorced from discussion on the technical aspects of delivering information to the parent or other recipient. Ratings can have broad notice and educational purposes; and how Member States generally fashion and administer them is discussed in chapter 2. Further, accompanying media education campaigns and media literacy policies are vital components of any rating or labelling policy. This is true whether a rating or labelling system functions with or without a technical device. These considerations are discussed in chapter 3. In this chapter, the study explores a much more specific issue: When the decided function of advisory information is to trigger a blocking or filtering action what impact does the design of the triggering device have on the design of the label? The question can also be put in the converse: If the conditions of an ideal (or close to ideal) rating or labelling system are known, what technical device or set of devices can make that system operative?

BACKGROUND

Rating and labelling systems originated in the world of film and have several purposes. Rating and labelling function, *inter alia*, to determine whether a film can be released at all (at least in some Member States) and to inform parents and others for which groups a film was suitable. In some cases, film theatres are required to refuse admittance to a person because of the unsuitability of a film to that person's age.

The history of film ratings offers a guide to the issues that will be raised by implementing rating and labelling systems in the television sphere. Clearly, the primary purpose of television ratings is to provide information for potential viewers, but the other objectives of cinema ratings apply also to the debate over television ratings. For example, establishing a rating to determine whether a film should be released at all (or be played in theatres generally open to the public) has its correlative in the question of continued broadcaster responsibility: whether a given rating determines that a programme cannot be shown; can only be shown after the appropriate watershed; or can only be shown on earmarked, encrypted, or subscriber channels. The study will return to this question when examining the relationship between rating and labelling systems and continued areas of broadcaster responsibility.

For television, a technical device may prove to be the desirable equivalent of the box office manager refusing admittance to minors. Theoretically (and it was subject to some manipulation), a rating or label was an instruction to the ticket seller to refuse entrance to persons for whom the film had been classified as inappropriate. Like the ticket seller, technical devices for parental choice act as a gatekeeper, with the capacity to determine, even if approximately, whether someone who wishes to gain access is qualified to do so.

The Search for a Technical Device: North America and the V-chip

The divined Golden Fleece of empowerment is a technical device that will allow a parent or guardian to control the television receiver so that programmes deemed undesirable will not be accessible to a minor under their care. Obviously, a rating or labelling system alone, while beneficial, does not sufficiently empower modern parents who, for a variety of reasons, may not be in custody of the receiver at the time that a programme decision is being made.

The V-chip, invented by a young Canadian engineer, Tim Collings, appeared to be the magic instrument for such parental empowerment. Originally, the V stood for viewer, as in viewer choice; later, it metamorphosed into V for violence, to mark the particular kind of undesirability that was the motivating reason for adoption and promotion of the technology. As the debate in Canada and the United States matured, the meaning of the V-chip was broadened to include its use in rating explicit sexual content as well as violent content.

At any rate, the V-chip provided the internal mechanism that would allow a parent to act, in advance, on information that was embedded in the programme. The technology promised to allow the parent to be an effective gatekeeper. The parent, using an instrument like a remote control, could direct the television receiver to block out programmes that had particular triggering signals.

In 1997, in Canada, after a period of study and research in which the broadcast industry, other groups, and the Canadian Radio and Telecommunications Commission worked closely together, the V-chip and an accompanying labelling system was finally adopted (Action Group on Violence on Television 1997). In the United States, with the 1996 Telecommunications Act, Public Law 104-104, the Congress ordered that the V-chip or similar technology be installed in all receivers of a minimum screen size and urged the broadcasting industry to develop an accompanying rating system on pain of further federal intervention. In 1998, a self-regulatory system for labelling was found by the Federal Communications Commission to be such an acceptable accompaniment.

The European Context

For a long time, Member States have had rating and labelling systems, more comprehensively for cinema but for broadcasting as well, and these are fully explored in chapter 2. These systems have varied in the degree of involvement of the state, the mode of communicating the result, the consequences of ratings, and the coverage of subject matter or age criteria. What has been common, until recently, is that the rating systems operate without a communication connection that triggers blocking or filtering activity at the home.

While the study reviews this rating history, the V-chip debate in North America inspired the question of whether or not European ratings and labelling systems could be linked to technical devices that would permit parents to be more effective gatekeepers. As a result, it was proposed under the revised *Television Without Frontiers Directive* in 1997 to analyse the opportunities and threats of technical devices. This proposal mandates the current study.

The Vital Place of Technology in Choosing Labelling Alternatives

Almost immediately, it became evident that technology is far more determinative than might have been anticipated. One facile way of approaching the problem would be to ask whether the V-chip system itself should be adopted in Europe; the combination of the proprietary patented chip and a version of the labelling and rating system developed in Canada and the United States. In these countries, the painful processes associated with this intervention have already been undertaken. Determining what labels should cover (for example, should they deal with age appropriateness or be more informative about content?), what elements could be called judgemental or informative, and who should develop the ratings had all been fought over and resolved, albeit on another continent, at least for the moment.

As it emerged in the beginning of this study, the issue could not, for technological reasons, be framed in terms of European adoption of the North American V-chip model. The North American solution was an accident of its own peculiarities of programme delivery design. The particular pathway for transmitting labelling and rating information to the chip integrated into the receiver, namely line 21, field 2, of the Vertical Blanking Interval (VBI), is not practically available in Europe. In itself, this obstacle to the adoption of the V-chip technology was important. But more vitally, it underscored a point that is often underestimated in the discussion over parental signalling. Available technological alternatives must be fully understood so as to appreciate the limits on which a parental choice signalling system can be adopted.

In the exploration of these technological limitations, some minimum characteristics can be defined: For a parental choice signalling system to function, the technical capacity must exist (a) to download the information to the receiving equipment and (b) for the receiving equipment to enact parental choice decisions based on that information. Information has to be downloaded with sufficient frequency so that it can be coordinated with every change of channel or programme. The system must also be tamper-proof. Parental choice, by definition, cannot be subject to easy override by the child. To be useful in a European context, a parental choice signalling system must also have some applicability in all Member States. The system must be comprehensible to the vast majority of parents and guardians and it must be of small cost to the viewer so that it can serve low-income families.

A second-order question is how the optimal technical system would provide parental choice. Would the most desirable European system provide parental choice by excluding undesirable content or by facilitating parental selection of desirable content, thereby controlling the realm of programming available to minors?

FACTORS IN THE EUROPEAN ENVIRONMENT AFFECTING CHOICE OF TECHNICAL DEVICE

At the outset, vital components in the analysis of the technological environment such as the transition from analogue to digital, direct and indirect transmission, the need for a 'pipe' or 'pathway', gateways, bit capacity, and the need for the system to be tamper-proof should be set forth.

The Transition From Analogue to Digital

Most important, any government policy relating to broadcasting must be sensitive to the underlying transition from analogue to digital broadcasting. We conclude that the architecture of a rating and labelling system will change as the shift to digital intensifies. This transition, fortunately, should permit the adoption of policies and technical systems in analogue that will facilitate the provision of a parental choice architecture in digital. Available analogue technologies and interfaces permit a useful, if not entirely unproblematic, technological system for providing a user-interface platform compatible with the burgeoning digital context. Nonetheless, this transitional status and the technical shortcomings of analogue militate against mandating an analogue-dependent device.

However, facilitating the voluntary introduction of certain parental choice methods within this analogue context is very likely to serve several important purposes. It is likely to promote the evolution of an adequate regime of analogue parental choice technologies (that is, rating/information encoding, transmission signals, and receiver devices) to be available to parents during this transition to digital and as the use of analogue legacy sets persists. It will also enable households to use a generally effective device within the particular transmission and technical environment of their geographic region. It will orient parents and viewers to the kinds of rating and information that should be made available to viewers, acclimating them to selecting among plural (that is, nonstate, non-monopoly) rating and information sources, and it will permit more detailed programming related information as an alternative policy to intrusive devices in a technically problematic analogue setting. These are four very important goals in the establishment of parental control mechanisms within the transitory analogue environment.

Direct and Indirect Transmission

There are other overarching characteristics of technical devices that must be understood as well. For example, there is the difference between direct and indirect transmission of programme-related information. 'Direct' transmission implies a mechanism that allows the parental choice information to track the programme itself, to be imbedded in it, and to arrive simultaneously with it. An indirect mode of transmitting parental choice information can be effective, but it poses different challenges and uses different signals and devices. Some technical devices have specific blocking or filtering devices automatically triggered by the parental choice information incorporated within them. Some technical devices are adaptable in ways that make circumvention difficult; others are not. In many instances, the mode for circumvention is the use of the VCR where the technical device transmits data in such a way or at such a speed that it cannot be recognised. In other cases, minor rearranging of the aerial to separate the two information streams can foil technical devices.

Need for a 'Pipe' or 'Pathway'

It is difficult to find a universally available location for downloading information in Europe. In North America, line 21, field 2 of the VBI, was reserved for closed captioning and is available for this purpose. The V-chip system of parental choice depends on this pathway for information, which permits sufficient data to accompany a programme and provide the necessary trigger for blocking purposes.

Space that is consistently and universally available for the transmission of parental choice information does not exist in any Member State. None of the array of Teletext-based delivery modes (packet 8/30, format 1; Video Programming System (VPS); Wide Screen Signalling (WSS); packet 31; packet 31 with embedded slow data rate component) is available throughout the European Union's many regions. Furthermore, owing to the particular arrangements for transmission protocols in the Member States, there is no convenient alternative. Perhaps the delivery mode with greatest reach in Europe is 'packet 8/30, format 1'. Philips Semiconductors has selected this path as the transmission mode of its TACS system for programme blocking. (Kinghorn 1997). While the prospective reach of this transmission system may justify the product development by Philips and other manufacturers, the unavailability of packet 8/30, format 1 in a large number of regions among the Member States precludes its introduction as a comprehensive parental choice delivery system at European-level. A universal answer with a common decoder facing a common mode of transferring information is not a solution in the present analogue environment.

Certain technological trends and the adoption of particular signalling technologies by broadcasters and receiver manufacturers are providing promise for the future of analogue. Yet, as explained later, the chain of technologies needed to effectively, robustly provide technical capacity for parental choice systems in analogue are not yet proven. Particularly, the technical differences in delivery modes (such as satellite, cable, and terrestrial) present serious difficulties in ensuring that adequate protection against circumvention can be presumed. Even assuming that the most viable chain of technologies was sufficiently effective to justify regulatory action, the necessary complements of signalling technologies have not been acquired by broadcasters to a significant enough degree to warrant the institution of requirements concerning analogue signalling systems standards at European level.

The anticipated digital environment, through the work of groups such as the Digital Video Broadcasting Project (DVB) and the Digital Audio-Visual Council

(DAVIC) (to be discussed later), is being primed to maximise interoperability, standardisation, and protocol establishment. These standardisation efforts show noteworthy foresight and should be appreciated for the extent that they facilitate the creation of a technical platform for a best-case parental choice technical environment within Europe. These developments stand in contrast to the tremendous differences in standards and protocols from state to state in the analogue context. These differences in analogue transmission are, to a significant extent, offset by the television manufacturing industry's efforts to establish technological platforms adequately capacious to operate among the varied environments. Nonetheless, there are important limitations to what can be and has been achieved by the industry on this front and thus cautious policy in this analogue setting is warranted.

Gateways

Gateways (usually in the form of set-top boxes) will play a vital role in the expansion, within the analogue setting, and in the introduction, within the digital setting, of parental choice mechanisms based on electronic programme guides (EPG).[1] As substantiated below, electronic programme guides provide a useful interface for the mobilization of technical devices in the protection of children. Standardization of transmission gateways and interoperability with new analogue sets is necessary in the analogue context in order to maximise the accessibility of EPG-based information.

In the digital setting, gateways can mobilize the information capacity of digital technology. Set-top boxes will not only function as the gateway for proprietary subscription services, but will provide the translation of digital signals to analogue televisions. It is anticipated that the diffusion of this EPG information will be vital not only in so far as it informs viewers of content, but also in the way in which it can contribute to the development of third party rating and information providers. The generation of plural providers is a pivotal matter and is dealt with more fully in the discussion of positive approaches versus negative approaches to parental choice, found in this chapter's concluding section.

Bit Capacity

One of the key interactions between the nature of a technical device and the allowable rating system is 'bit capacity' or 'bits per second'. 'Bit capacity' or 'bits per second' refers to the available space for data transmission over Teletext. A data packet, made up of bits, is the means by which programming information,

---

[1] For the purposes of the present study, gateways refer to the intermediary technical devices that process transmission signals so that they may be interpreted by a given television receiver.

such as ratings or other information, is delivered to the television receiver. The rate of 'bits per second', for example, determines the strength or robustness of the signal and thereby affects the level of corruptibility of the signal. Most available analogue devices have very little bit capacity, or room for sending signals that convey information to the viewer or to the device that is programmed for off–on, blocking, or filtering functions. The less the bit capacity and the information that can be conveyed, for example, the more likely the rating or labelling system will be terse and judgemental. Similarly, there is a correspondence between bit capacity and the capacity for grades of nuance among levels or criteria such as violence. In the digital environment, these bit considerations are no longer important. Thus, issues of robustness so significant in analysing analogue possibilities are utterly moot.

Tamper Proof

One important design element, limited by technology, is whether a technical device is more or less impervious to tampering. In analogue, there are acute trade-offs between programme information capacity and signal corruptibility. Possible analogue technical regimes may, for example, allow more information in bit capacity, but are more susceptible to tampering, such as separating the flow of programme-related information from the programme itself or by using 'time-shifting' to avoid the blocking function. 'Time-shifting' is the process of accessing blocked programmes by using intermediate steps. The predominant technique is the use of a VCR that is incapable of responding to blocking signals to record a programme for later viewing by the child. In digital, to overcome these limitations, the rating and information encoding may be utterly intertwined. The prospects of tampering in the digital context appear much less significant than in the current analogue environment.

TECHNICAL DEVICES IN THE ANALOGUE SETTING AND STANDARD RATING SCHEMES

The following section presents an overview of several of the technical devices that have been discussed in the European marketplace. The devices reviewed here have all been developed in the context of analogue broadcasting. Though, as indicated earlier, Europe is moving to digital broadcasting and digital approaches are making substantial headway, the present is predominantly one of analogue. Even in the future, analogue devices will be important because analogue sets frequently become the legacy of children. Table 1.1 demonstrates the levels of televisions and computers in childrens' bedrooms in 1998.

In this transition from analogue to digital, gateways that can translate the digital signals in order to be interpreted by analogue receivers will be increasingly ubiquitous.

As discussed later in this chapter, the likely pervasiveness of legacy sets coupled with the rise in the use of digital-to-analogue and other gateways in children's bedrooms should inform the development of policy during the digital transition and analogue legacy. As will be seen, each of the devices discussed herein has, because of their technical composition, consequences for the design of a partner rating and labelling system.

Teletext

Teletext provides important examples of technical systems using a direct mode of sending parental choice signalling information in an analogue environment. Several teletext-based systems may be made available within Europe. Two representative teletext systems, teletext packet 8/30 and teletext packet 31, will be discussed in the immediately following section. A third teletext-based system, analogue Electronic Programme Guides (EPGs), possesses features that distinguish it from the other teletext systems and thereby warrants a separate discussion later.

Teletext packet 8/30 provides the capability for sending information important for parental choice in an analogue environment. As it happens, in the current mode of transmission of teletext, there is a reservation for future use of bytes 22 to 25 designated under what is called 'packet 8/30, format 1'. According to the European Association of Consumer Electronics Manufacturers (EACEM), the optimal data rate to ensure standard error protection would deliver 18 bits per second, sufficient for basic parental choice signalling information (1998).[2] This '18 bits per second' scheme is twice the capacity of the North American V-chip.

Under this teletext system, the signalling information data is directly transmitted with the TV signal. Because it uses spare capacity in the Enhanced Teletext Specification (ETS 300 706), no new packets are introduced and it can be used in existing teletext hardware. An essential advantage of the teletext system is that the decoding data can be contained in the same packet. The system is compatible with all existing teletext-appropriate television receivers, although software modifications are necessary. The marginal cost of implementing this system is low.

---

[2] EACEM represents the joint interests of companies, national industry associations, associated national federations who manufacture in the European Union. Although as much as 32 bits are available in this mode, delivering just 18 bits frees up 6 bits for a error protection safety net to be transmitted simultaneously with data to ensure that breaks in the primary data transmission will not cause a total failure in the delivery of the information, that a simultaneous transmission with the same information is sent as a back-up.

All the news is not good, however. There are problems in coordinating this particular technology, in VCR avoidance, and in preventing signal corruption from the manipulation of the receiving aerial. Under most schemes, teletext data are transmitted at a rate much higher than can be recorded on most VCRs. Unless there is a modification of format, of transmission mode, or of VCR technology, the parental choice device can be avoided by a child by 'time-shifting'; that is, by recording the programme and viewing it later.

Technology that overcomes this high teletext transmission rate problem will soon be introduced to the market. These VCRs will be able to record content data along with the content itself, thereby allowing a blocking function to be performed when the recorded programme is played back.

TABLE 1.1
Children's Media Equipment, TV-Based, and PC-Based[a]

Percentage of Children with Television, Video, and Cable or Satellite at Home and in Their Bedrooms by Age Group.

Country	Television				Video				Cable/Satellite			
	6–7	9–10	12–13	15–16	6–7	9–10	12–13	15–16	6–7	9–10	12–13	15–16
Denmark	100	98	98	98	91	92	91	95	52	50	55	56
	32	58	72	84	12	28	32	50	10	19	28	31
Belgium*	92	91	97	97	89	84	88	92	–	–	–	–
	6	14	30	41	5	9	11	19	–	–	–	–
Finland	97	92	95	96	92	92	86	93	40	29	32	38
	21	30	42	59	6	14	17	22	2	6	8	18
France	99	99	98	100	91	92	92	91	26	26	24	19
	16	25	30	40	4	8	14	9	3	2	3	3
Germany	98	98	100	99	87	84	88	88	74	83	84	87
	17	29	48	64	6	6	10	22	6	19	33	46
Italy	–	–	95	95	–	–	81	79	–	–	22	19
	–	–	52	54	–	–	19	17	–	–	6	4
Netherlands	99	97	100	97	95	92	91	90	–	–	–	–
	12	20	39	48	2	2	5	8	–	–	–	–
Spain	97	92	96	98	77	53	75	85	13	23	25	21
	21	27	37	32	7	11	9	10	3	2	3	5
Sweden	10	96	94	98	97	91	92	93	63	50	64	76
	25	37	51	64	8	11	19	35	8	9	22	33
UK	85	99	99	97	70	90	91	88	31	37	35	40
	50	57	69	75	11	18	24	32	5	2	5	8
Average	86	96	97	98	88	86	88	91	43	43	49	45
	22	33	47	56	7	12	16	22	5	8	15	19

TABLE 1.1 (continued)

Percentage of Children with Computers and Internet at Home and in Their Bedrooms by Age Group.

Country	Computer with CD-Rom				Computer without CD-Rom				Internet Link/Modem			
	6–7	9–10	12–13	15–16	6–7	9–10	12–13	15–16	6–7	9–10	12–13	15–16
Denmark	33	56	61	62	70	68	76	80	20	27	27	26
	3	17	19	26	9	25	27	32	1	5	5	7
Belgium*	34	26	63	44	53	47	6	68	20	16	49	36
	2	3	12	16	7	10	15	26	1	1	4	6
Finland	33	47	53	47	35	33	32	37	19	24	30	30
	5	14	18	19	7	13	12	12	2	5	8	11
France	20	11	31	21	50	49	58	46	7	4	12	5
	3	1	8	3	17	23	17	16	1	1	4	1
Germany	25	34	44	50	12	14	16	19	8	8	10	9
	1	6	18	26	3	6	7	7	0	0	1	3
Italy	–	–	37	34	–	–	29	33	–	–	11	12
	–	–	23	20	–	–	17	18	–	–	5	6
Netherlands	39	47	47	48	77	86	84	90	18	18	15	20
	1	2	3	7	5	8	14	16	1	1	0	3
Spain	29	31	41	51	19	12	15	18	3	8	11	11
	3	10	13	22	5	6	5	7	0	1	4	3
Sweden	27	40	52	55	59	50	66	69	18	21	33	38
	2	8	16	23	8	12	23	30	1	3	8	13
UK	18	27	28	27	18	27	21	31	4	7	8	7
	3	2	6	4	7	11	8	14	1	1	1	1
Average	29	35	46	44	44	43	40	49	13	15	21	19
	3	7	14	17	8	13	15	18	1	2	4	5

Note. Shaded=home, Unshaded=bedroom. * Flanders only.

[a] These figures are the result of a multidisciplinary, multinational project investigating the diffusion and significance of media and information technologies among young people aged 6–17 years. The project was directed by the British team—Dr. Sonia Livingstone, Katherine J. Holden, Moira Bovill—and conducted by national research teams in eleven European countries (including Switzerland) and Israel. The national approaches followed a common conceptual framework and methodology, incorporating qualitative methods and a large-scale survey involving some 15,000 children and young people across the twelve countries during 1997–1998. The results will be published by Lawrence Erlbaum Associates in 2001. (Livingstone & Bovill 2001).

This technology would be adequately comprehensive if accompanied by a proliferation of television receivers containing teletext-based parental choice systems.

Otherwise, time-shifting would be executed in conjunction with set-shifting. After recording an intended-to-be blocked programme, the child would then playback the recording on a television that does not have the teletext parental choice system.

Given the very high level of multiple television households throughout the Member States, this prospect is quite likely and time-shifting circumvention is not, in practice, likely to be eliminated. Further, the teletext signal is easy to corrupt (where the aerial is portable), by moving or shifting the aerial. In sum, it is apparent that this teletext system is imperfect. It is subject to avoidance through both aerial manipulation and time shifting.

Teletext packet 31 (also known as Independent data lines [IDL], at first blush, provides great versatility and robustness in comparison. It may be transmitted as an independent information stream or it may be inserted transparently into existing teletext streams. It can be transmitted on any available line in either field in the VBI. This IDL structure, specified in the 'Data Transmission Within Teletext' specification (ETS 300 708), is able to deliver up to 36 bytes-per-packet. The availability of this 36 bytes delivery is merely dependent upon the likely occurrence of otherwise unusable VBI capacity.

However, Packet 31 cannot be carried by all existing networks, is not receivable by the majority of current teletext decoders, and also suffers susceptibility to time-shifting circumvention.

Wide Screen Signalling (WSS)

This system, like the most feasible forms of teletext, uses existing and available European data packets and recorders. It takes advantage of the fact that there is space available in the information packet sent to signal to receivers whether a programme is in a wide screen or normal screen format. In some settings, this packet of information also triggers a 'surround sound' system. The use of this packet approach has advantages over teletext. Because the information is transmitted more slowly, VCR adjustment to its use is possible. Many of the advantages of immediate use that are characteristic of the teletext model are available in the WSS context.

There are obvious disadvantages to the WSS system over the teletext system. The major difference is information provided by the bit data capacity. Because there is only one spare bit of capacity, relatively little information can be transmitted. Thus, if the signal were more than a simple on–off signal, it would have to build up over a number of frames and would increase the system's response time. This rate of transmission impinges on the room for 'hardware error integration'. Hardware error integration refers to the transmission's capacity to send signals to the receiver in addition to and simultaneously with the primary signal.

The serial data stream of WSS, a stream in which the signal to be decoded is built up over a series of delivered packets of one bit, has no capacity to send a protection stream as a back-up in case of transmission or reception error in the primary signal's delivery. While it is true that this system is theoretically compatible with VCR recordation, no VCR decoders fitting this system are in production or use.

There are other analogue technical devices that use other pathways. In general, they share similar constraints on the nature of rating and labelling systems that can be operative in conjunction with them and similar susceptibility to manipulation and avoidance.[3] For these reasons, they present neither feasible nor desirable options at European level.

Audioband

A French manufacturer, Communications SA, is currently developing a device that would be triggered by signals affixed to the audio band within both analogue and digital transmission modes. This prospective device avoids the very crowded video band and would be readily transmitted from any present broadcaster.

The technology appears to avoid the common pitfalls of most analogue devices designed to function via video band signals. The device is purported to be able to read evaluative information as well as content indicators such as violence level and even a more qualitative description of a violent scene.

Unfortunately, the device is still under development and technically unproven. Further, while it appears there is significant room for information on multiple levels, it is far from certain that the device and its corresponding signal would be able to carry multiple levels of information from multiple information providers.

SHIFTING THE PARADIGM: TECHNICAL DEVICES AND PLURAL RATINGS

The limited pathway and limited bit capacity of most technical devices, including the V-chip, reinforce the tendency toward judgemental rating systems (due to the structural limitations on descriptive qualities), and also encourage single, rather than multiple ratings. Chapter 2's ratings discussion presents these issues exhaustively. Assuming for now that the appropriate goal is a rating and information environment that facilitates both multiple sources of information and

---

[3] Video Programming System (VPS); packet 31 with embedded slow data rate component; and page-format Teletext are the relevant transmission modes referred to but not discussed here.

nuanced rating and information systems, the task is to identify the technical regime(s) that would permit such a system. In other words, our inquiry in the present chapter is to characterise technical approaches that may be anticipated to enhance parental choice in a decentralised, more multifocal manner. Such an approach would be more sensitive to the needs of different social and cultural groups and the needs of different Member States.

The multifocal approach also changes the way information is handled. In this approach, the most useful, viable way to employ the information provided is via an affirmative, selective manner rather than an excluding, negative way. Seeking desired content rather than designating types of undesired content is the best way to mobilise parental choice in this new television information environment. The use of electronic information to determine a list of programmes that will be filtered in rather than a list of programmes that will be blocked out may be among the consequences of the shift to a multifocal approach. Such a system might allow third parties to provide an electronic list of preferred programmes in a scheduled fashion. Individual viewers, rather than subscribe to pay services (for example Disney or Canal Plus), might subscribe to channels that organise programmes from all available information sources. In addition to determining what level of violence or sexual explicitness might be included, a group, for instance, might select a wider range of programming in French or Italian or more news and fewer 'reality' programmes.

Electronic Programme Guide Technologies in the Analogue Mode

Electronic programme guide (EPG) technologies and the adaptation called NexTView are perhaps the most vital possibilities for parental choice in the analogue mode. NexTView is an open standard developed by nineteen multinational manufacturers of televisions within Europe (Philips Consumer Electronics 1997). It is founded on the notion of a system designed to give information about specific programmes and schedules, offer means of ordering the recording of programmes in advance, and means of facilitating or pre-ordering shifts from one channel to another to organise television use in the increasingly complex multi-channel world. It is adaptable to a parental choice system because the system is so enmeshed in programme choices based on information about the programmes. Already, in the minimum service, information is often embedded in the broadcast about age suitability ratings. By including a decoder, information can trigger a parentally programmed block.

NexTView presents promising technical features and enjoys a virtual consensus among manufacturers that it is the preferred standard for electronic programme guides. However, its analogue transmission mode shares the propensity for being corrupted and the reliability concerns that burden other analogue modes. It shares the same corruptibility problems as the other Teletext-based and video-band based technologies discussed above. It suffers reliability problems because it is a parallel signal, delivered alongside the content transmission. As a result of this parallel delivery, the EPG timekeeping may not always map precisely with the actual boundary (that is, the beginning and ending) of programming. Thus, in blocking scenarios, the suppression process would be based on *expected* transmission time.

Similarly, in whitelisting scenarios the reception of programmes would be based on the expected time and, in cases when the programme mapping did not correspond precisely with the EPG timekeeping, would run the risk of inadvertently picking up unintended and undesirable programming. The NexTView technology includes Programme Delivery Control (PDC), a real-time switching signal that is designed to compensate automatically for imprecise programme delivery timing, allowing for blocking in real time rather than expected time via transmission of a unique PDC code. This PDC code may be sent for each programme and delivered once per second throughout the programme's duration.

In the long-term analogue context, this PDC technology will figure prominently in the mobilisation of EPG capabilities as either filter or block. However, at present, there is highly uneven availability of PDC signalling by broadcasters in the Member States.[4] Further, there are substantial limitations to using PDC signalling via satellite or cable delivery.[5] Serious reliability concerns for services from these delivery modes militate strongly for a cautious endorsement of PDC signalling as a comprehensive solution to the time mapping problem. Nonetheless, carriage of PDC transmissions in analogue should be encouraged among the Member States. PDC does show promise as an important modality that should be anticipated to provide an integral component in the effort toward EPG mobilisation as a parental choice technology in the analogue setting. NexTView's use of this technology potentially as both a filter and block should precipitate its broader pan-European embrace.

Notwithstanding these concerns, the NexTView electronic programme guide provides the best approach within existing and foreseeable analogue possibilities. It provides value to households by facilitating selection and blocking choic-

---

[4] For instance, in 1998, BBC1 and BBC2 broadcast a fully operational PDC service in the United Kingdom, except for Scotland where it remained experimental (Wiseman 1998). Although PDC is a European standard (despite not being ratified by the EBU), few remaining United Kingdom broadcasters have adopted the service and few broadcasters in other Member States have elected to provide this service.

[5] The primary difficulty with using PDC on satellite and cable is that to do so requires the changing of the channel to look for the programme identity label (PIL) in order to identify the date, channel and start time of the programme. For most video's, this it is impossible to change the satellite or cable channel.

es and it contributes to the general orientation of television viewers towards programming-related information. The premium on programming-related information applies regardless of the transmission mode. The changing transmission mode of television from analogue to digital should not bear negatively upon the orientation of households to this information. Rather, the change in the capacity of transmission modes and receivers to provide information should be a spur for emphasising analogue technologies that provide levels of information comparable to what can be expected from the digital environment.

While the NexTView technology relies on Teletext (the various pitfalls of which have been outlined earlier), it nonetheless provides the best means within the analogue setting for the provision of programming-related information. Moreover, within a positive approach to parental choice in which, *inter alia*, specific programming, particular channels, designated timeframes, and third party-provided programme packages are selected from an EPG menu by parents, corruption of the EPGs Teletext signal would completely disable the television. This is starkly different from the use of the EPG under a negative approach. A disabled EPG under a negative, blocking orientation would disable the parental choice mechanism itself and permit all content to make it to the screen. Thus, many of the corruption and circumvention shortcomings in analogue are obviated when EPGs are deployed positively rather than negatively. An elaborated discussion of the differences between and implications of positive versus negative approaches is provided later.

EPG Prospects in the Analogue Environment

Our qualified and limited recommendation of analogue EPGs prompts a further inquiry. Namely, what is the present and foreseeable future availability of this technology within European television households? The question of household penetration is multi-faceted. One part of the answer is a function of the anticipated purchasing of TVs with the NexTView open standard. The other part of the answer examines the likelihood of an EPG signal standard for other set-top box gateways. The most sensible way to discuss the NexTView standard's expected presence in European households is to first look at general television purchasing trends and to then consider the likely effects of the availability of digital-only sets on the analogue market and the anticipated overall market share of NexTView sets.

The determination of NexTView household presence must be based on the television replacement cycle throughout Europe, and the predicted levels of NexTView market-share in the new television market. Reliable figures for the rate of television replacement among European television households are not readily available. Within the United Kingdom, between 10 and 15 years is cited.

At any rate, the preeminence of United Kingdom households in spending on TV-sets, as demonstrated in Table 1.2, will bear greatly on the overall market for new analogue televisions. Table 1.2 compares the spending on television sets across 15 European countries during the years from 1988 to 1996.

While United Kingdom households will be within the ambit of some of the world's heaviest digital programming saturation, paradoxically they are quite likely to be able to receive analogue signals longer than any other Member State due to their public broadcasting history and policy commitment to universal access. Thus, whether and, if so, when Sky's digital programme offerings attain a critical mass and effectuate the transition to digital transmission remains an open question. Among the possible implications of this indeterminacy is that it is likely that the NexTView standard will have a healthy market in Europe. For one, the United Kingdom's analogue history and likely persistence of analogue transmissions long into the digital era point to a relatively healthy analogue set market. Philips, a leading manufacturer of televisions within Europe, asserted that by 2000, over 40 percent of new televisions purchased within Europe will possess the NexTView technology, even a substantially more conservative estimate would warrant the view that this technology will enjoy significant household penetration.

TABLE 1.2
Household TV Set Expenditure 1988–1996 in Millions of ECUs.

Country	1988	1989	1990	1991	1992	1993	1994	1995	1996
Austria	211	233	256	287	277	294	307	297	273
Belgium	200	218	244	254	274	277	284	302	296
Denmark	133	169	186	179	173	178	214	217	207
Finland	165	184	172	191	145	157	152	150	136
France	1768	1790	1984	1859	1897	1894	1876	1850	1745
Germany	1623	1741	3086	2793	2940	3093	3140	3174	3101
Greece	242	323	350	213	218	222	152	159	163
Ireland	54	42	50	52	58	55	94	93	91
Italy	1212	1280	1602	1494	1382	1140	1119	1010	1043
Luxembourg	10	11	12	13	13	13	13	13	13
Netherlands	420	386	457	466	481	477	498	494	512
Portugal	154	144	182	207	220	201	147	135	120
Spain	759	795	949	1026	878	809	822	848	839
Sweden	282	326	326	324	286	240	277	273	277
UK	1361	1243	1160	1184	1134	1061	1148	1109	1263
EU-15	8426	8655	10793	10343	10248	10013	10180	10055	9987

Source: Statistical Yearbook 1998, European Audiovisual Observatory

While figures for European household TV set expenditures generally hover at 10 billion ECUs, the level of digital acquisition in the immediate future is not anticipated to cut dramatically into this figure. As a result, it is not unlikely that the NexTView technology will attain a very high profile in European households.

Determining the maximum diffusion level of analogue EPGs requires more than pacing through the NexTView household penetration inquiry outlined above. It requires examining the possibilities for the establishment of an open standard for analogue EPG signals and identifying the foreseeable level of set-top box presence within European television households. This examination pre-supposes the establishment and use of an open (or at least quasi-open) standard analogue EPG signal interoperable with the NexTView protocol.[6] While this should not be flatly presumed, for this inquiry, we will assume an industry-wide requirement or embrace of such a standard. After the immediately following set-top box penetration inquiry, the discussion will return to the merits behind and likelihood of establishing and proliferating such a standard.

To determine the existence of an opportunity to extend the presence of ana-logue EPGs in European television households, data regarding the penetration of subscription services must be evaluated. While the front lines of the transition to digital are surely in the subscription television territory, it is nonetheless helpful to examine the household penetration rates of cable and satellite (with their accompanying gateways and the dynamics of this transition period in mind). With subscription services come gateways. At minimum, gateways function to allow subscribers to receive their subscribed services and to prohibit non-sub-scribers from receiving programming for which they have not paid. These gate-ways, beyond their conditional access function, can also provide the technical locus for proliferating EPGs to a larger number of analogue households.

As demonstrated in Table 1.3, penetration levels for cable and satellite are quite varied throughout Europe. The Benelux countries have very high levels of cable households: Belgium, 97 percent; Luxembourg, 95 percent; and Netherlands, 94 percent. The rates within these small states are roughly double the median percentage of penetration among the remaining states. Denmark with 56 percent, Finland with 44 percent, Germany with 44 percent, Ireland with 44.9 percent, and Sweden with 50 percent have substantial degrees of cable (and to lesser extents, satellite) penetration, while Italy at 0.2 percent, Greece, with less than 1 percent, Spain at 3.6 percent, and Portugal at 11.3 percent are outliners in both cable and satellite categories. The combined average of all 15 Member States for cable households is 39.8 percent, and the average for satellite house-holds is 13.4 percent.

---

[6] Compare Directive 95/47/EC, Article 4(d), wherein the licensing requirements of industrial property rights holders to 'ensure that this [license granting] is done on fair, reasonable and non-discriminatory terms'.

TABLE 1.3
Household Penetration Rates of TV, Cable, and Satellite in 1996/1997.

Country	Number of Total Private Households (TPH) in 000s	Television Households (TVHH) in % of TPH	Cable Households in % of TVHH	Date	Households with Satellite in % of TVHH	Date
Austria	3282	99.0%	37.4%	End 1996	36.1%	End 1996
Belgium	3759	96.0%	97.0%	1996	5.0%	1996
Denmark	2328	98.0%	56.0%	End 1997	42.0%	1996
Finland	2150	97.0%	44.0%	End 1996	12.0%	End 1996
France	22889	94.0%	9.7%	Jul-97	5.7%	End 1997
Germany	35272	97.0%	44.0%	1996	30.0%	1996
Greece	3646	96.0%	*	1996	1.0%	1997
Ireland	868	97.0%	44.9%	End 1997	9.0%	1996
Italy	22285	100.0%	0.2%	End 1997	4.8%	End 1997
Luxembourg	140	100.0%	95.0%	1995	5.0%	1996
Netherlands	6400	98.0%	94.0%	End 1997	4.7%	Jul-97
Portugal	3574	98.0%	11.3%	End 1997	8.0%	1996
Spain	15080	99.0%	3.6%	End 1997	8.2%	End 1997
Sweden	3889	96.0%	50.0%	End 1997	10.0%	End 1997
UK	21528	97.0%	10.0%	Feb-97	20.0%	Feb-97
EU-15	147090	97.0%	39.8%		13.4%	

* Exact data not available, however, total number of television households passed by cable is less than 1%. Sources: European Commission, Information Society Project Office, European Survey of Information Society, January 1998; European Market and Media Guide, December 1997.

The significant penetration levels in most States are due, in large measure, to the burgeoning digital market. This digital context is discussed in a later section, but for the purposes of the present discussion it should be noted that the digital market's growth is outpacing the analogue subscription services. Importantly, all pay-per-view broadcasters transmitting in analogue at present are scheduled to transmit in digital mode by the end of 1998 as demonstrated in Table 1.4. While these channels do not envision ending their analogue transmissions anytime in the near future, and legacy sets should be expected to receive analogue signals for years to come, this is still an important development.

TABLE 1.4
European Pay-Per-View Operators (Excluding Sports Only), 1997–1998.

Operator	Services	Transmission		Broadcasting		Launch
		Analogue	Digital	Cable	Satellite	
TeleDanmark (Denmark)	Tvbio Channel 1	x		X		Nov-96
TeleDanmark (Denmark)	Tvbio Channel 1012		x	X		Feb-98
Canal Digital/ TeleDanmark (Denmark)	Kiosk Channel 24		x		x	Mar-98
Canal Digital (Finland)	Kiosk Channel 24		x		x	Mar-98
Canal Satellite (France)	Kiosque		x		x	Apr-96
CGV Cable (France)	Kiosque Channel 10		x	x		Apr-96
Lyonnaise Cable/FT Cable (France)	Multivision Channel 2		x	x		1994
Télévisioin Par Satellite (France)	Multivision Channel 7		x		x	Nov-96
DF1 (Germany)	Cinedom Channel 16		x		x	Jul-96
Deutsche Telekom Cable (Germany)	Cinedom Channel 8		x	x		Jul-96
Deutsche Telekom Cable (Germany)	Premiere PPV Channel 4		x		x	Nov-97
Telepiù (Italy)	Telepiù PPV Channels 8-12		x		x	Mar-98
A2000 (Netherlands)	Moviehouse Channel 5	x		x		Mar-97
Casema (Netherlands)	Casema Plus Channel 6	x		x		Mar-97
Mediakabel (Netherlands)	Mediakabel PPV Channel 14		x	x		Nov-98
Canal Plus Nederland (Netherlands)	Canal Plus PPV Channel ?		x		x	1998
Canal Satélite Digital (Spain)	Taquilla Channel 25		x		x	Mar-97
Via Digital (Spain)	Canal Palco		x	x	x	Nov-97

TABLE 1.4 (continued)
European Pay-Per-View Operators (Excluding Sports Only), 1997–1998.

| | | Transmission | | Broadcasting | | |
Operator	Services	Analogue	Digital	Cable	Satellite	Launch
Canal Digital (Sweden)	Kiosk Channel 24		x		x	Mar-98
Telecential, Comtel (UK)	Take One Channel 4	x				Dec-97
TeleWest, NTL, Diamond Cable, General Cable (UK)	Front Row Channel 4	x		x		Jul-98
BSkyB (UK)	Sky Box Office Channel 4	x			x	Dec-97
BSkyB/Cable & Wireless Communications (UK)	Sky Box Office Channels 40-50		x		x	1998

NB. By the end of 1998, all analogue pay-per-view broadcasters will start transmission in digital mode in addition to analogue. This does not mean, however, that analogue pay-per-view will cease to exist. On the contrary, the conversion of the existing analogue subscriber base will be a long process in those markets that have not yet launched digital transmission.
Source: Statistical Yearbook 1998, European Audiovisual Observatory.

Perhaps of greater significance is the fact that many of the new digital satellite stations are transmitting in digital mode solely. Nonetheless, simultaneous analogue and digital transmissions should continue to co-exist for many years in most Member States. The scheduled shut-off of analogue signals has been mandated in several states (for example, Germany, 2010; Spain, 2012; Sweden, 2008); however, the persistence of analogue signals as the predominant transmission mode for many if not the majority of European television households does not seem to be in jeopardy for a number of years. In the context of the present discussion, it is noteworthy that this predominance does not necessarily correspond to an increase in subscription services and their corresponding gateways. The likely persistent analogue signal broadcasters will be the traditional terrestrial channels, located in countries like Italy were terrestrial analogue provides what is commonly deemed as a sufficient array of programming. In these areas, the incentive to seek services that would introduce gateways to households is lacking.

It is readily apparent that speculating on the trajectory of analogue subscription services is precarious given the present state of flux outlined earlier. At a minimum, it does not appear prudent to anticipate that analogue gateways will be increasingly introduced into households at a significant level. Whether this consideration supersedes the potential benefits of standardising analogue EPG trans-missions in conjunction with other analogue initiatives is not necessarily certain. As indicated above, the NexTView open standard is likely to have a significant penetration within the European market. Despite these less than compelling find-ings regarding analogue gateways penetration, establishment, and use of an open, or at least quasi-open, standard, an analogue EPG signal is still worthy of further consideration. While the earlier gateways discussion does not clearly point to an increase in analogue gateways, it does not conclusively indicate a decline. Further analysis may indicate that it would be sufficient impetus to facilitate sig-nal standardisation merely if the current analogue gateways household penetra-tion levels sustain.

In the past, Directives concerning television transmission standards have been promulgated with the aims of generating a single European broadcast mar-ket (*Directive* 86/529/EEC; *Directive* 92/38/EEC). While these Directives did not achieve this goal, the idea that standardisation could not attain less ambitious aims should not be deduced from this failure.[7] This said, would promulgating an open standard interoperable with the NexTView standard be economically oner-ous for any of the implicated industries? Given that the European Association of Consumer Electronics Manufacturers (EACEM), the consortium of television manufacturers, has adopted the NexTView standard, manufacturers should not anticipate injury due to such standardisation. Similarly, broadcasters are also free to adopt the open NexTView standard. Whether such adoption is overly costly to the broadcaster is a separate matter, but the market leverage the NexTView stan-dard is likely to attain in the analogue domain should warrant broadcaster adop-tion of this standard regardless of other interventions. Thus, it appears that mar-ket pressures alone may very well obviate regulatory action on this front.

Voluntary EPGs as a Primer for the Digital Environment

In spite of the limitations to this technology as a blocking mechanism, facilitat-ing a voluntary analogue EPG environment in anticipation of a more technically robust digital environment may serve several purposes. First, it is likely to help parents and children orient themselves to the use of the technology and to the use of the accompanying programming-related information. Second, it can con-

---

7 Richard Collins observed, 'the Directives on television transmission standards [...] express the dominant assumptions in the Community of the early and mid 1980s; that a single broadcast market would unify the Community culturally (and therefore politically) and would assist the development of the Community's audio-visual hardware and software industries. However, neither Directive established the single market, which they were conceived to implement' (1994: 114; quoted in Goldberg, Prosser, & Verhulst 1998: 54).

tribute greatly to the generation of plural rating and programming-related information providers.

Given that the digital transition will progress over many years and that both analogue transmission and analogue receivers will persist in Europe for decades into the future, policy should strive to import the promise presented by digital technology to the foreseeable analogue future. To this end, extant EPG technology within analogue should be anticipated to be increasingly pervasive and, in several ways, an adequately robust means of delivering a level of information comparable to that enabled within the digital setting. The greatest shortfall of EPGs as a parental choice mechanism in the analogue setting is their vulnerability to circumvention. EPGs in an analogue setting represent, if not an invulnerable measure, at least a valuable precursor to technically more sound parental choice mechanisms to be found in the digital setting.

As discussed earlier, standardisation of signals for programming-related information is essential for ensuring that the presently proprietary configuration of set-top boxes and other gateways converge to share standards for the transmission of signals concerning rating and programming information. As in the case of the United States, industry groups should be allowed to lead (either by market forces, policy articulation, or a combination of both) in the designation of digital and analogue signal standards at European level (FCC 1998). The formal standardisation of transmission signals can be seen to subsequently effectuate a de facto standardisation among manufacturers of receiver devices. In the European digital arena, DVB and DAVIC have achieved a tremendous level of standardisation. This trend should be further encouraged so as to ensure the establishment of a European API standard.

The proliferation of analogue EPGs can also provide what would amount to an incubator function for plural rating and programming-related information providers. The promotion of plural providers (as discussed in chapter 2) should be permitted to become a defining feature of parental choice within the digital context. The analogue EPG is a useful predecessor to the future digital environment. The information capacity of analogue EPGs is comparable to the capacity within the digital context. Similarly, abundant capacity to store information and the significant integrity of the signal as a parental choice mechanism mobiliser are anticipated to be indispensable properties for prospective digital devices serving the multinational, multicultural Europe. Thus, the technical capacity to transmit signals encoded with information provided from multiple sources is within reach. However, in order to have these plural providers of rating and programming-related information, the generation of a place and function for these third parties must begin well before the transition is complete. The corresponding need for information providers to at least supplement the traditional rating providers will steadily increase with the growing volume of programming.

A seamless vocabulary and reaching common descriptive criteria are also concerns for parental consent mechanisms. The analogue third party providers' role should be crafted to allow a seamless transition to the digital forum. To this end, structuring the format of ratings and programming-related information in correspondence to the envisaged technical platform is an appropriate measure. Given the anticipated latitude within the expected protocols or 'syntax', such structure should not effect the functioning of programming-related information providers within the analogue setting.[8] Establishing a rating vocabulary is of a high order for ensuring a seamless transition from analogue to digital in the provision of rating and programming-related information. Such a vocabulary will be needed to provide the vitally important common descriptive criteria at European level. Again, the technically imposed restrictions upon such a vocabulary should not prove to be overly limiting. Rather than present these considerations in the abstract, the further explication of a rating vocabulary is provided within the digital framework discussed later.

Information as an Alternative to Technical Devices

The technical limitations of the analogue environment preclude compulsory adoption of any technical regime. Nonetheless, this study appreciates the multiple benefits of encouraging the use of EPGs. Above all else, though, EPGs within the analogue setting must be appreciated for their functioning as an *alternative* to technical devices. It is not the capacity of this analogue technology as a blocking or filtering mechanism that militates for its broader availability among Member States. Rather, it is the technology's premium on information that is ultimately most compelling. Whether EPGs may be trusted as a signalling system, as outlined earlier, in an important sense is beside the point. No technology in analogue can be totally dependable.

The technical capacity latent in the digital future enables the deployment of an optimal rating/information environment as a signalling medium for parental choice mechanisms. Such an environment will help address the culturally and socially variegated European Union. However, in the foreseeable digital future, selection of programming rather than the exclusion of undesired programming is the most viable way for using parental choice mechanisms.

The importance of endorsing this technology in the analogue setting is three-fold. First, it allows for the voluntary use of a technical device and is probably

---

[8] 'Syntax', in this case, represents the grammar for the embedded labels that form the foundations of the descriptive language for rating and programme information. The primacy of this technical grammar can best be appreciated from its role in the Internet-based PICS (Platform for Internet Content Selection) system. Syntax provides the genetic coding for the expression of metadata.

the best analogue option for parental choice albeit one that is ultimately too susceptible to circumvention. Second, it provides a way to orient parents and viewers to both the kinds of rating and information that should be made available to viewers and acclimates them to plural (that is, nonstate, nonmonopoly) rating and information sources. Third, the provision of more detailed programming-related information is the best alternative to a problematic analogue setting.

TECHNICAL DEVICES
IN THE DIGITAL SETTING

While substantial digital availability across Europe is far off and the recently established technical protocols and standards are subject to change, the promise of a technical capacity to store and provide multiple rating and information sources in a transmission mode with low vulnerability should not be ignored. Hence, an elaboration of the relevant Digital Video Broadcasting Project (DVB) and the Digital Audio-Visual Council (DAVIC) standards are provided here in order to substantiate this study's basic recommendations concerning technical protocols.

Preliminarily, the study indicates that the establishment of these standards under the onus of DVB and DAVIC would ultimately address the relevant technical considerations adequately. This, in turn, should provide a technical platform that may enable the introduction of Europe-wide common description criteria. Such common criteria may permit the evolution of an optimal rating and programming-related information environment at European level. The contours of the present and recommended rating and programming-related information environments are outlined in the following discussion.

Digital Television at Present

As indicated in the introduction, the digital future poses a transformative opportunity for parental choice signalling information. The architecture of digital signalling expands the way from a unitary and centralised rating system to one that is multiple and largely nongovernmental. The very specific flaws that are characteristic of the analogue environment are not present in the digital era. The digital 'pipe' that ties the receiving set to a source or sources of information about the programme is very substantial, in many respects beyond comparison to analogue levels of receiving data flow.

The United States' V-chip experience demonstrates that establishing standards within an analogue setting greatly constricts what is possible in the ensuing digital setting. The digital standards established under the onus of the United

States Consumer Electronics Manufacturers Association (CEMA) have regrettably inherited the limitations of the preceding analogue system. Consequently, the rating regime structured around the carrying capacity in Closed Caption has constrained the subsequent digital transmission standard to using only a fraction of its information capacity. Fortunately, Europe is not inhibited by such a legacy. Were the converse the case, it would be hard to envisage a viable European approach to parental choice mechanisms. Europe's multicultural constitution requires a more sophisticated technical architecture in order to carry the information of multiple rating providers.

These ratings considerations, however, presuppose the actual deployment of digital television. Incrementally, digital television is becoming a European reality (see Table 1.5). This is indicated, in part, by the dramatically increasing percentage of satellite households within the United Kingdom (due to the onset of digital satellite stations courtesy of *Sky*), and the substantial proliferation in other states as well. *Premiere* of Germany and Austria has added a significant number of subscribers in the past few years as have the various *Canal Plus* satellite stations dispersed throughout Europe. In Spain, a newer satellite station, *Cineclassics/Cinemania*, had a tremendous growth rate of 139 percent between 1995 and 1996 alone (Broadcasting mode of pay-TV channels and subscription growth rate). It is important to note that several satellite stations, particularly the *Film net* channels in Belgium, and Scandinavia and *Sweden's TV1000* have suffered precipitous declines in the past years. Nonetheless, the aggregate trajectory for increased penetration for subscription services is ascending.

Initial efforts within Member States may be examined to determine whether useful directions are being taken. Within several of these new digital services, basic blocking services have been made available. An overview of the available blocking modalities provided in these different digital channels follows. It must be noted that these initial steps severely under-use the technical capacity inherent within the digital setting. This under-use, to a significant extent, is a function of the lack of rating and programming information.

Digital blocking modalities as they exist today should be examined in order to evaluate further development in this area. In Germany, there are two digital satellite channels, *Premiere* and *DF1*. *DF1* uses a set-top box named the 'd-box'. This gateway enables blocking of specific programmes as well as entire channels through an EPG menu. This particular 'd-box' has received heavy criticism within Germany because of its complexity.[9] It has been criticised as being difficult to use. While this technology is accessed through an electronic programme guide,

---

[9] The umbrella organisation for German media regulators, Direktorenkonferenz der Landesmedienanstalten (DLM), commissioned the Jugend Film Fernsehen Institute to investigate the possibilities for technical devices applicable to digital and encoded television programmes. This investigation unambiguously criticised the utility of the d-box: 'Technical devices for protection of minors irrelevant to practical parental guidance' (Theunert 1998).

the absence of a specific menu for the 'protection of minors' mode has lead parents to describe the use of the device as 'uncomfortable' and 'impracticable'. The problem does not appear to be the rating system or information itself, but rather the interface which parents must employ to act upon that information.

In Spain, the satellite platform of *Via Digital* is a useful example of a pioneering digital technology. Beyond requiring a smart card in order to decrypt the signal, this digital satellite platform provides an EPG with filtering software. The present filtering possibilities through this EPG are very basic. Parents may lock particular channels or block programmes according to three options: one of two age group ratings (age 14 or age 18), or according to sexual content. If age group 18 is selected, then the programmes labelled as having sexual content are also automatically filtered. This is an example of the use of an information-poor rating system with an information-rich digital platform. Similarly, Spain's *Canal Satelite Digital (CSD)* requires a satellite dish and set-top decoder. The decoder includes EPG navigation software. The main menu of the EPG allows parents to lock entire channels.

Sweden is also experimenting with digital broadcasting and parental choice mechanisms. Terrestrial digital network television was introduced in 1999 and the Swedish government plans to completely phase out the existing analogue during 2008 (Sweden Digital Television 1998). While information concerning parental choice mechanisms and detailed information regarding electronic programme guides are not presently available, *SVT*, the State-owned television company, has indicated that EPGs should be neutral, national, and include all distribution modes (terrestrial, cable, and satellite) (Sweden Digital Television 1998). The *SVT* also recommends that the EPGs should possess links to EPGs for all the other Nordic countries to facilitate the Nordic States becoming a single market, potentially countervailing broader European imperatives.[10]

The Swedish national broadcaster recommends that suppliers of services and equipment decide on a common standard for decoders, thereby allowing Nordic viewers to receive broadcasts from all of the distribution modes. At present, there is a lack of standardisation among the three modes of distribution as well as within the cable and satellite modes individually. Again, the Swedish are recommending that decoders be standardised not only within and across transmission modes, but also among the Nordic States (Sweden Digital Television 1998).

Within the United Kingdom, the emphasis has been on introducing digital terrestrial television as outlined by the United Kingdom Government in the Broadcasting Act 1996 (Chapter 55). Digital Terrestrial *(DTT)/Ondigital* was launched 15 November 1998; Digital Satellite *(Dsat)/SkyDigital* started its ser-

---

[10] Such a regional orientation may be seen to transgress the European Union's internal market principles, for example, the Treaties establishing the European communities as amended by the Treaty on European Union and the Treaty of Amsterdam.

TABLE 1.5

Broadcasting Mode of Pay-TV Channels and Growth of Subscription 1993–1997 in Thousands*

Country	Channels	Terrestrial	Cable	Satellite	1993	1994	1995	1996	1997	Growth 1995–1996	Growth 1996–1997
Belgium	Canal+Belgique	x	x	-	149.8	161.7	171.6	181.3	181.50	5.6%	0.1%
	FilmNet Vlaanderen		x		165.0	185.0	200.0	157.0	-	-21.5%	n/a
	Canal+Vlaanderen		x		-	-	-	159.2	161.00	n/a	1.10%
	Supersport		x		-	-	80.0	-	-	n/a	n/a
Denmark	FilmNet Scandanavia			x	80.0	100.0	52.0	-	-	-42.2%	n/a
	Canal+Denmark		x	x	-	-	-	-	-	n/a	n/a
	TVS	x		x	-	-	-	-	-	n/a	n/a
Finland	FilmNet Scandanavia			x	42.0	48.0	65.0	50.0	-	-23.1%	n/a
	Canal+Finland		x	x	-	-	-	-	-	n/a	n/a
	PTV				-	8.0	14.0	-	-	n/a	n/a
France	Canal +	x	x	x	3708.4	3870.0	4070.0	4466.9	4593.20	9.8%	2.8%
	Cinécinémas		x	x	195.0	293.0	375.4	421.0	-	12.1%	n/a
	Cinécinéfil		x	x	170.0	267.0	340.9	384.0	-	12.6%	12.6%
	Multivision		x	x	-	-	-	-	-	n/a	n/a
Germany	Premiere		x	x	723.0	860.0	1011.9	1337.0	1455.00	0.0%	8.8%
Greece	TV Plus			x	6.0	6.0	-	-	-	n/a	-
	Filmmet		x	x	-	3.0	-	-	-	n/a	-
Italy	Telepiù	x		x	544.0	650.0	800.0	-	-	n/a	n/a
	Tele +				-	-	-	865.9	868.20	n/a	1.3%
Netherlands	FilmNet Nederland		x		155.0	180.0	190.0	-	-	n/a	n/a
	Canal+Nederland		x	x	-	-	-	166.4	224.10	n/a	34.7%
	Supersport		x		-	-	150.0	-	-	n/a	n/a

TABLE 1.5 (continued)

Country	Channels	Terrestrial	Cable	Satellite	1993	1994	1995	1996	1997	Growth 1995–1996	Growth 1996–1997
Spain	Canal+España	x	x	x	767.6	969.6	1204.6	1366.1	1464.90	13.4%	7.2%
	Cineclassics			x	-	21.0	41.0	98.0	98.0	139.0%	n/a
	Cinemania			x	-	21.0	41.0	98.0	98.0	139.0%	n/a
Sweden	FilmNet Scandanavia			x	185.0	215.0	200.0	148.0	-	-26.0%	n/a
	Canal+Sweden		x		-	-	-	-	-	n/a	n/a
	TV 100		x	x	305.0	288.0	296.0	235.0	-	-20.6%	n/a
	FilmMax				13.0	12.0	-	-	-	n/a	n/a
UK	The Movie Channel			x	351.2	356.0	-	4006.0	-	n/a	n/a
	SkyMovies		x	x	576.2	560.0	-	-	-	n/a	n/a
	SkyMovies & TMC			x	1800.0	3000.0	3085.0	4068.0	-	31.9%	n/a
	SkySports 1		x	x	-	2800.0	3123.0	4176.0	-	33.7%	n/a
	SkySports 2		x	x	-	-	-	-	-	n/a	n/a
	Disney Channel		x	x	-	-	2792.0	3850.0	-	37.9%	n/a
	Zee TV		x	x	-	80.0	95.0	130.0	-	36.8%	n/a
Austria	Premiere		x	x	32.0	42.0	51.8	67.0	-	29.3%	n/a
	Teleclub	x	x		-	-	-	-	-	n/a	n/a

All of these channels started transmission of their signals in analogue mode, the majority, however, progressively moving towards digital transmission. Due to the transition period it is difficult to say which stage of a trial or implementation phase each of these channels has reached. Source: Statistical Yearbook 1998, European Audiovisual Observatory.

* Portugal has two pay-TV services (Tele Cine 1 and Tele Cine 2) provided by the cable operator TV Cabo since 1997 but subscriber figures are not available. Luxembourg is not included in this list as there are no pay-TV services; it is possible that some households subscribe to foreign pay-TV (Canal+, Canal+ Belgique) in which case they are included in the figures for the country providing the service. The same goes for Ireland where households may subscribe to BSkyB; subscribing households will be included in the figures for the United Kingdom.

vices in October 1998; and Digital Cable *(Dcab)* in mid-1999 (Special survey of technology and entertainment 1998; Digital TV 1999). Recently, broadcasters, mainly the BBC, aired concerns over proprietary operating systems that will not work satisfactorily with free-to-air services on a competitor's platform. Oftel (Office of Telecommunications) therefore clarified that any integrated television set that cannot receive and display all free-to-air services, with full functionality, will be in breach of the *Advanced Standards Television Directive* and associated regulations (BBC Says Digital Televisions Must Guarantee 1998). Full functionality for free-to-air services can be achieved by embedding the open standards selected by Britain's network broadcasters in sets.

At present, *Sky Digital* EPG is, to an extent, representative of the way in which EPGs can function as parental choice devices. The EPG provides a title and synopsis of each movie/episode; it provides British Board of Film Classification (BBFC) movie certificates; and it has 'Reason Code' fields with high levels of Sex, Violence, Language, or Mature Themes. An S, V, L, and/or M can be indicated in the Reason Code field on a voluntary basis. The *Sky* EPG also has its own parental choice device, allowing parents to require a PIN for viewing particular programmes or channels. In addition it also allows parents to set a threshold price for pay-per-view events such that if an event exceeds that threshold, a PIN number is required to purchase the event.

The Future of Digital Parental Choice Systems

The present array of blocking and filtering devices within the digital context does not fully exploit the technical capacity inherent within this environment nor does it give a full sense of the digital future from the point of view of enhanced parental empowerment. In the future, the screening, filtering, and blocking environment (as indicated above in the discussion of Electronic Programme Guides and NexTView), will become more plural, more organised by groups in society, more voluntary, and more varied.

The major effort to develop the technical standards to make this possible, as alluded to earlier, is the Digital Video Broadcasting Project (DVB). This is an organised effort to establish European standards that may provide a platform for the optimal use of digital technology in presenting programming-related information and effectively deploying parental choice mechanisms. DVB, constituted by over 220 broadcasters, manufacturers, network operators, and regulators, was formed with the aim of establishing a 'family of standards' for the delivery of digital television. DVB has provided a standard, MPEG-2, for the compression of image and sound data prior to transmission (Implementation guidelines for the use of MPEG-2 systems 1997). This digital standard was created with the goal of providing high levels of commonality and compatibility among the four digital TV formats: (a) Limited Definition, (b) Standard Definition, (c) Enhanced Definition, and (d) High Definition.

Within this MPEG-2 architecture, the DVB also has a standard for viewer–signal interactivity. This standard, called Digital Video Broadcasting–Service Information (DVB–SI) intimates the programming information possibilities available within the digital setting (Specification for service information 1998). DVB Service Information is designed to 'act as a header' for MPEG-2, the digital containers of compressed image and sound described earlier. DVB–SI establishes the point of contact with any type of digital receiver, indicating the technical nature of the attached MPEG-2 container. This 'header' function, by its purpose of identifying programmes, is a primary step in mobilising any blocking or selecting technology.

The decoder and the user can use the DVB Service Information system to navigate through the array of digital services offered. DVB–SI adds information that enables automatic tuning (via a DVB Integrated Receiver Decoder [IRD]) to particular services and allows services to be grouped into categories with relevant schedule information. These latter categories can be conceived as 'bouquets'. The DVB–SI table architecture, discussed later, has established a specific protocol for this bouquet function.[11]

Thus, DVB–SI is partly dedicated to providing a foundation for a digital Electronic Programme Guide and also to providing the capacity for distinct encoding for each state.[12] Hence, the DVB Service Information protocol provides the beginnings of a platform for programming-related information in the European digital TV environment. The DVB–SI standard, as is the goal for any interoperability standard, provides the minimum technical specifications for basic interoperability. More sophisticated EPGs can be layered on to this foun-

---

[11] This bouquet architecture may enable the positive approaches suggested in this chapter. (Specification for Service Information 1998: 27–32).

[12] The manner of presentation of the information is not specified, and IRD manufacturers have freedom to choose appropriate presentation methods. It is expected that Electronic Programme Guides (EPG) will get a feature of digital TV transmissions. The definition of EPG is outside the scope of the SI specification, but the data contained within the SI specified here could be used as basis for an EPG. The present specification describes Service Information (SI) for use in broadcast MPEG-2 bitstreams. The MPEG-2 System layer specified SI which is referred to as Programme Specific Information (PSI). The PSI data provides information to enable automatic configuration of the receiver to demultiplex and decode the various streams of programme within the multiplex. (Digital Video Broadcasting: Specification for Service Information in DVB systems. Scope and field of application). Thus, specific ratings as determined within a given Member State may retain their connection to that state. However, this technical feature cannot, by itself, address the issues of providing rating information for programming from one state in accordance with another state's standards and criteria. In other words, programming originating from state A and assigned a rating by state A's rating entity may be delivered within state B without any evaluation using state B's rating criteria even though the technical capacity to affix this rating information exists.

dation through a data service or a particular receiver interface (Specification for Service Information 1998: 13–25). This SI would allow applications running on a set-top box to use the DAVIC Service Consumer System specifications.[13] Applications would need these specifications in order to implement electronic programme guide applications that are not built into the particular set-top box but can be 'dynamically downloaded'.

These technical trends strongly indicate that EPGs, while vital during the analogue transition, have an even greater function in the digital environment regardless of their prospective use as parental choice mechanisms. EPGs are the perceived means for making sense of and navigating the volume of channels and programming that will be available within the digital setting. Thus, viewer familiarity with this interface will be a patent feature of digital television. Also, a user-friendly and straightforward EPG/parental choice design should be anticipated to arise from these consensually based protocol and standardisation efforts.

Returning to the particular technical concerns implicated by parental choice mechanisms, the DVB–SI platform is necessary for ensuring the universal access of programming-related information regardless of the source of the information or the transmission location of the corresponding programming. This SI architecture may provide the capacity for the desirable level of programme information within the multicultural European context. However, in addition to the DVB–SI protocol, a deeper level of interoperability must be achieved in order to realise the optimal technical environment. While significant strides toward comprehensive interoperability recently have been made, remaining steps must be taken. The following discussion outlines some of these steps that are necessary for an optimal technical environment.

Movement to Presentation Layer Interoperability

In digital television, the application programme interface (API) is essentially an application execution engine. In other words, it serves a somewhat analogous function to a computer's operating system. The establishment of API interoperability is needed to enable broadcasters to develop interactive applications that can run on different receiver and set-top box platforms across Europe. This API interoperability is required in order for a digitally based parental choice regime resembling what has been outlined earlier.

---

[13] DAVIC is a nonprofit Association based in Switzerland, with a membership of over 175 companies from more than 25 countries. It represents all sectors of the audio-visual industry: manufacturing (computer, consumer electronics and telecommunications equipment) and service (broadcasting, telecommunications and CATV), as well as a number of government agencies and research organisations.

Attaining this interoperability is, in principle, a core goal of both DVB and DAVIC. As efforts to create Europe-level interoperability are afoot, there is a simultaneous effort by some of the more powerful players and industry groups to create a global standard for presentation layer interoperability.[14] For European policy makers, it is beside the point to anticipate which standard would be adopted if this global effort ultimately succeeded; Europe has the opportunity to select a viable, open platform. Such leadership likely would militate strongly against subsequent efforts by the likes of Intel or Microsoft to establish a global standard incompatible with even a nascent European standard, assuming that such an European protocol was not encumbered by onerous licensing royalties and was not prohibitively costly or memory intensive.

This assumption that a European protocol would avoid these licensing and technological pitfalls requires greater scrutiny. As of late, the effort in Europe to obtain this standard has grown more contentious and problematic.[15] DVB has recently articulated the group's aspiration to establish a protocol with a next-generation API, focusing upon creating a Java-compliant protocol with three separate profiles: 'enhanced broadcasting', 'interactive TV', and 'Internet access' (The DVB Interactive TV Debacle 1998). Superficially, at least, these developments signal important progress toward finally creating a standard. However, the backdrop against which these developments are set makes the scenario more complicated.

As recently as March 1998, DVB's working parties on interactive TV had reached a consensus: The DAVIC, MHEG-5 standard would provide the future for digital in Europe. However, shortly after this inchoate consensus was made apparent among broadcasters, *Canal Plus* announced its embrace of a version of MHEG-5. Rather than a critical endorsement, this move was perceived by the broadcasting community to be an attempt to usurp the non-proprietary standard. This profound apprehension amplified the scepticism concerning MHEG-5's technical capacity to deal with an increasingly Internet-based environment.

Curiously, the scepticism over MHEG-5's technical prowess did not translate into greater support of a Java-based API. The robust Sun/Javasoft solutions are perceived with perhaps even more critical eyes. The cost and hardware requirements of the memory-hungry Java-solutions make many in the industry nervous.

---

[14] Intel, Microsoft, and America's Advanced Television Systems Committee (ATSC) are at the forefront of the effort to establish a global standard (Field report 1998).

[15] In addition to the difficulties surrounding the operation layer protocol discussed here, establishing more rudimentary interoperability in digital signalling and receiving, at state levels, has also suffered substantially from the conflicts between proprietary interests. For instance, the row between British Digital Broadcasting (BDB) and BskyB over set-top box, conditional access systems and EPG interoperability has, at least at the early stage, lowered consumer approval of digital services as indicated by the opinion poll conducted by NOP Media (United Kingdom: Consultant's report 1998).

Most important is the uncertainty over whether the proprietary Java can be a quasi-public standard with licensing royalties at a level that will not prevent its broad adoption. Clearly, creating an API standard has become a less than straightforward endeavour.

In November 1998, DVB officials met in California with Sun Microsystems to discuss adoption of a Java-based system (Yoshida 1998). The Java effort was hitting full stride, with DVB and Sun in serious negotiations. DVB as well as its American counterpart, Advanced Television Systems Committee (ATSC), expressed their concerns over Java-licensing issues with increasing emphasis (Yoshida 1999). It is not unlikely that within the foreseeable future, DVB will establish standards to enable presentation layer interoperability.

The progress of this API situation should be monitored. It is not sufficient that a standard be reached. For an API standard to be viable in Europe it must be clear that it will not subject the implicated industries to onerous royalties and that it will strike the difficult balance between technical robustness and modest memory requirements. It is not entirely certain that such an appropriate standard is guaranteed to result from the work of the industry groups and software entities. Given the vital importance of the API for the functioning of parental choice systems (let alone the fundamental importance of API interoperability for European digital television as a whole), it is incumbent upon the Commission to follow very closely the progress of this standardisation effort. The viability of digital parental choice systems hinges upon true API interoperability.

With the creation of a common API at European level or in accord with a global standard, the digital environment may allow for the standardisation of programming information syntax. The syntax standardisation would, in a way not dissimilar from PICS in the Internet context, provide a technical platform for the provision of information about content that far exceeds the explanatory power of simple labels or icons (Resnick 1996: 87–93). While such icons are important and useful in certain respects (as outlined and espoused later), they are ultimately limited, particularly in a multicultural European context. Thus, the standardisation of an API in conjunction with the creation of a programming information syntax would enable both the optimal level of content information that may be provided in an electronic programme guide and the formation of a generative environment for multiple, independent labelling and information providers.

To allow for seamlessness both in the long co-existence between analogue and digital as well as in the encroaching transition from analogue to digital, shared labelling and information vocabularies at European level should be encouraged in order to provide a common descriptive criteria. As in the digital environment where a standard API will enable a technical platform for syntax for receivers to receive labels and information, the analogue signals will also require standardisation (most likely the NexTView standard) to ensure interoperability.

To the extent possible within these two platforms, a shared 'labelling and information vocabulary' should be facilitated at European level.

Such a vocabulary existing within the parallel digital and analogue environments will obviate potential rating and description discontinuities created by differences in the delivery mode (that is, analogue or digital) of the programming. As these delivery differences should not have implications for the content, they should, as much as technically possible, also not implicate the nature of their associated labelling and information. Thus, a shared vocabulary is necessary. To advocate for this harmonisation is not, however, to assert that the vocabulary of this singular digital language should not include multiple dialects. In other words, the overarching vocabulary for content labels and information should affect the difficult equipoise between accommodating the range of cultural and linguistic diversity within Europe and sustaining a shared language, as it were, at European level.

TECHNICAL DEVICES, RATINGS, AND WATERSHEDS

One oft-expressed goal for improved rating and labelling systems is to improve on the obsolete watersheds and other forms of broadcaster responsibility, as described in chapter 2. There could be a time when parental choice technical devices have high penetration in television receivers and the social context is such that these devices are responsibly used by parents and adequately observed by minors. However, it is unlikely, given current imperfections in the capacity of analogue-specific technical devices, that this level of use will take place during the foreseeable future of the digital transition.

Broadcasters across Europe, as a rule, take their responsibility toward programming content very seriously. Awareness among broadcasters of the expectations of their viewership is keen. Dire consequences are anticipated for betraying this confidence.[16]

Use of watersheds are embraced by broadcasters as the most efficient, effective means for providing content that may be inappropriate for children in a manner that permits parents to share responsibility with broadcasters. It allows them

---

[16] Both public service providers (e.g. RAI in Italy, TV2 in Denmark, Bayerischer Rundfunk in Germany) and private broadcasters (e.g. Canal+ and TF1 in France) strongly expressed these sentiments in surveys conducted during this study. Broadcasters have an interest in overstating their commitment to this public confidence as well as the close relationship between broadcasters and audiences; they rightly fear burdensome regulation and being saddled with new technical and rating requirements. While these sentiments are likely overstated, it is hard to argue that they are fundamentally inaccurate. These responsibilities and relationships are long-held and enforced by negative audience responses as well as state governmental intervention.

to broadcast such content at a time when children are least likely to be viewing television.[17] The arguments that support watershed requirements today are very likely to be just as convincing tomorrow. Governments may wish to measure the actuality of parental exercise of responsibility as a barometer for the suspension of watersheds. They may wish to discontinue watershed requirements at a time when parental choice can be more easily facilitated (through greater notice of programme content and the existence of technical devices) than is true now. But neither condition is likely to occur.

In a somewhat distant future, digital television may gravitate toward more demand-driven delivery architecture. Rather than broadcasters (or, for that matter, narrowcasters), providing set programming timetables, programming menus may allow viewers to simply select from a menu and then receive the chosen programme. While this kind of delivery is available, in some instances, within pay-per-view services, this orientation may ascend from the margins to become the mainstream, due, in large part, to the technical capacity inherent in digital. Such a shift in the way in which programming is made available would require a corresponding total re-evaluation of how the protections normally achieved through watersheds can be maintained. Beyond identifying this possibility, it is past the scope of the present study to address the implications of this prospective shift.

In the foreseeable future, it is more likely that self-regulation will become a more varied, more inclusive process and will include third party interventions. Already, institutions like Internet Watch Foundation have sprung up in the multi-jurisdiction environment of the Internet to provide labelling or rating structures that can facilitate the use of EPG or digital filtering and screening mechanisms. Even industry-led self-regulation of the future is likely to involve establishing or supporting third party entities or allowing access to programme information by preferred and approved third party entities.

Convergence and the New Digital Environment

It is important to invoke 'convergence' when addressing the potential for parental choice signalling systems in this new digital information environment. This convergence is a meshing of television rating and labelling systems with mechanisms developed for the Internet. Already, there is stand-alone filtering software commercially available that allows parents to choose what material to block.

---

[17] The earlier-stated sense of broadcaster responsibility is indicated most strongly by the critical role of watersheds among nearly all Member States. At bottom, national regulatory muscle undergirds watershed functions. On the surface, the long-standing social reliance on watersheds evinces the sense of shared responsibility between parents and broadcasters so frequently mentioned in the survey responses of broadcasters. Generally, broadcasters viewed watersheds as the most effective means to effecting the desired protection of children.

These are often imperfect, at least at the present stage of development, and are both underinclusive and overinclusive when filtering. Some computer retailers bundle stand-alone filtering software loaded onto the computer's hard drive. Much criticism has been directed at these filters, but the methodology there can be adjusted for television in a new parental choice environment.

Finally, there will be a convergence between television rating and labelling systems and the web-based Platform for Internet Content Selection (PICS) filtering for third party rating mechanisms. Ideally, any organisation can create third party labels, self-label their own content, and use other labels to filter or organise web access. To date, the use of filtering devices by third party groups has not been rapid and the concept is still in the process, itself, of permeating civil society, though it is likely that the involvement by these organisations will increase. However, the question remains, should such a world in which third parties play the dominant role in rating, labelling, and filtering be encouraged as compared to centralised rating and labelling by the state or reliance on self-rating and labelling by producers and broadcasters?

As illuminated in this study's discussion of rating systems (chapter 2), the carry-over of the limitations in existing approaches to rating and information provision would be the retention of an unnecessary and undesirable vestige of prior administrative and technological limitations. The two greatest values of digital technology writ large are that interoperability readily may be established and that digital has tremendous storage and transmission capacity. These two features must not be merely acknowledged in policy making for the digital era, rather they must inform policy.

Thus, not only are the present issues concerning exposure or protection of children from harmful content fundamentally different from those in previous, purely analogue, periods and in other media, they are not constrained in the ways which limited policy in the past. The macro-level orientation to parental choice must be crafted to ensure that the regulatory milieu facilitates the optimal uses of technologies, recognises the qualities of television media particular to the digital area, and addresses the salient points of policy forged by this technological area.

For reasons amplified in the section immediately below, a positive approach to media technology is imperative. A positive approach is grounded in the pragmatics of the digital content onslaught. It is designed to foster a market for programming-related information rather than to obtain this information through coercion and dis-incentives.

THE COSTS OF A NEGATIVE APPROACH
AND THE BENEFITS OF A POSITIVE
APPROACH TO CHILD PROTECTION

As indicated earlier, the technical limitations within the analogue setting pre-empt a cost–benefit analysis of the available devices and their corresponding system. While the study recommends broader availability of EPGs and a corresponding expansion in the arena of rating and information provision, it is clear that compulsory technical systems within the analogue setting are not a sensible policy option. Within digital, the study has identified the powerful standardisation movement afoot under the auspices of DVB and DAVIC. The resulting protocols should be anticipated to provide the sufficient technical platform for the best-case rating and programming-related information environment at European level. In essence, the parental choice delivery system is a 'free-rider'. The technical standardisation creates the enabling environment for the necessary systems at European level. This standardisation is moving forward without any aid from parental choice efforts in any form. Thus, the technical costs of a digital technical regime, on this level, are nonexistent.

Although the cost of the technical system in and of itself may be properly seen as a collective consumption good, cost does become an issue for consumers and manufacturers. While signalling standardisation is the important technical determination, manufacturers will design signal receiver elements to this standard at varying costs. It is correctly anticipated that the cost passed to the consumer should range from nominal to negligible; however, it may nonetheless be a small consideration. The cost of developing devices is partially offset by the establishment of standards.

Rather than individual manufacturers bearing their own research and development costs for each technical system and device element, these costs are essentially shared and distributed throughout the entire industry. Furthermore, the costs appertaining to parental choice systems are not separable from the general costs of manufacturing the related technical systems and devices. For instance, the standardisation of an application-programming interface (API) is a necessity not merely for a universally accessible EPG interface, but is imperative for the establishment of a multimedia home platform. DVB endeavours to create such a platform for the general goal of optimising interoperability of media content vis-à-vis receivers. In other words, the industry seeks such a platform aside from prospective concerns of providing parental choice mechanisms. As indicated in the earlier discussion, interoperability protocols provide a minimum technical requirement. Thus, different manufacturers and software designers will tailor or build upon these standards. The preceding establishment of standards may then be seen to have enabled the further investment of manufacturers and designers to build upon this industry-wide foundation.

At present and for the foreseeable future, parental choice delivery systems on this level are 'free-riders' within the digital context. This is not to say, however, that cost does not play a tremendous role in shaping appropriate European policy.

The Cost of Providing Programming Related Information in the Digital Era

The imposition of providing ratings, indeed, detailed ratings, from the standpoints of both producers and broadcasters would prove quite substantial in the approaching digital era. Further, requiring adequately sophisticated ratings and textual descriptions of content at a programme level, let alone at a scene-by-scene level as has been suggested by many, will prove to be quite costly.[18] The orientation to ratings that logically follows from the strategy of blocking harmful content would require a tremendous degree of oversight in order to achieve its aims. The ascription of ratings, in a monopoly ratings context, would prove to be a cumbersome and costly undertaking and would likely receive systemic resistance and evasion from producers and broadcasters alike.

It is well known that digital transmission provides the promise of 500 channels. Whether and from where producers provide the content for these channels is an open question. Residually, the prospect of mandating sufficiently sophisticated ratings, indeed rating and evaluation that would be of use to viewers and parents, for this volume of content is a near impossibility. Its social cost in administrative machinery and escalation of cost to producers and broadcasters would be dear.

In contradistinction to this negative approach to harmful content, the prospects of cultivating an affirmative, selective television environment for children presents strong structural inducements to the producers and broadcasters to both provide detailed and sophisticated information about ratings and, simultaneously, greater access to their content for third party rating and information providers. In this positive environment, programming would be whitelisted or selected by households as within the range of programming available to their children.

This approach to children television viewing may also address the problem of 'channel-hopping'. It is hard to advocate that 'channel-hopping' provides any benefit to children's consumption of and exposure to television, especially in light of the sheer amount of time spent daily viewing television. See Table 1.6

---

[18] The discussion of the implications of such policies for artist's rights is taken up in the following chapter.

for an outline of how long children spend watching television or video or play-ing with games consoles. Less 'channel-hopping' is ultimately desirable. Children's viewing habits, whether determined by their caretakers or parents, or self-directed by the child, should be specific in purpose and temporally delimit-ed. In an affirmative, selective television environment, rather than moving from channel to channel as a form of television consumption in itself, intentional tele-vision watching may become the way in which children approach television.

Thus, as in the online environment, the information about and evaluation of television content would attain a high value. Just as browsers are the gateway through which Internet users access online content, EPGs and related program-ming menus from a multiplicity of rating providers would provide the means by which parents would affirmatively attain programming for their children. Consequently, programming information and evaluation would be sought and selected based on the credibility of the information provider. For instance, a Catholic family in Ireland who is not so concerned about the programming broadcast from Ireland, but is concerned about some content coming from out-side of Ireland, could refer to a programming menu put forward by the Archdiocese.

Whether this menu is ultimately palatable or credible in the eyes of the indi-vidual family is a function of whether what appears on the television comports with that family's conception of what is desirable and appropriate.

TABLE 1.6
Children's Viewing Indicators:
Average Number of Minutes per Day Spent by Children
With TV, Video, and TV Linked Games Machines

Country	Television			Video			Games Console		
Ages	9–10	12–13	15–16	9–10	12–13	15–16	9–10	12–13	15–16
Belgium*	95	105	115	14	21	20	11	19	14
Denmark	143	158	168	51	48	49	55	49	35
Finland	117	156	155	47	40	27	27	22	27
France	74	91	103	-	-	-	-	-	-
Germany	88	105	115	18	18	20	-	-	-
Italy	-	-	-	-	52	50	-	38	28
Netherlands	111	134	134	80	94	111	43	50	56
Spain	129	134	143	37	31	26	49	34	19
Sweden	114	140	145	40	45	46	38	26	26
UK	142	164	171	43	39	36	30	32	36
Average	102	120	126	35	41	41	27	28	25

* Flanders Only

To continue the browser analogy, those who use the Internet select their browsers based on the quality, breadth, and reliability of the array of webpages that are retrieved. It should be expected that people would select programming menus based on similar criteria.

All of this is not to say that blocking information and capacity should not be available if desired. Technically, the platform for providing information to facilitate positive strategies to programme selection would just as readily support the blocking strategy. However, as a matter of public policy, the most effective way to provide baseline protection to children is through selecting the universe of images and sounds to which they may be exposed. The blocking strategy is most appealing because it is a single decision that can function indefinitely. Once a rating level is selected all programmes at or above this level are blocked.

Intentional television, television that employs an affirmative strategy to protecting children, is more labour intensive. However, the fact that time may be spent on selecting channels, programmes and time-frames has two strong positive consequences. First, this creates a demand for information and selection systems that are easy to use and expedite the process of assessing the volume of programmes; second, this approach requires parents themselves to be more deliberate about what their children may watch. The degree to which parents create whitelists will vary; parents may select a number of channels, they may select channels but only within certain windows of time, they may identify a menu of individual programmes from which their children may select, or they may select a menu designated by a cultural, religious, linguistic, or other group.

At a policy level, the important implications are several. The process of describing and evaluating content will be plural, diffused, competitive, and thus better suited to the culturally variegated European Union; a positive strategy is the more viable way to provide protection of children from harmful content in a manner that is not overly restrictive; children will be acculturated to viewing television as an intentional activity, rather than using channel-hopping as a diversion or recreation in itself; the pressure of information and the environment in which programming is affirmatively selected will put a positive, and needed, pressure upon producers and broadcasters to increase the access of third parties to their content, and provide more and better positive programming for children.

The Access to Content Problem

Attaining an adequate level of sophisticated rating and description and facilitating plural providers of these services is contingent upon third parties outside of the conventional monopoly rating providers gaining access to the content. In a negative, blocking strategy approach, compulsion is the ultimate mechanism for providing access to third parties. As stated earlier, the volume of the content as well as the number of content providers and channels are serious impediments to the effectuation of the necessary environment for providing adequate coverage. In contrast, a positive, selection-centred approach applies economic inducements to not only greater responsiveness and breadth of coverage from the monopoly institutions, but the incentive to make programming content accessible to third party providers. Facilitating a market for the information about content and the ascent of 'brand' recognition (for example, UNICEF, the hypothetical Basque Cultural Authority) of content information providers will create incentives for allowing access to content for evaluation purposes to the greatest number of groups.

Ultimately, both the negative and positive approaches will use the same information currency. The technical platform recommended here enables the conceptual platform for the provision of descriptive information about content from a multiplicity of sources with a multiplicity of standards using a shared information vocabulary or descriptive criteria. This descriptive information may mobilise blocking techniques equally, as well as it may mobilise selecting techniques. The standardisation of the transmission of this information may universalise the access to this information. The shared rating information syntax between the digital and analogue transmission modes may allow a seamless transition to the era of digital transmission dominance.

The market forces that have already shaped the EPG industry will continue to intensify in Europe, providing serious competition for comprehensible, easy-to-use interfaces with the relevant information. The technical and rating environment may enable the parent to elect whether to block or to whitelist. Both options will be available. Public policy that encourages and educates parents and caretakers on the importance of creating a household culture of intentional television viewing for their children may overcome the 'channel-hopping' orientation.

A clear policy enabling the positive approach to the harmful content question is the best way to foster the necessary incentives to providing plural and expansive coverage of content. It is the most viable way to address the concerns predicated on the ever-increasing volume of programming and the concomitant and serious concern about the nature of this content. If the usurpation of the process by purely commercial interests can be avoided, this approach may be the strongest engine for facilitating the protection of children from harmful content in the optimal European television environment.

2

Rating Systems: Comparative Country Analysis and Recommendations

At the core of every parental control mechanism lies its rating or labelling system. That system both identifies the appropriateness of media content for children and determines the means by which children's access to that content may be controlled. Rating systems define whether a programme can be shown within the watershed, how it should be encoded for a specific technical device, and what type of visual warning system should be used. They should give sufficient information to empower parents to make efficient and deliberative decisions concerning children's access to media content. The challenge of every rating design is thus to develop a system complex enough to give relatively detailed information about a programme, but still simple enough for both labellers and parents to use.

In this chapter, we aim to furnish adequate data for analysing and evaluating the design of rating systems. We do not ultimately rate the rating systems. That cannot be fully done, since each rating system is the product of its own history, its own background in areas such as cinema ratings, its own tradition of monopolistic public service broadcasting and transitions to private broadcasting, and its own historical sense of government imposition of taste as a form of political censorship. In a report written in 1996, Joel Federman emphasises that the best remedy for mass media evils may not be ratings. He proposes that there are methods for 'minimising the risks and maximising the usefulness' of rating systems (Federman 1996: Conclusions and Recommendations).

Ratings are often the product of industry fear of harsher measures, demanded by a public in the wake of a spectacular crisis, for example, but can also be used to empower consumers, giving them a greater ability to choose media content consistent with their personal tastes and values. Our survey may assist in enabling states better to design rating systems. As part of that process we examine the rating systems already applied in the European Member States to provide a firmer foundation for assessing them, and to identify what are perceived as best/worst practices. This data will also assist in determining where there are similarities and differences, and which practices could be the basis for a European wide and/or cross-media rating system.

GENERAL FRAMEWORK AND CONCLUSIONS

In chapter 1, the study focuses on the relationship of rating systems to technical devices. However, almost all television rating systems in Europe have developed in the absence of technical devices into which they may be integrated. Secondly, for the foreseeable future, most parents will use rating systems without the empowering characteristics of technical devices. In this chapter, we build on a study of rating systems throughout the Member States and across media.

Several interim conclusions can be drawn from our survey of practices as included in this chapter. Member States have highly differentiated approaches to the process of rating and labelling, and, moreover, regarding the information released and its design. Very few of the approaches depend on the existence of empowering technical devices. The rating and labelling systems of the Member States reflect their own internal media history and, to some extent, political history and social construct.

As a result, the foundation does not exist, at this point, for extensive harmonisation. The primary function that the Commission and bodies at the European level can play at this stage in the development of rating and labelling systems is to encourage transparency, to provide information about the comparative experiences in various countries, to incite the sharing of experiences and practices via a European platform, and to deal with specific issues that affect transfrontier broadcasting. At the present time, rating and labelling systems are not a significant barrier to transfrontier broadcasting, but there are signs that this may become the case and the Commission should pay particular attention to this.

Within this complex evolution of Member State rating and labelling approaches, there are other specific issues which require European attention and actions. If plural, private descriptive approaches are to become more common in the digital era, and if pluralism in rating services is considered a public good, the Commission can facilitate this process through:

1. Working to ensure greater access to programme information by third parties in a timely fashion. It can ensure that industry rating systems, together

with Member State review, do not become a barrier to entry by third party rating providers.

2. Encouraging broadcasters as well as Teletext or EPG service providers to convey information prepared by third party rating providers (including information on technical devices where they are adapted to such ratings).

3. Monitoring the relationship between use of rating and labelling systems and watershed and encryption measures.

4. Encouraging European Union wide or coordinated media education and literacy campaigns (see chapter 3).

TYPOLOGY OF RATING SYSTEMS

Since the introduction of rating systems as a vehicle for addressing concerns about violent and other potentially problematic media content, several systems, such as watershed, acoustic warning, visual icons, or standard categorisation, have been designed and implemented. In general, systems:

1. Are administered by state, industry (board or single enterprise), or third party bodies (groups or individuals);

2. Are founded on either a specific methodology or an opaque judgement, and;

3. Provide different sets of information and/or symbolic representations such as age thresholds, acoustic warning, or visual icons.

Therefore, if rating systems as such are not so different and numerous, the information they provide, the way this information is processed as well as its design can, and usually does, vary among countries, within countries, within a given medium, and across media. This is especially true in Europe, as will be shown, where no common approach towards rating exists. Moreover, in some Member States, such as Spain, it has not even been possible to establish a common national classification system for TV. In others, such as the United Kingdom, an attempt to develop common principles has been made. All this makes a European-wide classification system seem extremely difficult.

Evidently this divergence reflects significant cultural differences between and within countries, which are, nonetheless, subject to common directives regarding transfrontier broadcasting. Furthermore, it reflects the different regulatory approaches taken to, for instance, broadcast media in comparison with cinema and video. This has always been justified on the basic grounds of the scarcity of airwaves, public service, and the pervasiveness of the medium. This final rationale for different approaches to regulation is often cited in discussion of the protection of children or parental control.

Media differ in the kinds of blocking, selecting, and organising filters practically available to them. It is easier to block videocassettes, because cassettes are individual and separate units of consumption. They can be put on high shelves or locked behind counters in shops. It is also easier to control admission to cinemas. Therefore—as Jack Balkin argues—if broadcast media are special, they are special in this respect: Broadcast media offer limited practical means of filtering (1998: 59–90). How this will change with the arrival of new rating and filtering techniques remains to be seen. In what follows we try to create a typology of issues that will make the analysis between countries and media in the field of rating systems feasible.

Technical Devices and Rating Systems

One important aspect of ratings history is that all existing rating systems were developed without the knowledge of the currently available technical devices for delivering them in an efficient and operative way. At the same time, most rating systems developed for television are derived from or related to rating systems established for earlier forms of media, predominantly cinema. During the development of cinema ratings, questions about the nature of ratings developed: should ratings be descriptive or evaluative; should there be specific criteria or should such standards emerge from a history of practice; and can there be consistency and reliability? In film, as with its successor media, questions arose as to whether ratings should be determined by official or governmental bodies on the one hand or by self-regulation on the other. And in film, too, questions arose as to whether some films should be forbidden rather than subject to the discretion of parents, and whether watersheds or other mechanisms for filtering and creating dual markets could be established. All these questions, developed in the context of the cinema, are now being applied to the present discussion on ratings.

For films, as now for television ratings, the process must be efficient and operative to be useful. By efficient, we mean a rating system must provide a package that allows parents to act within the constraints and demands otherwise placed upon them; by operative, we mean a parental control signalling system that allows the preprogramming, blocking, or filtering of a class of television broadcast through a technical device. In cinema, the action of the box office or turnstile was the operative item. An efficient rating indicated age appropriateness, such as barring those under 14. The equivalent to a technical device is the discretion of the gatekeeper.

What we have seen from the previous chapter is that the choice of technical device in the television setting can have a substantial effect on the kind of rating system that is feasible. In the analogue setting, for example, most Teletext-based systems have limited capacity for the transfer of bits or bits per second.

The pipe or pathway for information is extremely constrained. For a rating system to use these technologies, it needs to be strictly limited to a few criteria with something approximating an off-on choice for the recipient.

These techniques are also most efficient where there is a unitary rating scheme, whether it originated with the government of with the industry. On the other hand, if an indirect Electronic Programme Guide approach (such as NexTView) is employed, the programme-related information provided can be abundant and multisourced, even in an analogue environment. Similarly, if broadcasting is of a digital nature, then the possibilities for a rating system can be quite different. With this in mind, we can now examine the existing models for rating systems using the typology developed herein.

Administration and Organisation

Rating systems are in the first instance a product of an institutional framework. They can be deployed, issued, and governed in four ways:

1. State or governmental rating (usually via sub-entities, or regulatory bodies, e.g. France, Portugal).
2. Industry rating (e.g. Film by FSK in Germany).
3. Third party rating (e.g. America Online for all countries).
4. Self-rating (content providers e.g. video industry, Internet).

The composition and organisation of the rating provider will differ depending on its type. State rating is usually done by a body composed of departmental representatives, civil servants, professional representatives, experts in various fields (for example, childhood development, law), and in some rare cases, children's representatives (for example, in the cinema classification in France). An industry body is mainly composed of relevant professionals (for example, French broadcasters have implemented rating boards that are generally composed of members of the staff, with the notable exception of M6's board, which is composed of mothers of children under 12). A third party board is typically constituted by entities with a vested interest in the issue (for example, industry, children's representatives, educators, and consumers). Self-rating is carried out by the content provider (for example, producer, video editor, or Internet content provider).

One specific discernible trend within the broadcasting sector across countries is the further development of industry rating bodies. Broadcasters prefer to have full editorial independence including classification. Furthermore, we have identified certain reluctance on the part of public and private broadcasters to cooperate with each other in rating and labelling, such as in Germany and Italy.

This development differs from cinema and video regulation, where state rating is the most common approach, a product of the historical evolution of rating systems. However, because of the abundant amount of information and jurisdictional confusion the online industry relies exclusively on self-disclosure and third party rating. Moreover, the European Union recently urged the adoption of similar codes of conduct to ensure 'systematic self-rating of content' by Internet Service Providers (Council Recommendation 1998: 48).

It is clear that with the increasing flow of information, concerns exist that those persons and organisations that administer the organisation, rating, and presentation of information for others will increasingly determine the shape of media consumption. Delegating rating and filtering procedures to bureaucratic and rather monopolistic institutions, whether operated by government or by private industry can have some serious drawbacks. Rating mechanisms are not neutral means of organisation and selection. They have important effects on what kinds of material are subsequently produced and how social arrangements are subsequently organised. The risks of governmental control are perceived as particularly serious, involving the potential politicisation of ratings and the prospect that government ratings could be used as a springboard for further media content legislation. This fear is especially pronounced in some countries, such as Spain, Greece, and Portugal, where ratings may be seen as similar to censorship experienced under dictatorial regimes. The dangers of an industry-run system are that the ratings classifications may be designed less with the goal of informing consumers than with the intention of minimising their economic impact on the industry, and that ratings may be implemented in ways that favour one dominant segment of the industry over others (Federman 1998: 97–129).

Isolating the ratings process from such political and economic influence is of paramount concern in many settings. A step in the appropriate direction is a decision-making body whose board of directors is unconstrained by majority control by the industry being rated and completely independent of government. Such an organisation could be made up of a mix of individuals, representing constituencies relevant to the rating process, such as experts in child development and psychology, as well as parents and teachers. The gathering of such experts is a common pattern in the cinema environment but is nearly absent within the television industry. These constituencies would certainly include representatives from the media industries in question, but these would not have majority representation on the board. Should the media industry gain majority representation, strong checks would need to be organised in order to prevent any untoward commercial or economic influence.

Some have sought to avoid the problem of undue political or economic influence in the rating process by providing 'self-disclosure ratings', such as those developed by the Recreational Software Advisory Council (RSAC) in the video industry in the United States, which involves the creation of a standardised questionnaire (Roberts 1998: 157–177). Another advantage of the self-disclosure approach is that it minimises the organisational structure necessary for the rating process. This would be particularly useful in a multichannel environment, where the volume of programmes to be rated can exceed several thousand hours per day. Thus, producers can rate their own shows rather than programmers or some centralised ratings entity rating them.

A concern however with 'self-disclosure rating' is the level of reliability of the rating providers. This can partly be solved through public scrutiny and transparency, to the extent that open access to a reliable system is guaranteed. Anyone should be able to check the label or rating given to any programme at any time. The idea underlying this requirement is that if it is easy for anyone in the public to raise questions or objections in those instances when they do not agree with the rating (using, of course, the same rating system), then the threat of such checks keeps rating providers reliable. A 'complaint reporting system' designed for viewers may then be organised together with, possibly, a control exercised by the body in charge of broadcasting activities (either on a random basis, on content selected on its own initiative, or on the basis of viewers' claims).

Furthermore, as developed in chapter 1, the trend is toward a digital world, in which it is desirable to decentralise and enable other and more groups/spheres to administer rating systems. Groups based on family values may offer their own ratings system, employing their own conception of what is child-friendly and what is not. Consumers can then subscribe to the ratings system of their choice, much as they now subscribe to magazines. This will, however, largely depend on the available space on television systems. Furthermore, there may be economies of scale in producing a commercially viable ratings system. If so, then the number of ratings systems that survive will be quite small. But the more interesting prospect is that ratings systems can and will proliferate within the newer services. Consumers will be able to insulate themselves in increasingly specialised programming universes. By delegating their choices to specialised media rating companies, they can filter out the great mass of programming to focus narrowly on their own special interests. Some will see this as the ultimate vindication of autonomy, others will mourn the loss of a common television culture. In any case, this scenario produces a more plural and participatory model of parent empowerment and should be encouraged.

To conclude we recommend that during the transition period a system in which industry rating combined with third party or self-disclosure rating develops in order to prepare and adapt the current institutional framework to the digital setting, where the current online model will prevail.

Classification

Classification forms the main methodology and basis for media ratings. The first concern when classifying content is how an assessment of the programme content will be made: Will it be based on specific criteria or an opaque judgement? The second question is what type of judgement one delivers on what type of content. The final issue is what type of information concerning the classified programme is disclosed to the audience, and in which format. Classification systems are to a certain extent determined by the history of a family viewing policy in a certain country and in a certain medium.

Content Assessment

To make an assessment of the content, the rating body will in general apply a deterministic methodology, a nondeterministic methodology, or a combination of these two—semideterministic (Martin & Reagle 1997: 412). A deterministic rating process is based upon some objective methodology in which the final rating is the result of following the methodology. A nondeterministic rating process is based on the opinions of the rating body. A semideterministic rating process is a combination of these two processes and is the most widely used. It is more or less based on the case law of the rating body and corresponds with a so-called 'common-law' approach.

One example of a semideterministic rating system is the French Film Classification system. This system is based on the opinion of the members of the Classification Commission but refers, to some extent, to tendencies displayed by former members. For example, 12+ are movies that might shock the sensitivity of children (horrible images, representation of traumatic relationship between parent and children, and so on). The perception of a horrible image or a traumatic relationship may vary from one commission to another (panel is renewed every two years) but the criteria exist.

An example of a deterministic rating system is the system used by the French public broadcaster, France 2. France 2 tried to make certain criteria objective. The broadcaster implemented guidelines containing some extremely rigorous principles to be applied in rating violent content. There is a *fiche* (or brief memorandum) drafted for each programme. These notes are drafted based upon formal criteria established on the basis of popular surveys conducted in order to assess audience perception and the effects of violent images. Persons employed specifically to write these fiches classify each programme according to these criteria. The *fiche* is then passed on to the internal commission, composed of 12 members, to evaluate the question of scheduling.

At the moment, classification is mainly nondeterministic throughout broadcasting in Europe—apart from those used by France 2 and the FSK in Germany—there are no clear definitions of classification criteria. In cinema, a semideterministic approach is more developed (among half of the Member States) wherein content is classified based on mainly written subjective criteria (either internally or legally defined) as well as case-law and precedents. The decision criteria are transparent to a certain extent but the consistency of these criteria cannot be ensured. The same applies for video, as the body in charge of rating videos is, in most cases, the one also in charge of movie classification. Online categories—such as those defined by the United States-based RSAC, used as basis for the United Kingdom IWF and the Italian IT-RA—are purely descriptive, this being mainly a result of the self-disclosing nature of the rating system. Nonetheless, an evaluative rating applies in Germany.

The consistency and reliability of the system used, be it deterministic or otherwise, is essential. A reliable system means that any two individuals using the coding procedures correctly will describe or rate a programme identically. It is clear that this requires concrete and detailed definitions of everything to be described or a clear overview of the precedents in place. The idea is that no matter how different the individuals, if they use the same objective definitions or apply the same case law correctly, they should assign the same labelling or rating to a programme. In addition, these results should be reliable over a long period of time and across raters.

If it appears—and there is little evidence that this is now the case—that distinctions in rating requirements impede cross-national trade in programming, then efforts should be made towards cooperative approaches that yield more common standards and definitions. In this case the range of categories within the system must be sufficiently broad to allow users from different countries and cultures to be able to filter out the sorts of material that they are most concerned about. The creation of a European platform could be envisaged to bring together national content classifying bodies, as well as specialists, such as educators and psychologists, in order to share experiences and practice and, to the extent possible, work towards common criteria.

Furthermore, as the analysis of the research literature has shown (see chap. 3), though many studies argue that the proliferation of violent depictions on television is in itself harmful, most researchers will acknowledge, to a greater or lesser extent, that other factors influence the degree of harmfulness produced. This offers a case for ratings systems that take into account the context in which violence is portrayed, rather than judging a programme according to frequency of violent incidents. It also reemphasises the need for media education, by which children learn the skills to deconstruct programming so that content is less harmful.

In conclusion, deterministic rating has our preference and recommendation because it is considered more reliable, transparent, and consistent than semideterministic and nondeterministic rating. Moreover, in a digital setting, where plural third party rating across countries will be more likely, a common set of definitions will be needed. Of course, nondeterministic rating gives more flexibility to a contextual assessment than is the case with deterministic rating and should be considered a complementary system. In fact, all depend on the environment in which rating bodies operate. A situation where rating providers act in a monopolistic or quasimonopolistic environment should require a sufficiently sophisticated deterministic methodology so as to preserve equity of treatment for content providers and transparency of the rating decision for viewers. In a pluralistic environment this requirement is less relevant as existence of the rating providers will depend on their credibility, which in its turn, is derived directly from the confidence viewers and content providers may place in them.

Judgement

The question here is whether a content advisory should make an evaluative judgement about what a child should see, on the one hand, or on the other hand, should provide descriptive information about the programme, allowing parents to make the evaluative judgements appropriate to their personal beliefs, value systems, and the maturity of their child? There is a broad distinction between evaluative/judge mental and descriptive/informational ratings. Descriptive ratings tend to focus on relaying information about media content, while evaluative ratings tend to make judgements about the appropriateness of media content for particular audiences.

Some have referred to this distinction as one between 'rating' and 'labelling' (Federman 1996: 25). The fundamental difference is one of providing information about content and allowing consumers to make decisions (good or bad) rather than subjecting consumers to restrictions or prohibitions that are based on someone else's evaluation of the information and judgement about the capabilities and/or vulnerabilities of potential consumers. Federman's examples of descriptive ratings include: contains some violence; nudity/sex level 3; violence: blood and gore; language: mild expletives, contains extreme violence; and brief nudity (BN). His examples of evaluative ratings include: parental discretion advised; teen: ages 13+; R: restricted, adults only; Mature: ages 17+; and PG: parental guidance (1996: 101).

Currently, there is a tendency towards combining evaluative/descriptive rating within the European broadcasting industry. Strong differences exist, however, among countries in the way information is represented. Moreover, descriptive information is rather limited and sometimes not sufficient to empower parents in their decisions. Except for Greece, where a more informational approach is taken, cinema and video rating is mainly judgemental emphasising age descriptions. Online rating is mainly descriptive, apart from Germany where an age classification system is suggested.

The usefulness of the information depends on how clear, specific, and relevant it is to a given consumer. Assume, for example, that one wishes to avoid—or select—content depicting violent or sexual behaviour. In this case, a label explicitly describing the kind and amount of such behaviour and content is more helpful than content-free proscriptions that simply alert the viewer to the presence of problematic content but do not state its nature (for example, TV-14). In other words, informational systems assume that the primary function of content advisories is to inform viewers about what to expect, and that the more fully they do this, the better. An informational system leaves both the question of appropriateness and the selection decision to the viewer.

Judgemental approaches, that is, most film classification systems, generally do not provide much descriptive information. Rather, they make judgements about what is or is not appropriate for particular audiences—specifically, for different age-groups of children. Thus, a TV-14 rating tells consumers that somebody has judged that something about the content is inappropriate for children younger than 14, but says little or nothing about what that content is (for example, violence, sex, inappropriate language, and so on). In the most extreme cases, such judgements become proscriptions. For example, in the United States, youngsters under 17 years old are prohibited from attending an R-rated film unless accompanied by an adult. In other words, judgemental approaches hand over to someone other than the consumer the question of what is appropriate, and in some cases, the selection decision.

In short, several reasons can be given why descriptive ratings are preferable to evaluative ones (Federman 1996: 102).

1. Evaluative ratings run a greater risk of having boomerang/backlash effects, as in the case of Channel 4 in the United Kingdom, whose ratings affect the viewer in a manner opposite from how they were intended to affect the viewer. By contrast, descriptive ratings, such as 'This film contains some violence' or 'This film contains extreme violence' have not been shown to have that effect.

2. Evaluative ratings are less likely to be consistently applied than descriptive ratings. An evaluative rating system combines divergent dimensions of behaviour that requires that each rating decision include a judgement of the relative importance to the rating of the sexual, violent, or language component in that media product. According to Joel Federman, such a process 'individualises' rating decisions, which must then ultimately be made on an 'I know it when I see it' basis. By contrast, informational ratings can be applied more uniformly, since the level of judgement is lower and simpler to apply.

3. Because of their relative lack of consistency, evaluative ratings are less reliable as a source of information for those making media consumption choices. An Italian person living in the United Kingdom may have a different view on what level of nudity is allowed than the average United Kingdom citizen. In contrast, by providing specific content information, descriptive ratings allow these very different consumers to make choices according to their values and preferences. This point is especially relevant to the implementation of technical devices. Using an evaluative rating system, content would be blocked according to the rating provider's decision about what is appropriate or inappropriate for particular audiences, rather than according to the specific values and tastes of individual consumers concerning sex, violence, and language.

4. Descriptive ratings are less likely than evaluative ones to be misinterpreted as a value system for society. All media ratings run the risk of assuming a moralistic tone, and this is dangerous because ideas—or 'unacceptable' portrayals of behaviour or attitudes—can be suppressed in ways more subtle than direct government intervention. This is of particular concern for television ratings, since television is currently perceived as the most pervasive and influential medium. Evaluative television ratings run the risk of appearing to represent quasiofficial values for the society as a whole.

5. It is also worth mentioning that some studies (see chapter 3) have found that prosocial programming, which imparts information and provokes discussion, has been found to change attitudes, particularly when reinforced by discussion. A descriptive approach would allow the consumer to select programmes of positive value.

In order to meet differing cultural requirements in different countries via a more common European approach, it is imperative—as mentioned above—that the descriptive label should offer an entirely objective description of the content, free of cultural values or legal references specific to a particular country.

In contrast, two rationales are offered for adopting a judgemental as opposed to an informational approach. Firstly, it is argued that given the thousands of hours of media content produced each year, there is no way to develop a descriptive system complex enough to identify the kinds of content differences that proponents of informational systems would like to describe, but still simple enough to be employed by whomever is charged with the task of labelling. Secondly, even if such an informational system could be developed, proponents of judgemental systems say that it would be far too complex for most consumers to use. Rather, they argue, parents are more likely to use a system that only requires them to make a single, simple, and age-based choice.

Clearly, informational content labelling systems are preferable to judgemental systems. There is, of course, the possibility of combining the two approaches—of both telling the consumer what is in the package and providing judgements about its age-appropriateness. But it is important to keep in mind that even though content advisories are intended to help parents monitor and guide their children's media consumption, youngsters also see and respond to these ratings. Nor can we ignore the fact that content decisions are under the control of some children most of the time and of most children at least some of the time. It follows that how children respond to content advisories also warrants careful consideration. Indeed, as already mentioned, basic warnings or recommendations such as a red circle denoting erotic scenes, or the announcement of the unsuitability of the content for minors aged 15, is generally considered as having an attractive effect rather than a deterrent one. Substantially descriptive information would not present such high risks.

Another related question in designing ratings is of course what to label, that is, what type of harmful content and what type of programming. In general, three content dimensions—violence, sex, and language—are considered. However large differences across Member States exist concerning the relative importance of each dimension. The Nordic countries, for instance, are more tolerant towards sexually sensitive programming in comparison with the United Kingdom. Violence, though, is perceived in all European countries as equally harmful and is thus also the area in which a common European approach is most feasible. No real differences exist across media where cinema is generally used as the common denominator of the approaches.

Concerning the type of programming, pre-screening and the voluntary or mandatory character of rating plays an important role. First it is clear that, under the current regime, programmes can be rated only if they can be reviewed beforehand. Therefore, programmes, such as news reports, that are generally not prepared too far in advance and live performances, present difficulties. One reason for a preference for digital and pluralistic ratings is that the areas to be covered can be more varied and customised, and the relationship between electronic filtering and information concerning programme material can be flexible and interactive. There may not even be a moment of 'review'.

Warning System

The rating process culminates in its audience warning system. The traditional warning systems have been based on time through the use of watersheds, place (cinema versus home) and manner (visual versus acoustic), and are usually linked to the method adopted by the rating body as described earlier. Typically, an age classification used as part of the warning system is considered an evaluative process while the issuing of a set of indicators to warn corresponds to the descriptive system.

A programme can be preceded by a voice-over or visual parental warning system advising about rated content. Again several systems and icons have been developed across Europe in the television field. This may have serious drawbacks regarding the requirements of the new TV environment. Cinema, online, and video almost exclusively use visual warning systems, whereas broadcasting may also use acoustic warnings as a complementary warning system. Furthermore, the use of announcements at the start of television programmes is perceived more as 'information' rather than constituting a 'warning' in the accepted sense. European cooperation or coordination of on-screen icons should be considered to increase the acceptance of transfrontier distribution of European works, and thereby enhance the protection of children. But such coordination will certainly present some limits due to the absence of consensus on the use of such warnings and, where used, the absence of common standards on their design and what they should represent.

Ratings and classifications may also be used to determine whether the programme can be scheduled before the watershed. From our study presented below it is clear that all countries have accepted and implemented the watershed with success. Some would argue that with the arrival of technical devices, the watershed has lost its value and indeed, in some countries watershed rules have been revisited in order to take into account the specific characteristics of encoded TV services. We believe, however, that there should be continued emphasis on broadcaster responsibility, and attention should be given to use of watershed approaches (except Luxembourg) to minimise the consequences of harmful programming.

Warning systems may change significantly within the digital TV setting. As already stated and will be made clear in the following sections, descriptive information is the type to encourage. As to the representation of this information, the acoustic representation presents certain drawbacks due to its nature (intervention of a human factor, short-lived location at the beginning of the programme) that will not permit it to challenge both the countless number of programmes to be delivered and the necessary selection to be exercised by the viewer. Visual icons may eventually respond to these requirements but can be expected to provide only basic representations of the content to be displayed, such as the intensity and quantity of detrimental scenes and their contextual justification, unless presented in a variety of forms that would overcome imprecision at the likely expense of confusing the viewer.

We prefer a textual description of the content that uses and incorporates more or less standardised descriptive criteria that is then carried by the broadcaster, EPG, or Teletext services. Given the fact that this may be excessively time-consuming for the viewer, a preselection function may be preferable. In this system, broadcasters or TV satellite operators would have to use key words or standardised categories such as Action, Comedy, or History, to describe their programmes and then the viewer would preselect an acceptable quantity of programmes prior to exercising his selection on the grounds of any potential set of content indicators. *Canal Satellite* in France and *Vía Digital* in Spain have already created this.

COMPARATIVE COUNTRY
AND MEDIA ANALYSIS

In this section, we provide an overview of the way rating systems are designed and carried out across media and in each Member State. Our goal is to demonstrate how the technological and policy alternatives manifest themselves, yielding a few noticeable patterns but remarkable differences within the Union. An understanding of how Member States have negotiated in the past, with its own tumble of media technologies and challenges to taste, can provide a basis for suggesting the problems and opportunities for harmonisation in the future. Such a study provides guidance on how industry and public authorities involved in the rating process may respond to challenges emerging from the coming digital TV environment. We can assess whether the necessary regulatory culture and historical capacity exists to perform the new tasks implied. We can better assess whether state mechanisms will continue to evolve in their current environment, will shift dramatically or, as a consequence of changes in technology, become wholly redundant.

There are many ways of presenting a picture of Member State rating systems. In the next chapter, for example, we provide existing data, at this moment, on the efficacy or social efficiency of ratings. It might be suitable, though we do not do so, to study the impact of different rating systems, by country, on the production of creative material, industry by industry. We have organised the material in the following way: we look at rating systems by medium (film, video, broadcasting, and Internet) and, within those categories, by country of national origin. We pay special attention to a number of aspects that can be used to describe a rating system. These include: the administrative process of the classification; the nature (evaluative/descriptive) and range of content information to be provided; the standards that may guide the delivery and/or the substance of the information; and the nature of the icons or audio and visual signals that represent the conclusion.

Using terminology adapted from other scholars, we can ask whether the methodology developed for the rating process is—in large—nondeterministic, semideterministic, or deterministic. The nondeterministic approach means that the rating body provides the classification of the work based solely on its opinion and does generally not rely on established criteria. The semideterministic methodology is more elaborate in the sense that the rating body, even if the decision is made based on its opinion, takes into account some principles and criteria that are more or less flexible. This methodology is particularly important in a European context as it permits us to identify whether or not a certain age group is viewed in the same way or differently in terms of its presupposed weakness and susceptibility to violence, sex or anti-social behaviour.

Presentation of this history and picture of the present has a specific purpose: We know that television is leaving its antiquated mass-media label further behind every day as it moves towards fragmented and variable content supplies, as well as it relinquishes its purely broadcasting function to enter the interactive world. In consequence, the passive relation of the viewer towards content will change (quantitatively—amount of content/qualitatively—selection of content) and, therefore, tools must be offered to the viewer to empower his new 'active' status. Some elements of the solutions developed in the past for cinema or video or broadcasting may be instructive (such as those delaying with the mechanisms of decision-making) while other elements are not (such as those which are the result of the scarcity qualities of the medium).

Our study of the background of ratings is designed to help us understand the needs of the digital future: the way in which the viewer, working with an avalanche of available content, must first identify and categorise the imagery and then act according to this identification. And the viewer may act not just for the purposes of self, but also for organising the viewing of the family circle. The past, as we present it, is a complex set of lessons, largely inadequate, about how to inform the viewer about the proposed range of content in such a way as to permit him to navigate through it make his selection. The range of TV content available in the future will approximate the wide range of content offered on the Internet and that will present a sea change from the past. Content selection solutions developed for the Internet are of particular relevance and significance for the new TV setting and, therefore, take their place in this study.

Cinema

Cinema may be viewed as the progenitor of the long history of ratings (though one could go beyond to books and to art itself to find more ancient rating systems than the ones used since the age of cinema). The apparatus of rating films has been so complex and has evolved in such an intricate way that in some jurisdictions there is a comprehensive range of precise ideas about the type of scenes and behaviour deemed harmful for specific segments of the population (children, teenagers, persons of particular sensibilities). A mapping of each state's approaches to the influence of film images would provide an intriguing insight into how content is perceived in various parts of the continent. But one immediately obvious fact is that conclusions are not always transparent and criteria, guidelines, and principles not always so clearly articulated. What is obvious is the following: ratings and labelling systems have historically been media-specific; ratings and labelling systems have been local and distinctive in terms of structure and outcomes. It is possible that the evolution of the cinema rating system within a country is an indicator of the evolution of a system for other media, but that is not certain. And, finally, just as cinema itself is in the depository of different cultures, so are the ratings that accompany them. That may inform the way TV ratings are approached on a European level. Paradoxically, cinema rating systems are both *sui generis* and guides to the establishment of the systems for technologies that followed film.

At a time when self-regulation is most appealing, it is useful to note that the pattern for rating bodies in charge of film classification in the European Union is clearly one of strong ties to government, with the notable exception of the United Kingdom and Dutch system. This means that the rating body is mandated and fully organised by law, ordinarily derives its power from the public authorities on which it is more or less dependent, that rating cinema works is a delegated task, and that generally the certificate is delivered on behalf of the Minister in charge of culture (see Table 2.1).

In Germany, the distinction is complicated. While the *Freiwillige Selbstkontrolle der Filmwirtschaft* (FSK) is nominally an industry body, there is the right of the state 'tutelary' authority to review the certificate issued by it. The FSK is a self-controlling body under private law that acts in the name and at the request of the Supreme Youth Authorities in the Federal States.[1] The Federal States are permitted to make diverging decisions and to impose them if they do not agree with a decision of the FSK. Notwithstanding, this rating entity is a voluntary body, every film that will be shown publicly must be rated by the FSK. Without a rating, the film may only be shown to adults.

The United Kingdom system does not follow the same scheme. The British Board of Film Classification is an independent, nongovernmental body, which exercises authority over the cinemas. The cinemas, by law, belong exclusively to the local authorities. The Board was set up by the film industry in 1912 in order to bring a degree of uniformity to the standards of film censorship imposed by the many very disparate local authorities. The aim was to create a body which, with no greater power than that of persuasion, would seek to make judgements which were acceptable nationally. Statutory powers remain with the local councils, who may overrule any of the Board's decisions on appeal.

---

[1] Its specific character is reflected by the wording of the certificate of release: 'This film is released by the Supreme Youth Authorities in the Federal States according to §6 JÖSchG of 25 February 1985 to be shown publicly to children and young people from the age of ... years.'

TABLE 2.1
Cinema Rating Bodies

Country	Body	Nature	Mode
Austria	Jugendfilmkommission	State	Voluntary[a]
	Province Advisory Board	State	Voluntary
Belgium	Commission intercommunautaire de contrôle des films	State	Mandatory
Denmark	Media Council for Children and Young People	State	Mandatory
Finland	Valtion elokuvatarkastamo	State	Mandatory
France	Centre National de la Cinématographie	State	Mandatory
Germany	Freiwillige Selbstkontrolle der Filmwirtschaft	Industry	Voluntary[b]
Greece	Cinematograph Commission	State	Mandatory
Ireland	Censor	State	Mandatory
Italy	Censorship committee	State	Mandatory
Luxembourg	Commission de surveillance	State	Mandatory
Netherlands	Nederlandse Filmkeuring	Third-party	Voluntary[c]
Portugal	Secretariado do Cinema e do Audiovisual	State	Mandatory
	Comissão de Classificação de Espectáculos	Third-party	Voluntary
Spain	Instituto de Cinematografía y Artes Audiovisuales	State	Mandatory
	Communidades Autónomas (Catalonia)	Regional	(either one
		Authority	or the other)
Sweden	Statens biografbyrå	State	Mandatory
UK	British Board of Film Classification	Industry	Mandatory

[a] In the absence of a rating, the film may only be shown to children over 16 years.
[b] In the absence of a rating, the film may only be shown to adults.
[c] In the absence of a rating, the film may only be shown to children over 16 years.

The Netherlands has also developed a regime, which bridges the line between dependence and independence: the *Nederlandse Filmkeuring* (NFK) is administratively independent from governmental authorities but members of this rating board are appointed by the Minister of Public Health, Welfare and Sports.

Cinema rating providers act in a monopolistic environment, with the exception of Germany, Portugal, Spain, and Austria where two or more rating providers co-exist. In Germany the second rating provider is a more specialised Government entity, the BPjS, which is not a rating body as such, but is in charge of controlling the legality of cinema films and whether they should be put on the 'index' and prohibited for minors.

In Spain, a competitive rating may be offered by any *Communidades Autónomas*, but so far only Catalonia has implemented such a regional rating entity and, in practice, the Director General of the ICAA rates nearly all films.

Nonetheless, a company owning the exploitation rights in a film, which has its headquarters in Catalonia, may choose whether to have the film rated by the Catalan Department for Cultural Affairs or by the ICAA, with the exception of films that may be classified as 'X' films, which can only be rated by the ICAA. In addition, if a film is rated in Catalonia, the rating provided will be valid throughout Spain.

It has to be noted that Portugal is unique in having a Catholic noncommercial entity, the *Secretariado do Cinema e do Audiovisual* (SCA), which rates all films and competes within the government rating body. Finally, In Austria, due to its Federal nature, there are governmental rating entities in each federal province. Ratings provided in one province are not automatically valid elsewhere. To render the system more unified, however, there is also the central *Jugendfilmkommission*, the Youth Film Commission, affiliated with the Federal Ministry for Education and the Arts, which provides ratings valid for each federal province.

In most states, film producers are mandated to submit their works to the rating entity. Three countries apply a voluntary system, namely Austria, Germany, and the Netherlands. Two of these, Austria and the Netherlands, stipulate that showings of unrated films will be restricted to persons of 16 years and over. In Germany, such films may only be shown to adults. These are default ratings and producers have the opportunity to obtain a more favourable rating by submitting their works to the relevant classification agency.

However, even if applying a mandatory system, two countries have developed a singular system with the intention of overcoming difficulties that may be inherent to bureaucratic functions. Spain and Italy have established a specific procedure, by which if, in a certain given time, the classification body has not rated the work submitted, the rating may be proposed directly by the applicant. In Spain, for instance, this period is 1 month.

A characteristic of European cinema ratings is that they are mainly evaluative and refer to a specific age under or above which a film is considered as suitable or unsuitable. See Table 2.2 for a breakdown of age classifications among the different countries. Only Greece offers a descriptive classification and the nongovernmental Portuguese rating provider applies a semievaluative rating scheme (as discussed later).

Certain age gradations seem to be common to most of the countries, namely 12, 16, and 18 (seven countries use 12 and 16 as break points while nine countries use age 18). Some important differences survive. In Belgium, there is only one marker: 16 years of age. Italy does not follow the commonly agreed 12–16 gradation, which generally is thought to correspond to the beginning and end of adolescence, but uses 'over 14' and 'over 18'. The same is true of Spain, which has only one teenage cut- off, fixed at 13.

TABLE 2.2
Age Classifications

Country	1	2	3	4	5	6	7
Austria	All	6+	10+	12+	14+	16+	18+
Belgium	All	16+					
Denmark[a]	All	All, but NR 7-	11+	15+			
Finland	All	16+[b]	18+				
France	All	12+	16+	18+	Complete P		
Germany	All	6+	12+	16+	18+		
Greece							
Ireland	General	Under 12 if PG	12+	15+	18+		
Italy	All	14+	18+	unsuitable for all			
Lux.	All	14+	17+				
Netherlands	All	12+	16+				
Portugal (CCE)	R4+	R6+	R12+	R16+	R18+		
Spain	Specially R for children	For all	NR 7-	NR 13-	NR18-	'X' rated films[c]	
Sweden	All	7+	11+	15+			
UK	'U' (Universal)	PG	12+	15+	18+	Restricted 18[d]	

Note: R = recommended / NR = non recommended / P = Prohibition

[a] In accordance with the *Film Act of 12 March 1997*, it is permitted for children of the age of 7 and above to watch any film in the cinema, as long as the child is accompanied by an adult.

[b] Age categories 6, 8, 10, 12, and 14 may be used. There is also a PG-option '3 years younger may attend if accompanied by a parent (or legal guardian)'. May use: PG-8, PG-10, PG-12. (Finnish Board of Film Classification website 2001).

[c] Pornographic films and films that positively depict violence.

[d] To be supplied only in licensed sex shops to persons of not less than 18 years.

Luxembourg does not recognise any limit over 17, but it does use an 'over 14' rating. Apart from Spain, Italy, and Luxembourg the countries that do not use a 16-year breakpoint have used 15 years of age as the point of demarcation, namely Denmark, Ireland, Sweden, and United Kingdom.

While ratings systems usually first concentrate on controls on the distribution of imagery during adolescence, some of the countries nonetheless pay particular attention to childhood. This is the case in Austria, Germany, and Portugal where a specific rating requiring that children must be older than 6 to be admitted to certain films has been implemented. In Portugal, there is an 'over 4' rating. Spain has deployed a specific label, which recommends a film for children and fixes a seven years old threshold for some films. This rating is also used in Denmark and Sweden and is under consideration in the Netherlands. In the latter, the NFK would also like to introduce a 'PG' classification to add to the 'all ages' category, and an 'all ages' rating accompanied with the label, child friendly/family film.

As mentioned already, the rating scheme of the SCA in Portugal is of a semi-evaluative nature. As shown in Table 2.3, there is no specification regarding suitable age, but a few generic categories ('all', 'adolescent', and 'adults') and a general assessment of the content.

Cinema ratings are usually nondeterministic or semideterministic, as outlined in the introduction to this chapter. The principles on which this semideterministic methodology relies are variable. First, criteria may be incorporated into law though this may have drawbacks. A 'rigid' approach to cinema contents may lead to criteria that cannot adapt to the evolution of cultural norms or take into account the creative ways to depict sensitive issues. In other words, the context of film violence or sex may affect the content's impact.

TABLE 2.3
SCA Rating System

1	2	3	4
'For all'	'For adolescents and adults'	'For adults'	'For adults with reservations'
Films that are entertaining and easy to understand.	Films that present a complexity that makes them hard to be understood by children that may hurt their sensibility or distort their vision of the world.	Films that, due to their structure or content, may not be totally understood or adequately analysed by adolescents, films that contain problems which are not appropriate for individuals without full maturity and experience of life.	Films that present gravely distorted situations, due to their level of violence and/or degradation or exploitation of matters, which may hurt the viewer's sensibility.

Because of the need for flexibility in cinema, ratings criteria are generally formulated in such a way that they are easily adaptable by the rating provider to each of these two requirements. This is the case in Denmark, Italy, Germany, and Sweden, as shown in Table 2.4. The need for flexibility is also why some countries (such as France and the United Kingdom) follow a case-law approach. In the case-law approach certain definable criteria such as full-frontal nudity and explicit sex are used in combination with more contextual approaches that are determined by case-law. This, if it does not offer complete security to the consumer and the content creator/producer, is at least more flexible and adaptable to certain contexts, contents, and time.

Even more interesting than the methodology itself is the transparency, where it exists, of the criteria on the grounds of which the content is assessed, and the methodology applied, as they permit a direct comparison of what is considered harmful in the various European countries, and for each age category. Transparency mainly depends on the methodology adopted. In other words, with rare exceptions, sophisticated case law approaches or legal frameworks are a necessary characteristic of a transparent methodology.

TABLE 2.4
Methodology

Country		Nondeterministic	Semideterministic
Austria			Written subjective criteria
Belgium			
Denmark			Legal subjective criteria
Finland		Opinion of the panel	
France			Case-law approach
Germany			Legal subjective criteria
Greece		Simple pass or fail	
Ireland		View of individual censor	
Italy			Legal Subjective criteria
Luxembourg			
Netherlands			Guidelines and classification forms
Portugal	SCA	Moral judgement by SCA	
Portugal	CCE		Written subjective criteria
Spain		Decision of the Director General	
Sweden			Legal subjective criteria
UK			Case law approach

The criteria used by European countries are more or less precise according to the country considered (see Table 2.5). For example, the Portuguese rating entity refers to general and ambiguous assumptions such as psychological trauma or excessive exploration of sexuality. The same applies in Italy where erotic and violent scenes cited without being subject to more detailed explanation, which would permit identification of certain degrees of eroticism or violence. The French film board classification provides a generic approach to content (shocking work, incitement to dangerous behaviour, incitement to violence), but accompanies these criteria by more detailed categories or definitions (particularly horrific images, those that glorify suicide, drugs or terrorism). Criteria are more specific in the Netherlands and the United Kingdom.

Some common concerns may be observed from the criteria used, such as excessive violence, which uniformly entails age restrictions and may not be seen by anyone younger than 12. Another general concern is the influence that a film's depictions may have on children and teenagers inciting them to immoral and/or antisocial behaviour (drug use, incitement to suicide, hatred, and so on).

Other particularities can be observed. In the United Kingdom, sex/nudity related content appears with very sophisticated gradations in each of the categories (except suitable for all), which denotes the particular attention that is paid to the contact that minors may have with this aspect of life, and leads to tight controls on graduated admission of minors to films with this kind of content. This concern is not expressed in such a detailed way, nor regulated so carefully in the other countries, and, indeed, in some of them sex is not even perceived as detrimental for minors. This assumption is generally made when considering the Nordic countries, which express more concern regarding violence. The film *Sex, Lies and Videotape* was rated 18+ in United Kingdom while it obtained a 7+ certificate in Sweden and would have been released within a general audience certificate if it had not contained a violent scene.

The European Commission itself recognised that 'there is a wide gap between the Nordic countries, which are tough on violent material but easygoing where sexually explicit material is concerned and the Latin countries, tough on sex but less so on violence' (Commission of the European Communities 1996: 483 final, annex 3.II). The United Kingdom rating system is in fact rather more sophisticated than any of the others presented earlier. The full range of precise content criteria might imply more or less automatic classification in such or such a category. Nonetheless, the BBFC's view is that context, treatment and the intention of the film-maker are as important as the actual images shown. Virtually any theme is acceptable if the treatment is responsible, and the same images may be acceptable in one context but not in another.

TABLE 2.5
Comparison of the Rating Criteria (When Transparent)

Country	Sex	Violence	Language	Behaviour	Other
DE	Sexual deviation and pornography (18)	Representation of violence (18)		Incitement to racial hatred, glorification or playing down the consumption of drugs (18)	Glorification of the Nazi ideology or war (18)
DK	Sexual description (with graduation for children under 7, 11 and 15)	Brutalising effect, namely by weakening inhibition towards use of violence			
FI	Quantity and quality of sex determine the age suitability Hard core pornography (18) Sexual violence, animal pornography or child pornography (ban)	Quantity and quality of violence determine the age suitability Depiction of fictional graphic or sadistic violence (18) Brutal violence (ban)			Obscenity, Psychologically disturbing (ban)
FR	Pornography (18) pornographic films with children films depicting sexual relations between humans and animal (ban).	Horrible images, traumatic relations between parents and children, excessive violence (12)		Positive images of suicide, drugs, etc (16) positive images and glorification of violence inciting viewer (positive images of crime, terrorism, etc.) (18)	
IT	Represent erotic scenes (14/18)	Violent scenes against human beings or animals, hypnotic phenomena or shocking surgical operations (14/18)	Vulgar content (14/18)	Excite immoral behaviour, use of drugs, promote hatred and revenge, induce to imitation of crimes or suicide (14/18)	Obscene or against public morality (18)

TABLE 2.5 (continued)

Country	Sex	Violence	Language	Behaviour	Other
NL	Pornography	Frightening scenes, brutalising violence horrible, impudent, sadistic		Risk of excessive identification, racism, sexism, discrimination, alcohol or drug use	Intimidation, field of tension without possibilities to escape, bad ending/open ending, fascism, political extremism
SW	Depicts sexual violence or coercion or present children in pornographic situations	Brutalising effect, explicit or protracted scenes of severe violence to people or animals			Emotional shock, causes psychological damage
United Kingdom	Occasional brief non-sexual nudity bed scenes but no serious suggestion of actual sexual activity (PG), implications of sex (12), full-frontal nudity in a non-sexual context, impressionistic sex (15), complex sexual relationships explicit simulated sex, full nudity in a sexual context (18)	Mild violence (PG) more realistic violence limited in length and intensity (12), mildly graphic violence and horror with some gore (15), no details of harmful or criminal techniques (PG/12/15), graphic violence, provided that it does not encourage sadistic pleasure or glamorise dangerous weapons (18)	Limited scatological language but no sexual expletives (PG), stronger language, but only a rare sexual expletive (12), more extensive use of expletives (15), frequent use of sexual expletives (18)	No drug use or condoning of immoral behaviour unless mitigated by context (PG/12), no undue emphasis on weapons (PG), soft drugs may be seen in use, but not so as to condone or normalise (15), unglamorous use of hard drugs when justified by characterisation or narrative (18)	Controversial religious subjects (18)

In addition to the fact that a classification may be decided by one entity for the entire population on the grounds of criteria more or less univocally decreed, the question arises of whether or not these rating decisions are mandatory and must be respected both by those responsible for the cinema houses and parents, or whether the classification is perceived as a mere recommendation made by a specialised body in order to give some limited guidance to the audience, who, in this case, may make their own decision as to a film's suitability. The issue is of importance as it may highlight differences regarding the freedom of viewers and social responsibility. Indeed, two distinct approaches appear within the countries treated here, which deserve special attention due to the existence of specific historical factors. That Spain, Portugal, and Greece were dictatorial regimes for several decades has caused citizens to be more resistant to any kind of mandatory regulations regarding their behaviour, especially in the cultural sphere. This is one explanation of why the ratings issued by the bodies in charge of classifying film in these countries only recommend and do not prohibit films. In all the other countries the rating issued is binding, meaning that the whole industry must respect it and, more particularly, that the management and staff of theatres may be held responsible for allowing minors to view a film prohibited for their age group.[2]

Video

Since films are the dominant subject of videos, it is not surprising that video and cinema ratings have a strong relationship. One could distinguish between them in the impact of the large screen and the small one, or because there is the gatekeeper of the movie house as opposed to the gatekeeper of the video store, or even that the impact and context of the home is different from that of the public theater. Still, it is not a surprise to find that in most cases, the body responsible for the classification of films is also the one that rates videos, applying to this alternative medium the same procedure, the same criteria and issuing the same type of rating (see Table 2.6). This is the case in Germany, where the body authorised to rate video films is the FSK, which applies the same procedures as for film. This is also the regime applied in Denmark, Portugal, Spain, Ireland, Sweden, Finland, and United Kingdom.

However, in the United Kingdom, a new classification has been especially created for video, the 'Uc' label, emphasising the particular suitability of a given work for a young audience. In contrast, in Spain, two categories of cinema ratings have specifically designed for children disappeared for video, namely the

---

[2] The United Kingdom rating, strictly speaking, is not mandatory, as it can be removed by the local authorities who are officially in charge of classification through the Cinemas Act 1985.

'specially recommended for children' and the 'not recommended for under 7's' labels. In Finland, the 18+ rating has also disappeared, with just the 16+ age limit remaining. A film rated 18+ or that would have been rated 18+ is banned for video distribution.

Videos either based on a cinematographic work or originally created for video are rated as for a film, using the same criteria, following the same methodology and procedure, and granting the same graduated ratings. Moreover, generally the rating given for the cinema is reapplied to the video version. However, it must be noted that this is not the case in all the Member States. First of all, two countries do not apply any rating system to video. This is the case in Austria and Luxembourg. In Greece, the film regime is supposed to be applied to video but, the system has not really been implemented as yet.

Second, in Sweden, while ratings are compulsory for cinema films, they become voluntary for video. The video distributors assign ratings to their products with the exception of films containing depictions of realistic violence that are for hire or sale to children under 15 years. The ratings to be displayed on video packaging remains the same (All, 7+, 11+, and 15+). A system of voluntary examination by the classification board has been implemented, whereby charges can be brought against films that have not been previously examined where video films containing unlawful violence have been offered for hire or sale.[3] Charges cannot be brought in the case of films that have previously been approved by the Board.

Finally, in France, a clear distinction is made between the two possible origins of video products, which has some consequences for their system. Video products originating from the cinema have to carry the certificate issued by the film classification commission. Original video works escape this procedure and adopt a voluntary scheme regulated by a Code of Ethics enacted by the *Syndicat de l'Edition Vidéo* in 1995. This code requires the editor to display a warning when he considers that the work contains shocking scenes likely to harm the sensitivity of the consumer. The classification is issued directly by the different video editors. It is not a visual symbol system but only a display of information/recommendations. This is due to the fact that editors think they do not have the legal legitimacy to act as censor. There are no guidelines and no precise or harmonised criteria. For noncinematographic works the *Syndicat* refers to the classification system of the *Conseil Supérieur de l'Audiovisuel* (CSA) for TV programmes. It is interesting to note that the same medium will thus refer to the cinema system for some of its products and the TV system for others.

---

[3] Unlawful violence includes depiction of sexual violence or coercion or explicit or protracted severe violence to people or animals (Penal Code, chap. 16, section 10).

TABLE 2.6
Video Ratings: Austria, Belgium, Denmark, and Finland

	Austria	Belgium	Denmark	Finland
Ratings	Ø	All	A (All ages)	G (general)
		12 (12+)	T.f.A (7+)	Restricted for
		16 (16+)	T.O.11 (11+)	persons under 16
			T.O.15 (15+)	Banned
Amount	Ø	3	4	3
Required	Ø	Voluntary	Law[a]	Law[b]
Placed on	Ø	Packaging & cassette	Packaging	
Authority	Ø		Media Council for Children and Young People	Valtion elokuva-tarkastamo[c]

Video Ratings: France, Germany, and Ireland

	France	Germany	Ireland
Ratings	All	White (All ages)	R All
	12 (12+)	Yellow (6+)	R PG
	16 (16+)	Green (12+)	R 12+
	X (18+)	Blue (16+)	R 15+
	Recommendations (if purely video work)	Red (18+)	R 18+
Amount	4	5	5
Required	Law[d]/Voluntary[e]	Law	Law
Placed on	Packaging & cassette	Packaging & cassette	Packaging
Authority	Cinematographic works - CNC	Freiwillige Selbstkontrolle der Filmwirtshaft	Official Censor of Films

Video Ratings: Portugal, Netherlands, and United Kingdom

	Portugal	Netherlands	United Kingdom
Ratings	R4	AL (All ages)	Uc (All,+children)
	R6	PG	U (All ages)
	R12	12 (12+)	PG
	R16	16 (16+)	12 (12+)
	R18		15 (15+)
			18 (18+)
			R18 (restrict 18+)
Amount	5	3	7
Required	Law	Voluntary	Law
Placed on		Packaging & cassette[f]	Packaging & cassette
Authority	Comissão de Classificação de Espectáculos	Raad van Toezicht Videovoorlichting; RvtV[g]	British Board of Film classification

TABLE 2.6 (Continued)
Video Ratings: Italy, Luxembourg, Spain, and Sweden

	Italy	Luxembourg	Spain	Sweden
Ratings	For All	Ø	R All	All audiences
	Under 14		R 13+	7 (7+)
	(14+)		R 18+	11 (11+)
	Under 18		X	15 (15+)
	(18+)			
Amount	3	Ø	4	4[h]
Required	Mandatory	Ø	Law	Voluntary[i]
Placed on	Packaging	Ø	Packaging & cassette	Packaging
Authority	Censorship Committees	Ø	ICAA, Comisión de Calificación de Películas Cinematográficas	National Board of Film Censors

Source: International Video Federation, Country Reports—Programme in Comparative Media Law and Policy. No information was available for Greece.

[a] The Minister of Culture established MCCY in April 1997. Chapter 6 of the *Film Act of 12 March 1997* establishes the legal setting and outlines the mandate. At the same time, the State Film censorship was closed. Departmental Order No. 30 of 16 January 1998 regulates mCCY activity.

[b] Act on the Classification of Video and Other Audiovisual Programmes, 1987.

[c] Finnish Board of Film Classification.

[d] (*Décret du 23 February* 1990: title II, article 5, al. 3) This law mandates the video tape editors to display the certificate delivered by the classification commission of films on the tape's cover.

[e] Code of ethics approved on 25 March 1995, Article 6. This concerns only purely video products. Producers have to display information regarding the content when they consider it as potentially harmful.

[f] Voluntary video industry supervisory board under the charge of NVPI (*Nederlandse Vereniging van Producenten en Importeurs van beeld- en geluidsdragers*—The Dutch Federation of Producers and Importers of image and sound carriers); new self-regulating system for all audio-visual media to enter into force in 2000.

[g] Voluntary video industry supervisory Board.

[h] In addition, some times, the distributor also uses the category 'from 18 years.'

[i] The video distributor assigns, on her own, an age category. This is voluntary with the exception of films containing depictions of realistic violence that are for hire or sale to children under 15 years as well as of films showing at a public gathering or entertainment.

In the Netherlands, as in France, text must be displayed on the cover (in addition to the age rating), categorising the video (Child and Youth, Family, Drama/Classic, Humor, Sports, Music, Educational, Science Fiction, Action adventure, War, Western, Thriller/Crime, Horror, Racy Humor, Erotic and Porn) and giving an accurate impression of the content of the video.

Online Services

Rating solutions for the Internet are far from being the norm in Europe. Thus far, only three states have developed a true rating system, namely Germany, the United Kingdom, and Italy. Rating solutions used for Internet content are of direct relevance for the purpose of this study since, as stated earlier, it is very likely that the amount of television content available in the future will be similar to the wide range of content offered on the Internet. Therefore, content rating solutions developed for the Internet are of particular significance for the new television setting. The three cases of Germany, the United Kingdom, and Italy highlight the fact that both rating options—evaluative or descriptive—may be used for television.

In Germany, the entity in charge of software classification is also authorized to rate Internet content. This is the *Unterhaltungssoftware Selbstkontrolle* (USK), the Entertainment Software Self-Regulation Body, created on 1 October 1994. The USK has supervised network contents and online games since 22 August 1997. To this end, it applies the same procedure as the one used for software. It refers to the age categories included in the relevant legal provisions and has developed objective points for the age classification of computer and video games that are also of use for Internet content.[4] For instance, a game is always said to contain gratuitous violence if the player is placed in the role of the killer, if the death of opponents is rewarded, if the idea of the game is exclusively to allow aggressive behaviour, as well as if the effects of violence are clearly shown. However, the decision regarding the ratings is based on the opinions of the examination committee on the basis of these criteria. It could be said that the system employs a semideterministic methodology.

In principle, the USK exerts voluntary control. The aim of the USK is to guarantee the protection of minors by means of voluntary self-regulation on the part of the suppliers, even before the publication of products. By awarding its ratings the USK is ensuring that a given software is suitable for distribution and complies with the legal provisions regarding the protection of minors. The USK only acts on request of content providers.

However, German department stores have decided to sell only video and computer games that have been controlled by the USK. The suppliers and manufacturers as well as the information and communication service providers that are members of the Association of Entertainment Software in Germany (VUD)

---

[4] These criteria have been developed on the basis of the provisions of GjSM 1985 and are very similar to them.

recognize the USK as their self-regulation body for the software available for purchase and other public use.[5] The association is supported by the association for the Support of Young People and Social Work.

The USK is composed of an Advisory Council (*Beirat*), which is the policy-making and controlling body of the USK, and of expert examiners. The Advisory Council is made up of members of various groups of society for example, in the field of science, politics, culture, and protection of minors. The expert examiners must not be active in the computer hardware or software industry. They are independent and their function is honorary. They are only reimbursed for their expenses. They are obliged to attend the advanced training events organized by the USK. These relate to evaluations and examining activities and also advanced training on selected areas of assessment of computer and video games. The experts are selected on the basis of their professional experience and training.

The USK in principle examines everything submitted regarding its content and permissibility. It controls whether the content is compatible with the provisions of the Criminal Code and which age classification should be assigned to it. The USK then delivers a report to the content or service provider (*Strafgesetzbuch-StGB* [Criminal Code] §86a, 130, 131, 184 (3)). The USK awards age classifications (evaluative rating) for 5 levels and is displayed on the product by means of stickers as demonstrated in Figure 2.1.

FIGURE 2.1
The USK Rating System and Stickers Used

1	2	3	4	5
No age restriction	Suitable for ages 6 and over	Suitable for ages 12 and over	Suitable for ages 16 and over	Not suitable for persons under the age of 18

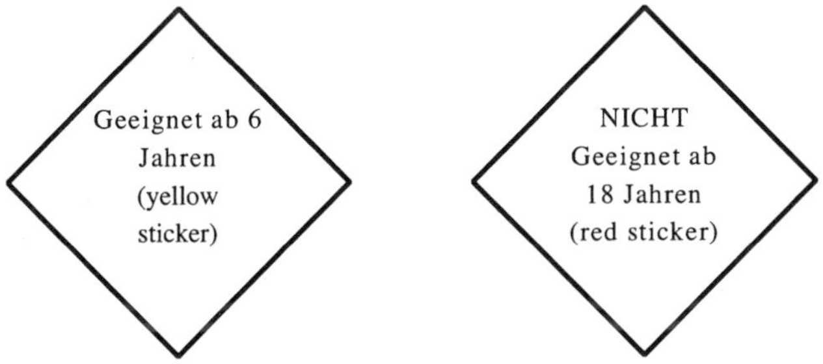

Geeignet ab 6
Jahren
(yellow
sticker)

NICHT
Geeignet ab
18 Jahren
(red sticker)

---

[5] The VUD is composed of developers, distributors, and licensees from the entertainment, information and educational software industry, such as Acclaim Entertainment GmbH, ACTIVI-SION, ak tronic Software and Services, ART DEPARTMENT GmbH, BLUE BYTE Software GmbH etc. The members do not rate their products themselves but give them to VUD, which passes them to the USK to be rated.

The USK maintains that the age groups categories should be updated. However, they regret that current theories regarding psychological development have not been studied in a sufficiently scientific manner on the basis of the computer game practices of children and young people.

In addition, there is no legal obligation relating specifically to the USK rating. However, the relevant general legal provisions regarding rating are complied with by the USK, partly because of the fear of bad publicity following the attribution of an inappropriate rating. This prevents voluntary self-control organizations acting in the interests of the companies financing them. The ratings of the USK are not binding in the legal sense, but are supplied mainly for consumer information.

The USK's rating capacity is limited because of the size of the organization. Only 5 people are employed, and there are 27 experts and 7 observers. So far they have received requests from 195 organizations from 6 countries. It requests fees for the examination of websites: 300 DM for a maximum of 25 pages; 500 DM for a maximum of 75 pages; 750 DM for a maximum of 100 pages; 1000 DM for a number of pages exceeding the limit of 100.

As to the solution deployed in Spain for the classification of videos, the USK guarantees that an examination will take place no later than 21 days from application for a rating, and the applicant is informed of the results by fax. The USK is a national system, but the fact that Germany is, in the field of entertainment software, the second biggest market after the United States motivates foreign firms to participate in this voluntary self-control organization.

In Italy, the solution deployed is also nongovernmental. The collaboration between the Information Science Degree Course of the University of Cesena (who prepared the operating environment) and the *Association Cittá Invisibile* (who defined the rating system) has recently given birth to a pilot Italian rating agency: IT-RA.

The IT-RA rating system is evaluative and voluntary and uses a Platform for Internet Content Selection (PICS) rating system, which is a system elaborated within the Word Wide Web Consortium (W3C). It grants PICS labels to content providers who autonomously rate their documents by completing application form available online. Table 2.7 reproduces the IT-RA descriptive criteria. Based on the level of content as rated by the content providers, IT-RA issues the relevant PICS label (metadata), which is then associated with the Internet content. When access to the document is sought the software browser reads the level of each category and blocks access when the level is higher than the one selected by the user. The IT-RA system applies to advertising as well.

TABLE 2.7
IT-RA Rating System

	Level 0	Level 1	Level 2	Level 3	Level 4
V	No express or implied violence	Materials denouncing violation of human rights—NHM	Implicitly violent	Expressly violent	Inducing or inciting to violence
S	No references to sex	Scientific material on sex and sexuality—NHM	Alluding or relating to erotica	Moderately sexual and non explicit	Sexually explicit and pornographic
L	No vulgarity	Materials on the use and diffusion of dialects—NHM	From time to time vulgar or dirty	Vulgar and/or blasphemous	Verbally violent
A	No advertisement	Advertising—NHM	Also advertising products for minors	Subliminal advertising contents	Prevailing expressed advertising contents
R	No references to religion	Material on religion	References to a particular religion	Proselitical religious references	Religious or non religious intolerance
P	Non political	Material on politics—NHM	Generic political references	References to political associations	References to political parties
R	No racial references	Racial material—NHM	Subliminal racial references	Explicit racial references	Inciting to racial hatred
D	Highly didactic and based on accurate scientific materials appropriate for minors	Highly didactic and based on accurate scientific materials appropriate for adults	Medium didactic with good scientific basis	Low didactic with poor scientific basis	Nondidactic

Note. V=Violence; S=Sex; L=Language; A=Advertising; R=Religion; P=Politics; R=Racism; D=[
NHM=Not harmful to minors.

The United Kingdom has also opted for self-regulation. An independent organization, the Internet Watch Foundation (IWF), was created in April 1997 to implement the proposals jointly agreed on by the Government, the police, and the two major United Kingdom service provider trade associations, ISPA and LINX. It is funded by the United Kingdom industry on a subscription basis and is controlled by a Management Board drawn from the subscribers and a Policy Board drawn from a wide range of stakeholders in the Internet including industry, child and education, consumer, libertarian, and other media organizations.

The principle is the same as for the IT-RA system. The provider rates its own content according to the range of categories provided by the IWF, as shown in Table 2.8. It is a descriptive system, developed in close coordination with the one created by the Recreational Software Advisory Council (RSAC) and contains 10, more or less detailed categories. To assist users in their choices, IWF also recommends that 'off-the-shelf' profiles be introduced so that a familiar classification of content, such as the equivalent of a film certificate rating, can be chosen.

TABLE 2.8
IWF Rating System

	Level 0	Level 1	Level 2	Level 3	Level 4
N					
SE	No reference	Romance Affection	Passion	Groping, touching (erogenous), clothed unclothed	Other (not covered above): masturbation, intercourse, sexual violence, deviance.
SA	No reference	Emotional/ relationship issues (with no explicit sexual content)	Adolescent/ emotional issues with sexual content: puberty/period, and so on.	Sexual relations (hetero/ homo)	Other sexual matters: sado-masochism, and so on.
L					
V					
PD	Not requested 'Nothing of relevance'	Non-verifiable or default (such as, e-mail address)	Verifiable detail (such as, name and address)	Financial detail (such as, credit check-style detail)	
FT	Nothing of relevance	Expenditure from a pre-agreed fixed ceiling account (already committed)	Direct expenditure from bank, credit card, and so on, (real money)		

TABLE 2.8 (continued)

	Level 0	Level 1	Level 2	Level 3	Level 4
T	None of these--no relevance to this category	Neutral (non-prejudicial) reference to groups or attitudes to them	Reference to a group or groups which imply or assert a degree of inferiority or superiority by virtue of real or imagined membership	Maligns or deprecates one group and/or advocates discriminatory treatment of its members (not including physical harm or violence)	Advocates action which would cause physical, psychological or economic harm or violence against the group
H	No reference	Reference without promotion or advocacy	Promotion of, or instructions about any activity which is normally considered safe for children only if supervised by an adult (such as, water sports)	Promotion of, or instructions about, any activity not considered safe or advisable for children and/or which can be harmful to adults (such as, smoking, consuming alcohol)	Promotion of, or instructions about, any activity which has a reasonable possibility of leading to serious injury or death (such as suicide advice)
A					
C					

Note. N=Nudity; SE=Sex: Erotic; SA=Sex: Advice, Information; L=Language; V=Violence; PD=Personal Details; FT=Financial Transactions; T=Tolerance; H=Potentially Harmful Subjects; A=Adult Themes; C=Context Variables.

Television

As to television-based rating solutions developed to date, the principal conclusion that emerges from the data is that there is no single approach among the Member States and no approach that seems to serve as the basis for a harmonization or unification of rating systems. Some of the countries have opted for extremely elaborate procedures, such as France, while others have not implemented any specific systems, such as Luxembourg.

The method by which a rating system is implemented is important for its operation and this, too, varies from country to country. In some Member States, law requires labelling systems. Law plays an important defining role in Austria, Denmark, Finland, The Netherlands, Sweden, and Italy (in conjunction with the implementation of a code of conduct). In Spain, rating television content is mandated by law either at a national or regional level, and the *Communidades regionales* have authority to implement their own rating system (as for cinema). However, Catalonia is the only region to have done so. In Belgium, because of its constitutional federal structure that encompasses the three Flemish, French, and German linguistic communities, the legal structure provides that rating solutions vary from one community to another. While the French community is in the process of adopting a visual signalling system, the Flemish Community has opted for an acoustic warning solution and the German Community has not yet implemented any regime.

In some other countries legal provisions have addressed the protection of minors but leave the door open to self-regulatory initiatives. This is the case in France, where there is no mandatory provision regarding the introduction of a specific rating system, but rather a requirement, in general terms, for the *Conseil Supérieur de l'Audiovisuel* (CSA) to oversee the protection of minors. In consequence, a labelling system was implemented in 1996 by the terrestrial broadcasters under the initiative of the CSA and introduced into the licenses of the broadcasters concerned.[7] The same process was followed in Portugal, where the *Alta Autoridad para a Comunicação* came to an agreement with the broadcasters on 9 July 1997. In Germany, the system was implemented under the sole initiative of the private broadcasters, with public service broadcasters separating themselves and relying on their own 'in-house' system.

Cultural differences are extremely evident in this domain as they are for cinema ratings. In Spain, Greece, or Portugal, the dictatorial regimes' legacy may have created certain resistance within the population to state influence on behaviour, especially where cultural choices are involved. The same reluctance applies to content providers, who are not so enthusiastic about implementation of parental control mechanisms. In these states, where content regulation is implemented, it is done so in a free and competitive way (see for instance, Spain discussed later). There are cultural determinants of ratings, of course, other than the hand of an oppressive past. In Ireland, for example, some Catholic pressure groups oppose labelling systems to alert the public if they authorize an infringement of the 'social contract' not to broadcast detrimental programmes. As a consequence, broadcasters act as self-censors and refuse to broadcast any kind of material that might endanger the audience, and consequently, their own image.

Because of these cultural and historic differences and because of differences in the legal and structural origins of television rating systems, there are signifi-

---

[7] This system was recently reviewed, giving birth to a new visual icons regime, implemented in September 1998. The system primarily addresses TF1, France 2, France 3, Canal + and M6, the visual warning system was introduced in the licences of RFO, La Cinquième, Canal Antilles, Canal Calédonie, Canal Réunion, Canal Polynésie and Canal Guyane. for RFO (*Official Journal* 1998a; *Official Journal* 1998b).

cant differences in the way rating systems have evolved in the different European Member States. They do, however, display a few similarities. One common point is that most of the countries (except Luxembourg) have developed watershed rules and time-scheduling corresponding to these rules are mostly identical. The second half of the evening (beginning between 9:00 p.m. and 10:30 p.m.) is generally perceived as the limit before which detrimental content for minors is prohibited.

In Austria, the watershed rules stipulate that before 8:15 p.m. programmes must be family-friendly and cinema works rated 16+ or more have to be broadcast after 10:00 p.m. In Belgium, fiction works which due to number of scenes or to their atmosphere are likely to harm sensitivity of minors under 12, when broadcast before 10:00 p.m. must have an icon that appears throughout programme (including credits) for unencrypted channels and for one minute at the beginning of the broadcast for encrypted channels (including credits). When these works are broadcast after 10:00 p.m. the icon must appear for 1 minute at the beginning of the broadcast (including credits and for 15 seconds after each break. Works with erotic character or intense violence must broadcast an icon throughout programme (including credits) whatever the broadcasting time (prior to or after 10:00 p.m.).

In Denmark, the Public Service Television Danmarks Radio uses an informal watershed of 9:00 p.m., and there is also a standard provision for all broadcasters that those programmes that are considered harmful to minors can only be shown after 12:00 p.m. A watershed is not necessary if a decoder is used to receive programme.

In Finland, Programmes unsuitable for children must be broadcast after 9:00 p.m.

In France, cinema works rated 12 +, as well as television works likely to disturb a young audience, notably when they contain systematic or repeated psychological or physical violence, have to be broadcast after 10:00 p.m. However, broadcast of such work may be possible before 10:00 p.m., if an icon is displayed throughout. Such exceptions are not permissible on Tuesdays, Fridays, and days preceding non-working days. For encrypted channels, broadcasting time is left to the assessment of the broadcaster, however, the enterprise must take particular attention to the fact that programmes dedicated to young audience as well as programmes and trailers broadcast immediately after the said programmes do not contain scenes likely to harm young viewers

Also in France, cinema works rated 16 +, as well as television works with erotic character or intense violence, likely to impair physical, mental, or moral growth of minors under 16 have to be broadcast after 10:30 p.m. Trailers for these works must not contain scenes likely to harm youth audience sensitivity and cannot be broadcast before 8:30 p.m. For encrypted channels these programmes cannot be broadcast on Wednesday before 8:30, Saturday, or Sunday morning. The trailers for works containing violent scenes or scenes likely to harm the sensitivity of a young audience cannot be broadcast during the unencrypted part of the programming as well as Wednesday before 8:30 p.m., or Saturday and Sunday morning.

In Germany, the watershed is the only system in use. Broadcasts that may endanger the physical, mental, or emotional well-being of children or adolescents may only be transmitted between 11:00 p.m. and 6:00 a.m. Films rated '16' can only be broadcast between 10:00 p.m. and 6:00 a.m. Films rated '18' can only be broadcast between 11:00 p.m. and 6:00 a.m. Broadcasts whose contents are completely or basically the same as publications included in the Index can only be broadcast between 11:00 p.m. and 6:00 a.m. Exceptions to these time restrictions are also permissible if the broadcaster makes sure by specific means such as encryption that children or adolescents do not have access to the programme. However, this needs to be confirmed by the competent regional regulatory authority on the basis of a proposition for a decision of the Joint Office for the protection of Youth and Programming.

In Greece, less harmful programmes have to be broadcast after 9:30 p.m. and more harmful programmes have to be broadcast after 12:00 p.m. In Ireland, adult viewing may solely be broadcast after 9:00 p.m.

In Italy, motion pictures that have been certified by the censorship committees as unsuitable for minors under the age of 14 can be broadcast only within a strict time period[8]: between 10:30 p.m. and 7:00 a.m.[9] This watershed rule applies also to advertisements of audiotext services such as hot lines, chat line, and one-to-one services.[10]

There are no watershed rules in Luxembourg, but in the Netherlands, films which have been rated by the Dutch Board of Film Classification (NFK) for an audience over 12 years of age, may not be shown before 8:00 p.m. Also in the Netherlands, films which have been classified '16 and over' may not be broadcast before 10:00 p.m.

In Portugal, violent and shocking content should be broadcast after 10:00 p.m. In Spain, broadcasts that may endanger the physical, mental, or emotional development of children may only be broadcast after 10:00 p.m. In Sweden, programmes unsuitable for children must be broadcast after 9:00 p.m.

In the United Kingdom, the terrestrial channel watershed starts at 9:00 p.m. and lasts until 5:30 a.m. Cable and licensed satellite services operate with the

---

[8] Law 223/1990 of 6 August 1990 (the so-called "Mammì Law"), section 13.

[9] It has been pointed out by many studies, that the effectiveness of this provision may be frustrated given that children's television viewing time appears to include a good deal of night hours.

[10] Law Decree No. 545 of 23 October 1996 converted into Law No. 650 of 23 December 1996.

standard 9:00 p.m. watershed for all channels, except for specially encrypted services with restricted availability to children, which have two watersheds: one at 8:00 p.m. (equivalent to the 9:00 p.m. change on other channels) and the second at 10:00 p.m. when material of a more adult nature can be shown. Other cable and licensed satellite services are expected to follow similar standards to the terrestrial channels. The watershed does not apply in the same way to pay-per-view services given their stricter security systems. '18' rated films are allowed at 8:00 p.m., '12' and '15' rated films may be shown at any time. Similar arrangements will apply to variants, such as (Near) Video on Demand.

One logic that is emerging is that encrypted services receive different treatment (see Denmark, France, Germany, and United Kingdom) in terms of ratings and watersheds. This may be a harbinger of the ways a watershed system could be adapted to the digital environment and for new services such as pay-per-view. Unlike the general broadcasting scheme, encrypted services, whether terrestrial, cable, or satellite based, apart from the fact that they offer basic technical means to prevent direct viewing, presuppose that viewers have expressed positive and active consent to the content carried by those services. As such, regulation that applies contents received by passive means may be, and generally is, adjusted to take into account this particular aspect. In Germany and Denmark this peculiar type of broadcasting may even exempt the broadcasters or operators concerned from applying the relevant watershed rule. A recent Italian Bill also proposes such a specific regime for encoded programmes.[11]

In addition to the watershed, an acoustic warning is often included among the protective devices. Acoustic warnings are to be found in the structures of several countries, namely Belgium, Denmark, Finland, Ireland, the Netherlands, Portugal, Spain, Sweden, and United Kingdom as a possible means of protection. However, acoustic warnings may not be the panacea for the new TV setting. There are built-in restrictions to this technique. The necessary intervention of a direct human factor will make it difficult to process the amount of content needing to be rated, and this old-fashioned method of recommending or alerting viewers may be in contradiction with the new bias towards delegating decision-making power directly to the viewer regarding selection of programmes. In other words, this will in no way inform the viewer well in advance. And a mechanism that provides a warning in advance may be necessary if the goal is to allow the viewer to block or pre-select programming.

Visual icons as a means of empowering parents in controlling contents broadcast on TV is widespread, and is more likely, to some extent to have a future within the next TV environment.

---

[11] A recent Proposal (Proposal in favour of friendship between children and TV') sets out, *inter alia*, that time limitation concerning performance of programmes not suitable for minors cannot be applied to codified broadcasting.

Nevertheless, this system has not yet been implemented in every European country and may not be for some time. The reasons for this are diverse. The United Kingdom and Germany believe that it would have a perverse effect. In Ireland, social pressure has halted its implementation and the Belgian Flemish Community have not accepted it because of a lack of European harmonization in this field. Even where it is in use there are divergences as to the design and what it represents.

The countries that have opted for visual icons systems are Austria (Table 2.9), Finland, The Netherlands, France (Table 2.11), Portugal (Table 2.12), Spain (Table2.14), Sweden, Belgium (Table 2.13), and Italy (Table 2.10). Catalan has its own system of icons, demonstrated in Table 2.15.

TABLE 2.9
Visual Icons: Austria—Evaluative
(Only applied by the public broadcaster ORF,
Bundesgesetz, mit dem das Rundfunkgesetz 1993)

Rating	Indicator
Not for children	X
Only for adults	O
Recommended for Children[a]	K+

[a] This third symbol does not appear on the screen but only in the ORF Teletext, in press releases, and via the Internet.

TABLE 2.10
Visual Icons: Italy—Evaluative (Only applied
by the commercial broadcasters *Canale Cinque*, *Italia Uno* and *Retequattro*)

Rating	Indicator	
Not suitable for children		(A child is represented in a red circle)
Parental Guidance Advisable		(A child and an adult are represented in a yellow circle)
Suitable for all		(A child is represented in a green circle)

Note: The indicators portrayed here are artistic renditions of the actual icons and are meant as examples. They do not represent the exact icons used by the broadcasters.

TABLE 2.11
Visual Icons: France—Evaluative/Descriptive (Terrestrial Broadcasters)

Rating	Indicator
All audiences	 (Green with white interior)
PG desirable *Works containing scenes likely to harm young* *audience*	 (Blue with white interior)
PG compulsory/Cinema works rated 12 + *TV works likely to disturb young audience, notably* *when plot contains systematic or repeated* *psychological or physical violence*	 (Yellow with white interior)
Adult audience/Cinema works rated 16 + *TV works with erotic character or intense violence,* *likely to impair physical, mental or moral growth of* *minors under16*	 (Red with white interior)
Pornographic or extremely violent work, likely to *seriously impair physical, mental or moral growth of* *minors*	 (Purple with white interior)

Note. Canal Satellite uses a descriptive rating. Content is displayed via EPG and divided into categories (Film, documentaries, animation, sports, and so on) and subcategories (Film-action, Film-history, Film-pink square (X), and so on).

TABLE 2.12
Visual Icons: Portugal—Descriptive

Rating	Indicator
Violent, shocking scenes	O

TABLE 2.13
Visual Icons: Belgium—Evaluative/Descriptive
(to be revised by the Belgian authorities)

Rating	Indicator
Parental guidance: Fictional programmes which, due to number of scenes or to their atmosphere, are likely to harm sensitivity of minors under 12	(orange)
Prohibited to minors under 16: Works with erotic character or intense violence	(red border)
Prohibited on channels other than encrypted: Works with pornographic character and/or gratuitous violence	(solid red)

TABLE 2.14
Visual Icons: Spain—Specific to the Broadcaster

Canal Plus Spain—Evaluative

Rating	Indicator
All ages	◦→ (Green key) Age Group
Prohibited to minors under 13	◦→ (Blue key) Age Group
Prohibited to minors under 18	◦→ (Orange key) Age Group
X rated films	◦→ (Violet key) Age Group

Canal Satélite Digital—Descriptive

Rating	Indicator
Subcategories: such as drama, comedy, horror, and eroticism.	EPG facilities divide content into these subcategories.

TABLE 2.14 (continued)

TVE—Evaluative[a]

Rating
Specially recommended for children
For all
Not recommended to children under 7
Not recommended to person under 12
Not recommended to person under 18
X rated films

Via Digital—Evaluative/Descriptive[b]

Rating	Indicator
All audience	• Title, author, date of creation, language, and so on • Category: documentaries, sports, series, • Basic content description: violence, sex, etc
Prohibited to minors 14	• Title, author, date of creation, language, and so on • Category: documentaries, sports, series, • Basic content description: violence, sex, etc
Prohibited to minors 18	• Title, author, date of creation, language, and so on • Category: documentaries, sports, series, • Basic content description: violence, sex, etc

[a] The information assessing the content appears on the TV screen prior to each broadcast. The rating is displayed on a blue screen containing basic information such as the title of the film, its author, the audio facility (mono or stereo), and also the age group to which the film content is most suitable. This age group classification is the same as the one used for the cinema, apart from the 13+ threshold, which becomes a 12+ limit.

[b] No icons correspond to these ratings. The information is displayed on the screen by pressing a button on the remote control to access the ratings, which can refer both to age classification or type of content. It may be possible to block content that does not correspond to a certain age group using the age classification. The descriptive information displayed, at the moment, may be subject to improvement. The idea under development is to insert colours for each category of content such as yellow for films.

TABLE 2.15
Visual Icons: Catalan Cable TV operators—Descriptive.

Rating	Indicator
Programmes which may harm the sensitivity of minors due to their physical or psychological violence or eroticism	(solid red)
Programmes which may harm the sensitivity of minors due to their pornographic nature or gratuitous violence	(solid red)

In Austria, the visual icons apply only to the Public broadcaster ORF. In Finland, they are dedicated to TV guides and Teletext. In the Netherlands, visual icons are used on a voluntary basis. In Sweden, the icons only apply to TV 1000. In Belgium, the icons are still under development. In Italy, the icons have been adopted but not yet implemented. Visual icons also exist in Greece (ERT) and United Kingdom (Living, Bravo), but on a completely voluntary basis. In France, as well as in Portugal and Finland, the design of this icon applies to the different broadcasters, while in Spain and the Netherlands, when applied, this design varies from one broadcaster to another. In France, in 1998, the visual icon regime applied solely to the terrestrial broadcasters with the exception of ARTE (created under the Bilateral Agreement between France and Germany, 30 April 1991), but was expected to be extended soon to cable channels.

Belgium is also in the process of implementing a visual system that will be common to all broadcasters. Because of the recent change in the French icons, the Belgian authorities are revising implementation there so as to maintain an approximation of them. The Belgian system will, however, not be identical to the French system because of different regulations regarding admission to cinemas. A recent Italian proposal requires that all broadcasters should adopt a visual symbols regime, but rules have not stipulated any principles regarding the design of the icon to be displayed on screens so competing solutions may exist. A self-regulatory regime adopted by Italian commercial broadcasters, which are members of the FRT (Federation of Radio Television Commercial Broadcasters), has been implemented. A self-regulatory visual icon system may also be developed in Luxembourg (the public authorities have pronounced in favour of visual signalling, but would leave broadcasters to implement their own system).

The design of icons and the complexity of iconic systems differ from state to state. From one single icon in Portugal, 5 different icons in France represent the visual system, while Belgium is considering three different icons and Canal Plus Spain has developed a 4-icon system. The example of Canal Plus Spain is symptomatic of the difficulty of envisaging a transfrontier labelling solution. As part of the Canal Plus group, this broadcaster could have adopted the labelling system already implemented by its parent company. However, the Spanish company preferred to create its own system, claiming that the approach taken in France was too complex and multilayered.

Similarities exist, however, as to the nature of the rating provider. In France, the ratings issued are, in the main, similar across broadcasters, holding programs constant, even though the rating procedure is the responsibility of the individual broadcaster. Each broadcaster is free to organize the administrative procedure as it wishes, and free to organize the composition of the rating body, which may be either internal or external. These are mainly internal for the reason that the broadcasters are reluctant to delegate any power that might have an impact on their editorial policy. M6, a French private broadcaster, has a variation on this theme: it has developed a procedure based on the successive opinion of two committees constituted of persons external to the channel (and representative of its audience—mothers and youth). The managerial staff of the channel, however, make the final decision.

Similar approaches to autonomy (broadcasters rating their programme) apply in most of the other countries, as demonstrated in Table 2.16. In Belgium, it is anticipated that the responsibility for the visual icons system will be given to the broadcasters. In Italy, a code of conduct adopted in 1997 requires each broadcaster to appoint a screening committee. The TV operators have not yet implemented these structures. It is interesting to note however, that in this country there is a specific twist: a law adopted in 1995, provides for producers, distributors, and broadcasters who intend to transmit TV films and fictional programmes during the daytime, which may significantly impair minors, must apply to the film censorship committee to obtain a certificate to do so. The specific section within the censorship committee responsible for administering this law has not yet been established.

In Germany, the system is distinctive: private broadcasters delegate the rating decision to an external body, the FSF, while the public broadcasters rate their programmes (that is, decide the broadcasting schedule) in-house. It is clear that in most cases the responsibility for rating lies with the broadcasters. As to the methodology followed by the rating bodies, given the fact that it is in-house, it is quite secret. As transparent criteria are not generally communicated outside the organization, it may be concluded that the process is mainly nondeterministic.

TABLE 2.16
National Rating Systems

Country	Body	Process	Mode	Represent-ation	Control
AUT	Broadcasters	TV departments	Mandatory[a] from 1.1.1999	W/V	*Kommission zur Wahrung des Rundfunkgesetzes*
BEL	Broadcasters	Producers/ programme dept/channel directors	Mandatory[b]	W/A/V (common) Flemish community	*CSA, Commissariat voor de Media*
DNK	Broadcasters	Programme department	Mandatory[c]	W/A	
FIN	Broadcasters	Internal boards or programme responsible	Mandatory[d] from 1.1.1999	W/A/V[e] (common)	Telecommuni-cations Administrative Centre (TV programmes) Consumer Ombudsman (advertisements)
FRA	CNC (film) Broadcasters	Internal committee	Mandatory[f]	W/V (common)	*Conseil Supérieur de l'Audiovisuel*
DEU	FSF[g] Broadcasters	Compliance officer	Mandatory[h]	W	FSF/ *Landesmedienanstalten*
GRC	Broadcasters	Programme department	Mandatory[i]	W/V(v)[j]	
IRL	Broadcasters		Voluntary	W/A	Broadcasting Complaints Commission Independent Radio and Television Commission
ITA	Broadcasters/ Cinema rating body[k]	Internal committee /additional sections	Mandatory[l]/ Voluntary (FRT code of conduct)[m]	W/V(v)	*Autorità per le Garanzione nelle Comunicazioni*
LUX	Underway				

TABLE 2.16 (continued)

Country	Body	Process	Mode	Represent-ation	Control
NLD	NFK (film) Broadcasters[n]		Mandatory[o]	W/A/V(v) (vary)	Commissariat voor de Media
PRT	SCA (movies) Broadcasters	SCA programme director	Mandatory[p]	W/A/V (common)	Instituto para a Comunicação Social
ESP	CPCC (movies) Broadcasters	CCPC/ program or channel providers[q]	Mandatory[r]	W/A/V (vary)	
SWE	Broadcasters	Programme dept	Voluntary	W/A/V[s]	Granskningsn-ämnden for radio and television[t]
GBR	Broadcasters	Compliance officer	Mandatory	W/A/(M)/V (v) (vary)	Independent Television Commission

W = Watershed; A = Acoustic warning; V = Visual symbol; (v) = voluntary.

[a] Section 2a of *Bundesgesetz über die Aufgaben und die Einrichtung des Österreichischen Rundfunks* (Broadcasting Act) as amended by *Bundesgesetz, mit dem das Rundfunkgesetz und die Rundfunkgesetz-Novelle* 1993 *geändert werden* (Federal Act to Amend the Broadcasting Act and the 1993 Amendment to the Broadcasting Act), *Federal Law Gazette* 1999 I 1.

[b] Decree of 28 April 1998 (Flemish community). The Decree of the French community is still not yet adopted.

[c] Broadcasting Act of 19 February 1998.

[d] Act on Television and Radio Operations , 22 September 1998.

[e] Visual icons are solely published in TV magazines and Teletext. The symbol 'K' refers to forbidden programs (K stands for Kielletty). For Swedish programs, the symbol 'F' (forbjuden) is used. The symbol is printed after the titles of programmes that have been labelled as unsuitable for children.

[f] Inserted in broadcasters' licence (see, supra, note 44).

[g] Competent only for private broadcasters.

[h] Agreement between the Federal States on Broadcasting in United Germany, 31 August 1991, last amended on 25 November 1997 (Rundfunkstaatsvertrag - RStV).

[i] Law 2328/95 entered into force in August 1995.

[j] As already mentioned, ERT, the Greek public broadcaster, voluntarily implemented a visual system.

k Law No. 203 of 30 May 1995—This is designated for television films and fictional programmes which, given the violent or sexual content, may significantly impair minors. This has not yet entered into force due to the delay in appointing the competent sections to operate within the censorship committee.

l Law 223/1990 of 6 August 1990.

m Adopted on 19 May 1993. Signatories are Canale Cinque, Italia Uno, and Retequattro.

n As a result of discussions in recent years on media violence in society, the NFK has been asked to rate media products concerning films for television.

o Media Act, enforced in 1987.

p Law 31-A/98, 14 July 1998.

q Concerns Satellite Digital Platforms: Canal Satellite Digital and Vía Digital.

r Article 17.2 of Law 25/1994 of 12 July 1994.

s TV 1000 has only developed visual symbols.

t Swedish Broadcasting Commission.

In France, the rating situation differs from one broadcaster to another, but the common trend is that the assessment is nondeterministic, with the notable exception of France 2, that has developed some objective criteria on the basis of qualitative investigations. This may be due to the particular responsibility that public broadcasters feel is vested in them, though it is not possible to draw firm conclusions as, for example, France 3 has not taken this option. The same applies to Spain as the responsibility for ratings assessment rests with the broadcasters and appears to be nondeterministic for each of those who have implemented such a system (TVE, Canal Plus Spain, Via digital, Canal Satellite digital, and Catalan cable TV operators).

In Germany, the system aspires for greater objectivity in ratings. Private broadcasters delegated classification to a common and external body, the FSF and guidelines have been drawn as assurance of impartial rating and respect for the editorial freedom of the content providers. The standards employed are interesting as well. For example, programs should not have the effect of making children emotionally insecure, frightened, or disturbed because of excessive depiction of violence or the blurring of reality and fiction. Broadcasts must not lead to social or ethical disorientation of children, for example, through the identification with violent characters or through the representation of strategies based on violence to resolve conflicts. However, these guidelines leave a great deal of room for a subjective approach on the part of the rating board. The methodology may therefore be described as semideterministic.

CONCLUSIONS

Some conclusions emerge from this review of the actual rating regimes existing in Europe.

Acoustic Warnings

Guided to some extent by the *Television Without Frontiers Directive*, acoustical warnings are widely used in Member States. This mechanism is generally seen as more likely to avoid the perverse effect of the 'forbidden fruit' phenomenon. Acoustical warnings are also a way for the broadcaster to avoid the stigma of having part of its programmes 'marked' as presenting certain risks for a part of the population. This technique presents serious drawbacks partly because it is limited in time: The warning is presented at the beginning of the programme and is not repeated afterwards, meaning that the viewer will have no capacity to be informed on the potential detrimental effect of a given programme if he missed the announcement that was made (visual icons may also present this weakness where they are not imposed throughout the duration of the programme). In addition, this system will not permit a parent to organize television viewing in advance. It is an antiquated means of alerting and informing, not responsive to challenges brought about by digital technology.

Visual Icons

The most developed rating system at the moment, in terms of information disclosure, is the use of visual icons, which may carry both evaluative and descriptive information. However, this system has certain limitations. Icons have not been adopted in all European Union countries and are far from being adopted in some of them. This is due to cultural reasons as in Ireland, social motivations as in Germany and the United Kingdom, or historical legacies as in Greece, though ERT, the public broadcaster has developed a visual system, even if not prescribed by law. These circumstances are not likely to alter significantly within the near future. Another reason may also be the lack of coordination regarding visual information that, due to the increase of cross border broadcasting, has led to some confusion among the viewers. That is why the Flemish community of Belgium has not implemented any visual information.

Where visual icons are adopted there are divergences regarding the design. There is no clear common understanding of a specific format to represent a specific content or a specific age group, even if, apart from the *Canal Plus Spain* case it appears that a 'Triangle' commonly represents danger and harmful content and a restricted access to teenagers while 'Orange' and 'Red' colours are used in most cases to denote violence or erotic content.

There is some divergence regarding what visual icons should represent, that is, evaluative or descriptive information, or a combination of the two. And whether evaluative or descriptive is opted for, some countries, for cultural reasons, will not see the point of icons that alert the viewer to certain contents, such as nudity in Nordic countries.

There is some divergence in the scope of application. Common icons are applied to all broadcasters in Portugal, Finland, and Belgium. Common icons are applied only to terrestrial broadcasters in France and, in Austria, to the public broadcaster only. Each broadcaster in Spain applies specific and different icons. The broadcasters in the Netherlands as well as in Italy or Luxembourg will probably also apply specific and different icons in the near future.

This visual icon system is also not sufficient. The icon in itself, while it can refer to two or three basic considerations about the content (eroticism, traumatic relationship, or physical violence), may not have the capacity to explain precisely what is represented within the content. For example, the two red triangles of the Catalan cable operators refer to pornography or gratuitous violence, the orange triangle of the French Community of Belgium refers to erotic character or intense violence. These are the limitations of a simple icon system. The viewer knows that nudity, sexual relations or death may appear on the screen, but he will not know whether these depictions are put into an appropriate context or simply appear crudely. The choice to watch the content will not be a fully informed one. Attributing more descriptive references to a given icon will lead to the opposite unsatisfactory result that the viewer will not know exactly to which of the specific contents the icon refers. A solution may be to offer each icon within the range in a variety of forms, but this would run the high risk of confusion among the viewers and would probably not be approved by those in charge of its implementation. A clear and written description of the content to be displayed on the screen would be more satisfactory.

In addition visual icons, unless embedded in a mechanical device or recorded and displayed in a programme guide, do not allow the viewer, especially the parent, to organize viewing in advance. It is an instantaneous information source, which requires an instantaneous reaction.

For all these reasons it would be difficult, from a European perspective, to rely on this type of rating system to significantly improve the ability of the viewer to make a comprehensive choice (either positive or negative) among the types of programmes to be broadcast in the new TV setting. Visual or oral information is useful to warn the passive viewer, but can not be sufficient to inform the active viewer who will need to find his way among the countless number of programmes that the receiver will transmit. Nevertheless, this form of warning and its coordination at a European Union level should be encouraged within the existing TV setting during the transition period, but it is not a significant option for the future. Rating structures and procedures need to be reassessed to meet the challenges raised by digital opportunities and must accompany efficient technical facilities offered to viewers.

In either a selecting or blocking environment the issue is less the design of the rating system than the information embedded in the programme. The first attempts to display descriptive and textual information appertaining to a given programme in a digital setting, as shown by the two Spanish digital operators, demonstrates an appreciation for this concern and may help to support this change in orientation to the provision of programming related information.

Watershed

The situation is somewhat different for the watershed. A watershed is akin to a rating system but cannot be qualified as a rating system as such since it does not contain any transmitted information to the viewer. Rather, in the European environment, the watershed can be defined as a contract between the broadcaster and the viewer. The broadcaster assures that no detrimental material will be broadcast before a certain time and the parent-viewer can rely on that programming strategy to organize its family viewing policy. This system is commonly applied in European Union countries (with the exception of Luxembourg). Broadcasters strongly believe that it is the best way to assume their duties and responsibilities towards viewers and the latter have a good understanding of the terms of this 'contract' (see chapter 3).

Assuming that parents perform their role conscientiously, the contract is currently the most efficient way to ensure that viewers, especially child viewers, are protected from exposure to certain kinds of unsuitable content. This assumption is valid in the 'passive' scheme in which the viewer is ordinarily situated. This, however, may change in the future as subscription to specific thematic channels or broadcasting services, such as pay-per-view, involves a more transparent determination of the content or the necessary determination of the programme to be 'booked' and implies an active consent from the viewer towards the nature of the content to be displayed. This new parameter in the relations between the viewer and TV suggest that certain safeguards such as the watershed do not present the same need and would merit revisiting. Some countries have introduced graduated watershed rules according to the nature of the broadcasting service; namely, whether the service in question is encrypted and whether it requires a specific action from the viewer in order to be activated.

However, even in a digital setting where such broadcasting services may grow, watershed rules may still represent, if not perfect protection, at least a strong insurance that undesirable exposure to detrimental content will be prevented even when parents are not intensively careful about what their children watch. Nevertheless, this may be difficult to apply to services such as the pay-per-view. The commercial interests of pay-per-view hinge on the provision of selected content at a selected time. Fortunately, the necessity of payment means such as credit cards may act as a safeguard towards undesired viewing by children. It is well advised to strengthen this 'gatekeeper' as much as possible.

Prospects for a Digital Setting

What protects minors most consistently, and in a way is the most healthy for society, is not regulation but the integrity and care of parents, on one hand, and the recognition of responsibility by content producers and broadcasters on the other. This relationship suggests the adoption of a public policy that buttresses these vectors of self-implementation. One element is to encourage broadcasters to produce and disseminate content responding to the needs of children within times corresponding to child viewing habits. A second element is to encourage broadcasters to supply sufficient information so as to support parents and other guardians in the fulfilment of their responsibilities as well to encourage a critical approach among viewers toward TV content.

Because the principal idea is to engage parents and other guardians in the enterprise, to assist them in making decisions as opposed to making decisions for them, the tendency ought to be to favour the expansive use of descriptive information as opposed to what is more generally called evaluative labels. Evaluations are efficient, simple to administer, and lend themselves more easily to blocking and filtering solutions. But descriptive information more readily permits those with the most relevant responsibility (parents and guardians) to adapt TV viewing to the expectations and maturity of particular children. In the next section, the uses and abuses of each approach are identified.

What Kind of Information is Needed?

The extent to which the choice between descriptive and evaluative is critical depends on emerging technical developments and expectations of viewer behaviour. A preference for evaluative rather than descriptive ratings turns on many factors: these include a societal decision about the very existence of a parental role and how the parents play this role in the lives of their children. It turns on whether parents wish to engage in evaluation themselves, or wish for a set of proxies, whom they trust, who conduct the evaluation for them. As a rule, descriptive information responds most favourably to these concerns.

Evaluative Information. If blocking is desired, evaluative ratings (such as age suitability), would be the most efficient. Age classification categories, with their tradition in the cinema environment, are well understood and long established in most of the countries. In addition, broadcasters have not tried to ignore them or establish competing approaches. In some cases, such as France, broadcasters are required to display an evaluative rating with a film, since film labels must be carried regardless of the medium in which they are played.

If an age-based evaluative approach for original television programming is desirable, then integration of the experience with the cinema rating entities may be required. At present, most of the broadcasters provide descriptive information, if at all, rather than an age suitability evaluation. One might attribute this to a lack of experience in this domain, but it may more likely be because of an approach that favours a shared responsibility between broadcasters and parents for determining what is suitable for the children.

But, can an evaluative approach be harmonized at European level? As we have seen, age categories are not the same across the Member States; none of the European Union countries' specific age categories have been created for original television programs and none have grown up under the sole initiative of the broadcasters. In addition, law generally introduces these age categories. Harmonization is difficult to envisage and would be very State-sensitive.

Some analysts have comtemplated a rating conversion system for all European Union countries. An age recommendation or certification performed in one country would correspond to a given European Union formula that would link it with a corresponding age recommendation or certification in another country (see Table 2.17). The conversion system would rely on the relevant rating entities 'pegging' their ratings hierarchy to the European Union standard. For example, the Irish rating entity could decide that a movie rated 12+ in Ireland corresponds to a rating of 'suitable for all' in Finland or a 'Recommended 7+' in Spain. This would have the advantage of facilitating the movement of programmes across national jurisdictions while preserving ratings and avoiding the heavy work involved in the reclassification of programmes by operators of the country of reception.

Adapting the film evaluation systems might allow harmonization among European Union ratings; but it would still require that programmes be rated in their own country in a way that allows the rating entity to determine an age suitability, and that is far from being the case at the moment. In addition, cross-boundary evaluations for age purposes may be inherently simplistic, imperfect, and unable to take into consideration the motivations and criteria which yield particular classifications in any of the separate European Union countries. What may lead to a rating of 12+ in Ireland may not necessarily lead to a 'Recommended 7+' in Spain.

TABLE 2.17
Cinema Ratings conversion

AUT	A	R6	R6	R10	R10	R12	R12	R14	R14	R16	R16	R18
BEL	A	A	A	A	A	A	A	A	A	16	16	16
DE	A	6	6	6	6	12	12	12	12	16	16	18
DNK[a]	A	A	R7	R7	11	11	11	11	15	15	15	15
FIN	A	A	A	A	A	A	A	A	A	16[b]	16	18
FRA	A	A	A	A	A	12	12	12	12	16	16	18
DEU	Ø	Ø	Ø	Ø	Ø	Ø	Ø	Ø	Ø	Ø	Ø	Ø
IRL	A	A	A	A	A	12	12	12	15	15	15	18
EU	**1**	**2**	**3**	**4**	**5**	**6**	**7**	**8**	**9**	**10**	**11**	**12**
ITA	A	A	A	A	A	A	A	14	14	14	14	18
LUX	A	A	A	A	A	A	A	14	14	14	17	17
NLD	A	A	A	A	A	12	12	12	12	16	16	16
PRT	R4	R6	R6	R6	R6	R12	R12	R12	R12	R16	R16	R18
ESP	A	A	R7	R7	R7	R7	R13	R13	R13	R13	R13	R18
SWE	A	A	7	7	11	11	11	11	15	15	15	15
GBR	A	A	A	A	A	12	12	12	15	15	15	18

A=All

[a] In accordance with the *Film Act of 12 March 1997*, age classification may be circumvented as it is permitted for children of the age of 7 and above to watch any film in the cinema, as long as an adult accompanies the child.

[b] Age categories 6, 8, 10, 12, and 14 are used. There is also a PG-option: children '3 years younger (than the given age) may attend if accompanied by a parent (or legal guardian)'. The following PG categories are possible: PG-8, PG-10, PG-12.

The main difficulty of an evaluative formula is that it hides the social, psychological, or cultural motivations leading to the placement of a certain age suitability. The varied motivations found in each European Union country would be highly difficult to harmonize as they are strictly linked to the approach countries may have towards contact of children with potentially detrimental content. The high transparency of descriptive criteria, where exempt from judgemental parameters, should overcome this issue and allow adherence to each country's belief system and desire to protect children from harmful content, however that is defined.

While reductive evaluations like the ones displayed in Table 2.17 are well suited to a blocking approach, the drawbacks must be reiterated. To be effective, a blocking facility has to be based on one-dimensional criteria such as age or a basic content descriptor, such as sex, violence, incitement to immoral behaviour, or crude language, possibly presented in a variety of forms, such as Sex Level 1, Sex Level 2, or Sex Level 3. As a consequence, works to be rated in such a way will not be appreciated in their complexity and will be rated without an appreciation for context. Risk is also high that certain programmes that would have been of interest for children (as has been already widely mentioned for the Internet filtering facilities), will fall under these too simplistic criteria and thus never be displayed on the screen.

In giving parents or guardians the faculty to block programmes responding to certain criteria, the risk is high that the blocking will not be revisited frequently. In extreme circumstances, children may be deprived of opportunities to access content corresponding to their development needs. The UN Convention on the Rights of the Child explicitly stresses the importance of the mass media in the development of children and requests states to act with awareness of the functioning of mass media in disseminating beneficial information and material to children.[12] Finally, by reducing incentives, blocking facilities may also have indirect and deleterious implications for the creation of work.

Descriptive Information. One of the main drawbacks of evaluative rankings is that they obscure the exact nature of the content. Parents should be informed directly of the content contained in a programme so that they can judge whether their child is mature enough to view it. What we call descriptive information is that set of data that permits judgement to be adequately exercised.

Here, too, there are fundamental assumptions about the viewing and decision-making context both of viewing and decision-making. A choice for descriptive information is based on presuppositions about the availability of time, cultural familiarity with the terms used, and ability of the parent or guardian to process that information. It is hard to conceive of a situation in which long-form

---

[12] The UN General Assembly Convention on the Rights of the Child, (12 December 1989), was signed by all countries except Somalia and United States. Article 17:

States Parties recognize the important function performed by the mass media and shall ensure that the child has access to information and material from a diversity of national and international sources, especially those aimed at the promotion of his or her social, spiritual and moral well-being and physical and mental health. To this end, States Parties shall:

(a) Encourage the mass media to disseminate information and material of social and cultural benefit to the child and in accordance with the spirit of article 29;

(b) Encourage international cooperation in the production, exchange and dissemination of such information and material from a diversity of cultural, national and international sources;

(c) Encourage the production and dissemination of children's books;

(d) Encourage the mass media to have particular regard to the linguistic needs of the child who belongs to a minority group or who is indigenous;

(e) Encourage the development of appropriate guidelines for the protection of the child from information and material injurious to his or her well-being, bearing in mind the provisions of articles 13 and 18.

descriptions, sufficiently detailed to encompass the whole, are adequately available. And, as with evaluations, any decision about labelling or rating sets forth the subject matter (sexuality, violence, and so on) that is to be the subject of the process. Digital services will permit the viewer to receive a huge amount of programmes and ample information about each of them, but that does not answer the question of how such information will be processed.

A more easily solvable problem than the viewer processing question is the question of whether the rating providers can manufacture such information about so many programmes. This problem is termed the mirror problem, and may be surmounted via the emergence of a plurality of providers. As an example, a subscriber to Canal Satellite probably receives, at present, approximately 100 channels. The EPG of Canal Satellite could permit the viewer to make a preselection for a given day (up to 7 days in advance), within or without a given time and within or without a given channel according to various categories presented in a variety of forms. For example, for documentaries they may choose: Doc-cinema, Doc-culture, Doc-discovery, Doc-escape, Doc-history, Doc-music, Doc-nature, Doc-portrait, Doc-sciences & techniques, Doc-society, and/or Doc-sport. For movies they may choose: Film-action, Film-animation, Film-history, Film-laugh, Film-passion, Film-pink square (X rated), Film-science-fiction, Film-shiver, Film-society, Film-suspense, Film-tenderness, and/or Film-thriller.

When choosing a category, a selection of programmes appears on the screen containing the title of the programme, the duration, the channel, and the starting time. By clicking on the title of the programme the viewer may obtain more details about it such as the director, year of creation, country of origin, credits, and a brief. Navigation facilitates preselection (understood as the capacity for the parent to select, at a given moment or for a given period, a certain type of content). To be effective both on the rating side and on the selecting side, a pre-selection function must introduce categorization: Content descriptions will be filtered through the prism of criteria brokered, over time, between the parent and the TV operator.

Out of this informal pattern of brokered descriptive ratings, it is likely that common descriptive criteria would evolve. These descriptive criteria would emerge both from the repertoire of those engaged in description and the preferences for information selected by parents and other viewers. A function, at the European level, is to encourage harmonization through the observed evolution of a common practice of description. The exercise of evaluating content criteria applied by cinema rating bodies throughout Europe illustrates how the following content descriptors outlined in Table 2.18 may be obtained.

TABLE 2.18
Descriptive Criteria

Sex	Violence	Language
• Sexual Deviation: child pornography, sexual relations between humans and animal, sexual violence or coercion • Sexual Description: pornography, full nudity in a sexual context, explicit simulated sex, complex sexual relationships , impressionistic sex full-frontal nudity in a non-sexual context, implications of sex non-sexual nudity	• Physical Violence: excessive violence scenes of severe violence to people or animals, graphic violence, horror with some gore, horror, mildly graphic violence, realistic violence, shocking surgical operations, mild violence • Psychological Violence: psychological trauma, traumatic relations between parents and children, excessive exploration of pathologic forms, hypnotic phenomena	• Scatological Language (limited, strong) • Sexual Expletives (rare, more extensive, frequent) • Vulgar Content (rare, more extensive, frequent)

TABLE 2.18 (continued)

Behaviour	Other
• Risk of Identification: positive images of immoral behaviour or suicide, soft/hard drug use, violence (emphasis on weapons, glamorized dangerous weapons, details of harmful or criminal techniques, induce to imitation of crimes) brutalizing effect (weakening inhibition towards use of violence) • Incitement: encourage sadistic pleasure, promote hatred and revenge, incitement to racial hatred, sexism, discrimination	• Obscene or against public morality • Controversial religious subjects • Glorification of the Nazi ideology • Glorification of war • Intimidation • Field of tension without possibilities to escape, • Fascism, political extremism • Sadism • Emotional shock • Bad ending/open ending

The list in Table 2.18 should be elaborated. Actual rating bodies and specialists such as educationalists and psychologists may have the required competence and legitimacy to perform such a task. A European platform bringing such experts together should be encouraged for this purpose. The result would be an armoury of key content descriptors that would provide the basis for judgement by the viewer. To the extent possible, these should be limited to neutral descriptions of the content without any judgement from the rating provider, though this goal may be difficult to reach with behavioural content. Thus, these descriptions would sensitively negotiate the cultural differences within the Member States.

Current descriptive systems are too limited to support genuine content selection by the viewer and therefore need to be elaborated. Titles of the films, name of the author, linguistic versions available, and a brief survey of the story may not be sufficient to inform viewers about the specific type of content they would find within the work. In this sense, cinema rating bodies have developed a case-law approach or transparent criteria that may serve as a starting point.[13] But the process of building, without overt government involvement, a descriptive process that is serviceable, efficient, and has integrity is a difficult one.

Who Might Perform This Task?

At present, rating procedures mainly rely on the broadcasters. By controlling ratings, they also maintain contact with their audience and have an influence on them. A digital television environment, with its abundant programmes, will challenge this structure, and may produce competing rating entities.

In the future, the structure of rating and labelling, the process of providing evaluative and descriptive information, will change markedly. We foresee the growth of third party entities who for self-generated interests or for a fee provide the appropriate information to parents and other viewers. We foresee, as well, an environment in which key entities exist to provide benchmarks within particular Member Sates and for Europe as a whole.

How Will This Evolve?

Content Producers, Content Providers. The now dominant rating providers in broadcasting are the content producers and, moreover, broadcasters and narrowcasters themselves. The next years will determine whether they can perform this function adequately, notwithstanding the commercial stake they have in the outcome. It is possible to imagine, as an analogy to the Internet set-

---

[13] This may be even more useful as cinema rating bodies are usually the ones that have developed the more sophisticated approaches toward the assessment of content (resulting from their long experience, establishment of criteria, case-law approach). Descriptive standards developed for the Internet could also be considered but, given the nature (mainly static content) of Internet content, these approaches may prove overly simplistic and fail to take into account a contextual approach.

ting, that content producers may rate and label their content directly according to criteria developed by more neutral entities. These entities may emerge from the industry itself, or may be standard-bearing entities, with some relationship to government. Such an entity may both help evolve descriptive criteria and, *a posteriori*, provide a check on whether producer or provider ratings are credible. A complaint procedure may also be a possibility, following schemes already devised in the Internet setting. Alternatively, a state or industry body may monitor rating schemes, either on a random basis or following viewers' complaints.

In addition to the necessarily simplistic label, it could also be required of the content producer to make available a sufficiently comprehensive, and possibly standardized, explanation of the content in order for the operator to organize a preselection function and for the viewer to use it. The use of sophisticated and listed descriptive criteria as indicated earlier may be of high relevance.

Monopolistic Third Party Body. An alternative is for the standard-setting entity to provide descriptive or evaluative information in addition to its other functions (that is, a governmental body or a monopolistic third party body composed of representatives of the various segments of the society). This system is not consistent with pluralism or with minimizing the state function; in addition, such single bodies would be incapable of evaluating all the content provided in the new digital setting. This shortcoming is already obvious with video games, software, and Internet rating. In addition, content producers as well as viewers in certain countries which may harbour a strong 'state-resistant' feeling (such as Portugal, Spain, or Greece) may be reluctant to delegate content to a state body unless the description of the content is provided through a genuinely transparent methodology and procedure.

Plural Third Party Entities. A more likely and preferred option is that various competitive third party entities provide either evaluative or descriptive content assessment. These third party entities will be cause-driven or market-oriented: They will be answerable to their own constituents or to the market. Parents will, if they so desire, subscribe to competing content screening organizations, which can be religious, value, linguistically, or national identity based.

From a social perspective, one measure of such a system is whether various cultural, social, ethical, ethnic, political, and religious concerns of the inhabitants of a given country or at European Union level are well represented. Pluralism is fostered only if a parent has a variety of points of view especially where evaluative ratings are on offer. This option depends on the involvement of groups in the evaluative process who have not been involved before. The European Union and the Member States may have a role in educating groups as to the opportunities and responsibilities in providing a pluralistic third party rating structure. In the case that part of the population does not find its values or expectations represented within the range of operational rating providers, the need for ratings normally perceived as 'consensual' may become compulsory. These required ratings could be performed by a single body, composed of representatives of the different segments of the society, concentrating on certain types of programmes such as movies, TV fictions, documentaries, and animation.

Third party entities may also act as preselectors of content for the viewers who accept the values the entities represent. Indeed, in a pluralistic setting, some entities rating and recommending programmes will merely approve a list of offerings rather than go through the far more cumbersome process of rating or providing sophisticated information. Content screening organizations will download the unique programme identifiers of screened programmes to those consumers who have selected them as screening provider and only those programmes will make their way to the consumers' TV screens. With respect to the Internet, screening entities that specialize in selecting children sites already exist. This process can be extended to television programmes.

However, close attention must be paid to potential conflicts of interests. This may support action to ensure that preselecting entities are completely independent (financially, administratively) from content producers and providers.

How May the Rating be Performed?

Geographical Level.   We have discussed the question of descriptive versus evaluative ratings and the nature of the rating entity. A final question is what role should be played at the pan-Europe level as opposed to the state level?

The answers to our questionnaire, sent to key actors, (see Annex 2) suggest that there is little support for strict harmonization in the domain of ratings, the establishment of common age categories, or common content descriptors. Most broadcasters believe that a European approach may be useful but only to the extent that it is limited to cooperation. The main support posited for this position was the difficulty inherent in overcoming the many cultural differences. At the European level, there can be the exchange of opinions and sharing of experience via, for example, the creation of a platform for constant dialogue.

On the other hand, plural rating providers and screening entities as defined above do not have to be restricted to State boundaries. Many such entities have concerns—ethnic, political, religious, or philosophical—that are not limited by any cross-border motivations and thus may be represented at a higher geographical scale than the territory of the state. Linked to the fact that satellite developments will significantly increase cross-border movements of audiovisual services, third party groups may rate not only programmes dedicated to their national territory but also others.

A role at the European Union level would be to encourage common descriptive criteria, or the use of common terms in describing similar programme content. This solution is the most likely to have a pan-European potential. If third party pluralistic entities are to be encouraged, it is virtually assumed that there will be a variety of evaluative criteria. Perhaps all that can be required is that a third party entity, if it is sponsored by an interest group, makes known what values lie behind a particular approach to evaluation. We have described the processes described earlier that might permit a rating in one Member State to be converted to the evaluative currency of another Member State. One possible role at the European Union level is to experiment with such conversion criteria. But, once again, the recommended approach is to develop descriptive criteria as a result of the sharing of experiences and practices of the actual rating providers, combined with the insights of experts of childhood.

Methodology. There is a debate about the methodology to be followed by rating entities and the role of government in establishing a methodology. Consistent with our discussion of pluralism in rating entities, we favour flexibility in methodology, so long as that methodology is transparent.

Some favour strongly what might be called a deterministic methodology, meaning that decisional criteria are articulated and consistently used. Given a deterministic rating system, one rating provider would achieve the same result as another with the same programme. Other things being equal, consistency in process is desirable; but here, there is an emphasis on pluralism, disclosure, and community decisions as to which entities should survive. Furthermore, as to the descriptive ratings, there is less of a specific need for deterministic and transparent methodology where the information provided tends to be more neutral and does not imply any judgement regarding the content.

A different analysis arises when it comes to evaluative ratings. There, classification often camouflages the process that resulted in the rating. The more monopolistic or oligopolistic the rating system, the more pressure is warranted for disclosure and consistency. A pluralistic situation where a high number of rating providers exists does not require the same attention because the existence of ratings will depend directly on the credibility granted to the rating entities. This loop of credibility should be anticipated to eliminate, over time, rating providers who fail to match the expectations of their consumers. A certain degree of deterministic methodology is therefore only required in the situation where a monopolistic/oligopolistic evaluative rating is performed.

Support. Encouraging third parties to perform the evaluative and information tasks also raises the question of their access to the content. Voluntary access may be forthcoming as it may attract audience. However, broadcasters may resist making programming available in advance, especially if a rating might be restrictive. One role, at the European Union or Member State level, is to develop processes that will permit such access as a way of avoiding or minimizing government evaluation. The most prudent step to be taken on this path points to positive approaches to technology and rating mobilization. As explained in the previous chapter, a selective approach to the EPG technologies will place a premium on information about programming content. A positive approach will offer a potentially strong economic inducement for producers to distribute their programmes to information providers, who, as with the Internet, will be their means of reaching the consumer. Facilitating a market for the information about content and the ascent of 'brand' recognition of information providers will create incentives to allow the greatest number of appropriate groups access to content for evaluation purposes. Though producers may still be reluctant to offer their product widely, for fear of negative reaction from certain groups, if they are to reach those segments of the market place that require an endorsement from a particular information provider, they will have no choice but to take that risk.

Self-regulation might also yield improved opportunities for viewers to select among rating entities. Broadcasters will often be the gatekeepers for rating systems and can make access easy or difficult. This role may also be played by Teletext or EPG service providers. How this plays out may be an area for European Union scrutiny. An obligation or a strong recommendation to provide information for viewers may be inserted in the licenses of the content providers.

Finally, the European Union might monitor the evaluation and labelling process to determine if leaders emerge, standard setters that could provide excellent service to parents interested in preselecting or having greater control over programmes for their children. The function of such leaders could be strengthened or at least information about their methods and performance considered and distributed. This task may be performed by a single body, commonly identified by citizens of a given country as being an authority in the field of broadcasting activities. Rather than recommending particular rating entities to viewers, this single body could provide viewers with the necessary information permitting the viewer to assess the relevance of these rating bodies as to its requirements and values. Information such as the values and aims of the rating provider, its field of coverage and type of programmes rated, and the way to access these ratings, such as identification of broadcasters, EPG service provider that carries the ratings, or need for a subscription or not, would have to be made available to viewers by such means as brochures, Internet postings, or newspapers.

Control. This study has already indicated that controls on the rating entities may be exercised via several means directly available to the viewers, such as hotline or by choosing whether to subscribe to a given service, or in the hands of a control body in charge of supervising the appropriateness of the rating performed (following viewers complaints and/or on a random basis).

Given the power that comes with rating, there might be pressure to license entities that engage in the rating or labelling process. A license delivered by the relevant national authority might mandate that ethical rules be respected. But regulatory measures are likely not the first appropriate action on this front.

Alternatively, one could envisage the adoption of a code prescribed by the industry and adopted voluntarily by all the various key actors. The European Union could be involved in the fashioning of such a common code of conduct, though it is possible to envisage different codes of conduct taking into account different modes of rating and different kinds of rating entities. Respect for the code(s) might be enforced by sanctions pronounced by a board or committee composed of representatives of the signatories and could lead, for example, to the exclusion or suspension of the violator. Such boards or committees could act on their own, supervising on a constant or random basis the good application of the rules formulated or be the recipients of complaints formulated via hotlines. Following the framework already drawn in the recent European Commission Recommendation on the protection of minors and human dignity, an European Commission instrument could draw the framework in which such codes may be elaborated and implemented (European Council Recommendation 1998: 48).

3

Family Viewing Alternatives: Economic Justifications, Social Efficiency, and Educational Support

In the previous chapters, we discussed what is at the heart of the European Union's concern over parental control: What prospect is there for a technical device that will assist parents to exercise choice within their homes? Furthermore, we provided an analysis of the rating and labelling systems that are the backbone for such technical devices and, in addition, those increasingly common systems that function without technical devices, but provide efficient and useful information to parents and others.

We conclude with a discussion of three extremely important questions. Firstly, in a time when government intervention in areas touching upon personal choice and rights of freedom of speech is often questioned, what can economists tell us about the justification for these labelling and rating systems? Secondly, if ratings and advisories have been introduced, how effective and efficient are they in protecting children from harmful content? And finally, for these systems to work, what needs to be done to educate the public as to the nature of television viewing and to increase the capacity for television consumption to be an activity that is approached critically, with an awareness of its costs and effects as well as its pleasures and benefits? These issues are intertwined, because an analysis of the inadequacies in a 'market' or parental television empowerment demonstrates the need for education as well as rating and labelling systems.

ECONOMIC EFFICIENCY
AND REGULATORY INTERVENTIONS

We start with a brief economic analysis, examining issues of efficiency and equity in the context of protecting minors by way of public regulation of content. There are several key questions that need to be addressed. First of all, what do we mean by choice? Do consumers really enjoy the greatest possible choice of suppliers, information, and audio-visual services in the current broadcasting setting and is their situation likely to improve in the future digital setting? Are there any income or socioeconomic factors associated with the ability to receive information and to make rational choices? These are important issues because of the assumption that the 'choice' and/or information available to parents is full and unproblematic, making intervention to repair 'market failure' unnecessary.

Second of all, can regulation enhance any of the various aspects of efficiency and equity, by: (a) improving the content information provided to consumers and (b) facilitating parental control of minors? Obviously more information is usually preferable to less, but we need to ask why the market does not provide all the necessary information itself and who, among the population, is disadvantaged by the current form in which information is distributed or by the absence of certain information. Lastly, are there substantial efficiency and equity benefits associated with having public compulsory intervention rather than a pure free market supply?

The current (and future digital) audiovisual markets are likely to be affected by familiar problems associated with imperfect and asymmetric information; namely, that content is, and is likely to remain, influenced by a small number of operators, with serious consequences for efficiency and equity. Information is imperfect because there is little market for the kind of data that tells consumers not to buy. Information is asymmetric because it is understood or used more readily by some consumers than others. Making information less imperfect and its distribution less asymmetric improves all consumers' control over the content they wish to view or which they desire for their children. That is or should be the goal of public intervention.

Appropriately coordinated government action (which might take the form of encouraging self-regulation) serves efficiency grounds if, as should be the case with a properly structured rating system, it can expand competition while improving consumers' information. Multiple ratings and labels can ensure a proper evaluation of content and the quality of the product, as well as its possible benefits. At the same time such a system ensures stimulation of competition. Furthermore, from an economist's perspective, there is another way in which effective ratings and labelling systems—those that allow parents to use technical devices to perform parental functions without being at home—improve social welfare. Assisting parental control by means of technical devices may have positive benefits for family income, since time allocated to watching with children and/or making prior judgements about appropriate television programmes for children's viewing decreases time available for work. This not only reduces earnings directly, but indirectly, by slowing down the growth of the parent's career.

There is legitimate social concern about changes in the broadcasting environment, since its regulation is similar to that of a public utility, affecting all households simultaneously (for example, rating and labelling systems which might lead to channelling and blocking of programmes). Moreover, the introduction of rating and labelling systems may have external benefits, or benefits that extend to others than the parents and children themselves. This would be the case if such benefits improve parental supervision and if improved parental supervision yields better young people and better citizens. The provision of a more propitious broadcast environment for children brings satisfaction to other members of society, who benefit indirectly from an improved society. Hence, the usual conditions for a 'market failure' argument apply; namely where there is a public good and an externality.

The argument for public intervention in the supply of content information is also important from an equity perspective. Obtaining the information necessary for parental control has a cost, which can be significant. The problem of this cost is greater for lower socioeconomic groups. Accordingly, television consumption patterns of children in these groups may be more unbalanced than might otherwise be the case, for example, excessively violent or inappropriately dependent on particular aspects of audiovisual culture. Moreover, parental activities, which often turn on the mother, have a negative effect predominantly on the labour and earnings of women, which are already subject to discrimination. By decreasing the parental control activity of mothers, regulation may—at the margin, to be sure—redistribute resources to women, help reduce the *feminisation* of poverty and improve the well being of poor lone parent families. Voluntary action may fail due to the incentive to free ride. The market failure argument applies again and concerns about equity concern should lead to public intervention.

Technological devices that enable a faster selection of content and filter unwanted products may facilitate parents' control of their children's education and decrease restrictive public interventions (those related to delinquency or worse). The transmission of appropriate and multiple ratings would allow each household to determine the broadcast environment best suited for their children. However, the presence of an externality may lead towards more drastic solutions and, as is the case with education, there may be arguments in favour of stronger regulation if parents cannot always be trusted to act in the best interests of the child, either due to insufficient information or a lack of parental initiative.

It is difficult to determine social benefits or aggregate individuals willingness to pay, since households have incentives to mislead the policy-maker, seeking to reduce required contributions by understating their willingness to pay, or, where acting as free-riders, overstating it in order to increase their benefits.

However, as far as parental control activities are concerned, we can separate parents' expenditure of time (in control activity) from other expenditures (net flow of commodities) that increase child welfare, and examine the impact of a given audiovisual regulatory environment. Reducing control activity through regulation allows parents to devote more time to income-producing activities, other parental activities, and leisure. Improvement of the children's broadcasting environment generally increases the benefits from work and parental activities, since the household becomes more productive by being able to spend more time in work and other parental activities. Moreover, regulation implies additional benefits through the reduction of problems caused by (a) uncertainty about the future environment (that is, the option value of regulation) and (b) the irreversible harm, which, in the absence of a regulated environment, stems from ex-post insufficient parental control.

The benefits deriving from the time saved in parental control activities can be measured by the potential for increasing consumption, that is through the compensating variation measure of the benefits (the amount of money the household in the original environment should be allocated to make it as well off as the household in the environment improved by regulation). In an approximation that uses earning data we can consider the monetary value of parental control activity—no longer required in the regulated environment—in order to reach the same level of welfare for children.

Regulatory benefits and costs may vary among different socioeconomic groups, even perversely. However, once the financing of regulatory social costs by progressive taxation is considered, the system as a whole is likely to improve equity. In any case, an unequal distribution of the regulatory net benefits is not the necessary outcome and can be avoided with the right technical design.

SOCIAL EFFICIENCY

Given the economic justification offered for interventions such as ratings, what social benefits do they offer, and how efficient and effective are the systems currently in place? To date, there is surprisingly little research on the efficiency of ratings and advisories (verbal or written warnings). This fact is noted in the National Television Violence Study, conducted in the United States, and the country experts participating in this study and leading organisations engaged in children and media issues have stated it repeatedly. However, this is less surprising if one considers that visual ratings in contrast to verbal warnings are relatively new in most countries. As a result, the most comprehensive research has been carried out in the United States, where the history of monitoring violence stretches back to the 1950s and has prompted the study of the efficiency of advisories. Following the more recent development of visual symbols and acoustic signals, studies have also been conducted in Belgium, France, Italy, and in the United Kingdom, as outlined later. Where possible, the findings have been grouped into the various issues related to efficiency such as awareness, understanding, satisfaction, utility, appropriateness, impact, and need for improvement. Special attention is also given to the United States.

Belgium

A study by Herman and Leyens investigated the impact of verbal warnings on the audience in Belgium during the years of 1972–1975 (1977: 48–53). The study focused exclusively on films, and audience sizes were compared for films broadcast with and without verbal warnings. The main conclusions drawn from the study were that films broadcast with a warning about violent or sexual content attracted larger audiences. This may prove that the contrary effects associated with visual symbols (such as attracting a young audience) also apply to verbal announcements.

France

An opinion poll conducted by the *Conseil Superieur de l' Audiovisuel* (CSA) in 1998 researched the effectiveness of the French rating symbols.[1] At the time, the system consisted of three visual symbols: a green circle for programmes containing scenes likely to harm young viewers, an orange triangle for programmes unsuitable for viewers under 12 years of age, and a red square referring to films unsuitable for viewers younger than 16. The survey revealed interesting results.

For the category 'Level of Awareness Amongst Parents', the survey revealed that 80 percent of the people interviewed were aware of the existence of the visual symbols; for the parents of minors the figure was 88 percent.

For the category, 'Level of Viewer (Parents and Children) Understanding of the Warnings Provided by the System', the meaning of the icons was best known for the Red Square. 63 percent gave a fully or at least partly correct interpretation of the meaning of the red square. Awareness of the meaning of the orange triangle was lower, with 53 percent, and only 34 percent were able to give a definition for the green circle.

---

[1] The opinion poll refers to the former rating system, which was replaced in September 1998. The introduction of the new rating system was partly a result of the findings of the study.

For the category 'Level of Satisfaction', of the people interviewed, 63 percent said that they considered the visual icons as very or relatively useful.

In the category, 'Perceived Utility for (a) Protecting Children (b) as an Educational Modality', 75 percent of all children between 8 and 14 years of age interviewed say they take the icons into account when choosing a programme for themselves (80 percent for the 8 to 10 age groups).

For the category, 'Perceived Appropriateness for the Range of Proposed TV Programmes, and Perceived Need to Extend System to Additional Programming such as News, Sports, and Advertisements', 11 percent of people questioned said that the classification 'is very relevant' and 47 percent said that the classification was 'rather relevant' regarding the level of violence of the programme.

For the category, 'Impact on the Viewing Policy of the Family', 84 percent of parents stated that they take into consideration the signals provided by the icons for their children's television consumption 'at least sometimes'. This shows a considerable increase since a previous opinion poll was taken in January 1997, when only 53 percent of parents used the signals. 79 percent of all adults claimed that they do not use the signalling system for themselves.

For the category, 'Degree of Need for Improvements Perceived by Viewers', of the parents in favour of the rating system, 19 percent thought that it needed to be improved and more details needed to be provided in order to make it more effective. Ideas for improvement of the current system included the complementary use of an acoustic signal. Others suggested the extension of the symbols, currently applying to films and fiction only, to other programmes such as documentaries about war or prostitution. The CSA concluded that the system ought to undergo some improvements. Amongst other suggestions, the CSA recommended changing the colour of the green circle, due to the substantial amount of confusion surrounding its meaning, and prolonging the presence of symbols on screen if not displayed permanently (to 1 minute at the beginning of the programme and 15 seconds after commercial breaks).[2]

A qualitative study carried out by SORGEM in November and December 1997 established that when asked which criteria guided their programme choice most parents said they trusted the schedule and believed that violent programmes were not broadcast during daytime. They also thought that programme guides were the best way to select a programme. The majority considered the current system of coloured symbols as effective; some parents, however, stated that their children had a better understanding of the signs than themselves, and that they needed to learn the meaning of the symbols before they were able to explain them to their children.

---

[2] In the new rating system the orange and red triangle are present throughout the duration of the programme.

As with the CSA survey, there was a great deal of confusion about the green circle; some interviewees even associated it with the 'go' signal given by a green traffic light and interpreted it as 'suitable for all children'. Many parents believed that the symbols merely performed the function of a complementary tool, together with other sources of information (TV guides friends). The symbols were perceived as a real warning for children, but on the other hand their efficiency was doubted if they were not present on the screen throughout the broadcasting of the programme.

Italy

In January 1994, the private broadcaster Mediaset introduced a colour-code, the so-called 'traffic light system', for its channel Canale Cinque, at the time the only initiative of this kind in Italy. The system was introduced following a lengthy survey conducted by a team of university researchers, psychologists, educators, and audio-visual experts. All scheduled fiction programmes are classified as to content, with particular reference to scenes featuring sex or violence. The classification criteria were established with the help of a team of external experts who assisted the editorial staff. Three different coloured symbols are used: green to indicate programmes that children can watch without any concerns, yellow to suggest 'parental guidance', and red to mark programmes unsuitable for children. Each coloured symbol contains a graphic logo to make the message clearer in case the colour alone is insufficient. TV programme guides and announcers draw attention to the symbol, which also appears on the screen during the broadcast and immediately following commercial breaks. The 'traffic light' symbols are also shown in trailers, announcements, newspapers, at the beginning of every fiction programme, and after every commercial break.

Since February 1997, the channels Italia Uno and Retequattro have also adopted the scheme, by using the same classification criteria and identical symbols. In order to apply the same labelling principles for fiction programmes shown on networks with three completely different types of schedule, regular liaison meetings were held with editorial staff, marketing directors, and a team of psychologists and educators.

In July 1994, R.T.I. carried out a telephone survey to verify the level of awareness and effectiveness of the traffic light system. During the course of the survey, 1140 people aged over 14, and representative of the Canale Cinque audience, were interviewed.

For the category, 'Level of Awareness Amongst Parents,' the study established that 53 percent of respondents were aware of the existence of the colour-coded symbols. Out of these, 57 percent were able to recall them spontaneously, while 43 percent recalled them when prompted.

For the category, 'Level of Viewer (Parents and Children) Understanding of the Warnings Provided by the System', 81 percent of respondents judged the symbols to be very clear or fairly clear at all events. There was some degree of uncertainty with respect to the correct interpretation of the various symbols. Among the respondents who were aware of the colour-coding system, 30 percent were able to provide a spontaneous correct answer and complete interpretation of the symbols used. When asked to choose from a series of preset interpretations, more than 50 percent of respondents correctly interpreted the green and red symbols, 38 percent correctly interpreted the yellow symbol.

For the category, 'Level of Satisfaction', 83 percent of the respondents thought that the traffic light system was 'certainly a very useful initiative'. 7.5 percent considered the system ineffectual, as they perceived its meaning as unclear.

For the category, 'Perceived Utility for (a) Protecting Children (b) as an Educational Modality', 91.5 percent of respondents stated that they interpreted the symbols as aimed at families and at parents with young children.

In the category, 'Perceived Appropriateness for the Range of Proposed TV Programmes, and Perceived Need to be Extended to Additional Programming such as News, Sports, and Advertisements', 82 percent of respondents thought that other networks should also introduce the colour-coding system, as an intelligent and effective tool to safeguard children and assist parents in choosing films for their children.

In the category, 'Level of Need for and Nature of Additional Accompanying Measures', some viewers asked for more detailed information to be provided by the broadcaster, and some asked for audience training in respect of the meaning of the symbols used.

United Kingdom

In the United Kingdom, awareness and impact of the watershed has been monitored since 1975. An unpublished report by the ITC reveals valuable conclusions, drawn from a survey about the efficiency of the watershed (Overview of 27 Years of Annual Surveys 1998).

In the category, 'Level of Awareness Amongst Parents', the report suggests that until the mid-1980s, overall awareness of a fixed watershed time remained at around 60 percent of adults. In the mid-1980s, the levels climbed sharply and have remained stable at around 90 percent. This increase coincided with a major publicity campaign mounted by the ITC and the BBC in 1986. The watershed is now firmly established and widely understood—both by parents and other adults. In a recent survey by the Broadcasting Standards Commission the watershed timing was placed correctly at 9:00 p.m. by 79 percent of the respondents.

Compared with overall awareness of watershed times for terrestrial channels, the figures for cable and satellite are low, although they have improved markedly since 1990. In 1991, 34 percent of viewers were aware of the existence of a Family Viewing Policy for cable and satellite channels; in 1997, this figure rose to 55 percent. However, it is clear from research that there exists a high level of confusion with the longer established terrestrial watershed time of 9:00 p.m. Unlike terrestrial channels, film channels and adult channels are subject to somewhat different scheduling restrictions. For films, those with a '15' certificate cannot be shown prior to 8:00 p.m., while '18'-rated films can only be screened after 10:00 p.m. 'Adult' channels can only show explicit material after 10:00 p.m., and generally targeted cable and satellite channels have a 9:00 p.m. watershed.[3]

In the category, 'Level of Satisfaction', for the majority of viewers, the degree of regulation of television channels is felt to be at about the right level; possibly verging on too little rather than too much. This overall balance of opinion has been found regularly since 1989 for the main terrestrial channels. Very similar views have been documented for satellite and cable viewers about non-terrestrial channels since 1991.

For the category, 'Perceived Utility for (a) Protecting Children and (b) as an Educational Modality', in the United Kingdom, parents say generally that the time of day is a useful guide to them for a programme's suitability for their children; a large majority of parents (72 percent) feel that transmission time is an indication of a programme's content (Millwood-Hargrave 1995).

In the Category, 'Impact on the Viewing Policy of the Family', parental responsibility for children's viewing is considered vital and parents in particular are clear that they have to play their part in monitoring children's viewing, especially after the watershed. Nearly six in ten (56 percent) of all respondents had watched television recently with children and nearly half of these (43 percent) had occasion to switch off/over. A recent Gallup Poll commissioned by Pace Micro Technology has also revealed that 75 percent of parents censor their children's viewing (Pace Report 1998).

In the category, 'Level of Viewer (Parents and Children) Understanding of the Warnings Provided by the System', the 9:00 p.m. watershed is a well-recognised and understood principle. Many children accept that it is there to protect them. The participants were also questioned on information about programme content, on-air pretransmission warnings. These were deemed the most useful by 37 percent of poll respondents; well ahead of on-screen symbols (19 percent).

---

[3] NB Cable and satellite subscribers have a 'technological' advantage, since they have access to channel blocking or filtering, either through PIN numbers to prevent access to specified channels, or through removal of the satellite receiver smart card. Despite this fact, however, only 37 percent of parents with multichannel access in 1997 knew that such facilities were available to them. Only one in ten of these said they had in fact used them to prevent children's access to programmes or channels. (Regulating for Changing Values 1997).

For the category, 'Level of Need for and Nature of Accompanying Additional Measures', the Gallup Poll mentioned earlier has revealed that nearly half of children (47 percent) go to bed after 9:00 p.m. during half term and other school holidays. The same poll shows that 47 percent of parents interviewed want broadcasters to extend the current 9:00 p.m. watershed to protect children from exposure to unsuitable television programmes. Of this group, 72 percent would like a 10:00 p.m. watershed with the majority of the remainder (23 percent) wanting the present watershed to be moved to 11:00 p.m. In last year's Pace report, 60 percent of parents stated that the watershed should continue to apply to digital channels with only 20 percent feeling that it should not be required.

United States

A survey among adults in Georgia, conducted by Wurtzel and Surlin in 1978, found that almost all respondents recalled having seen advisories on television (1978: 19–31). However, only 24 percent said that they had had an impact on their viewing. Of the respondents familiar with the advisories, 39 percent reported that they had resulted in their not watching the programme and 24 percent said they actually prompted them to watch the programme with greater interest. Of the respondents with children, 54 percent stated that the advisories had influenced their decisions about their child's viewing, with the overwhelming majority (81 percent) not letting their child watch the programme as a result.

In 1973, a nation-wide *TV Guide* survey reported that 53 percent of those questioned were in agreement with a rating system for television programming, and by 1993 a United States *Weekend* reader survey reported that 73 percent of their readership would be in favour of this initiative (Federman 1993).

A more recent unpublished study by Hamilton looked at the Nielsen ratings for prime time films on network television between 1987 and 1993 (1994). He noticed a significant drop among viewers in the 2–11 age band, whereas the advisories did not have a significant impact on the teenage or adult group. This suggests that advisories can help protect minors; the study does not, however, address whether the warnings resulted in parental interference or whether the minors decided not to watch the programmes themselves.

A major issue regarding ratings and advisories has been whether they have their desired effect, namely the protection of viewers, and in particular minors, from harmful content, or whether they actually achieve the opposite by making the content seem more attractive and interesting, especially to children. Although it is commonly agreed that ratings and advisories are directed at adults to inform them about content and to allow them to protect their children, one cannot ignore the question of how children respond to these messages, as children's viewing decisions are often made in the absence of the parent.

An experiment conducted as part of the National Television Violence Study involved 297 children aged 5–14 years, from a variety of schools in Madison, Wisconsin. The children were given programme guides and asked to choose from a variety of films. One group was given a guide with accompanying ratings, the other was given a guide listing the same films without ratings. The experiment concluded that ratings and advisories could have a significant impact on children's viewing. This impact depends on a number of factors, including aspects of the advisory or rating and characteristics of the child.

The well-known advisory 'parental discretion advised' had a strong and positive impact on boys' interest in viewing reality-action programmes, with the strongest effect for the boys aged 10–14. The same advisory had no impact on girls' tendency to choose such a programme. In contrast, another frequently used advisory, 'viewer discretion advised', did not increase boys' interest in viewing police-detective shows, but it decreased the number of choices of such programmes for girls, and especially for the younger ones. The Motion Picture Association of America (MPAA) ratings, 'G', 'PG', 'PG-13', and 'R', also strongly affected children's desire to see a film. Older boys were especially interested in a film when it was rated 'PG-13' or 'R', and completely avoided it when it was rated 'G'. Younger girls, on the other hand, were most interested in the film when it was rated 'G'. For older girls and younger boys, interest in the film peaked when it was rated 'PG-13'. All of these findings suggest that ratings and advisories are important factors in children's choice of programmes, but do not necessarily influence their choice in the way intended.

Also worthy of mention is that half of the children's comments about rated films implied their appeal; for example, some children said 'the cooler the movie the higher the rating'. The study also found that children whose parents set limits and were more involved in their television viewing were less likely then other children to choose programmes with parental advisories and films with more restrictive ratings. These findings suggest that parental involvement may become internalised and have beneficial effects when the child selects programming without adult supervision.

In October 1997, the television industry in the United States began implementing a new system for rating all programmes other than news and sports shown on broadcast and cable. The rating system, designed to work in conjunction with the V-chip device, provides for both age-based ratings and content descriptors (V for violence, S for sexual behaviour, D for sexual dialogue, L for adult language, and FV for fantasy violence in children's programmes). One year into the launch of the new system, the Kaiser Foundation conducted a study to explore how it had been applied during its first year of operation.

Overall, the study found that the television industry had done a good job in complying with the new policy, because across all networks and programmes reviewed, only 4 percent of programmes that qualified for a rating failed to receive one. The findings also suggest that the age-based ratings were applied accurately to general audience shows. However, the study found that the rating system does not flag most sex and violence for parents, but most who use it assume it does.

A companion survey of more than 500 parents found that two thirds of those who use the ratings say the content descriptors provide the most useful information (13 percent say the age-based ratings do). In fact, however, content descriptors are not being used on the vast majority of general audience shows containing sex, violence, or adult language. Of all the programmes with an age-based rating, only 23 percent received a content descriptor; 65 percent received an age-based rating only and 7 percent were MPAA rated. More than three out of four programmes with violent content and nine out of ten with sexual content do not receive the appropriate V or S content descriptors. Yet, the majority (55 percent) of those who use the TV ratings believe that the V content descriptor is supposed to be used on all programmes containing violence. As a result, parents who wish to use the ratings to prevent their children from viewing content of this nature may not be aware that there is still a significant amount of 'moderately intense' sex, violence, and adult language in programmes without content descriptors. In the words of Vicky Rideout, Director of the Kaiser Family Foundation's *Program on the Entertainment Media and Public Health*, 'The bottom line for parents who want to use the V-chip is clear. Parents cannot rely on the content descriptors, as currently employed to identify most shows containing sex, violence, or adult language' (Major New Study of the V-Chip 1998).

Conclusions

Studies addressing the social efficiency of ratings and advisories have produced very mixed results. On the one hand their findings suggest that visual symbols and verbal warnings have their desired effect, namely the protection of the viewer, especially children, from potentially harmful content. On the other hand, despite fairly high levels of awareness and satisfaction, it is clear that there is a list of shortcomings—confusion about the meaning of symbols, misinterpretation and sometimes even a counterproductive effect. The latter, in particular, demonstrated quite clearly by the results of the National Television Violence Study, and to some extent by other studies, is a cause of great concern. Boys approaching adolescence and juvenile males have a particular tendency to be tempted by high ratings; and yet it is specifically this group that plays a substantial part in the occurrence of violence in the United States.

Ratings and advisories can play an important part in protecting the viewer, but one cannot deny their 'side effects'. They are a strong influence on the choice of children's and young people's viewing, and this influence is not always positive. It seems that their role should be more that of a complementary tool; this suggestion has been made by parents in particular and has emerged from various studies. Furthermore, as the study by the Kaiser Family Foundation reports, the majority of parents prefer content descriptors; these can, however, only fulfil their purpose if applied across the whole spectrum of programmes by the broadcasters.

MEDIA EDUCATION AND LITERACY

As we have seen from the economic analysis, regulation, by providing information through rating and labelling systems, is a means of facilitating parental control and choice. It compensates for market failure by assuring that information is made available. However, it is clear from the social efficiency analysis that other forms of providing information can complement rating and labelling systems, and are sometimes necessary to make rating and labelling systems effective. Ultimately, the goal is to enhance the power of the parent by making that parent informed (and able to act on that information). For this reason, the substantial experience of the Member States in encouraging media literacy among both young people and families is an essential adjunct to any discussion of ratings and labelling systems. Furthermore, information about programmes—the essence of rating and labelling systems—is inadequate unless the public is advised of the existence of these systems and educated in their use. The enhancement of children's media literacy and critical viewing skills is a necessary component of any broad approach to avoiding harm from adverse television viewing. Our study of comparative practices suggests that media literacy is not given a high priority, even though the research literature on harmful effects from media emphasises the significance of media education in developing healthier viewing habits.

Though many studies argue that the proliferation of violence depictions on television is in itself harmful, most researchers will acknowledge, to a greater or lesser extent, that other factors influence the degree of harmfulness produced. This seems to be particularly true of research conducted in European countries, which has focused more on audience perceptions of violence in order to determine whether the context in which violence is shown has a bearing on its harmfulness. Such studies have found that both adults and children are capable of making varied and complex judgements about violent content, despite a widespread belief that the young are much less able to comprehend the context in which violence is shown, and are therefore more susceptible to harm. Various factors have been found to affect the audience's response to violent images. These include the degree to which viewers can identify with characters and with the setting in which violence is depicted; the extent to which they understand what is happening within a scene or what the likely outcome is to be; the viewers' perception of the victim's innocence; and the level of detail and/or disturbing effects used in a violent scene.

The more we know about the context of viewing and the consequences of various viewing styles, the more we will understand how to develop media literacy skills. For example, distinguishing factual from fictional material is a skill that can be taught in primary schools from an age as early as seven. In order to foster deliberate, informed selection practices, a comprehensive, well-defined media literacy campaign should supplement the establishment and use of technical blocking devices, engaging parents and children in all aspects of media literacy including reading and writing; speaking and listening; accessing new technologies; critical viewing; and the ability to create personal media content, using a wide range of technologies, including cameras, camcorders, and computers (Hobbs 1998). Finally, a greater understanding of the relationship between children and media should result in the improvement and augmentation of programming for young people.

Media Literacy: General Framework and Recommendations

In most circles, even academic ones, media literacy is an amorphous concept. The ambiguity of media literacy implicates how and to whom it is taught (Dyson 1998: 155-166). In recent years, it has come to include the ability to analyse competently and to utilise skilfully print journalism, cinematic productions, radio and television programming, and even computer-mediated information and exchange. This study defines media literacy as 'the ability to access, analyse, evaluate, and produce communication in a variety of forms' (Aufderheide 1992).

A media literacy campaign can not only facilitate informed, positive television viewing, it can assist in the development of citizenship skills, promoting the development of information literacy skills, offering access to diverse sources of information, and providing opportunities to practise leadership and responsible self-expression (Aufderheide 1992). A media literacy campaign should involve partnerships between broadcasters, community and nonprofit organisations, families, educational institutions, and the government body responsible for education. Media literacy clearinghouses such as the Media Literacy Online Project, The Media and Communication Studies Site, Canadian Association of Media Education Organisations (CAMEO), and The Center for Media Literacy are on the Internet for the development of comprehensive media education strategies for families, schools, community organisations, and broadcasters. The roles of those stakeholders in media education and literacy are described later.

Broadcasters

We recommend that, as part of a self-regulatory process, the broadcasters agree to the development of a continuous on-screen effort to create general awareness of ratings and parental control mechanisms. Such a campaign would differ from Member State to Member State, but the prospects of cultivating an affirmatively selected television environment for children presents strong structural inducements to the producers and broadcasters to both provide detailed and sophisticated information about and, simultaneously, greater access to their content by third party rating providers. In such a positive environment, programming would be whitelisted or selected by households as within the range of programming to be available to their children. This approach to children's programmes would facilitate a dramatic and desirable departure from the 'channel-hopping' habits of children watching television today.

Children's viewing habits, whether determined by their parents or caretakers, or self-directed by the child, should be specific in purpose and temporally delimited. Thus, as has happened in the online environment, information about and evaluation of television content would attain a high value. Just as browsers are the portals through which Internet users obtain information, EPGs and related programming menus from a multiplicity of rating providers would provide the means by which parents could positively select programming for their children. Initial steps in this direction have been taken by the U.S. television industry, with the development of websites such as 'The TV Parental Guidelines', which provides a detailed description and explanation of their television ratings system for the benefit of parents, and as a resource for broadcasters.

The United Kingdom Film Education organisation is an interesting example of industry-led education. It is a registered charity funded by the United Kingdom film industry, whose aim is to encourage and promote the use of 'Film and Cinema within the National Curriculum.' This states that teachers should give pupils the opportunity to analyse and evaluate a wide range of media, including film. Study resources include film specific study guides, generic study guides, BBC Learning Zone programmes, study videos, CD-ROMs, and educational Internet pages, plus an information booklet for cinema managers working with schools. We recommend developing a similar system for broadcasting and in particular for parental control mechanism.

Community/Non-Profit Organisations

In order for families to effectively utilise industry whitelist mechanisms, increased participation by community and nonprofit organisations can assist in informing parents about means of parental control. Parents can work with groups such as religious organisations, schools, ethnic and cultural bodies, parents' associations, teachers' unions, and youth organisations, which have a stake in building and reinforcing loyalties and assist members in shaping identities as part of their activities. Programming information and evaluation could be sought and selected according to the credibility of the information provider or third party rating provider as perceived by the particular group.

Whether any given menu is ultimately palatable or credible in the eyes of the individual family is a function of whether what ultimately appears on the television comports with that family's conception of what is desirable and appropriate. Those who use Internet browsers select their browsers based on the quality, breadth, and reliability of the webpages that are retrieved. In a similar manner, programme content/ratings guides can be developed to provide parents with a proactive mechanism for deliberative television viewing. Using models provided by associations such as 'Screen It! Entertainment Reviews for Parents', organisations can develop detailed programme/ratings guides to inform parents fully about television content. One example of an organisation providing detailed ratings is The Movie Mom. This information can be made available both online and in print form, and designed to complement industry-developed on-screen programme guides.

Parental Initiatives

Parent and family involvement is a significant component of effective, long-lasting media education. Understanding the different rating systems and devices that apply to media is also an important step in becoming a better-informed parent. Media literacy strategies for parents should begin with a focus on more parental involvement in children's media habits: the location of computers and electronic media in central places in the home (living room, study, and so on), discussion of programming, monitoring, and intentional television viewing (including the maintenance of viewing diaries/logs). Descriptive rating systems can assist parents in undertaking this educational process. The encouragement of family-focused media education will require resources for a determined, long-running campaign. To implement this, partnerships with other agencies are vital.

Supplemented by public service campaigns, announcements, materials from nonprofit organisations, guides for parents on viewing television with children, and strategies for parents to use media as a catalyst for educational opportunities, parents can create a culture of informed, responsible television viewing in their homes. In the online guide 'Taking Charge of Your TV. A Guide to Critical Viewing for Parents and Children', Renee Hobbs advises parents to become more aware of TV programme production methods and techniques; establish limits on how much TV the family watches each week; develop family guidelines for programme selection; and 'Talk back to the TV', by expressing opinions of what is seen and heard (Hobbs 2001). Parent education strategies such as workshops by 'The Television Project' can provide parents with both specific activities and strategies to assist them in developing television viewing policies for their families and facilitate the use of programme/content guides developed by broadcasters and independent nonprofit organisations.

Educational Institutions

For myriad reasons, the practice of watching television programming together as a family has declined and will decline further in a multichannel, multiset digital era. We recognise the need to empower parental control of television viewing when parents cannot be with their children, or are unable to directly monitor programme consumption. School-based media literacy initiatives can directly support and supplement efforts in the home and community, fostering the development of youth as informed, responsible television viewers. However, several observers and projects around the world have also underscored the need to train teachers for media education. Teachers must have administrative support and the necessary resources to study media phenomena. The latter can be initiated by the relevant government authorities in the respective countries.

Research indicates that Great Britain, Canada, Australia, Scotland, Germany, and other nations include media literacy as part of the language arts programme in primary and secondary schools. The practice is not so widespread in the United States, but North Carolina, Massachusetts, New Mexico, and Texas include media literacy in their curriculum frameworks. Current United States efforts employ models provided by British scholars, including Len Masterman, David Buckingham, David Lusted, and Cary Bazalgette.

Difficulties have arisen in school-based media literacy initiatives. These include teachers' use of media texts and other materials for noneducational purposes such as rewards for good behaviour, to keep students quiet, for passive viewing (without discussion, reflection), and as a 'filler' to free up time for other tasks (Hobbs n.d.). In addition, media analysis in schools has often been a teacher-centred practice, viewed as a process of media 'demystification' for youth, which often disregards students' prior knowledge and assumes their passivity (Buckingham 1990). Media production work is often relegated to vocational education, an esteem-building exercise for 'at-risk' students only or purely for entertainment purposes.

To fully realise the educational benefits of media literacy programs, well-developed media literacy curricula should be implemented with proper institutional support and comprehensive teacher training. Classroom practices, particularly the nature of student—teacher dialogue, must be re-examined. A school-based media literacy initiative should be an academic discipline, employing both media analysis and practical work to facilitate the development of youth as informed, active viewers. Curriculum examples are available free-of-charge or at low costs, from organisations such as YTV Canada, Inc. (Andersen and Ventura n.d.), the Just Think Foundation, which provides a professional development model for educators among its services, and Creating Critical Viewers, a partnership between educators and broadcast professionals that produced this online handbook.

At the European level, the European Association for Audio-visual Media Education (AEEMA/EAAME) was founded in 1989 under the joint auspices of the European Commission and the Council of Europe. It benefits from the recognition of Eureka Audiovisuel and regularly liaises with the European Parliament on matters concerning media, education, culture, and young people. Its purpose is to develop the identity of audiovisual Media Education and to foster the idea of an audiovisual culture amongst the public at large. AEEMA/EAAME has nearly 300 members who represent the key protagonists in a wide variety of national scenarios. It aims *inter alia* (a) to promote the teaching of the languages of image and sound; (b) to convince young people, the public at large, the authorities both local and national as well as the professionals that such education is necessary; (c) to prepare young people to use new means of communication; (d) to encourage a critical approach to audiovisual media by practical exercises; (e) to establish a permanent inventory of audiovisual education in Europe; and (f) to exchange information on the methods used in training and in the audiovisual creation in Europe.

Curriculum development is the responsibility of the Department of Education in most Member States.[4] In order to develop a successful parental control environment education departments should be involved in the creation of a supportive education system. At European level, DGXXII is responsible for education, training, and youth. The Maastricht treaty's articles 126 and 127 respectively specify that the European Community 'shall contribute to the development of quality education by encouraging cooperation between the Member States and, if necessary, by supporting and supplementing their action'. They should also 'implement a vocational training policy which shall support and supplement the action of the Member States'. In both cases, the Member States maintain full responsibility for the 'content and organisation' of their national education and training systems. DG XXII has developed three 5-year programmes: SOCRATES for education, LEONARDO DA VINCI for training, and Youth for Europe, a new programme for young people outside formal education and training systems. We recommend stimulating the use of these programmes for the further development of media education in Europe.

---

[4] See the education information network in Europe (EURYDICE) for more information. It is a reliable source for national and comparative information on European education systems and policies.

Comparative Country Analysis

Austria

Since 1973, all primary and secondary schools in Austria have been required to integrate media education across the curriculum. In theory, every teacher addresses the basic principles of media education in every subject. In practice, this means that the teaching of media education depends upon the personal commitment of individual teachers.

Denmark

A group of committed teachers introduced media education in Denmark in the 1930s. While the 1950 Education Act ignored their initiative, the 1961 official education handbook devoted a whole chapter to screen education. The subject was offered as an optional course for older students, and focused on film as an art rather than as a medium. When the Danish curriculum underwent a major revision in 1969, media education lost its designation as a separate subject. Since the mid-1970s, the National Media Research Association has encouraged the integration of media education across the curriculum. And, while many teachers of history, social studies, and Danish feel media education to be an important part of their subject, some teachers complain that such teaching interferes with their own course material.

Research has shown that Danish students prefer courses in production to courses in analysis and critical awareness. Currently it is suggested that students 'might' or 'ought to' be taught media education as part of other courses. There are a number of dedicated teachers who are doing just that, with both critical analysis and production.

England

In the 1970s, the sociologists and the semiologists put their marks on British media education. The sociologists concentrated on media in a collaborative industrial form, and encouraged its study from such viewpoints as that of ownership and control, audience, and the ideological role of media. They gave more attention to what made media what they were, rather than to media texts themselves.

Media education in Britain evolved in the 1980s with Len Masterman's work. His approach is essentially interrogative and informed by critical mass communication research. His questions are based on the assumptions that the mass media construct their own realities. These questions cluster around four general areas: (1) The sources, origins, and determinants of media constructions. Who constructs media reality? (2) The dominant techniques and codings employed by media to convince us of the truth of their representations. How is this process of representation carried out and achieved? (3) The nature of the 'reality' constructed by media and the values implicit in media representations. What are the characteristics of the world so represented? (4) The ways in which media constructions are read or received by their audiences. How are these representations read and understood by the people who receive them?

For primary students, the English national curriculum currently requires a minimal element of media literacy within the reading attainment target for English, which can be taught by using print texts only. Secondary students have been offered courses in media literacy since the early 1960s. At present there are courses available—Film and Media Studies, Media Studies, and Media Studies Advanced—in both the GCE (General Certificate of Education) and the GCSE (General Certificate of Secondary Education). Teacher training programmes are available in many colleges throughout England, such as the University of London and the University of Southampton.

One institution has been central to the development of media education in Britain, the British Film Institute (BFI). This organisation receives government funding to foster public appreciation and the study of film and television. The BFI's operations include the National Film Archive, the National Film Theatre, and the Museum of the Moving Image. Its London offices house large libraries of books, periodicals, photographs, publicity materials, and a database on film and television. The Education Department of the BFI works with people in education and training to develop knowledge, ideas, and ways of teaching about film and television. This work includes research, teaching and advising, publishing teaching materials, and organising courses and conferences.

Finland

In the curriculum of Finnish schools, media education is described as a 'pervasive' subject. This means that while mass media education has no course of its own, it is taught at certain points in Finnish, art, history, social studies, and study of the environment.

There have been two significant projects in Finnish media education. In the first, organised during the mid-1970s by the National Board of General Education in cooperation with the Finnish Newspaper Publishers' Association, students received—for a period of one week—teaching about newspapers and mass media. The second, the Mass Media Entertainment Project, took place during the 1978–1979 and 1979–1980 school years. This National Board project focused on different forms of mass media entertainment, and getting teachers and students to discuss their use. The Board provided material aimed at developing students' critical viewing skills. Both the Association of Film Clubs and the

Finnish Broadcasting Company also produced materials, which have continued to prove useful. The National Board has indicated that it considers media education an important subject, yet there are few textbooks in the area and there is no adequate training for teachers. Moreover, many educators feel the subject would work best as a separate course.

France

Media education—especially in the area of film study—has a long history in France, though generally not as part of the formal system of education. Traditionally it has been an extracurricular activity carried on by film societies, school clubs, and youth activity groups. By the late 1970s, there were hundreds of thousands of these film societies (Cine-Clubs) organised into federations.

One of the first initiatives in teaching media within the school curriculum began in the mid-1960s and continues today. Known as '*Langage Total*', it was developed at the *Institut du Langage Total* in Lyons under the direction of Brother Antoine Vallet in conjunction with the Catholic University of Lyons and the Catholic University of the West at Angers. Programmes are taught in over 200 French primary schools and more than 100 secondary schools. The *Langage Total* method is also used in other European countries, the Near East, Latin America, and French-speaking Africa.

On the initiative of a research-action team from the Centre Régional de Documentation Pédagogique (CRDP) in Bordeaux, René La Borderie directed the development of the project known originally as Introduction to Audiovisual Culture (ICAV) and now called Introduction to Communication and the Media (ICOM).

As ICAV, the project introduced an integrated approach to the study of image forms transmitted through advertising, newspapers, and educational publications to schools. Until 1982, education authorities recognised the project only as a provisional programme allowed into schools attached to the Ministry of National Education (primary and secondary schools). In 1982, there was a new definition of the Introduction to Communication and the Media project, formulated and adopted at a national meeting.

Within this new definition, ICOM wants education to cover all media and all situations involving communications. In 1979, the various government ministries involved in educational activities for young people—the Ministries of Agriculture, Education, Family, Leisure, Youth, and Sport—conducted a joint nation-wide experiment in educating young television viewers. *Le Jeune Téléspectateur Actif* (JTA) (Young Active Television Viewers) lasted until 1983. The project urged all who played a role in education—parents, teachers, youth club organisers, and so on—to integrate a consideration of the part played by television in the daily lives of the young into their educational activities.

After two years, JTA evaluated the changes that had taken place in the relationships between children and television. As was expected, the amount of knowledge acquired about television had increased. Furthermore, the young showed a change in their capacity for observation. They were paying more attention to the form of the messages, to the modes of representation and the prevailing meaning. They were also seen to have developed research attitudes towards the kinds of programmes watched. At the end of the experiment in 1983, a number of training courses in critical viewing skills were incorporated into in-service and training for teachers at various levels. It is also important to note that the new official curriculum published by the Ministry for secondary schools makes some important statements about media education.

The *Centre de Liaison de l'Enseignement et des Moyens d'Information* (CLEMI) was established in 1982 by the French Ministry of Education to help students develop critical thinking skills and to train them in the responsibilities of modern citizenship. CLEMI organises national and regional teacher training courses, publishes professional journals for teachers, and makes available its documentary resources on contemporary media education.

Germany

There are records to indicate that German schools introduced media education in the 17th century when the first newspapers were published. Scholars attribute the first mention of media education to Johann Amos Comenius (1592–1670) in *Schola Pansphica*. Comenius held that the study of newspapers 'would benefit the development of language skills, and provide basic information for current affairs and geography'. His educational philosophy insisted on a relevant curriculum—students must learn about the world around them.

By the late 1960s, German educators acknowledged that media were not only educational tools, but also worthy of study for their content. Gradually media education made its way into the curriculum as part of other subject disciplines.

Today media education is usually taught in such courses as Political Education, Knowledge About Society, or Social Studies. These courses must be included in the curriculum of each federal region's school system. Their function is to promote awareness of citizenship. A student is to be given an education that will allow the student to be involved in society decision making, develop the student's personality, and allow the student to take informed action.

A 1984 study commissioned by the *Institut Für Publizistik der Universitat Mainz* showed that of the 199 teachers surveyed, 91 percent had dealt with mass media in class and 72 percent dealt with the topic regularly. However, they placed most emphasis on analysing newspapers, despite the fact that West German adolescents at that time viewed 72 minutes of television a day on average and spent only 8 minutes a day reading newspapers.

Each federal region also has its own resource centre to help teachers. The major one is the *National Institut Für Film Und Bild im Wissenschaft und Unterricht* (FWU) (The Institute for Film and Image in Science and Education). Along with two journals, *AV Praxis* and *AV Forschung*, FWU has produced a portable case of materials for classroom use. The resource materials include a film cassette with three different commentaries, and the same script filmed from three different perspectives. These are used to demonstrate the constructed nature of media images and messages.

Media education is seen by some German parents as a useful way to protect minors from the 'dangerous' influences of media. Other parents see television as 'mere entertainment' and therefore not worth studying in school. And some see any kind of visual literacy as something that belongs to a left wing philosophy.

In 1984, the *Institut Jugend Film Fernsehen* in Munich completed a project for the German Research Institute. For four years the group had been developing a media education curriculum; by 1984, 4 textbooks had been piloted, revised, and published. Unfortunately, funding for the project was stopped. While the government gave teachers in the federal region of Bavaria permission to use the new curriculum, they provided neither training nor teaching aids.

Ireland

Although it is not officially included in the curriculum, a growing number of Irish schools are including some form of media education in their courses. Since the late 1960s, the Catholic Communications Centre in Dublin has conducted in-service courses in media for teachers. As a result of these courses—and courses organised by other groups—scores of individual teachers have attempted to introduce media education into such traditional subjects as English and Religion.

The first publication of the Curriculum and Examination Board, Issues, and Structures in Education (1984) made clear that media education would be a basic part of the new curriculum. With the support of the European Economic Community, a training programme was established and media education included within its 1-year syllabus. In August 1985, Ireland's first two media textbooks were published with the hope that they would be used to incorporate media education into other subjects.

Italy

In 1985, a new curriculum was announced for Italian primary schools. This went into effect in 1987 and was preceded by refresher training for all Italian primary teachers. Media education was included in the area known as Image, Sound, Music, and Movement. This area deals with the cultural and social values of nonverbal language and their role in the development of children.

Netherlands

As of 1990, Audiovisual Education (as media education is known in the Netherlands) was neither an autonomous nor mandatory subject in the Dutch national curriculum. Audiovisual Education takes place mainly within art education and as a result has a very aesthetic approach. Media are regarded as purposeful constructs whose form is highly significant.

Scotland

Growth in media education, especially in the secondary school system of Scotland, was stimulated and shaped by the Media Education Development Project (MEDP), which was established by the Scottish Council for Education Technology (SCET) in 1983. 1983 was also the year in which the Scottish Education Department began a reassessment of the curriculum in Scottish secondary education. In the midst of all these changes, there were many opportunities to develop courses in media education. The MEDP made use of these.

The curriculum development work of the MEDP differentiated between media education and Media Studies. In media education, components are inserted into existing subjects. Media Studies refers to a series of modules, which are taught as a separate course. These modules range from a general overview of all media, to eight specialised modules.

The Media Studies modules were written to have either an analytical or practical emphasis. Television, Radio, Press and Magazines, and Graphic Design and Photography were written into the practical domain. Students were asked to produce short television or radio shows, a newspaper, a magazine, or an advertisement. They were also asked to analyse professionally produced examples of media to help them with their own productions. In the analytical domain, specialised modules were developed in Film, Contemporary Popular Music, and Representations and Narrative Forms in Broadcasting. As early as 1984, over 100 institutions were teaching Media Studies using the first five modules to be published.

The MEDP's efforts in the area of teacher training included direct provision of in-service training, planning of locally based courses and involvement in the planning of National and Certificate courses. The Scottish Film Council has worked in conjunction the Association for Media Education in Scotland (AMES) to produce many teaching aids and a quarterly journal, *The Scottish Media Education Journal*.

Spain

The Department of Education at the Universidad Nacional de Educación a Distancia produces a number of books, audiotapes, and videocassettes on media education. A number of North American media education books are available in Spanish.

Sweden

The Education Department of Sveriges Radio (SR) has produced materials for media education in Sweden's secondary schools since the beginning of the 1960s. The courses developed were basically theoretical. While the emphasis has been on film study, some television has been included. The official policy is that media education should be taught so that students will have 'the ability to watch critically and make an independent judgement of the messages received from the different media, and the ability to talk about how one has experienced films and TV programmes'. This was made compulsory in 1980.

Annex 1
Comparative Analysis
of Rating Systems

CINEMA RATING SYSTEMS

From its first appearance, cinema has been widely considered to have an important impact on society in general and viewers in particular. This explains why Member States have taken care to regulate it strictly, particularly the content. At first, propaganda considerations dictated regulation of content, which was also intended to prevent a challenge to civic education through this medium. However, by the middle of the century the idea had slowly developed that content provided via the cinema could be harmful to specific groups of society (children, sensitive persons). Some specific rating bodies were then established, generally under the control of the public authorities, and acting as a monopolistic rating provider (with the exception of Austria, Portugal, and Spain). For the most part, this pattern is present in all Member States. Ratings issued are usually evaluative, assigning a suitable age category, which is decided using either a nondeterministic or semideterministic methodology.

Austria

Further to Article 15 paragraph 1 of the Bundes-Verfassungsgesetz (Austrian Federal Constitution), the legislative branches of the nine federal provinces may enact statutory provisions for the protection of minors. For practical reasons we have focussed here on the legal situation in the province of Vienna, which is typical of all the federal provinces.

Two acts are of interest in the context of protection of minors: the *Wiener Jugendschutzgesetz 1985* (Vienna Minors Protection Act of 1985) and the *Wiener Kinogesetz 1955* (Vienna Cinema Act). The Vienna Minors Protection Act applies to public film presentations, theatre performances, television, and video presentations; children under 6 years old may only attend when accompanied by a *Begleitperson*.[1] Furthermore, Section 9, paragraph 1 of the Act stipulates that children under 6 may only attend presentations to which the Vienna Cinema Act applies if their admission has been approved by the competent authority.

Children over the age of 6 and young people aged less than 16 years may attend public film presentations, as well as television and video presentations, to which the Vienna Cinema Act applies only if the admission of minors of that age has been approved by the competent authority.[2] Children and young people may not attend other public film presentations, as well as television and video presentations, if such presentations may be harmful to minors.

Notwithstanding, children are not allowed to attend public film presentations, theatre performances, or television or video presentations after 9:00 p.m. unless accompanied by a *Begleitperson* or with the approval of their *Erziehungsberechtigte*.[3] For young people the time limit is midnight.

Section 19 of the Vienna Minors Protection Act states that any violation of this Act is an administrative offence; the amount of the fine depends on the offender's age, and there are no fines for children.

Far more provisions on the protection of minors are found in the Vienna Cinema Act. As a general rule, people over 16 may only attend public film presentations; however, younger people may be admitted by the municipal authority, which has to take advice from the *Filmbeirat der Stadt Wien* (Film Advisory Board of the City of Vienna). This advisory board is composed of members from the *Stadtschulrat* (City School Council); the *Bundespolizeidirektion Wien* (Federal Police Directorate of Vienna); one educationalist; one expert from the field of youth welfare work; one expert from the field of national education; one representative of a parents' association and one of a youth organisation; 2 members from the film industry and a maximum of 3 other members. Landeshauptmann, the head of the provincial government, appoints the members and their deputies.

---

[1] 'Children' are defined as persons of less than 14 years of age, see definition in Section sub-paragraph 1 of the Vienna Minors Protection Act. A *Begleitperson* is a parent or other person/institution who/which has the right to raise the child, person who has been legitimately raising the child for a long period or forever, or person over 18 who is entrusted with the care of the child from time to time.

[2] Young people' are defined as persons aged at least 14 and less than 18. See definition in Section sub-paragraph 2 of the Vienna Minors Protection Act. However, young people who are either married or are members of the Austrian Federal Armed Forces (Bundesheer) are not considered to be young people within the meaning of the Vienna Minors Protection Act.

[3] An *Erziehungsberechtigte* is a parent or other person/institution who/which has the right to raise the child, or person who has been legitimately raising the child for a longer period or forever.

While the rating bodies can operate at a provincial level, in practice there is much more centralisation. In the Cinema Acts of some provinces there is even an express provision allowing for the transfer of such authority. Section 11 paragraph 5 of the Vienna Cinema Act, allows film ratings admitting under 16's given by other Austrian advisory boards or commissions, which also include members appointed by the provincial government, to be recognised as binding, if the classification is made according to the same principles that the Film Advisory Board of the City of Vienna applies.

Though there are governmental rating entities in the federal provinces, for the sake of simplicity there is also a central *Jugendfilmkommission* (Youth Film Commission), affiliated with the *Bundesministerium für Unterricht und kulturelle Angelegenheiten* (Federal Ministry for Education and the Arts). The Youth Film Commission was established in 1948 and is composed of experts drawn from education, protection of minors, youth organisations, parents' associations, churches, and the film industry. In addition, there is one representative from each federal province. The Commission is chaired by the head of the Ministry's competent service, described in section 2 of the Rules of Procedure. Film presentations usually take place once a week, and the members of the Commission are obliged to attend the entire presentation.

The regime is voluntary: It is up to the film producer/distributor to accept the age limit applied in each province. If they want younger viewers admitted, they may request the Commission to examine the admissibility of younger people

The methodology followed by the Commission is semideterministic. The *Jugendfilmkommission's* Rules of Procedure provide for criteria on which the opinion is based. However, these criteria are not so detailed as to dictate the commission's expert opinion entirely. The Commission bases its opinion on whether it suspects a film to have a potentially harmful influence on young people; notably on their physical health; their mental and/or moral development; their religious sentiments; and their democratic civic attitude. Notwithstanding the legal situation at provincial level, the categories of 'no age limit', 'over 6 years', 'over 10 years', 'over 12 years', 'over 14 years', 'over 16 years', and 'over 18 years' are applied in the Austrian *Jugendfilmkommission* classification system. The system is therefore an evaluative system.

The Austrian approach proves that despite responsibilities being divided among smaller entities such as federal provinces, ratings may be carried out on a higher level. However, the present structure is unlikely to be able to cope with the volume of existing and future television programming.

Section 8 of the Youth Film Commission's Rules of Procedure provides for film trailers and other short films (for example, newsreels, advertising films) to be rated on the same principles as main films (defined as films with a duration of more than 30 minutes).

Belgium

The rating system for films in Belgium is a result of the 'Cooperation Agreement' of 27 December 1990 between the French Community, the Flemish Community, the Inter-Community Commission of the Bruxelles-Capitale region, and the German Community, which establishes the composition, rules, and functions of the *Commission intercommunautaire de contrôle des films* (CICF). The responsible Ministers of each Community appoint members of this Commission.

This Commission has been subject to numerous criticisms regarding its rating system. Indeed the institution works on the basis of a law dated 1 September 1920 issuing only one age classification, which prohibits films to those less than 16 years of age. It is the only classification in force. The Commission does not take into account the category of film prohibited to those under 12 years of age whereas this category exists in media regulation of the Flemish and French community.

Reform of the Commission and the rating system is expected. However, the institutional issue (obtaining an agreement between the different Communities and the Bruxelles-Capitale region) makes the process slow.

Denmark

The rules applying to cinema in Denmark are contained in the Film Act of 12 March 1997. The body responsible for classification is the Media Council for Children and Young People (MCCY), which was established by the Minister of Culture in April 1997, to replace the State Film Censorship. Chapter 6 of the Film Act of 12 March 1997 establishes the legal setting, outlining the Council's mandate, and Departmental Order No. 30 of 16 January 1998 regulates its activity. The MCCY is central to the regulation of film, video, and computer games on CD-ROM. It is also part of its mandate to maintain a continuous dialogue with the national public service broadcasters, Danmarks Radio and TV2; in order to advise them on following the regulations stipulated by the Broadcasting Act and the subsequent ministerial order. However, private performances and films shown on television do not fall under the jurisdiction of the MCCY.

The MCCY's budget was 1.8 million Danish kroner in 1998. The estimated income in 1998 from producers and distributors paying for their films to be evaluated is 300.000 Danish kroner.

The MCCY has 7 members. Three of the council members are experts on children; 2 are experts on the film industry; one represents cultural and/or media views; while the last member represents consumer interests.

The principal task of the MCCY is to evaluate films and videos, analysing their suitability for children. It evaluates films from a general perspective including interaction between the actual story and the special effects, and evaluations are based on the criterion of harmfulness that is stipulated in the Film Act, albeit in very general terms.[4]

During the first year of the MCCY's existence, substantial time has been spent on formulating and establishing a consensus on the criteria for assessing harmfulness in film and videos. Given the ambiguity of the concept, the discussions are expected to continue. The notion of harmfulness changes as does the norms and moral of a society.

Age classifications issued by MCCY are: 'permitted for all', 'for all, but not recommended for children under the age of 7', 'permitted for children above the age of 11', 'permitted for children above the age of 15'.

It is important to stress that in the evaluation of films and videos, it is harmfulness rather than suitability that is expressed by the age limits applied. A film may receive a classification for 7-year-olds, due to its lack of harmful content, without thereby being particularly suitable for children through being able to interest them or being easy to understand.

In accordance with the Film Act of 12 March 1997, age classification may be circumvented as it is permitted for children of the age of 7 and above to watch any film in the cinema, as long as an adult accompanies them. This decision was received with approval within the industry and likewise among parents. The MCCY's understanding is that this rule resolves a situation that the audience used to find frustrating—the fact that they could not decide for themselves what their children should be allowed to see. It allows parents and children to decide jointly what is suitable for the children to watch, thereby applying the same situation to cinema visits as home viewing, where it is the parent who decides which programmes children may watch on television or video.

In addition to this work on evaluation of films and videos, the MCCY's role includes the provision of information, awareness raising, and the formulation of guidelines. It cooperates with other institutions performing similar roles (that is, The Danish Film Institute, public libraries, and children's film clubs), in passing on information to teachers, users, and parents about suitable films for children and about the importance of raising awareness among users.

---

[4] The criterion of harmfulness is reflected on in Note no. 38 of the Film Act, where emphasis is put on whether the film contain scenes presumed to have a brutalizing effect on children and youth, by weakening their inhibitions towards use of violence. Sexual descriptions contained in the film are also taken into consideration, with a view to restricting admission to children below 7, 11, and 15 years of age respectively. Further interpretations of harmfulness are thus left to the MCCY to administer.

Finland

The first Act on Film Classification in Finland was introduced in 1946. Before that date film distribution was self-regulated by the film industry. According to the Act on Film Classification (299/1965), all films (except when they are broadcast on television) must be viewed and classified by the *Valtion elokuvatarkasta-mo* (Finnish Board of Film Classification) before they can be shown in public. Only this body has the authority to ban and censor films. All audiovisual programmes to be shown in public are subject to film classification (except when they are broadcast on television or at film festivals exempted by application).

The censors must not authorise for public showing a film or part of a film that is obscene, contains brutal violence, or which is psychologically disturbing (by shocking or otherwise). Films that disrupt public order, threaten public security or national defence, or damage Finland's relations with foreign powers should also be banned. Furthermore, a film must be banned if it obviously violates Finnish law.

The Act on Film Classification is decreed in an exceptional way, by following the constitutional legislative procedure. Preventive film censorship is in conflict with the constitutional right of free speech, and, in addition, many of the criteria articulated in the Act on Film Classification are obsolete.

In 1995, the constitution was revised and a new clause was added to the paragraph on the freedom of speech. According to the new clause, 'audiovisual programme restrictions necessary to protect children may be prescribed by law'. Since 1995, the film classification system has been under revision, and according to the revised constitution, a Film Classification Act need no longer be decreed following the exceptional constitutional legislative procedure, if it only contains restrictions necessary to protect children—that is, rating restrictions only.

A committee on film examination finished its report on the revision of the Act of Film Classification for the Ministry of Education on 3 April 1998. The new law would aim to unite previous laws and regulations concerning the censorship and classification of audiovisual programmes. At the same time, previous Acts would be rescinded. The committee proposes that films, videos, and other audiovisual programmes for adult viewing would be exempted from preliminary examination, but that the showing of such films to people under 18 would not be allowed. Films should include ratings based on age. All films and programmes should be registered with the *Valtion elokuvatarkastamo* before being shown and distributed. In the proposal, freedom of speech and the equal treatment of different audiovisual media are emphasised.

However, programmes violating the penal code should not be distributed or shown. A programme should not be accepted for viewing if it is likely to disturb the psychological development of a child by shocking, or due to its violent or sexual content. Age restrictions set at 7, 11, 15, and general, should be included in television programme information.

According to the proposal there would no longer be a body responsible for censoring and banning films. The criteria of 'offensive, disrupting public order, threatening security or national defence, and damaging the nation's foreign relations' would be abolished. Interactive programmes, that is, video games or computer games that are targeted at audiences of all ages, are not currently subject to censorship, but if there were any reason to suspect an interactive programme, under the new proposal it should also be submitted for classification.

The establishment of the proposal for a new Act would mean an improvement in the equal treatment of different media. At the present time, for instance, programmes that may be aired on TV cannot be distributed as videotapes. The proposal has also been praised for its capacity to combine the previous Acts on Film Classification, and the Act Relating to the Inspection of Video and other Audiovisual Programmes. In line with the Constitutional right of free speech (10 §) it limits the restriction of free speech to materials that are suspected of having a potentially negative effect on children. However, the proposal has encountered some criticism. For instance, it does not attempt to control the selling or distribution of illegal films. The report was under revision in the Ministry of Education to be completed during the winter of 1999.

The current rating system is mandatory, since all ratings are necessary by law, and evaluative, as it provides a single rating indicator based on age. As it is based on the opinions of the rating body the system is also nondeterministic.

Since 1966, the classification has been executed by the *Valtion elokuvatarkastamo*. The law contains a provision as to the composition of the Board, with screening to be the responsibility of eight censors. The Ministry of Education appoints the chairperson of the board and the other 7 censors, who serve for a 3-year term, though reappointment is possible. The chairperson and 2 other censors work on a daily basis, examining programmes for 20 hours per week. Five other censors each work 4 hours weekly.

The Board has to meet the following criteria: (a) equal representation of men and women; (b) representation of both the Ministries of Culture and of Finance; (c) psychological, psychiatric, and pedagogical expertise; and (d) expertise in the social sciences and in film art.

The basic rating scale is divided into 4 categories: 'G' for general audience, 'Restricted for persons under 16', 'Restricted for persons under 18', and 'Banned'. In the second category, 'Restricted for persons under 16', age categories 6, 8, 10, 12, and 14 are used. There is also a PG-option, '3 years younger may attend if accompanied by a parent or legal guardian'. The PG categories: PG-8, PG-10, and PG-12, are also possible.

Three members of the Board, one of whom has to be either the chairperson or vice-chairperson, constitute a quorum. The decisions do not need to be unanimous. Two members of the Board can make a decision provided that they are in agreement and that they do not cut or ban a film. One member can even make a ruling relating to the age limit, if the distributor or producer agrees to it. Rating decisions are binding and the penalty for public showing of a film that has not been classified is a fine or imprisonment for up to six months.

If a film has been authorised for public showing it is not rechecked for home video distribution, except when it has been rated 18, in which case cuts are required in order to acquire a 16 rating. Programmes including hardcore pornography or depicting fictional graphic or sadistic violence are rated 18. Films or programmes, which contain sexual violence, animal pornography, or child pornography, are banned. Lower ratings are based on the quantity and quality of violence, sex, horror effects, and so on in films.

The decisions of the Board can be appealed to the Appeal Board, but the appeal process is open only to distributors or producers. The Appeal Board consists of eleven members, appointed by the government for a term of 3 years. The Ministries of Education, Justice, and Finance are each represented by one member. The other members represent different branches of society, for example, the press, the film industry, film critics, education, and psychology. If a distributor or a producer is not satisfied with the decision of the Appeal Board, they can appeal to the Supreme Administrative Court.

France

In France, the *Centre National de la Cinematographie* (CNC) was established by the law of 25 October 1946. It is a public body under the authority of the Ministry of Culture and the 'tutelary father' and 'nourishing mother' of the cinematographic industry. The Centre is responsible for classifying cinematographic works.[5] The Minister of Culture issues a certificate after advice from the Commission for the Classification of Cinematographic Works.[6] All French and foreign cinematographic works to be screened in France are subject to this procedure.

---

[5] Article 19 (Ordonnance n° 45-1464 of 3 July 1945, first Article—modified by law n° 92-1477 of 31 December 1992) of the Code of the Cinematographic Industry (Decree n° 56-158 of 27 January 1956—Law n° 58-346 of 3 April 1958): 'The representation and export outside European Economic Community of cinematographic works is subject to obtaining a certificate granted by the Minister of Information'. The certificate is now granted by the Minister of Culture.

[6] Composition and functions of this commission are fixed by Decree n°90–174 of 23 February 1990 as revised.

The classification commission is composed as follows: A president (chosen from the members of the *Conseil d'Etat*) and a substitute president, both designated by Decree of the Prime Minister, as well as 25 permanent members and 50 substitutes, divided into 4 colleges and designated by ministerial order (Ministry of Culture). All are mandated for 2 years. The four colleges are: First college; Second college: Professionals; Third college: Experts; and Fourth college: Youth.

The first college is composed of 5 permanent members and 10 substitutes representing Ministries of Justice, Education, Internal Affairs, and Youth and Social Affairs.

The second college is composed of 8 permanent members and 16 substitutes appointed from representatives of the cinematographic profession, after consultation with main organisations or associations of this field.

The third college is composed of 5 permanent members and 10 substitutes appointed from proposals made by Ministries of Justice, Education, Internal Affairs, and Youth, and Social Affairs. It also has 1 permanent member and 2 substitutes appointed from nominations by the *Conseil supérieur de l'audiovisuel* in addition to 2 permanent members and 4 substitutes appointed after consultation with the National Union of Family Associations and the Association of the Mayors of France

The fourth college is composed of 3 permanent members and 6 substitutes nominated by 18 to 25 year olds and appointed after consultation with the National Council for Popular Education and Youth. It also has 1 permanent member and 2 substitutes appointed from 18 to 25 year olds, on the grounds of an application list established by the general director of the CNC.

Promotional support made available by distributors to the theatres is also subject to a certificate issued by the commission. Posters of films prohibited to minors under 12 or 16 may only use images or illustrations approved by the Commission.

Specific legal provisions apply when a film is disseminated without a certificate or in infringement of the certificate issued. These provisions are administrative seizure by the film police authorities or possible judicial proceedings leading to fines, to which may be added a ban (permanent or temporary) from any form of work in the cinematographic industry.

Admission of minors to screenings prohibited to them also constitutes a breach and leads to the imposition of fines, as mandated by Decree n° 92-445 of 15 May 1992 concerning access by minors to cinemas.

The procedure for rating cinema in France is outlined in Figure 1.

FIGURE 1
French Cinematographic Rating Procedure

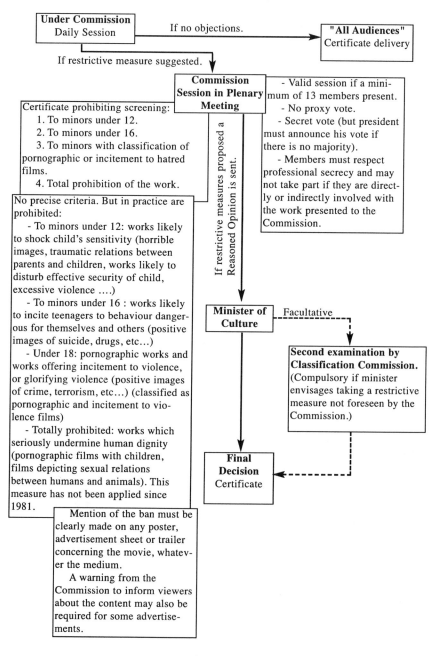

Under Commission
Daily Session

If no objections.

"All Audiences"
Certificate delivery

If restrictive measure suggested.

Commission Session in Plenary Meeting

Certificate prohibiting screening:
1. To minors under 12.
2. To minors under 16.
3. To minors with classification of pornographic or incitement to hatred films.
4. Total prohibition of the work.

- Valid session if a minimum of 13 members present.
- No proxy vote.
- Secret vote (but president must announce his vote if there is no majority).
- Members must respect professional secrecy and may not take part if they are directly or indirectly involved with the work presented to the Commission.

No precise criteria. But in practice are prohibited:
- To minors under 12: works likely to shock child's sensitivity (horrible images, traumatic relations between parents and children, works likely to disturb effective security of child, excessive violence ....)
- To minors under 16 : works likely to incite teenagers to behaviour dangerous for themselves and others (positive images of suicide, drugs, etc...)
- Under 18: pornographic works and works offering incitement to violence, or glorifying violence (positive images of crime, terrorism, etc...) (classified as pornographic and incitement to violence films)
- Totally prohibited: works which seriously undermine human dignity (pornographic films with children, films depicting sexual relations between humans and animals). This measure has not been applied since 1981.

If restrictive measures proposed a Reasoned Opinion is sent.

Minister of Culture

Facultative

Second examination by Classification Commission.
(Compulsory if minister envisages taking a restrictive measure not foreseen by the Commission.)

Final Decision
Certificate

Mention of the ban must be clearly made on any poster, advertisement sheet or trailer concerning the movie, whatever the medium.
A warning from the Commission to inform viewers about the content may also be required for some advertisements.

Germany

Strictly speaking, the only rating/labelling system in Germany is the one used by *Freiwillige Selbstkontrolle der Filmwirtschaft* (FSK), the voluntary self-regulation Board for cinema films. The *Bundesprüfstelle für jugendgefährdende Schriften* (BPjS), the Federal Examination Department for publications harmful to minors.[7] This is not a rating body as such, but it is in charge of controlling the legality of cinema films and whether they should be put on an 'index', listing publications which are likely to morally endanger children and young people, and which are prohibited for minors.

The FSK uses an evaluative rating system. The films are classified on the basis of age categories included in the law: §6II JÖSChG. These categories are: 'no age limit', 'children older than 6', 'children older than 12', 'Young people older than 16', 'young people older than 18'.

The system is based on legal provisions, which are completed by the examination criteria of the FSK. However, the system is semideterministic since the FSK enjoys a certain licence in interpreting the criteria under the principle of proportionality.

The FSK calls itself a voluntary body. However, every film intended for public screening needs to be rated by the FSK. In the absence of a rating, the film may only be shown to adults.

The FSK is difficult to define precisely within the system. The Federal States reached a specific agreement regarding the protection of minors in films on 1 April 1985, by which they decided to use the FSK as an expert body for rating cinema films. However, the FSK is a self-controlling body under private law, which acts in the name and at the request of the Supreme Youth Authorities in the Federal States.[8] The FSK describes itself as well-informed, independent, and representative of society. Even if, as is always emphasised, the Supreme Youth Authorities in the Federal States remain responsible for their decisions and no official transfer of rights has as yet taken place, the certification for release is effectively carried out by the FSK. For these reasons, the FSK might be classified as a government rather than an industry system. The Federal States are enti-

---

[7] The legal basis of the activity of the FSK is included in §6 of the law on protection of minors in public places (JÖSchG). The FSK was established after the war as an independent department of the Spitzenorganisation der Filmwirtschaft e.V. (SPIO). The first classification of a film took place on 18 July 1949. The BPjS was created on 14 May 1954 on the basis of §8 of the GjSM. It was originally under the administrative control of the Ministry of Internal Affairs, but is now under the Ministry for Youth, Family, Women and Health.

[8] Its specific character is reflected by the wording of the certificate of release: 'this film is released by the Supreme Youth Authorities in the Federal States according to §6 JÖSchG of 25.02.1985 to be shown publicly to children and young people from the age of ... years'.

tled to reach different decisions and to impose them if they do not agree with a decision made by the FSK. However, this has never happened in practice. The ratings of the FSK are also indirectly valid for the broadcasting of films on television, even if the FSK is only officially authorised for video and cinema.

The working committee is composed of 7 people (the permanent representative of the Ministry, an expert on the protection of minors, 2 representatives of the public authorities, 3 representatives of the film and video industry not currently active in the film and video industry). A simple majority is required for decisions.

There are two ways of dealing with appeals against decisions made by the FSK. Firstly, the High Committee (*Hauptausschuß*) is responsible for petitioners who are not satisfied with the result of the examination committee. It is also authorised to adjudicate in the event of there being a minority of the working committee that was outvoted. It is composed in the same way as the working committee with an additional representative each from the public authorities and the film industry. Secondly, the Supreme Youth Authorities in the Federal States and the SPIO are also entitled to appeal against a FSK decision. In this case, a specific appeal committee (*Appellationsausschuß*) is formed and made up of 1 lawyer (president), 2 experts in the field of protection of minors, and 4 examiners nominated by the Supreme Youth Authorities in the Federal States.

Legal provisions are the basis for decisions taken by the FSK. Moreover, the FSK has developed examination criteria to guide their interpretation. Following the examination, a rating certificate is granted. It has to be presented at the cinema counter if requested by the authorities responsible for security. The FSK also organises film screenings for young people to discuss the ratings with the age group concerned. An exchange of experiences also exists with similar organisations examining films in the Netherlands and Austria.

Around 400 cinema films are rated every year and about 600 to 700 video films per year. The FSK also supervises the conformity of advertisements (especially those concerning tobacco and alcohol) to the relevant legal provisions. If the examination committee comes to the conclusion that they are targeted towards minors younger than 16, the advertisements are prohibited for this age group.

The criteria used by the BPjS for the evaluation of cinema films are the legal provisions of the *Gesetz über die Verbreitung jugendgefährdender Schriften und Medieninhalte* (GjSM), the law on the dissemination of publications and other media morally harmful to youth. Further to these provisions, publications that are likely to morally endanger children and young people have to be inserted in an 'index'. This includes representation of violence, glorification of the Nazi ideology, incitement to racial hatred, glorification of war, sexual deviation, and pornography.

The list of §1 is not exhaustive, media that glorify or play down the consumption of drugs are also considered as harmful to minors. §1(2) contains exceptions to the 'index' system. The principle is that media may not be put on the 'index' on the grounds of their political, social, religious, and ideological content. However, they may be put on the 'index' when the danger for minors is not based on the abovementioned reasons, and media including content which is contrary to the Constitution may not take advantage of this principle.

The system is based on the legal criteria described earlier, but the criteria are also interpreted on the basis of case law, which defines certain legal concepts. Since this interpretation necessarily includes an element of subjectivity the system may be described as semideterministic.

This is neither a voluntary nor a mandatory system. The content producer is not required to have the films examined by the BPjS. The BPjS can only review a film on the basis of a request coming from one of the following institutions: (a) *Jugendämter* (youth welfare departments), (b) *Landesjugendamt* (youth welfare departments of the Federal States), (c) *Oberste Landesjugendbehörden* (Supreme Youth Authorities of the Federal States), and (d) The Ministry for Family, Elderly People, Women, and Youth. All together there are around 900 authorities entitled to submit a request for examination. Private citizens can only address themselves to these places. Once the BPjS has received a request, it is obliged to examine the publication in question.

The BPjS is a Federal authority with quasi-judicial functions under the administrative control of the Federal Ministry for Women and Youth. It is composed of full time members: the president, vice president, 2 lawyers, and five assistants, and honorary members: 50 members representing different groups of German society and 40 members representing the Federal States. However, further to §10 GjSM, its members do not comply with instructions as regards the examination procedure of the films.

The competence of the BPjS is limited to films which have not previously been rated by the FSK, for example, films which were either not presented to the FSK or which were refused a rating. The BPjS is also responsible for publications and other media. The decision to put a film on the 'index' is published in the *Official Journal*; otherwise, the decision is not valid.

The classification in the 'index' is not strictly speaking censorship, as these publications remain available to adults. The legal nature of this classification is an administrative act, further to 35 VwVfG (Verwaltungsverfahrensordnung). Consequently, it can be challenged before the administrative courts. Further to §§3–5 GjSM, the classification of a film on the 'index' creates limitations regarding its delivery, presentation, circulation, or advertising. More precisely, the film's appearance on the 'index' means it is prohibited to show or disseminate the films to children and youth.

Parents may not be held responsible under criminal law if they show indexed material to their children because of their constitutional prerogatives as parents. However, if parents infringe their custody rights, the Youth Authority may, according to §1666 of the Civil Code, request appropriate action from the court dealing with matters relating to guardianship. Criminal prosecution is a matter for the police or the state prosecutor.

To assess the work, examiners sit in a committee of 12 people (or 3 in the case of an obvious risk to young people). The committee members are people with specialised knowledge and representatives of different sectors of German society. The examination is not open to the public. This system is State-specific and is not designed to provide classification at the European level.

Greece

The rating system in Greece is the responsibility of the Cinematography Commission, which consists of officials from the Ministry of Culture. It is mandatory in the sense that the producer is required to have all films rated by an agency.

Broad legal provisions relating to content apply in the absence of specific provisions for cinema regulation. According to Article 29 of Law 5060/31 of 1931 (this law has been neither amended or repealed) on obscene and indecent material, it is a criminal offence to 'sell, distribute, exhibit, fabricate, transport, export, import, and generally circulate documents, publications, Articles, sketches, pictures, drawings, seals, photographs, motion pictures, or any other forms of objects considered to be indecent or obscene'.

Indecent or obscene material is defined by Article 30 of Law 5060/31 as that which 'according to general public sense, is offensive to public shame'. The same provision states that 'works of art are not indecent or obscene unless specifically offered for sale, hire, or distribution to people under 18 years of age'.

Though Article 86 of the Greek Penal Code restricts the import for commercial use of indecent or obscene works of art, court rulings in 1983 under these regulations held that pornographic films, although unsuitable for most public cinemas, catered to specific tastes. Thus, if shown in specialist adult cinemas where minors (that is, under-18s) were prohibited, they did not constitute violation of statutes. Such cinemas are now widespread in most Greek cities, with notices at entrance points barring under-18s.

Despite the regulations, in the last decade very few films have been confiscated after screening for violating public decency (particularly pornographic films). There have been a few incidents in which authorities closed down adult cinemas for admitting under-18s.

The procedure for classifying films is nondeterministic. Ministry officials classify film and script submissions on a simple pass or fail basis. However, the ratings issued are descriptive. It should also be noted that Articles 2 & 36 of Law 1597/86 set up a 'Youth Board' with the aim of classifying films according to the following classification system: (a) suitable for youths under 17 years of age; (b) limited suitability; (c) unsuitable; and (d) extremely unsuitable. However, that classification system never came into effect and the 'Youth Board' was never appointed due to ministerial non-decision-making.

Since in 1993/94 local authorities took over former police functions in licensing cinemas, it is reasonable to assume that the classification system will be placed in their hands in due course. Given that no significant incident has occurred during the last decade, expectations of the introduction of a more sophisticated classification system are limited.

Ireland

The body responsible for the classification of films in Ireland is the Official Censor of films established by 1923 Act. The rating procedure applied by the Censor is nondeterministic, depending on the view of the individual censor. The system requires all films for public viewing to be submitted in advance to the Censor with a view to obtaining a certificate. The Censor can grant such a certificate in full, or with conditions attached, or can refuse to grant one. Where conditions are imposed, they might relate to the class of viewer or place of viewing. A certificate can be refused altogether if the film or part of it is indecent, obscene or blasphemous, or tends to inculcate principles contrary to public morality or is otherwise subversive of public morality.

There is no definition of indecent, obscene, or blasphemous in the Act. However, the Censorship of Publications Act 1929 states that 'indecent': 'shall be construed as including suggestive of or inciting to sexual immorality or unnatural vice or likely in any other similar way to corrupt or deprave'. Where part of a film falls into any of these categories, the Censor must indicate which part to the applicant, who may then remove the offending part or appeal to the Appeal Board. Once a certificate has been granted no other pressure group may prevent its being screened publicly'.

The Appeal Board consists of nine people and operates with a quorum of 4. It has power to affirm, reverse, or vary the Censor's decision, and since 1965 has been reconstituted to allow it to grant limited certificates itself in the case of films that have already been rejected. The certificate ensures that a film may be shown, but an age classification system, outlined in Table 1, introduced in 1965 and later amended, also applies. The rating system applies to all films, advertisements, and trailers for films, and, by amendment Act of 1925, advertisements.

TABLE 1
Age Classification for Films in Ireland

Gen	PG	12	15	18
Fit for viewing by persons generally.	Fit for viewing by persons generally, but in the case of a child under the age of 12 years, only under parental guidance.	Fit for viewing by persons aged 12 years or more.	Fit for viewing by persons aged 15 years or more.	Fit for viewing by persons aged 18 years or more.

There is no uniform identity card system in operation in Ireland but children and young people seeking admission to cinemas are often challenged as to their age by cinema staff.

Producers are obliged to submit films for certification and to pay a fee to have the film categorised. The whole system was designed to be self-financing, by imposing fees on applicants for a certificate. The advantage is that the scheme is not a drain on the Exchequer. However, as the fees have increased over time to meet increasing costs and staff wages, the price of obtaining a certificate (approximately £700 for an average length film by 1988) has posed a problem for smaller films. Trying to recoup the outlay, as well as meeting advertising and promotion costs, can be difficult for small or alternative films showing at fringe venues. Various alternatives have been mooted, including linking fees to gross revenue, but since measures of that nature would involve the large American mainstream films essentially subsidising the rest, they have not been uniformly welcomed.

Fees are recoverable in the event of a successful appeal or if a ban is revoked. According to the Censorship of Films (Amendment) Act 1970, where a certificate is refused and an appeal is either not sought or unsuccessful, the situation may be reviewed after a period of 7 years.

Due to the financing system there is sufficient capacity to deal with any volume of material, subject to the fees not becoming prohibitive for all but the large American outlets.

There is no indication of any change being contemplated specifically with regard to control of content. The biggest development in this regard has been the inclusion of the Censor's office within the Freedom of Information Act 1997, which will allow more transparency into the whole process. However, the Government has recently established a Film Industry Strategic Review Group, whose terms of reference appear to be broad enough to cover control of content. The terms of reference include: (a) carrying out an objective evaluation of the effectiveness of the existing schemes and to make recommendations in regard to future measures and incentives to develop the industry; (b) analysing and identifying the fundamental issues facing the industry and making recommendations in regard to future measures in support of the film and television industry; and (c) formulating a strategic plan for the future of the sector in the next decade. The Group has invited submissions from interested parties (notice published in the national press on 27 October 1998).

As to the sanctions, under the 1923 Act it is an offence, punishable on summary conviction by fines, including daily fines (per diem) for continuing offences, to show an uncertified film in public or to permit one to be shown in breach of the terms of a limited certificate.

Italy

The Italian cinema rating system is evaluative and mandatory. Relevant guidelines concerning the rating system nature and process are set out in Article 21.6 of the Constitution, Articles 528 and 529 of the Criminal Code, Law 161/1962, and Presidential Decree D.P.R. 2029/1963.

Film screenings in Italy are subject to the release of a certificate, which has to assess the suitability of the work's content according to fixed guidelines. Article 1.2 of Law 161/1962 sets out that a special censorship committee operating within the Prime Minister's office grants the certificate after prior examination of the film.[9] Before releasing the certificate the committee has to evaluate, among other things, whether the film is suitable for minors given their particular sensitivity. In addition, Article 667.2 of the Criminal Code sets forth that, in order to (a) produce; (b) introduce into the territory of the State; (c) export; or (d) trade films prior notice to the Police Authority is necessary. The offender is liable with a fine up to ITL 1 Million or imprisonment for up to 1 month whether or not the violation is perpetrated against the Public Authority's order.

Therefore, in Italy (a) no films may be produced or distributed without prior notice to the Police Authority; (b) no films may be screened without the prior release of a certificate by the censorship committee; (c) cinema managers are held liable whenever minors attend the screening of a film certified as unsuitable for them; and (d) cinema managers are held liable whenever, given the age-limit certificate, they do not verify the age of the audience they admit.

---

[9] Article 668 of Criminal Code ('Non-authorised performances of films') establishes that anyone who screens films, which have not been submitted to prior censorship, in a public space, is held liable with a fine of up to ITL 600,000 or imprisonment for up to six months. Article 15 of Law 161/1962 reads that infringements of Article 5 (concerning films that have been granted a limited-age certificate or a certificate of non-suitability for minors) are punishable by a fine of up to ITL 50 Million. The same penalty is provided for screenings of films not submitted to prior censorship or denied a certificate, or screened in a different version than the one censored (Article 15.3).

The Italian cinema rating process is somewhat semideterministic. It is based on an (allegedly) objective methodology (that is, examination of the submitted work in compliance with the contents guidelines provided by the Law).[10] The broad definition of the committee's criteria (such as, for example, the public morality principle) allows its interpretation to vary according to social changes and sensitivity, with the result that the rating process is ultimately based on the committee's opinion. When a film's content is assessed obscene or against public morality a certificate is denied and the film may not be released.

Article 9 of Presidential Decree No. 2029 of 11 November 1963 (D.P.R. 2029/1963) adds further criteria for censorship with the purpose of protecting minors' sensitivity and development. It sets out that films, even where they do not offend public morality, are to be denied a certificate of suitability for minors when they: (a) contain vulgar content; (b) encourage immoral behaviour; (c) depict erotic or violent scenes against human beings or animals; (d) refer to hypnotic phenomena or disturbing surgical operations or to the use of drugs; (e) promote hatred and revenge; and (f) induce to imitation of crimes or suicide. The committee's assessment of the degree of seriousness of such elements will determine the suitability of the film for minors over the age of 14 or over the age of 18. The Administrative Court of Appeal has ruled that, in compliance with Article 9 of D.P.R. 2029/1963, the seriousness of vulgar or violent scenes — which determines denial of a certificate for minors — may be adequately assessed *only* if referred to the specific context in which those scenes are depicted (Consiglio di Stato sez. IV, judgement of 30 September 1988).

The censorship committee is a Special Committee operating in the Department of Entertainment of the Prime Minister's Office, which, according to Law 161/1962, Law 203/1995, and Legislative Decree 8/1998, is authorised to assess films. This committee in turn is composed of 8 sections; the composition and functions of which have been recently re-drafted in Legislative Decree No. 8 of January 8, 1998 and Law No. 203 of 30 May 1995. Accordingly, each section of the censorship committee must be composed of 8 members, among which 2 must be representatives of parents' associations. The remaining members are experts from other domains (such as the law, psychology, or pedagogy), 2 representatives of the cinema industry and 2 experts on cinema (such as journalists or authors). A University of Law Professor chairs censorship committees. According to Article 4 of Law 161/1962, certificates are granted by each section on approval by the majority of their members.

---

[10] (i) Article 21.6 of the Constitution, which prohibits all publications, performances and other expressions against public morality; (ii) Article 528 of Criminal Code, which declares liable those who show obscene films; and (iii) Article 6 of Law 161/1962, which provides for the denial of a certificate whenever the film represents, as a whole or in singular scenes, an offence to public morality and, (iv) case law interpreting all such provisions.

The previous composition and functions of the censorship committee raised various complaints among the public and, in particular, among parents' and viewers' associations. Membership of parents' representatives was only recently provided for by Law 203/1995, with the purpose of balancing different interests at stake. The fact that representatives of cinema interests (such as producers, distributors, and cinema managers) were included in the membership, while representatives of children's interests were not, was deemed to be the major reason for the release of an excessive number of certificates that did not comply with contents regulation and were thus injurious to the community's general interests. Moreover, before Law 203/1995 each section could issue a certificate on its approval by a simple majority of the members *present*.

It is worth mentioning, in light of this rule, that many critics argued that only the representatives of cinema interests were in the habit of attending all examinations, whereas members appointed to safeguard general interests, such as judges or Professors at University of Law, were too often absent. Therefore, certificates were granted following a brief evaluation carried out mainly by cinema representatives; and, consequently, very few films were denied a certificate. Notwithstanding Law 203/1995, the censorship committee is to date still operating under its previous composition established by Law 161/1962. New sections have not yet been appointed for a number of bureaucratic reasons.

The Associazione Genitori (A.G.E) is one of the most representative Italian parents associations, and will probably have one or 2 representatives among the members of the new censorship committees. According to this association, the bureaucratic slow pace is due to the interests of cinema's powerful lobbies, which prevail over those of the community. The main difference from the past will be the membership of parents' representatives and the new majority required to vote on a certificate. This will likely lead to a different interpretation of content regulation and a more accurate and strict valuation of submitted works, which will not be able to obtain a certificate as easily as before. The possible censorship committee outcomes are: (1) 'Suitable for all', (2) 'Unsuitable for all', and (3) 'Age limited', which is divided into: 'over the age of 14' and 'over the age of 18'.

According to Article 6 of Law 161/1962, in the event that the committee does not provide a decision within the prescribed time frame, the certificate is issued automatically under the rule of 'silent-consent', established in order to avoid bureaucratic inactivity, which could damage applicants. 'Applicants' is a term that encompasses producers, distributors, and importers. When the work is assessed as 'unsuitable for all' the applicant may appeal to the second-degree committee, which is formed by 2 sections of the first-degree committee different from the one that made the first evaluation.

However, according to Law 161/1962, applicants can appeal against the decision issued by the first-degree committee only when a certificate has been denied or has been assessed 'unsuitable for minors'. The second-degree committee may issue a new evaluation of the film, possibly subject to modifications in some scenes, sequences, or lines, balancing public interest with the producer/distributor's economic concerns.

In this case too, in the event that the second degree committee does not provide a decision within the prescribed time frame, a certificate is issued automatically under the rule of 'silent-consent'. Should the appeal be rejected by the second degree committee, the applicant has the right to take legal proceedings against the committee's decision before the Administrative Courts (that is, Administrative Tribunal and Administrative Court of Appeals), the decision of which prevails over the challenged decision (Article 8).

Whenever a film has been granted a certificate of 'unsuitable for minors' by the first-degree committee, provided that they have re-edited and modified the work, the applicants are allowed to request a second examination in order to achieve a broader certificate and thus access a broader audience. It is also possible to take legal proceedings against the second-degree decision before the Administrative courts.

The Administrative Court of Appeal, in fact, has ruled that the right provided by the Law for works which do not obtain a certificate may be extended to those that are given a restricted (age limited) certificate (*Consiglio di Stato*, judgement 734/1977). Some commentators have argued against this interpretation of the law. In fact, Article 11 of DPR 2029/1963 (integrating Law 161/1962) reads that 'works which do not achieve a certificate may be re-submitted for a new examination, provided that they have been re-edited and modified in some scenes, when modifications clearly guarantee that the work represents a different and new edition'.

As a result of the Administrative Court of Appeal's interpretation, interested parties have developed and perfected the practice of creating new versions of their work in order to obtain less restrictive certificates. Therefore, it is now possible to find many different versions of the same film on the market: one suitable only for people over 18, one suitable for people over 14, and another suitable for all. The availability of different versions is important in light of the requirement that only works that are suitable for all, or granted an age-limited certificate may be broadcast on television. However, while this practice ensures the work's exploitation in all media, it makes it more difficult to monitor each version in use. In addition, any version of the film (even versions which have been denied a certificate) is protected by copyright (Law No. 633, 22 April 1941) given that the law does not limit the author's protection to works, which comply with public morality and public order principles.

As to the current capacity of the censorship sections to examine the work submitted, the decision concerning the number of films to be examined during each section meeting is discretionary, and the responsibility of the Officers within the Department of Entertainment of the Prime Minister's Office.

There are currently various proposals for change. One the most important ones is found in the governmental Bill 3180 of March 1998. The Bill states that the present censorship regulation is no longer adequate in the current social context, nor does it comply with the principle of freedom of expression. The Bill, therefore, is meant to avoid freedom of expression being subject to limitations such as those constituted by certificates denying public performances of films.

Moreover, it deems that the constitutional 'public morality' principle can be appropriately guaranteed and pursued by the provisions concerning suitability of films for minors, and by the existing provisions of Articles 528 (obscene performances) and 668 (unauthorised performances) of the Criminal Code. The Bill, therefore, through modifications of Law 161/1962 provides that: (a) certificates may no longer prevent films from being screened and (b) certificates may only refer to the suitability of a film for minors.

The second important proposal for change was drafted by the *Associazione Nazionale Industrie Cinematografiche Audiovisive e Multimediali* (ANICA). ANICA, is the Italian association of cinema industries, which represents most of the producers and distributors operating in the Italian market. The proposal aims at replacing Law 161/1962 and its 'limited-age' provisions, which are deemed, according to the President of ANICA, to be the main problem of censorship in Italy.

It is inspired by the existing US rating system and is based on an understanding that cinema should be treated differently from television. While the audience makes a discretionary choice when visiting a cinema, it has no control over what programmes are broadcast on television. Its only method of control is to turn on or off the television or switch channels. Given this discretionary choice, preventive control of a cinema film's content is not necessary.

The proposal sets out a new voluntary rating system where the producer is also a self-rating content provider. It has been argued that this self-regulatory scheme, to be implemented by cinema associations, would most likely lead to a greater sense of responsibility on the producer's part. In fact, producers have already promised to make efforts to safeguard the sensitivity of minors by cooperating with all parties dealing with children. It is worth noting that A.G.E representatives object to this proposal on the grounds that it is exclusively aimed at increasing the earnings of the cinema industry and discarding all existing content regulations.

As to age limits, the proposal seeks to modify the existing thresholds (14–18 years of age) which are deemed to be too strict and not appropriate in a more diverse and varied social context, in which parental guidance concerning a film's contents should be preferred and implemented. Accordingly, prohibitions for minors should be articulated in the following way: (a) '*P.G*'.: suitable for children with parental guidance; (b) '*P.G. 13*': suitable for children over 13 with parental guidance; (c) '*R*' prohibited to minors under 17; and (d) '*NC*': prohibited to minors under 18.

Luxembourg

According to the Grand-Ducal Order of 14 November 1925 modifying the Order of 16 June 1922 mandating the establishment of the law of 13 June 1922 concerning monitoring of cinema establishments and public screenings, the *Commission de surveillance* is the public body in charge of film classification in Luxembourg. It consists of 2 sections, and is composed of a President, 4 permanent members, and 2 substitute members (in practice film critics, representatives of cinema theatres and civil society, and one lawyer). A vote is valid if only 2 of the members are present.

The Ministerial Ruling of 28 November 1977 concerning: (a) the submission of a request to proceed with a cinema screening accessible to minors under 17; (b) the publication and dissemination of the decisions of the Commission de surveillance; and (c) the recommendation of films with cultural and education value to young people, which was issued by the Ministry of Education and Cultural Affairs, provides guidelines on the procedure to follow for a certificate to be granted. According to Article 3 of the ruling, the release of a film authorised to those under 17 is subject to a prior demand that must be made one month before the date of its first release at the latest.

The government may pronounce the prohibition of the 'screening of any movie that engenders a scandal or is likely to jeopardise tranquility and Public Order'. It is, however, the responsibility of the judicial authorities to pronounce penal sanctions. The exception to this rule which is especially of note may be found in Article 4 of the ruling where the Commission may 'recommend to youth audiences some films with cultural or educational value'. As to the classification itself, two categories exist: (1) movies prohibited to minors under 14 and (2) movies prohibited to minors under 17.

The Netherlands

In the Netherlands, the *Wet op Filmvertoningen* (WOF), the Act on Film Exhibition, provides the legal framework for the Dutch film industry. The Act, which dates from 5 January 1977, was set up principally to abolish classification for adults and integrate a new rating system for youth.

The rating body is the *Nederlandse Filmkeuring* (NFK), the independent Dutch Board of Film Classification. According to Article 2, paragraph 5 of the Act, the rating is chosen by a majority of votes of at least 3 members but Article 15 paragraph 3 states that 5 members are preferable (Buwalda 1997: 79). In selecting the Board (out of at least 20 and up to 40 members of the NFK) an attempt is made to include a diversity of ideologies, expertise, age, sex and region *(Notitie* 1997: 11). The Minister of Public Health, Welfare, and Sports appoints the members of the NFK. Age categories are 'all', '12 and over', and '16 and over'.

Films are classified according to the Board's evaluation of their potential to damage persons under 12 or under 16. The Act on Film Exhibition states that children under 12 or 16 will only be admitted to public showings of films that have been rated in their respective categories. However, rating is voluntary; film distributors may decide for themselves whether or not to submit a film for rating, but films which are not submitted are automatically rated as '16 and over', and may therefore only be shown in public to persons over 16 years of age. The Act allows for films to be given a rating of '12 and over' and 'all ages' on the condition that appropriate cuts are made, but this has not so far happened, since NFK policy states that 'cuts will be avoided as much as possible'.

The Act on Film Exhibition also states that films that are shown in cinemas open to everyone must have an age certification. The ratings decisions of the Board are binding instruments. Article 1; paragraph 3 states that the cinema entrance must clearly display the age limit. And according to Article 6, cinema managers or film distributors who do not comply with a given decision of the Board, are committing an offence, and may consequently be punished with imprisonment of up to 2 months or a fine.

If at least 2 members of the Board object to the rating result, a request for reclassification can be made. The person submitting the film can also make this request for a second rating. The members involved in the first rating process may not participate the second time round (Buwalda 1997: 79–80).

In 1997, about half the films released were submitted for rating (Nederlandse Filmkeuring 1997). Economic reasons are probably an important factor in choosing not to submit a film: film distributors must pay 35 guilders for every 5 minutes for the rating process, and a rating of '16 and over' often attracts more adults (and even minors) to the film than a lower rating would. There are therefore films that, though officially inadmissible to minors, could have been open to them, if they had been submitted for classification. The Board believes that another reason for not submitting a film is that film distributors object to having their films rated and prefer a self-regulatory classification system.

The rating of the NFK is somewhat controversial for the liberal Netherlands. It is widely believed that children or their parents should decide for themselves what films they do or do not want to see. The *Raad voor het Jeugdbeleid* (Council for Youth Policy) has suggested substituting classification with the provision of greater information about the product (whether film, television, or video) (1996). At the moment the appropriateness of the age classification system, which is used by all media sectors, is questioned, particularly the rating 'all ages'.

The independent Dutch Institute of Psychologists suggested extending the ratings to include a category for '6 (or 7) years of age'; a classification already used by most other European countries. The Dutch Video industry is experimenting with using the 'Parental Guidance (PG)' classification (Notitie 1997: 15), used by several Anglo-Saxon countries, in combination with the 'all ages' classification(*Raad van Toezicht Videovoorlichting*, 1997: 5).

The Board of Film Classification believe that consumers should be better informed and are also considering introducing this classification, as well as the label 'child friendly/family film', to accompany the 'all ages' category (*Nederlandse Filmkeuring* 1997).

The age classification is issued following a semideterministic methodology. For rating, the Board uses its guidelines and classification forms with the following criteria: frightening scenes, brutalising violence, drugs, pornography, and an open criterion, which may be used by the rating provider in a film specific context. The use of open criterion is sometimes used for discriminating between aspects of a film or for the showing of excessive pornography. Guidelines are as follows: (a) the individual scenes should be judged in the context of the whole film but trailers, promo's, and commercials are judged on their own merits, without reference to the feature film; (b) the Board shall not enforce its right to make cuts to films; and (c) the Board aims to make as many films as possible available to young people, insofar as they are not likely to result in mental 'damage'.

Furthermore, the Board uses a score form, outlined in Table 2, with criteria for damaging material (*Commissariaat voor de Media* 1997). The score card has scores of 1 through 3. The NFK expects the rating system to expand, due to discussions of media violence becoming common in society. As a result of these discussions, the NFK has for a few years been asked to rate films for television, which is not part of its remit.

Portugal

In Portugal, there are 2 bodies rating cinema: the *Secretariado do Cinema e do Audiovisual* (SCA), a non-commercial Catholic body, and the *Comissão de Classificação de Espectáculos* (CCE), a government body.

TABLE 2
NFK Score Form

Score	Description
Score 1: General	• Intimidation
	• The risk of excessive identification
	• Insufficient understanding of the theme
Score 2: Fear	• Tension without means of escape
	• Shocking effects
	• Bad ending/open ending
Score 2: Violence	• Horrible
	• Malicious
	• Sadistic
Score 3: Film contains elements of:	• Sadism
	• Fascism
	• Racism
	• Sexism
	• Discrimination
	• Other forms of humiliation
	• Violence
	• Political extremism
	• Alcohol or drug abuse

The *Secretariado do Cinema e do Audiovisual* (SCA) analyses film content, and publishes its analysis and ratings in the *Boletim Cinematográfico*. It has been operating for 40 years. The system is voluntary, developed by an independent Catholic entity, and viewers do not have to take its ratings into consideration. It uses a nondeterministic method of rating, based on the moral judgement of the rating body, and the ratings issued are a mixture of descriptive ratings and evaluative ratings.

On the one hand, a judgement is made about the film. This subjective judgement is expressed in terms of age category; that is, the SCA decides the age groups for which the film is suitable to be shown. Moreover, the SCA also attempts to describe the film content and provides an abstract of the film plus a moral and aesthetic comment.

Occasionally, it characterises actors and performances with a description of the actor or performance's suitability and a summary of their qualities. The rating system includes 4 categories: 'for all', 'for adolescents and adults', 'for adults', and 'for adults with reservations'. Descriptions of these categories are laid out in Table 3.

TABLE 3
SCA Rating System

'For All'	'For Adolescents and Adults'	'For Adults'	'For Adults with Reservations'
Films that are entertaining and easy to understand.	Films that present a complexity that makes them hard to be understood by children, that may hurt their sensibility or distort their vision of the world.	Films that, due to their structure or content, may not be totally understood or adequately analysed by adolescents, films that contain problems which are not proper for individuals without full maturity and experience of life.	Films that present gravely distorted situations, being its level of violence and/or degrading exploitation of matters which may hurt the viewers sensibility.

In the mid-1980's, two categories were added: 'for adults with serious reservations'—considered 'harmful to the large majority of the viewers'—and 'condemnable'—films that, 'by their content, constitute a serious moral attack or defend blameworthy theories that pose severe danger to the audience'. According to those responsible for the SCA, the 'condemnable' rating may still be used in the case of pornography and in other 'really exceptional' cases.

The SCA analysis and ratings are published in the *Boletim Cinematográfico*, and frequently in local newspapers with close links to the Catholic Church. The SCA classifications are also provided to distribution and exhibition houses. Research confirms that occasionally managers of cinemas believe that the SCA classification originates from the government, not from a Catholic association.

Moreover, as described by the Head of SCA, Eng. Jorge Perestrello, the national private television channel, set up by Catholic associations, *Televisisão Independente* (TVI), broadcasts the ratings given by the *SCA*. Though the rating system has a reduced impact at national level, as the SCA views are usually conveyed by the regional/local press (mainly controlled by the Catholic Church), it may influence readers in terms of the films they should or should not see.

The CCE is an agency of the *Ministério da Cultura* (Ministry of Culture). It is regulated by the Law-decree 106-B/92 of the 1st of June. This piece of legislation gives the Commission deliberative power in terms of age and quality rating of films. In addition to the classification of films, it may issue opinions about proposed legislation in this field.

The Commission has up to 45 members, including representatives of ministries with responsibilities in the film arena, representatives of civilian associations and representatives of film industry interest groups (the latter may only express their views in the Commission plenary meetings). The CCE is organised in sections: (a) age rating; (b) quality rating; and (c) pornographic and nonpornographic rating. There is also an appeals sub-commission that examines and rules on submitted appeals and may alter or uphold the previously applied rating.

The system is mandatory because no film may be exhibited to the general public without being classified. Indeed, it is the responsibility of the *Inspecção-General das Actividades Culturais* (Inspector General of Cultural Activity), the autonomous administrative service with general responsibilities in the area of media regulation, to make sure that all films exhibited are properly rated and to monitor the observance of the ratings. The rating system is legally defined and therefore it has force of law throughout the national territory. In accordance with the 'spirit of freedom' of the post-1974 revolution era, the rating system is primarily of an informative nature.

The audience and educators are made aware of what is appropriate for different age groups and are also informed whether a film is 'pornographic' or not. They may also be given information about a film's 'quality'. The adopted classifications are provided in information about the films. Nevertheless, the implementation of the legislative construct depends mostly on the role educators perform. Until the 1970's, the view was punitive and authoritarian. Thus, for example, Article 15 of the Law-decree 41051 of 1 April 1957 stated: 'Parents, educators or indeed anyone who allows or facilitates the access of minors to films contra to what is written in this Law-decree will pay a fine of 100 to 1000 Portuguese escudos, and if the action is repeated, they may be imprisoned for up to three months.

According to information concerning the rating/labelling process provided by the President of the CCE, Eng. António Xavier, every 3 months, there is a Commission plenary meeting. It is the plenary which approves the rating criteria to be observed; though the Ministry of Culture is able to change them if it does not agree. The rating procedure is nondeterministic because the rating is not the result of an 'objective' methodology, but rather the expression of the panel's views and sensibility.

When a film is presented to the Commission in order to be classified, the president selects a panel, usually constituted by five *vogais* (elements of the jury). The panel watches the film and, taking into account the written criteria mentioned later, each of its members provides his/her opinion. The panel discussion is meant to reach a consensus. If a consensus is not possible, there is a simple majority vote. However, panel members who voted against the winning classification may appeal to the 'Appeal sub-commission'. Appeals are however extremely rare, and generally panels decide by consensus. Appeals from civilian groups and the film industry are even more scarcer.

Though the panel considers specific aspects of film content, the ratings issued are evaluative since the decision is taken according to the panel's opinion of the appropriate age groups to see the film. The current age rating was established by Article 2, No. 1 of the Law-decree 196/82 of 21 September 1982 and later regulated in *Portaria* 245/83 of 3 March 1983. There are five categories in the system, described in Table 4.

The 'pornographic' label is applied to a film which persistently and superficially explores 'sexual situations and acts with the main purpose of arousing the spectator' and has a 'low aesthetic quality'. However, in 'Soft-core' films there is no graphic exhibition of genitalia and sexual acts are simulated. 'Hard-core' movies include graphic presentation of genitalia and sexual acts are not performed or acted, but real. Finally, films might also receive a 'quality' stamp for being distinguished by their artistic, thematic, pedagogic, and technical aspects.

The Commission is supposed to classify all types of videograms (analogue and digital), thus including cinema, videos, video, and computer games. Nevertheless, video and computer games are not rated, although there is some concern about this. No rating system is applied to advertising.

TABLE 4
CCE Rating System

Rating	Description
For over 4's	Short and easy to understand; for this age group, films should not provoke fear and should not conflict children's fantasies.
For over 6's	Films that, due to their theme and/or length, are not adequate for lower age groups.
For over 12's	Films that, due to their length or complexity, may cause excessive fatigue and/or psychological trauma to the previous age groups.
For over 16's	Films that excessively explore sexuality and physical and/or psychological violence.
For over 18's	Pornographic movies and/or films which explore pathological forms of physical and psychological violence.

Note. In the Law-decree 41051 of 1 April 1957, films 'for adults' (over 17 year olds) were those which, although respecting the minimal conditions required to get authorisation from the CCE, might be harmful to the spiritual education and the moral and intellectual development of young people. Moreover, films for adults are those with the potential dangerously to excite youth sensibility and imagination, and those that might suggest fundamentally wrong notions about life and historical facts (article 8).

The maximum volume of programming this system can accommodate depends on the potential enlargement of the Classification Commission, which is a political decision that may be taken only by the Ministry of Culture

Spain

The rating body in Spain responsible for film is the *Instituto de Cinematografía y Artes Audiovisuales* (ICAA), an autonomous body deriving its authority from the Ministry for Education and Culture. Though the Autonomous Communities, the regional political entities, have the right to assume responsibility for films produced in their own region, only Catalonia has done so as evidenced by the Catalan Decree 495/1983, of 3 November 1983, on the rating of films and audiovisual works. A company with headquarters in Catalonia, which owns the distribution rights in a film, may choose whether to have the film rated by the Catalan Department for Cultural Affairs or by the ICAA, with the exception of films that may be classified as 'X' films, which can only be rated by the ICAA. If a film is rated in Catalonia, the rating provided will be valid throughout Spain. In practice, the Director General of the ICAA rates nearly all films.

According to Article 16.2 of Decree 81/1997, films are rated by the Director General of the ICAA, after obtaining the opinion of the *Comisión de Calificación de Películas Cinematográficas* (CCPC), which also belongs to the ICAA. The CCPC has been performing its functions since the abrogated Decree 1067/1983, of 27 April 1983. Its creation completed the transition from the severe censorship that existed until General Franco's death in 1975 to the current total freedom, with the Commission now playing an advisory role only.

According to Article 6 of Decree 7/1997, of 10 January 1997, on the structure and functions of the ICAA (Decree 7/1997), the Director General of the ICCA is proposed by the Minister for Education and Culture and appointed by the Council of Ministers. The CCPC, which assists the Director General, consists of 9–12 members: the Director General of the ICAA himself; the head of the Ministerial Department for Promotion of the Film Industry; and 7–10 members who are appointed for a 2-year period by the Minister for Education and Culture from nominations made by the Director General. Article 17 of Decree 81/1997 states that these members are chosen from people related to the film and audiovisual industry that are fit to carry out this duty.

The system is mandatory for content producers, who are required to submit their works to the ICAA before distributing, showing, or advertising them, and to clearly indicate the rating, according to Article 16.1 of Decree 81/1997, and Article 13 of the Ministerial Order 7 July 1997. The decision adopted by the rating authority is compulsory and the company that asked for the rating may not change the rating given by the Director General of the ICAA.

It is also mandatory for film distributors and exhibitors to show the film's rating in all advertisements for the film, at the box-office of the cinemas where it is being shown, and before the commencement of the film screening (Article 15 of Decree 81/1997, and, for films rated 'X', Article 6 of Law 1/1982 and Article 19.1 and paragraphs 3, 4, and 5 of Article 20 of Decree 81/1997). However, entrance to cinemas on the grounds of age may not be prevented, as the classification is a mere recommendation for parents.

According to Article 1 of Law 1/1982, the only exception to this is 'X' classified films, whose exhibition is restricted to cinemas with a special licence, to which the entrance of children under 18 is prohibited. Advertisements for pornographic films or films depicting gratuitous violence ('X' rated films) must not include any graphic representation, and must clearly state that the film may only be seen in cinemas with a special licence. The name of the film may not explicitly show its pornographic or violent nature. Article 6 of Law 1/1982 states that trailers and advertisements for these films can only be shown in the cinemas rated 'X' and in the cinema section of newspapers or other media.

Advertisements for films to be shown in cinemas must also be rated, following the same system used to rate films. This system is State-specific: the Spanish authorities must rate all films and audiovisual works distributed in Spain, and the rating provided by these authorities is only valid in Spain.

Though officially, according to Decree 81/97, the Director General of the ICAA is responsible for rating films, in practice the films are usually rated by the CCPC, which adopts its decisions by a majority of the votes cast, and the Director General makes this decision his own. The rating given is stated in a formal Resolution from the Director General.

If the film distributor does not agree with the rating given to a film, the film is usually viewed for a second time before the Director General of the ICAA adopts a final Resolution. This Resolution is an administrative act, which can be appealed before the jurisdiction for suits under administrative law. The system is nondeterministic, depending on the decision of the Director General, made after obtaining the opinion of the CCPC, which also follows a nondeterministic approach.

To prevent the marketing of a film being impeded in the event of there being too many films for the CCPC to rate at any time or the rating process taking too long, Decree 1/1997 establishes the principle that, if no rating has been provided within a month, it should be understood that the ICAA accepts the rating proposed by the applicant (Article 16.2 of Decree 81/1997).

The rating system is an evaluative system providing a single indicator according to a standard of harmfulness based on age groups (Articles. 15, 16, and 17 of Decree 81/1997). The ratings are: (1) 'Specially recommended for children', (2) 'for all', (3) 'Not recommended for persons under 13 years', (4) 'Not recommended for persons under 18 years', and (5) 'X' rated films (pornographic films and films that make a defence of violence) (Seventeenth Article of the Order of 7 July 1997).

In practice only pornographic films are given an 'X' rating, while films depicting gratuitous violence are rated as not recommended for children under 18 years. This rating system provides ratings for all existing films. In 1997, 456 films were rated, as well as 115 short films and 346 advertising spots of films to be shown in cinemas. 201 of the films rated came from the USA, and 76 from Spain. Since its creation in 1983, the CCPC has rated more than 5,000 films.

Given that the organisation of the CCPC could be changed to increase its rating capacity, by increasing the number of members or creating sub-commissions within the Commission, and given that ratings may be given implicitly if the Commission has not opposed the rating proposed by an applicant within one month, it is likely that the existing system would be able to accommodate all films and audiovisual works falling under the jurisdiction of the ICAA in the future; that is to say, all those which are shown in cinemas or distributed on video cassettes.

Infringement of the provisions relating to 'X' rated films (prohibition of screening these films other than in cinemas with a special licence; prohibition of access to these cinemas by persons under 18 years old), or breach of the provisions related to advertising of 'X' rated films are regarded as serious violations, and are punished with a fine of 500,000 to 5,000,000 pesetas, which is about 3,000 to 30,000 Euros (Article 9.2.c and Article 10.1.b of Law 17/1994). Infringement of the remaining rating provisions is regarded as a minor violation, and is punished with a fine of up to 50,000 pesetas, about 3,000 Euros (See Article 9.3.b and Article 10.1.a of Law 17/1994).

The Director General of the ICAA imposes the sanction for minor violations, and the Minister for Education and Culture sanctions serious violations, without prejudice to the sanctioning power of the authorities of the Autonomous Communities with responsibility in this field (Article 21.3 of Decree 81/1997 and Article 10.3 of Law 17/1994 and Article 21.3 of Decree 81/1997). According to Article 21.2 of Decree 81/1997, the proceedings to impose a sanction are to be conducted according to the Decree on Administrative Procedure for the Imposition of Sanctions of 4 August 1993. It is initiated by the Director General of the ICAA, who appoints a civil servant to investigate the facts of the case, without prejudice to the capacity of the Autonomous Communities with responsibility for rating films to determine their own administrative procedural rules and to decide who shall initiate and carry out the proceedings in their territories.

Sweden

The body responsible for rating cinema works in Sweden is the *Statens biograf-byrå* (National Board of Film Classification). The rules regarding classification are set out in the Examination and Control of Films and Videograms Act. The examination is mandatory, and all films must be approved and classified by the *Statens biografbyrå* prior to showing in a cinema. Section 1 of the Act states that 'the content of films or pre-recorded video recordings (videograms) shall be examined and approved by the National Board of Film Classification prior to showing at a public gathering or entertainment'.

Some exceptions are outlined in section 2 of the Act where films and videograms are broadcast by radio or cable, (provided that such broadcasts are retransmissions of satellite broadcasts or of broadcast transmissions or constitute autonomous broadcasts within the meaning of the Public Cable Transmissions Act 1991:2027 as amended by SFS 1991:2031 of January 1, 1992), consist of advertisements for goods or services, are shown at trade fairs, exhibitions or sporting events, unless the showing in itself constitutes a public gathering, or are shown at a museum in conjunction with the museum's normal exhibition activities and are of a documentary nature (as amended by SFS 1991:148 of July 1, 1991).

In addition, Section 3 states that 'the National Board of Film Classification may, for the purposes of a film festival or other artistic or non-profit making event, authorise the showing of films and videograms to persons over the age of 15 although they have not been examined and approved for showing. Such authorisation may be made subject to any conditions that the Board considers necessary.'

Statens biografbyrå is an authority under the domain of the Ministry of Culture. Its remit is based on law, ordinance, and instructions. It can decide to ban or cut a film, but the film can still be released in the video market. The Board does not take any action on religious or political grounds, nor does it act as an arbiter of taste, banning 'bad' and passing 'good' films. Its task is to judge whether films, or film sequences, are liable to have a brutalising effect on the audience. It determines whether they are likely to make young people more indifferent to violence and more inclined to accept violence as natural or appropriate for solving problems. The Board's judgements are based on expertise and experience.

The age limits that have been fixed take into account the likelihood of children in the various age groups being 'emotionally shocked'. Only a very limited amount of violence is allowed in films for young children. The censors also pay special attention to scenes that may have a very upsetting or terrifying effect, particularly where they involve characters with which children can easily identify.

This includes scenes that are difficult for children to understand and are liable to cause confusion and fear. An example of a film that would confuse and disorient a child could be a foreign film with subtitles that children cannot read or cannot finish reading before they disappear.

The classification system is evaluative and semideterministic in the sense that the criteria laid down by law leave a certain margin of judgement to the censors. The ratings that may be assigned to a film are: 'allowed for children', 'from 7 years', 'from 11 years', and 'from 15 years'.

In addition, *Statens biografbyrå* may ban a film from public showing as well as demand that a certain sequence or sequences be cut in order to be approved for showing. The criterion for determining the age limits for children is whether the film 'causes psychological damage'. Section 5 of the Act states that, 'the content of a film or videogram shall not be approved for showing to children under the age of 7, 11, or 15 years if it is liable to cause children in the relevant age group emotional shock.

The criterion for the limits for adults is whether the film 'has a brutalising effect on the audience'. Section 4 of the Act states that : '(1) The content of a film or videogram, or a part thereof, shall not be approved for showing if the events are depicted in such a manner and in such a context as to have a brutalising effect and (2) the assessment shall take particular account of whether the film or videogram contains explicit or protracted scenes of severe violence to people or animals or depicts sexual violence or coercion or presents children in pornographic situations.'

Persons who have not attained the minimum age fixed by the *Statens biografbyrå* shall not be admitted to public gatherings or entertainments where a film or videogram is being shown, except when they are accompanied by a person over 17 years.

United Kingdom

The British Board of Film Classification (BBFC) is an independent, non-governmental body, which exercises responsibilities over the cinema. By law, the cinema belongs exclusively to the local authorities. The Board was set up by the film industry in 1912 in order to bring a degree of uniformity to the standards of film censorship imposed by the many very disparate local authorities. The aim was to create a body, which, with no greater power than that of persuasion, would seek to make judgements and recommendations, which were acceptable nationally.

Statutory powers remain with the local councils, who may overrule any of the Board's decisions on appeal. In practice this rarely happens, and the local licensing conditions give the Board's categories legal status. A film distributor can however ask a local authority to award a local category for any film, whether it be one banned by the Board, passed by the Board in a category unacceptable to the distributor, or not seen by the Board at all.

Every film is viewed by at least two examiners, who write reports justifying the decision they have reached. In cases of doubt or disagreement, the film will be referred to another team, usually with a principal officer present at the screening. The Board views every film destined for public distribution in Britain, and in recent years it has seen around 400 films annually.

Specialist staff are employed to view foreign language works. A principal officer, any one of whom may be asked to view a film or video on appeal, must ratify all decisions. The President or Vice-Presidents will be consulted on difficult works, including those that may be refused a certificate altogether, and it is usually the case that such films are seen by most of the examining team before a final decision is taken.

The Board does not rely on a written set of guidelines but operates a system of precedent, so that every decision is taken in the light of previous ones. The BBFC's view is that context, treatment and the intention of the filmmaker are as important as the actual images shown, so that a list of prohibitions is unhelpful. Virtually any theme may be accepted if the treatment is responsible, and the same images may be acceptable in one context but not in another. The same applies to the boundaries between categories, although there are quite rigid rules on the sort of language allowed in the junior categories.

In questions of classification, the BBFC is primarily concerned with the protection of children, and the age-based category system was changed in 1982 so as to reflect changes in society, and to provide clear and concise information to parents and the public generally.[11] Only if a film fails to fall naturally into one of categories set up by the United Kingdom rating system, as displayed in Table 5, will cuts be considered.

It is an offence for the cinema manager to allow minors to view films with an age restriction, for which he or she would be liable to lose his or her cinema licence.

The Board does not receive any subsidy or grant either from the film industry or from government. Its income is derived solely from the fees it charges for its services; calculated by measuring the running time of films or video works submitted for certification.

---

[11] Since 1913, there were only 'U' and 'A' categories. In 1951, the 'X' was added, restricting audiences to those over 16. In 1970, an 'AA' was introduced limiting audiences to 14 and over, and the age for admittance for 'X' films was raised to 18. In 1982, the 'AA' was changed to '15' and the 'X' renamed '18'.

TABLE 5
United Kingdom Rating System

Rating	Description
'U' (Universal: suitable for all)	No theme, scene, action, or dialogue that might be construed as disturbing, harmful or offensive.
'PG' (Parental Guidance)	Mild violence; occasional brief non-sexual nudity; bed scenes but no serious suggestion of actual sexual activity; limited scatological language, but no sexual expletives; no drug use or condoning of immoral behaviour unless mitigated by context (e.g. comedy); no undue emphasis on weapons (e.g. flick-knives).
12 +	Implications of sex (within a relationship or in a humorous context); stronger language, but only a rare sexual expletive; more realistic violence limited in length and intensity, but no drug use.
15 +	Themes requiring a more mature understanding Full-frontal nudity in a non-sexual context; impressionistic sex; more extensive use of expletives; mildly graphic violence and horror with some gore. Soft drugs may be seen in use, but not so as to condone or normalise. As with lower age categories, no details of harmful or criminal techniques, (e.g. how to break into cars, pick locks, and so on).
18 +	Themes requiring an adult understanding (e.g. complex sexual relationships, controversial religious subjects); explicit simulated sex (or in some educational contexts real sex); full nudity in a sexual context; non-glamorised use of hard drugs when justified by characterisation or narrative; frequent use of sexual expletives; graphic violence, provided that it does not encourage sadistic pleasure or glamorise dangerous weapons.
'R18'	Consenting, non-violent sex depicted with a degree of explicitness limited only by the law

VIDEO RATING SYSTEMS

Austria

No specific measures for the protection of minors from harmful video content have so far been taken in Austria, though from time to time there is an initiative aimed at filling that gap. For instance, the social democratic Austrian youth organisation, *Kinderfreunde,* has recently launched a campaign, which, according to its title (*'Kein Mord am Bildschirm'* — 'No murder on screen'), focuses on television broadcasting activities, but also deals with the video sector, calling for an obligation to label brutal content also on video and computer games.

There is no rating mechanism in place, but general provisions on devices harmful to minors (cf. Section 18 of the Vienna Minors Protection Act: Children and Young people are not allowed to acquire, possess or use devices which could endanger their respect for human dignity) and on pornography apply.

Belgium

The only provisions in force for video rating in Belgium are the criminal ones. Criminal liability comes from Article 383 bis (law of 13 April 1995) and 380quinquies (law of 27 March 1995). It provides criminal sanctions against the dissemination of a pornographic film. The *'cour de cassation'* extended the *'bonne moeurs'* case-law application to dissemination of videotapes, even though Parliament has not issued specific provisions. The rating system used for film screenings does not apply to video dissemination.

Denmark

In Denmark, rules applying to video content are contained in the Film Act of 12 March 1997 and are exactly the same as the ones existing for cinema works (see Section 1).

Finland

In Finland, the Act on the Classification of Video and Other Audiovisual Programmes was passed in 1987. Prior to this the video industry had its own self-regulation body, called the *Videolevityksen valvontalautakunta*. The option exists to revive this body whenever necessary.

The Finnish Board of Film Classification also examines videos and the classifications applied are: (1) 'G' for general, (2) 'restricted for persons under 16', and (3) 'banned'. There is effectively only one rating. Otherwise, the programme is either passed for all or banned for all. If the programme has been or would be rated 18, it is banned on video.

The decisions may be accompanied by rating recommendations. Thus, *Titanic*, for instance, was rated 12 for cinema viewing, whereas on video it is exempted from classification and automatically passed for general audience viewing with the rating recommendation 12. The difference between rating decisions and rating recommendations is that rating decisions acquire the force of law, whereas recommendations do not.

The system is mandatory. No audiovisual programme may be offered for sale or for rental to the consumer unless passed by the Finnish Board of Film Classification. Home video classification concerns all linear audiovisual programmes—VHS, laserdisc, DVD, and so on—as long as they are commercially distributed for private use. There are a number of exceptions, most importantly: programmes that have already passed film classification, interactive programmes including videogames and CD-ROMs, and programmes produced by the Finnish Broadcasting Company. Additional content that may be exempted from classification includes education, science, product information, music, sport, documentaries, programmes for small children, travel, nature, and religion. The classification board may also order those programmes to be screened.

The criteria of restriction applied in video censorship include obvious violations of the law, obscenity, violence, and psychologically disturbing material. There are therefore fewer categories in video censorship than in film censorship. According to Antti Alanen, the manager of the Finnish Board of Film Classification, there is an urgent need to reform this aspect of video censorship. The boom in hard-core pornography sweeping the Western world has also struck Finland, where hard-core pornography gets the highest rating, that is, restricted for persons under 18. This means that there is effectively a video prohibition on pornography in Finland, which has led to the emergence of a huge black market with all its ramifications. Pornographic home videos are naturally submitted neither for classification nor for registration since they would be banned. Instead, police time is taken up with the seizure of pornographic material, and court time with the subsequent trials.

The Finnish Board of Film Classification will continue in its supervisory role but only for the setting of age restrictions. The need for the liberalisation of video censorship has been widely accepted, not least for practical reasons. Furthermore, television companies are not willing to follow the classifications of the Board of Film Classification.

France

Strictly speaking there is as yet no regulation regarding video classification in France. As to cinematographic works edited on video tapes, the Decree of the 23 February 1990 (Title II, Article 5, al. 3) requires producers of video tapes to display the certificate granted by the Commission for Classification of Cinematographic Works on the packaging. Video classification has only been dealt with under Fiscal Law, following the adoption of Article 18-4 of the Finance Act, 29 December 1984, which makes the transfer of rights in works distributed on video, which are pornographic or incite to hatred, subject to VAT (at the highest rate).

Nonetheless, where the video has not been released in the cinema prior to its distribution as a video, it does seem that, under the provisions of the New Criminal Code, Article 227-24 which states that 'when a message of pornographic or violent nature is likely to be seen by a minor a 3 year jail term or a fine of FF500,000 may be imposed', the producer may be obliged to issue warnings dedicated to the protection of minors. In addition to this Article, the Law No 98-468 of 17 June 1998, concerning the prevention and repression of sexual infractions as well as the protection of minors, was adopted recently. This law applies to any work transmitted in either magnetic format, digital format with optical reader recognition, or semiconductor support, such as videotapes, videodiscs or electronic games.

When, due to its pornographic character or its depiction of crime, violence, incitement to ethnic hatred, drugs, and so on, such a work may endanger youth, the administrative authority (Ministry of Internal Affairs) may prohibit (via ministerial order and after having consulted the Commission) its distribution to minors or its advertisement by any means (other than in premises prohibited to minors).

These prohibitions must be mentioned on each unit of the edited and distributed copies. However the decrees need to be finalised (in consultation with the Conseil d'Etat) before the area and modalities of the application of this law can be known precisely.

Nevertheless, and despite the absence of clear regulation in this area, the Syndicat de l'Edition Vidéo has developed a self-regulatory system. The code of ethics approved by the General Assembly of the Syndicat de l'Edition Vidéo on 25 March 1995 states clearly in article 6:

> Members of the 'Syndicat' undertake to operate with the following rules in mind: (1) Edited works, as well as the graphics used either for the cover of the tape or its promotion, shall respect human dignity; (2) When the editor considers that the edited work contains scenes, which are shocking or likely to upset the viewer, a warning explaining the content must be displayed.

The classification is issued directly by the different video editors. It is not a visual icons system but only displays information/recommendations (editors do not believe they have the legal legitimacy to act as censor). There are no guidelines, and no precise or harmonised criteria. For noncinematographic works the Syndicat refers to the classification system of the *Conseil supérieur de l'audiovisuel* (CSA).

Germany

In Germany, video films are rated either by the FSK under the same procedures as for cinematographic films, or by the BPjS, whose authority is limited to video films which have not been rated by or were not presented to the FSK, or those rated '18'. The 'index' creates limitations regarding the circulation of the videos.

They may only be shown in places where children or young people do not have access to them. Similarly, indexed videos may not be sold or rented outside shops, ordered by mail, rented in public libraries, or transmitted through electronic information or communication services. Middlemen must also refer to the abovementioned selling restrictions.

Video games are subject to *Unterhaltungssoftware Selbstkontrolle* (USK), the Entertainment Software Self-Regulation Body, which refers to the age categories included in the relevant legal provisions (evaluative). It also refers to the decisions made by the BPjS.

The USK has developed objective points for the age classification of computer and video games. These criteria have been developed on the basis of the provisions of 31 GjSM and are very similar to them. For instance, a game is always said to contain gratuitous violence if the player is placed in the role of the killer, if the death of opponents is rewarded, if the idea of the game is exclusively to display aggressive behaviour, and/or if the effects of violence are clearly shown.

The USK makes its decisions following the provisions of the BPjS and the FSK, which are mentioned in the USK criteria. These criteria clarify the points of examination. However, the decisions regarding the ratings are semideterministic in that they are based on the opinions of the examination committee according to these criteria.

In principle, the USK exerts a voluntary control. However, this voluntary character is limited by the fact that German department stores have adopted a policy of offering only USK rated products to their customers.

The USK only acts at the request of producers. The suppliers and manufacturers who are members *of Verband der Unterhaltungssoftware Deutschland e.V.* (VUD), the Association of Entertainment Software in Germany, recognise the USK as their self-regulation body for software available for purchase and other public use.[12] It is also supported by the Association for the Support of Young People and Social Work.

Thus, the aim of the USK is to guarantee the protection of minors by means of voluntary self-regulation on the part of the suppliers, even before the products are released. By awarding its stickers the USK attests that a given software is suitable for distribution and complies with the legal provisions regarding the protection of minors.

---

[12] The VUD is composed of developers, distributors, licensees from the entertainment, information and educational software industry, such as Acclaim Entertainment GmbH, ACTIVISION, ak tronic Software and Services, ART DEPARTMENT GmbH, BLUE BYTE Software GmbH and so on. The members do not submit their products themselves but give them to VUD, which submits them to USK to be rated.

The USK is composed of a *Beirat* (Advisory Council), which is the policy-making and controlling body of the USK, and expert examiners. The Advisory Council is made up of members of various groups of society, from, for instance, the field of science, politics, culture, and the protection of minors. The expert examiners must not be active in the computer hardware or software industry. They are independent and their function is honorary. They are only reimbursed for their expenses. They are obliged to attend the advanced training events organised by the USK, which relate to evaluations and examining activities and also advanced training on selected areas of assessment of computer and video games. They are selected on the basis of their professional experience and training.

The USK's other role is to provide information and clarification for the public regarding the opportunities and risks involved for children and young people from the use of entertainment software and interactive media. Parents and families are one of the main target groups for this work. The USK tries to encourage them to have an independent influence on the media socialisation of their children.

In principle, the USK examines all submitted software for its content and permissibility. The USK decides whether the software is a comparable image carrier in the meaning of §7 JÖSchG, whether its content complies with the provisions of the Criminal Code (§86a, 130, 131, 184 [3]), which age classification should be assigned to it, and whether a title should be prohibited.

Instruction books and the sales packaging are examined along with the software and the USK awards age classifications at the following levels: (1) 'no age restrictions', (2) 'suitable for ages 6 and over', (3) 'Suitable for ages 12 and over', (4) 'suitable for ages 16 and over', and (5) 'not suitable for persons under the age of 18'. The USK considers that these age group categories should be updated; however, they regret that current theories regarding psychological development have not been studied in a sufficiently scientific manner on the basis of the computer game practices of children and young people.

The USK's assessment is displayed on the product by means of stickers. There is no legal obligation relating specifically to the USK rating. However, the relevant general legal provisions regarding rating are complied with by the USK, partly because of the fear of bad publicity following the attribution of an inappropriate rating. This prevents voluntary regulatory organisations acting in the interests of the companies financing them.

The ratings of the USK are not binding in the legal sense, but only provide information for parents or retailers. As a consequence, shops buying USK rated products are not obliged to follow the USK decision.

Since its creation to August 1998, the USK classified 3500 titles. 17 titles were not rated, as they were considered not compatible with the relevant legal provisions. As to its capacity, it is limited because of the size of the organisation.

Only 5 people are employed and they receive requests from 195 organisations from 6 countries. They consult 27 experts and there are 7 observers. An average of 15 films is examined per week. The products classified by the USK constitute 90% of the entertainment industry's market. This proportion is only 50% for console programmes. The USK guarantees that an examination will take place no later than 21 days from application for a rating, and the applicant is informed of the results by fax. There also exists a special express procedure, which only takes 5 working days. The costs of the examination are defined in an agreement between the VUD and the *Förderverein für Jugend und Sozialarbeit,* the association for the promotion of social and youth work. The rating system does not apply to advertisements.

The USK is a national system, but the fact that Germany is the second biggest market in the field of entertainment software for PC after the USA motivates foreign firms to participate in this voluntary self-control organisation.

Greece

The group responsible for rating videos in Greece is the Cinematography Commission, and the same classification applies to video as that which covers films.

Ireland

In Ireland, the Video Recordings Act of 1989 extended the Film Censor's role to cover video. Video classification is mandatory—application must be made for a supply certificate declaring the video work fit for viewing. Unlike film, there is no provision for cutting videos, removing scenes or dialogue. Either the video will receive a certificate as it is or it will be refused one.

Video outlets require a licence and can be prosecuted for operating without a licence or in contravention of it, or for supplying uncertified videos. There is no penalty for supplying videos in breach of the age classification. Unlike the certification system, the age classification is not a binding system; it is intended only for guidance. When this system was adopted, there was disquiet that it would not go far enough towards controlling the availability of adult videos or 'video nasties' to children, but the legislators felt that a binding system would be difficult to enforce.

The parliamentary debates include discussion of the problem of striking a reasonable balance between the viewing rights of an adult and the quite clearly damaging effects of inappropriate material on children. Primary control was expressed as resting with the parents, not the State, which discharged its duty in providing guidance through the classification system.

A certificate will be granted unless the video work is likely to cause viewers to commit crimes; is likely to stir up hatred; may deprave or corrupt viewers, by reason of the inclusion in it of obscene or indecent matter; or depicts acts of gross violence or cruelty (including mutilation and torture) towards humans or animals (s.3.1). From 1991 to 1994, nearly 1,400 titles were refused certificates under the Act. Despite the reference to 'gross violence' as a ground for refusing a certificate, there is no definition in the Act of either 'violence' or 'gross violence'. Also, the exemption for video games has caused some debate and disquiet. Since they are not included in the Act, video games are subject to self-regulation or to the regulatory systems in the countries from which they originate, including age classifications.

The Act sets out a classification system, designed to indicate the suitability of the video for viewing by children. The age-based system, as amended, uses the same categories as for the cinema. A schedule to the relevant Statutory Instrument illustrates how the symbols denoting each class should be designed. The classification operates hand-in-hand with the certification system, as the certificate includes a statement of the appropriate age. This is intended for the guidance of parents and video wholesale, retail, and lending outlets.

All videos must be classified except those which, taken as a whole, are designed to inform, educate, or instruct, are concerned with music, religion or sport, or are video games. In these cases a certificate need not be sought unless the video contains matter that might be grounds for refusal of a certificate.

As in the case of the public viewing of films, it is an offence to supply, offer to supply, or possess with a view to supplying, a video work for which a certificate is not currently in force, unless an exemption under the Act applies. Penalties vary with the particular offence but include fines of up to £1,000 on summary conviction, and periods of imprisonment

Italy

The certificate granted to a film permits it to be shown in the cinema and in any other medium (thus including home video) throughout Italy's territory. However, obscene and pornographic films specifically produced for distribution only as home videos are also available on the market. These works have to be submitted for prior examination by the censorship committees, and are normally granted a certificate of 'unsuitable for minors' (mandatory). Accordingly, they may be rented or sold only to individuals over 18.

Finally, Article 75 of R.D. 773/1931 (Royal Decree No. 773 of 18 June 1931 concerning general provisions for public safety) states that 'anyone who produces, even periodically, motion pictures must give prior written notice' to the Public Authority (that is, the Police) in order to be granted a licence.

There is no specific content-related regulation in Italy that addresses video games, nor any specific rules concerning parental control systems that may be applied in this domain. Nevertheless, regulations on games in general are applicable to video games and their respective differences are not taken into consideration. Thus, rules on games in general apply to leisure and ability video games, both aiming at players' enjoyment; rules on gambling (or games of chance) apply to gambling video games (or games of chance); rules on games incompatible with the public interest apply also to video games with content incompatible with the public interest; finally, the regulatory framework on billiard-rooms applies anytime video games are provided. According to Article 110 T.U.P.S., the authority (that is, the mayor of the town) may prohibit (video) games where deemed incompatible with the public interest. In such cases, criminal provisions apply, punishing the licensee of the billiard-room where such games are available (Article 723 of the Criminal Code). General provisions concerning indecency and obscenity set forth in the Criminal Code, such as Article 528 and 725 also apply in this domain where the video game contains such material.

Luxembourg

In Luxembourg, only criminal provisions apply. It is compulsory to have a separate room for videotapes prohibited to minors.

The Netherlands

In the Netherlands, formal provisions for the video industry are provided by the Constitution's provision for the protection of freedom of speech (Article 7 paragraph 3), the Act on Film Exhibition, and the Penal Code (Articles 240, 240a and 240b).

Protection of freedom of speech applies to videos but the legislator can lay down rules regarding the showing or screening of videos to people under 16 years of age for the protection of good morals. Article 240a of the Penal Code states that providing and showing a picture or object to a person younger than 16 years of age, the viewing of which may be assumed to be damaging to a minor, is punishable. When videos are shown in public, the Act on Film Exhibition applies.

However, as the rental of video films is not considered to constitute a public showing, a rating system like the one for films cannot be introduced for rental videos. The responsible Secretaries of Justice and Culture have stated that the Articles 240 and 240a of the Penal Code concerning the penalisation of pornography only apply when a video is shown in public and that penalisation is not possible when videos are rented or sold. If the video has a pornographic picture on its box, Articles 240 and 240a may apply, and the video retailer/lender has to take this into account when placing these videos in his store. If the video contains child pornography, its sale and trade, which includes rental, is punishable according to Article 240b of the Penal Code. This exception is made in the hope that penalisation of the rental of child pornography will protect minors against exploitation for the purposes of pornographic production (*Raad voor het Jeugdbeleid* 1996).

The introduction of preventative limitations on viewing in order to protect minors was discussed with Parliament by the Secretaries for Justice and Culture. (Letter of the Secretary of Justice 1985–1986: 10). The Cabinet was of the opinion that minors run the risk of being damaged, but in the *Notitie Jeugdbeleid* of 1984, its memorandum on Youth Policy, it stated that Government should not in principle involve itself in private matters. Parents are expected to be responsible for the care of their children; government should, at most, create the best circumstances for them to be so. Consequently, the Cabinet has rejected any suggestion of legislation in this area (*Raad voor het Jeugdbeleid* 1996).

Nevertheless, the Cabinet did propose voluntary labelling of videocassettes to provide more information on their contents, including information on potential harm. As a result, the *Gemengde Commissie Videovoorlichting* (Committee on Information on Video) was set up, which has advised on a labelling system. Based on this, a 'gentleman's agreement' on self-regulation was reached on 14 October 1991 between the former Ministry of Welfare, Public Health, and Culture and the video industry. The latter was represented by the *Nederlandse Vereniging van Producenten en Importeurs van beeld—en geluidsdragers* (NVPI), the Dutch Federation of Producers and Importers of Image—and Sound Carriers and the *Nederlandse Video Detaillisten Organisatie* (NVDO), the Dutch Organisation of Video Retailers.

The *Raad van Toezicht Videovoorlichting* (RvtV), the Supervisory Board of Video Information, which was established by the industry itself, is responsible for the self-regulatory rating system. It meets once every six weeks, and its initial role was to monitor the system. On 6 May 1996, the 'gentleman's agreement' was tightened into the *Convenant en Reglement Videovoorlichting* (Covenant on Video Information), because of the popularity among minors of the video film, *Faces of Death*, which showed fatal accidents and killings. This time the Government party responsible was the State Secretary for Public Health, Welfare, and Sports, and the agreement was also signed by the *Nederlandse Vereniging Grammafoonplaten Detailhandelaren* (NVGD), the Dutch Federation of Record Retailers). As a result, the labelling showing the age classification will be examined by the RvtV; the labelling showing the age classification will be attached on the front and back of the video cassette in the same way; computer games as well as videos will be rated by age; video retailers will be more vigilant about the age of persons to whom they rent or sell extremely violent videos; self-regulation will expand to shops other than video stores, such as department stores; complaints may be addressed to the RvtV; and the RvtV may impose fines up to an amount of 5,000 Dutch guilders (Groebel and Smit 1996: 65).

The rating system is descriptive and evaluative. It is evaluative in the sense that standard age classifications are given—'all ages', 'Parental Guidance recommended', '12 years and over', and '16 years and over'. The criteria used for rating, and described in the Covenant on Video Information, are the same as those used by the Dutch Board of Film Classification, including an open criterion, which may be used by the classifier in a film specific context. The criteria are defined in the Covenant as follows:

1. Frightening scenes are those, which are unexpected, and are alien to the general ambience of the audiovisual work, and which could cause excessive terror or anxiety. This does not include those scenes, which are necessary to the story line and are resolved within it;

2. Brutalising violence, which has no motive and is used as a negative and destructive tool;

3. The use of drugs shown in an attractive way, or in a way that suggests they are 'not as bad as they are made out to be'. This does not apply to audiovisual works meant to warn youth about the damaging consequences of using drugs;

4. Pornography, where the object is to stimulate sexual arousal without showing revealing intercourse; and

5. Open criterion; used to identify racism and discrimination, offensive use of language, continuously frightening ambience and other disturbing elements which are not mentioned in the other four criteria.

The rating system is also descriptive because one of the goals of the RvtV is to provide the best possible video information for the protection of minors and for consumers in general. Therefore, a genre classification of video films is also given, including: Children and Youth; Family; Drama/Classic; Humour; Sports; Music; Educational; Science Fiction; Action adventure; War; Western; Thriller/Crime; Horror; Racy Humour; Erotic and Pornography. In addition, the accompanying cover text has to give an honest impression of the video's content.

The classification system could be described as a deterministic process. The use of a score form results in a classification and a genre definition, and the score form is given to the RvtV at least 6 weeks before the release of the video film so that the Board will be able to take action where necessary.

The rating of video films is voluntary for those importers/producers who are not members of one of the organisations ratifying the Covenant on Video Information; members of those organisations have to comply with the rules and regulations for Video Information. The ratings decisions are, however, not binding instruments.

Portugal

In Portugal, video films are rated in precisely the same manner as films exhibited in public cinemas and are covered by the same legislation. The rating of videos is mandatory and the *Comissão de Classificação de Espectáculos* (CCE) is the body responsible. Video films on the commercial circuit have to have an 'official' stamp with the following information: title, record number, copy number, and the classification attributed by the CCE. Specific rules regarding presentation and distribution of videos were set up in the Law-decree 39/88 of 6th February 1988.

If videos are copies of films that have already been rated for cinemas, they are automatically rated by the CCE, except for those films shown prior to the Law-decree 396/82 of 21st September 1982. If the video film has not been distributed in public cinemas, it is classified by the CCE by the same procedure as for cinema films.

Spain

In Spain, the responsibility for rating other audiovisual works belongs to the same bodies that have the responsibility for rating films (the Director General of the ICAA and the CCPC; and, in Catalonia, the Department for Cultural Affairs, which in practice hardly rates any audiovisual work at all).

The main problem for the rating authorities is software. According to the ICAA, there is neither the political will nor the means to rate software. The ICAA believes that self-regulation in this field could be the best possible solution, and in fact, a new association of software producers and distributors has been established, the *Asociación de Distribuidores y Editores de Software de Entretenimiento*. Its main goal is to protect the intellectual property rights of its members, but it also plans to adopt a common framework within the industry for a voluntary rating of software products.

State Decree 2332/1983 regulates the sale, distribution and public exhibition of audiovisual material in general. According to this Decree, all audiovisual material must be rated before being advertised, distributed, or sold to the public, unless it is a mere reproduction of a cinema film, in which case it is possible to use the rating given by the CCPC for cinema screening (See Article 1 of Decree 2332/1983, of 1 September 1983, and also Article 16 of Decree 81/1997 and Article 13 of Order of 7 July 1997).

As with cinema films, content producers are obliged to submit all audiovisual works to ICAA for rating (See Article 16.1 of Decree 81/1997, and Article 13 of the Ministerial Order 7 July 1997). The rating must appear clearly on the boxes of the audiovisual works, and if the rating is 'X', the box must have a notice stating, 'only for persons over 18' (See the Article 16 of Order of 7 July 1997). Audiovisual works rated 'X' may not be sold, rented, or given to minors, and they may not be within reach of children in premises where the entrance of children is not prohibited (See Article 19.2 of Decree 81/1997). Advertisements and packaging of these audiovisual works shall not include graphic representations or titles that explicitly show the pornographic or violent nature of the audiovisual work in question (See Article 19.2 of Decree 81/1997).

State Decree 488/1988 regulates public exhibition (for example, on buses, aeroplanes, hotels, and so on) of audiovisual works distributed in video format (See Article 1.2 of Decree 448/1988, of 22 April 1988 ['Decree 448/1988']). If audiovisual works distributed on video are exhibited in public, they must previously have been rated (See Article 2.1 of Decree 448/1988, and also Article 16 of Decree 81/1997 and Article 13 of Order of 7 July 1997). Audiovisual works distributed on video format that have been rated 'X' or recommended for persons above 18 may not be shown to the public on premises where children under 18 are allowed to enter (See Article 2.2 of Decree 448/1988, and also Article 8 of Law 1/1992, of 21 February 1992).

The admission of minors to premises where their entrance is prohibited is punishable by the local council with fines up to 50,000 pesetas (approx. 300 Euros) (See Articles 26, 28.1.a and 29 of Law 1/1992, of 21 February 1992). A breach of the provisions relating to selling, renting, or giving 'X'-rated audiovisual works to minors or displaying them within reach of children is sanctioned by the Director General of the ICAA, with a fine up to 500,000 pesetas (approximately 3,000 Euros) (See Article 9.3.b), Article 10.1.a and Article 10.3 of Law 17/1994).

According to the CCPC, all audiovisual works must be rated, regardless of the distribution format. However, it is not clear what constitutes an audiovisual work. Clearly, all cinematographic works fall into this category, whether they are distributed in cinemas, or on video, CD's, DVD's, CD-i's, and so on. All videos are also considered to be audiovisual works. As regards software or interactive works, the ICAA says that they may be considered to be audiovisual works, but that the rating authority is not prepared to perform its tasks in relation to products of this nature. So, while some Autonomous Communities expressly prohibit the distribution of pornographic or violent video games or other audiovisual materials, there is no rating system for products of this nature.

The system is therefore mandatory vis-à-vis the owners of exploitation rights of audiovisual works. For the public, the ratings merely provide a recommendation, with the exception of audiovisual works rated 'X'. The rating procedure is nondeterministic and follows the same process as for films. The ratings are expressly applied after the CCPC has seen the audiovisual work concerned, but it is also possible to obtain a rating implicitly. Decree 81/1997 establishes that, if an audiovisual work has been given to the CCPC for classification, and no rating has been provided within a month, it is understood that the ICAA accepts the rating proposed by the company that has requested a rating for the audiovisual work (See Article 16.2 of the Decree 81/1997.) The ratings issued are the same evaluative age based system as for films. The existing rating system provides ratings for all videos distributed in Spain. In the first semester of 1998, 1379 videographic works were rated in total.

With regard to video, the volume of programming that the rating system will accommodate may be increased by the creation of committees with rating capacity within the CCPC or an increase of the number of its members for example. As a government entity, the State has the legal and economic resources to increase the capacity of the existing system. This will depend on the rating needs of this sector and on the political will of the Minister for Education and Culture.

Sweden

In Sweden, the law applying to videograms is contained in the Penal Code, chapter 16, section 10, and reads as follows:

> It is a criminal offence to depict sexual violence or coercion or explicit or protracted severe violence to people or animals in photographs or in films, videograms, television programmes, or other moving pictures, with the intention of distributing such pictures or such depictions, unless this is justified in view of the particular circumstances.

The distribution of scenes of unlawful violence is a criminal offence under the Law on Freedom of Expression, which means that only the Office of the Chancellor of Justice can act as public prosecutor and that such proceedings are always jury trials. When charges are brought against a distributor or retailer, the National Board of Film Classification must notify the Office of the Chancellor of Justice of its opinion. Charges cannot be brought in the case of films that have previously been approved by the Board. It is also a criminal offence to sell or hire out video films containing realistic depictions of violence to persons under the age of 15. Over the years, the debate has also led to the following rules:

> Voluntary advance examination of video films intended for sale or hire to the public. This option is used as a precaution, since charges can be brought against films that have not been examined. (1)Advance examination is only compulsory in the case of video films shown at public entertainments. (2) Compulsory registration by the National Board of Film Classification of distributors of video films for private use. (3) A copy of every film (that is, every film of which at least 10 copies are distributed) must be sent to the National Archive of Recorded Sound and Moving Images.

A regional supervisory organisation that reports to the National Board of Film Classification monitors compliance with these rules and ensures that unlawful representations of violence disappear from the market.

The rating system, which has come to be applied to videos, which are sold or hired to the public in Sweden, can in practice be divided into 4 parts or forms. The first part is a voluntary classification with the exception of films containing realistic depictions of violence for hire or sale to children under 15. The age category, which a film is assigned when the National Board of Film Classification examines it in advance, is the same as when it is offered as a hire or purchase video. The second form is when the distributor voluntarily submits the video film for examination by the National Board of Film Classification in order to avoid any future legal proceedings. In the third form, the video distributor assigns his own age category. This is voluntary with the exception of films containing depictions of realistic violence that are for hire or sale to children under 15. In the fourth form, a video film may be distributed to persons 15 years of age or older if it has not been deemed to violate the abovementioned law (Penal Code, chapter 16, section 10). Since this is compulsory, some films are banned from distribution.

Age limits for the classification are the same as the ones used for cinema. In addition, sometimes the distributor also uses the over 18 age limit. As long as the age categories are taken from the National Board of Film Classification, the rating is evaluative and semideterministic. In some cases, when the distributor himself assigns the categories, there may be nondeterministic limits.

United Kingdom

All video works sold in the United Kingdom (unless specifically exempted) have to carry a rating issued by the British Board of Film Classification.

The BBFC uses the same age-based classification system as for film but the video industry has asked for an additional category, to be used for works to be stocked on the children's shelves of video shops: 'Uc'—Universal—Particularly suitable for young children. It is a criminal offence to supply an age-restricted video to someone below the relevant age.

Unlike for films, the BBFC ratings for videotapes are legally binding, but distributors may appeal against decisions to the Video Appeals Committee, an independent body set up as a requirement of the Act.

The Video Standards Council (VSC) advises its members on how to comply with the BBFC classifications. It was established in 1989 as a non-profit making body to develop and administer a Code of Practice designed to promote high standards within the video industry. In 1993, its brief was expanded to promote high standards within the computer games industry. VSC membership represents all segments of the video and games industries and has over 8000 registered retail outlets across the country. VSC supplies its retail members with a whole variety of in-store display items designed to remind staff and customers about the law relating to video and games. It also provides staff training guidelines, which include a staff training video for use by video and games retailers.

TV RATING SYSTEMS

Austria

Broadcasting activities are subject to a federal law in Austria, and to its restrictions. At present, there are 2 possible bases for television broadcasting activities. In the first instance, the *Bundesgesetz über die Aufgaben und die Einrichtung des Österreichischen Rundfunks*, commonly referred to as *Rundfunkgesetz* (Broadcasting Act), provides the legal basis for the Austrian public broadcaster, *Österreichischer Rundfunk* (ORF). It dates from 10 July 1974, and has recently been amended by the Federal Act to Amend the Broadcasting Act and the 1993 Amendment to the Broadcasting Act, to conform to the new *Television Without Frontiers Directive*. The Broadcasting Act covers terrestrial, cable, and satellite broadcasting.

In the second case, the 1997 *Bundesgesetz mit den Bestimmungen über den Kabel- und Satellitenrundfunks*, commonly referred to as *Kabel- und Satelliten-Rundfunkgesetz* (Cable and Satellite Broadcasting Act), serves as the legal basis for private cable and satellite broadcasting activities; a basis for private terrestrial television broadcasting, however, is still missing. A controversial amendment aimed at integrating this type of broadcasting activity and changing the name of the Act to *Privat-Rundfunkgesetz* (Private Broadcasting Act) could not be passed with the aforementioned amendment to the Broadcasting Act but is still under discussion in Parliament. The warning obligation laid down in Article 22 paragraph 3 of the *Television Without Frontiers Directive* as amended can be found in Section 16 paragraph 3 of this Bill.

Up to now, no legislative distinction between analogue and digital television broadcasting has been drawn. However, as it is likely that there will only be one licence for private country-wide television broadcasting, some interested parties advocate delaying the introduction of private terrestrial television broadcasting until digital television has superseded analogue television.

In April 1993, the ORF was the first German-language broadcaster (voluntarily) to adopt principles and guidelines regarding violence on TV (*Richtlinien zum Thema Gewalt im Fernsehen*). Apart from other measures to protect minors and human dignity, the ORF has introduced a watershed of 8:15 p.m., before which all programmes must be appropriate to the whole family. There are no legal provisions on 'harbours' or 'watersheds'.

The ORF voluntarily introduced time zones in its 1993 Guidelines. As a rule, films which have been rated '16 and over' by the *Östereichische Jugendfilmkommission* (Austrian Commission for Film and Youth) are not broadcast earlier than about 10:00 p.m. If an exception is made at all, then substantial editing takes place. The ORF also takes the recommendations of the *Östereichische Jugendfilmkommission* and other renowned institutions (for example, German *Freiwillige Selbstkontrolle Fernsehen* [FSF]) into account and cuts films according to what these institutions put on the 'index'.

Since 1 January 1999, when the latest Amendment to the Broadcasting Act entered into force, the ORF has also applied a rating system consisting of 3 parts, which is partly inspired by the *Television Without Frontiers Directive*. At present, no such activities can be observed on the part of the private Austrian (cable or satellite) television broadcasters.

The Austrian legislator decided to take up nearly *in extenso* the provision issued from the Directive and the ORF opted for the permanent visual symbols. The 3 signs used by the ORF are evaluative, they do not carry information on the contents. Although the ORF's watershed is based on the recommendations given by the *Östereichische Jugendfilmkommission*, there is no objective methodology regarding application of the visual symbols. The process may therefore be defined as nondeterministic.

The 3 different symbols introduced by the ORF each consist of bold black sign framed by a square. They are displayed in Table 6.

The third symbol was introduced at the request of the body representing the listeners and viewers, *Hörer- und Sehervertretung*. Whereas the 2 restrictive symbols are shown on the screen, the rating of K+ that recommends the programme for children is only given in the ORF Teletext, in press releases, and via the Internet.

This rating system is not applied to advertisements. Standard advertising contracts give the ORF the right to refuse to broadcast an entire advertisement for reasons of protection of minors, among others, but do not give the right to insert visual symbols.

TABLE 6
ORF Visual Symbols

Rating	Symbol
Not for children	**X**
Only for adults	**O**
Recommended for children	**K+**

The system is mandatory. The Austrian implementation of the new *Television Without Frontiers Directive* being in force, the ORF is obliged to rate the contents of its programmes. However, at present, the ORF is the only broadcaster obliged to provide a warning/identification. As, according to its own press releases, the ORF is in the habit of checking all films irrespective of the hour at which they are broadcast, the new regime should not cause a capacity problem.

Belgium

The adoption of visual icons is underway in Belgium. Otherwise, there are no definitive systems in place, as the French and German Communities are currently debating the matter. The Flemish Community appears to be distancing itself from the discussion, probably due to the fact that it fears the adoption of visual icons being circumvented by VT4, which broadcasts its programmes from outside Belgium, but is dedicated to the Flemish audience.

Belgium used to use the white square but does not seem convinced of its efficiency. They consider that it, 'more often offers the attraction of forbidden fruit, and there are greater numbers of viewers than usual when it is present on the screen' (French Community of Belgium 1997: 64). Nevertheless, the white square has never been officially rejected and has not completely disappeared from the screen. The white square is also part of a larger system. The broadcaster RTBF has, for example, established a double control system, which is still in use. The Director of Programmes invites producers to provide a list of the programmes that may be problematic.

In addition, a procedure of graduated warnings is in force. The first is 'implicit reservations'. In this case, the continuity announcer draws attention to any aspects of the programme that are likely to shock a significant part of the audience (violent or erotic images, rude language, particularly negative treatment of certain topics, and so on). These warnings do not imply a value judgement on the part of RTBF.

The second warning is 'explicit reservations'. In this case, the RTBF takes a position. The word 'reservations' is clearly expressed (programmes with risky material, but for which broadcasting is justified by their artistic or informative nature). In the third case, the white square is used to reinforce the warning of 'explicit reservations'. It is displayed throughout the programme.

Canal Plus Belgique is the only channel to adopt its own visual icons system. However, this system does not appear on the screen but only in its TV guide. It uses a colour code as follows: green (for all), yellow (when there are some reservations about the programme), red (adults only). This system is quite similar to the road code, and it is argued that it is therefore more easily comprehensible to viewers.

VRT uses a system similar to the graduate warnings system that depends in principle on channel directors. However, channels under the jurisdiction of the Flemish Community are in favour of acoustic warnings.

The newly adopted French visual icons system has led the Belgian political authorities to aim towards a system that will not create too much confusion for viewers. Nonetheless, the Advisory Committee of the CSA argues that the French system is not totally adaptable to Belgium due to different regulations, namely those regarding admission to cinemas. In addition, in Belgium a single category exists (prohibited to those under 16). However, 'the adoption of some of the icons used by the French broadcasters and widely distributed in Belgium would facilitate message comprehension for the viewer'. Meetings between the CSA of the French Community, and the French CSA have been organised to discuss this (*Les cahiers du CSA n° 2*).

A visual icons system is in the process of being adopted. However, a full range of initiatives has preceded it. To win the support of all the interested parties (public authorities, broadcasters, representative associations, educationalists, and parents) is one of the priorities. To this end, broadcasters from the French Community (RTBF, RTL, TVI, and Canal Plus Belgique) are represented on the Advisory Committee. The system to be adopted will have the approval of all parties involved in advance.

The French Community Parliament is supposed to adopt a decree that incorporates into domestic law the new *Television Without Frontiers Directive*. The Advisory Committee has just announced its position in the Opinion n° 4/98 of 10 June 1998, published in *Les cahiers du CSA n° 2*. However, this proposal will be modified due to the new French system.

The duration of the icon on the screen will depend on the category in which the programme is classified. For the programmes rated orange triangle but broadcast prior to 22.00 the icon must be present throughout the programme. This is also the case for all programmes rated in the 'red square' category, whatever time of day they are broadcast.

The programmes rated 'orange triangle' but broadcast after 22.00 need only display the icon at the beginning of the broadcast and after each break. This rating system may be adopted in principle, subject to a new debate to take the French changes into account. With broadcasters having been involved in its development, application of the ratings system should be respected all the more since it is their responsibility to classify the programmes.

Fictional programmes broadcast by public or private broadcasters, as well as encrypted programmes, may be rated according to 4 categories that each may correspond to a visual icon. These categories and their descriptions are displayed in Table 7.

TABLE 7
French Community's Suggested Television Rating System

Categories	Public	Duration
No Icons	All audiences	
Full Orange Triangle	Parental guidance: Fictional programmes, which due to number of scenes or to their overall character are likely to harm sensitivity of minors under 12.	*For programmes prior to 10:00 p.m.:* For the duration of the broadcast (including credits) for unencrypted channels and for one minute at the beginning of the broadcast for encrypted channels (including credits). During trailers (at minimum when announcing title of film and its broadcasting time. These trailers must not contain images likely to harm sensitivity of youth audience). *For programmes after 10:00 p.m.:* For 1 minute at the beginning of broadcast (including credits). For 15 seconds after each break During trailers (as above)
Red Square	Prohibited to minors under 16: Works of an erotic nature or depicting intense violence	*For programmes prior to and after 10:00 p.m.:* Throughout the broadcast (including credits). During trailers (at minimum when announcing title of film and its broadcasting time. Trailers must not contain images likely to harm sensitivity of youth audience).
Full Red Square	Prohibited on channels other than encrypted: Works of pornographic nature and/or containing gratuitous violence	*For programmes prior to and after 10:00 p.m. and only on encrypted channels:* Throughout the broadcast (including credits) During trailers (minimum when announcing title of film and its broadcasting time. Trailers must not contain images likely to harm sensitivity of youth audience.

According to the CSA, the visual icons system is the responsibility of the broadcasters. Nevertheless, the regulatory body has made the following recommendations to the Government. It is the responsibility of the broadcasters to consider the impact that their programmes may have on the physical, mental, and moral growth of minors.

Media and multimedia literacy must accompany visual icons. It is essential to develop real education skills among viewers and educators to work towards a critical understanding of images. Coordination between broadcasters in the French Community, the CSA, and the Inter-Community Commission for Film Control is desirable.

Visual icons should cover all kinds of fictional programmes in the broadest sense of the term. But they should not apply to news, which is covered by internal codes of ethics and the conventional provisions of the different channels. Parallel with the adoption of these icons, broadcasters from the French Community have undertaken to set up an internal commission for the classification of films.

Alternative methods, as expressed in Article 22.3 of the TWF Directive, will be applied in Belgium, the Flemish Community having opted for the acoustic warning, and the French Community for the visual symbol. It is difficult to tell at present whether the Flemish Community will follow the French Community in adopting a visual icons system, but debates preceding the adoption of the Decree of 28 April 1998 show a lack of enthusiasm regarding icons.

Nonetheless, it must be acknowledged that the Flemish position will depend to a large extent on the European environment. If legal mechanisms warrant a common rating system for all the Flemish speaking channels (the VT4 case), then nothing should prevent such icons (this is what the French Community is attempting to establish for French speaking channels). The Flemish position is not one of categorical opposition, but a reflection on the effectiveness of the system in the European context.

Denmark

Television in Denmark has a long tradition of public service broadcasting, originating with the beginning of radio broadcasting in the 1920s. Danmarks Radio (DR), at the time called *Radiosymfonien*, was created in 1925, around the time of the passing of the first Broadcast Act. One of the fundamental criteria in programme production and selection is that programmes should be generally of an enlightening and cultural nature.

The principle of enlightenment—historically conceived as a high-brow cultural discourse—has been challenged by the deregulation of broadcasting in Denmark. In cultural terms, a broad Danish consensus exists vis-à-vis prohibitive measures, where the general opinion is that prohibitions attract attention, radical actions, and feelings, and, in some cases, may lead to criminal behaviour. 'Forbidden fruit' is often considered attractive and tempting, so antipathy towards prohibition and detailed regulation is widespread.

Regulations regarding television (and radio) content are contained in the Broadcasting Act of 19 February 1998. This Act anticipates the development of digital television and will be renegotiated in the year 2000. Through this instrument the 2 national public service broadcasters, Danmarks Radio and TV2 have gained increased economic liberty, becoming independent of the Minister of Culture, and are able to determine the budget frame within which they operate.

On the other hand, their public service obligations have been extended and are to be accounted for in their annual reporting, as proof of fulfilment of their duties.

With explicit reference to the question of harmful content to children, chapter 2, § 3 in the Act stipulates as follows: 'The possessor of a broadcasting licence must ensure that no programmes are transmitted that could damage to any serious degree the physical, mental, or moral development of minors, exercising particular control over programmes that include pornography or unjustified violence. This also counts for programmes that can damage the physical, mental, or moral development of minors, unless it is ensured—by choice of programming hours or by installing of technical devices—that minors will not watch or listen to the programmes.'

With regard to children, all pornographic films are automatically rated at 16 years and above, but the Broadcasting Act contains no explicit regulations concerning the question of violence, nor any paragraphs explicitly referring to control of programme content.

Danmarks Radio uses an informal watershed of 9:00 p.m., and there is also a standard provision for all broadcasters that programmes considered harmful to minors may only be shown after midnight. The guidelines used by Danmarks Radio are inspired by the European Broadcasting Union (EBU). The normal procedure is acoustic warnings before films or TV series that may be harmful to children. Also, trailers for violent films are no longer shown during children's programmes—as sometimes happened in the past—but mostly during programmes aimed at an adult audience.

No explicit control mechanisms regulate the programme scheduling policies of the public service institutions in Denmark. They themselves decide on suitability and/or possible harmfulness of each programme. This is done on a self-regulatory basis.

However, the Minister of Culture, Elsebeth Gerner Nielsen, has recently instructed the broadcasting companies to operate a clearer line of information and orientation in order to prevent children from being exposed to harmful content on television. As a consequence of the Minister's communiqué, Danmarks Radio has clarified the following to their Departments: in both fiction and news programmes that contain harmful content and that are broadcast in prime time, the speakers or programme hosts must warn the viewer about the harmful content.

The initiative from the Minister is not a legal initiative, but a policy guideline. Thus, it falls within what one might call the formulation of an ethical code of conduct. Subsequently, Danmarks Radio has defined how to implement it for itself. Danmarks Radio's code of conduct will be included into their new/revised rules and regulations, which were to be adopted in February 1999.

Finland

The Finnish Broadcasting Company, *Yleisradio* (YLE) is the national public service broadcaster that offers the Finnish audience 2 nation-wide TV channels. YLE's primary sources of financing are the television licence fees and the operating licence fees. It is state-owned and supervised by an administrative council elected by Parliament. It does not require an operating licence since its operations are based on the Act on *Yleisradio Oy*. YLE owns the nation's broadcasting networks, transmitters, and links.

Since 1993, YLE has offered 2 channels, TV1 and TV2, whose programming carries no advertising. Two other nation-wide television channels, MTV3 (MTV Media Oy) and Nelonen (Channel Four Finland) are commercial. They pay the operating licence fees, which are typically allocated to YLE. Cable television operators no longer require an operating licence, but must register with the Telecommunications Administration Centre.

Traditionally, no rating systems have been applied on Finnish TV. The Administrative Board of the YLE accepted the following five programme policy rules in March 1987 (at this time the YLE operated on 2 channels and sold broadcasting time to a commercial company, MTV, which provided the programming for channel 3):

1. YLE and MTV will be cautious in the selection of programmes likely to convey violent behaviour models and calculated violence. Also, single serial films should be previewed and banned, if necessary. Continuous discussion should take place over the definition of the limits of programme practices.

2. YLE and MTV should release more programme information to newspapers. Product information concerning TV programmes should also be further developed. TV companies ought to answer questions appertaining to TV violence in their programmes on the basis of present research findings. Parents should be informed of the effects of TV violence. Research funds of the YLE will be directed to studies on TV violence.

3. The YLE and MTV are committed to observing the 9:00 p.m. watershed and broadcasting programmes unsuitable for children at later hours. Companies have to inform their audiences about the watershed policy effectively.

4. Positive attitudes to life and human dignity should be preferred in programme selections, as well as programmes promoting non-violent behaviour. Programmes conveying a respect for life and non-violent attitudes should be preferred in the selection of programmes for a young audience in particular.

5. The commercial channel, MTV, should also apply the principles of programme policy mentioned earlier.

Broadcasters have applied the 9:00 p.m. watershed. In addition, auditory announcements have been used in some cases to warn when a forthcoming programme contains shocking or violent material that could cause distress to some viewers.

On 22 September 1998, the Finnish Parliament approved government proposals for an Act on Television and Radio Operations; an Act on the State Television and Radio Fund; an Act on the Amendment of the Act on *Yleisradio Oy*; and the proposal for certain technical amendments to the Act on Telecommunications Administration and the Copyright Act. This legislation replaces the Radio Equipment Act of 1927 and the Cable Transmission Act of 1987, and incorporates the European Union's television directive into Finnish legislation. The Act, which emphasises freedom of expression and diversification in programme output, came into force on 1 January 1999.

In line with Article 22.2 of the *Television Without Frontiers Directive*, the section concerning programmes harmful to the development of children (§ 19) obliges a broadcaster to broadcast programmes with sexual or violent content that may be harmful to children's development at a time when children generally do not watch TV. If programmes unsuitable for children are broadcast, an announcement about the programme's unsuitability must be made prior to transmission, or it must be indicated by means of a symbol throughout the transmission of the programme.

Section 25 deals with the protection of children under 18 from television or radio advertisements. According to this section, advertisements should not cause moral or physical harm to children. The Telecommunications Administrative Centre (TV programmes) and the Consumer Ombudsman (advertisements) are to supervise compliance with the act with respect to the protection of minors.

In compliance with the new Act on Television, all national TV companies, that is, YLE, MTV3, and the *Ruutunelonen* (Channel Four Finland) have agreed on joint national frameworks for the self-regulation of television programmes unsuitable for children. From 1 January 1999 programmes will be divided into 2 categories, (1) those permitted for children under 16 years, and (2) those unsuitable for children under 16. Each company is responsible for the coding of its own programmes. Ratings will be made by certain boards or by people responsible for programme selection or editing.

As set out in Article 22.2 of the *Television Without Frontiers Directive*, companies have committed themselves to applying the 9:00 p.m. watershed in programme distribution. In line with Article 22.3, acoustic announcements indicating that the programmes are unsuitable for children, will be made prior to their showing. In addition, TV companies must provide newspapers and teletext services with regular programme information, with special symbols indicating the programmes unsuitable for children.

Television companies have agreed to pay attention to the content and distribution times of the trailers of programmes that may have possible harmful effects on children. YLE, MTV3, and Channel Four Finland have committed themselves to using similar programme symbols and codes. By having a standard of harmfulness and by providing a single rating indicator based on age, the rating system of TV programmes in Finland is evaluative.

It is also a nondeterministic rating process, because the ratings are based on opinions or judgement. The rating system is mandatory, since law regulates it. The programme producers make the ratings. Company programme policy personnel and programme purchase personnel will be responsible for the coding. This system can be expected to accommodate only the fictional programming of each company and will not be applied to advertisements.[13]

France

There is no specific law for television broadcasting regarding the protection of minors in France. Specific regulations are contained in the 'Youth' directives of the *Conseil Supérieur de L'Audiovisuel* (CSA) dated 5 May 1989. The law of 30 September 1986 on freedom of communication states simply in Article 15 that the CSA oversees protection of childhood and adolescence in programmes broadcast by audiovisual services.

The first television rating system was implemented in November 1996 by broadcasters on the initiative of the CSA after several months dialogue between public authorities, industry, family, and viewers associations. The preparation needed for this implementation began in October 1995, when a dialogue began with broadcasters on the means to reduce violence on TV. In July 1996, broadcasters near the CSA began to implement a 3-point system of protection of minors that involved (1) programme classification, (2) time scheduling for the more violent programmes, and (3) display of visual icons corresponding to the classifications. In October 1996, the implementation of a common visual icons system between TF1, France 2/3 and M6, with Canal+ keeping its own icons began. Finally, in November 1996 the system, as displayed in Table 8, was introduced.

The adopted rules were inserted in channels' licences. Once implemented it is up to the broadcasters to apply the system and the responsibility of the CSA to monitor application. To this end the CSA created an *Observatoire de la signalétique*, in charge of monitoring all rated programmes to assess the appropriateness of the rating applied, as well as the time scheduled for broadcasting.

---

[13] Regulations concerning the protection of children are included in the new law on television (744/1998, section 25): Television and radio advertisements may not cause moral or physical harm to children. It is forbidden for example, to show children in dangerous situations in TV and radio ads.

TABLE 8
The 1996 Rating System

Category Symbol	Description	Restrictions
I	All viewers	No restrictions
II ◯	Works containing scenes likely to harm young viewers Parental Guidance desirable Symbol: white circle with green border.	Broadcasting time is at the discretion of the broadcaster, but this work may not be broadcast during children's programmes. Particular attention to be paid to trailers for these works, when broadcast near children's programmes.
III △	Cinema works prohibited to under 12's, as well as TV works likely to disturb young viewers, notably when programme contains systematic or repeated psychological or physical violence Parental Guidance essential, prohibited to under 12's Symbol: White triangle with orange border.	To be broadcast after 10:00 p.m. Exceptionally, broadcast of such work may be possible before 10:00 p.m., if icon is displayed throughout. Such exceptions are not permissible on Tuesdays, Fridays, and days preceding non-working days. In addition these works may not be broadcast near children programmes.
IV ☐	Cinema works prohibited to under 16's, as well as TV works of erotic nature or containing intense violence, likely to impair physical, mental or moral growth of under 16's Adult audience, prohibited to under 16's Symbol: White square with red border.	To be broadcast after 10:30 p.m. Trailers for these works must not contain scenes likely to harm youth audience sensitivity, and may not be broadcast before 8:30 p.m.
V	Pornographic or extremely violent work, likely to seriously impair physical, mental or moral growth of minors.	Complete prohibition

Some differences between the CSA and the broadcasters regarding the appropriate ratings have generated regular meetings between these 2 parties. When the CSA considers a rating to be particularly unsuitable it examines the programme in plenary session and addresses written opinions to the broadcasters concerned. Each broadcaster created a viewing committee to process and issue the rating. The rating process is different for each channel (*Conseil Supérieur de l'Audiovisuel* 1997, 15 décembre).

For France 2, an internal commission composed of channel staff holds a session every week. Experts appointed by the broadcaster make notes on the programmes to be broadcast. The internal commission examines the notes to establish classification. The different criteria, on the basis of which the notes are made, were established according to a study conducted by a specialist institution, mandated by the CSA to understand how violent images are perceived and what their impact on children might be (qualitative investigations that were made in schools generally by the teacher).

If there are any difficulties the Commission refers to other members of the channel. France 2 said it has tried to identify objective criteria based on extremely rigorous principles already in existence (conditions and circumstances of depiction of violence, identification with heroes, 'reading keys' of violence) in order to avoid subjective assessment.

For France 3, an internal commission is composed of 6 members (consider that freedom and responsibility of the broadcaster is in any case subject to delegation). The broadcasting time is not a variable that is taken into consideration for the rating; meaning that the same criteria are applied whatever the envisaged time schedule. The commission tries to take into account evolution of mentalities.

At TF1, an internal is commission composed of one representative per programming unit (approximately 10 members). The members are in charge of rating their own programmes. This is checked by 2 people, one of whom is the programming Director, who may give a favourable or unfavourable opinion (in most cases the opinion is favourable). If there is debate, arbitration is made at the level of the General Direction or the President.

At M6, there are 2 committees.[14] The first is a selection committee: external committee composed of mothers and young people (representative of the M6 audience) who watch every programme prior to taking the decision whether to buy it. This committee gives a qualitative assessment as well as an initial classification of the programme in category 1, 2, 3, or 4. The decision to buy the programme is made according to its quality and to the icon that will apply. The second committee is a screening committee: external committee composed solely of

[14] M6 was the first free-to-air channel to adopt a signalling system in 1989.

mothers (with children under 12 who watch a lot of TV) who watch the programmes a second time 4 to 5 weeks prior to broadcast (films, whether or not prohibited to under 12's, TV films, documentaries or magazines which could cause problems, as well as series that are broadcast in the first, second, or third part of the evening). This committee confirms or modifies the first assessment regarding the icon to be displayed.

The committees do not make the decision, but make proposals and provide arguments. The final decision is made by the Programming Director, or, if there is dispute, the Assistant General Director in Charge of Programmes, the General Director or the President.

Canal + follows the rating of the Film Classification Board when a film is broadcast. Occasionally Canal + rates a film more strictly. There is no screening commission as such. The person responsible for programming watches the programmes and may receive opinions from the various programming units. If a debate occurs, there is no arbitration as the stricter opinion prevails.

For films prohibited to under 12's there is no restrictive regulation applying to Canal+, which is broadcast in an encrypted form. But the decision has been taken not to broadcast them during times where parental control may not be exercised.

Arte is part of the Groupement Européen d'Interêt Economique (GEIE), the European Grouping of Economic Interests, that consists of a French company, La Sept, and all the German public broadcasters (ZDF + ARD stations). It is not specifically the broadcasters that rate the programmes but the content providers (who are mostly broadcasters themselves in their own country, except La Sept). So each broadcaster providing a programme to Arte must: (1) verify if the programme is adapted to a youth audience and (2) indicate to ARTE GEIE the ideal broadcasting time.

Nonetheless there is a commission, named the *Conference des programmes*, which deals with contentious issues and other programmes of ARTE. A member of this commission is responsible for the protection of minors, and is completely independent. They must be consulted if any doubts are raised regarding a programme.

The most important difference from other channels comes from the (international) Treaty creating Arte, which states clearly that Arte is not subject to any Government or administrative authority. This is why Arte does not apply the visual icons system.

Countrywide, new visual icon regime was adopted in 1998 and implemented by terrestrial broadcasters from September that year. It makes a clear distinction between unencrypted and encrypted channels. The differences between ratings for encrypted and unencrypted channels are outlined in Table 9. The rating system itself is depicted in Figure 2.

FIGURE 2
Signalling System
(Applicable to all broadcasters,
but only used at the moment by terrestrial broadcasters)

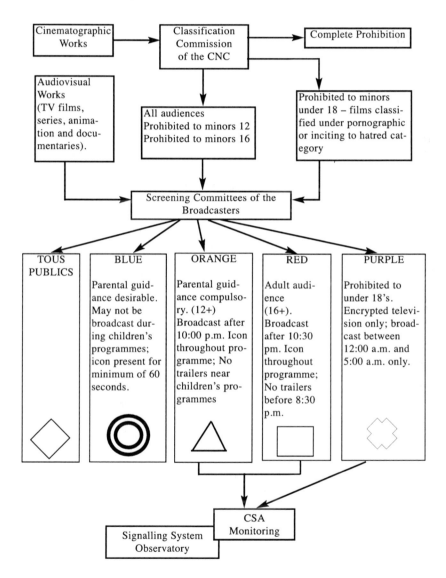

TABLE 9
The 1998 Rating System

Categories Symbol	Description	Unencrypted Programmes	Encrypted Channels
I Icon: Green circle with white diamond.	All viewers	No restrictions	No restrictions
II Icon: White circle with blue border.	Works containing scenes likely to harm young viewers. *Parental Guidance desirable*	Broadcasting time is left to discretion of the broadcaster, but work may not be broadcast during children's programmes. Particular attention to be paid to trailers for these works when broadcast near children's programmes.	Broadcasting time is left to the discretion of broadcaster, but must ensure that programmes dedicated to a youth audience and programmes and trailers broadcast immediately after said programmes not contain scenes likely to harm young viewers.
III Icon: Orange circle with white triangle.	Cinema works prohibited to under 12's, and TV works likely to disturb young viewers, notably when programme contains systematic or repeated psychological or physical violence. *Parental Guidance essential, prohibited to under 12's.*	To be broadcast after 10:00 p.m. Broadcast of such work may be possible before 10:00 p.m., if icon is displayed throughout. Such exceptions not permissible on Tuesdays, Fridays, and days preceding non-working days. These works may not be broadcast near children programmes.	Broadcasting time is left to the discretion of the broadcaster, but must ensure that programmes dedicated to a youth audience and programmes and trailers broadcast immediately after said programmes not contain scenes likely to harm young viewers.

TABLE 9 (continued)

Categories Symbol	Description	Unencrypted Programmes	Encrypted Channels
IV Icon: Red circle with white square.	Cinema works prohibited to under 16's, as well as TV works of erotic nature or depicting intense violence, likely to impair physical, mental or moral growth of under 16's. *Adult audience, prohibited to under 16's.*	To be broadcast after 10:30 p.m. Trailers for these works must not contain scenes likely to harm youth audience sensitivity, and may not be broadcast before 8:30 p.m.	May not be broadcast on the Wednesday before 8:30 p.m., on Saturday or Sunday morning. Trailers for works containing violent scenes or scenes likely to harm sensitivity of youth audience may no be broadcast during unencrypted part of programme schedules as well as on Wednesday before 8:30 p.m., on Saturday morning or Sunday morning.
V Purple circle with white cross.	Pornographic or extremely violent work, likely to seriously impair physical, mental or moral growth of minors Icon: Purple circle with white cross inside it.	Complete prohibition	May not be broadcast during the unencrypted part of the programme schedules. May not be broadcast either between 5:00 a.m. and 12:00 p.m.

On unencrypted channels, visual icons are shown throughout the duration of the trailer. For programmes with a category II rating, on an unencrypted channel, the visual icon is shown for a minimum of 60 seconds at the beginning of the programme or during the credits and at least 10 seconds after each break. The warning «parental guidance desirable» must be displayed for at least 10 seconds at the beginning of the programme or during credits.

For programmes with a category III rating, the visual icon is shown throughout the programme. The warning 'parental guidance essential', or where relevant, mention of the prohibition for under 12's, must appear for at least 10 seconds at the beginning of the programme or during the credits. Decree of 22 February 1990, Article 5, alinéa 2 states that in the case of a cinematographic work being broadcast by an audiovisual service, the audience must be informed of the certificate released by the film classification board, both during the broadcast and the trailers as well as in the TV guides.

For category IV, the visual icon should be shown throughout the programme. The warning 'adult audience', or where relevant, mention of the prohibition for under 16's must appear for at least 10 seconds at the beginning of the programme or during the credits.

Germany

The German system for television rating is composed of a combination of cinema ratings (FSK) based on age limits, observing watershed set by the legislation; voluntary ratings by a self-regulatory organisation, *Freiwillige Selbstkontrolle Fernsehen* (FSF) for private broadcasters (using the watershed) and controlled by the regional regulatory authorities; and a system of self-regulation for public service broadcasters also using the watershed.

There is consequently no unified approach. The system is also characterised by the importance of self-regulatory mechanisms. With the exception of the system used for cinema films, there is no 'individual rating system' as used in the US or in France. Researchers as well as broadcasters and regulators are not very keen on the idea of introducing visual or acoustic warnings. They fear the effect of the so-called 'forbidden fruit' towards minors, that is, that the minors would be made aware that they should not watch the programme and thus be enticed to watch this particular broadcast.

The FSF makes a judgement about content using legal standards of harmfulness. It recommends an appropriate broadcasting time depending on the age for which the programme is suitable and the likelihood of parents being present to watch with their children. The system is based on the opinions of the rating body (the examining board). However, the opinions of the rating body are based on certain principles for examination of broadcasts (*Prüfgrundsätze der FSF*), which have been developed by another organ of the FSF, the Committee (*Kuratorium*). These principles (especially §19 to §23) give guidance for scheduling broadcasting times. The principles also encompass a series of criteria aimed at helping the assessment of programmes (semideterministic). For example, children must not be made emotionally insecure, be frightened, or be disturbed because of a drastic depiction of violence or the blurring of reality and fiction. Broadcasts must not lead to social or ethical disorientation of children, for example, through the identification with violent characters or through the portrayal of strategies based on violence to resolve conflicts. These principles are mainly formulated for fictional programmes, which constitute the majority of the examined material.

The system is voluntary. Private broadcasters who are members of the FSF submit programmes if they have not been rated (by the FSK) or if they have any doubts regarding the validity of the rating.

Following a strong public debate about the increase in sex and violence on the screen, German private television channels decided to set up the FSF in November 1993 according to the model of the FSK for cinema. Their aim was to create a structure to render the necessity for stricter legal provisions useless and to stop or reduce the public discussion regarding the level of violence within their programmes. Several private broadcasters, such as (among others) Kabel 1, DSF, n-TV, Premiere, Pro Sieben, RTL, RTL 2, Sat1, and VOX, manage this organisation, established in April 1994. Its aim is to limit the portrayal of violence and sex on television to protect the moral, spiritual, and mental development of children and young persons over and beyond the limits set down by law.

This is expressed by Article 19 section 1 of its regulations for examination: 'the objective of the examination is to prevent the impairment or endangerment of minors, particularly ethical disorientation by means of television'. Public service broadcasters have refused to participate in the FSF thus far. They claim that the examination of programmes by an external organ would be a threat to their programme autonomy (French broadcasters claim the same). They are critical of the work of the FSF (Mohr 1998).

Private broadcasters submit all programmes that raise questions regarding the protection of minors to the FSF. Broadcasters submit broadcasts mostly in 2 cases. In the first case, films that are on the 'index' as, in order to broadcast them between 11:00 p.m. and 6:00 a.m., broadcasters need to put their justification in writing and to communicate it on request to the regulatory authority. In this case, they also communicate the FSF findings to the regulatory body.

In the second case, a request for exception to the watershed may be made. In this case, the regulatory authority will decide on the exception, but the FSF findings are communicated to the competent authority by the broadcasters as the basis of the request for exception.

The decision whether a programme shall be submitted or not is made by the Commissioners for the Protection of Young Persons, representing the private broadcasters. The commissioners have to send an application to the FSF stating the time the broadcaster intends to show the film. The examiners have then to decide whether the request may be accepted. They can also recommend a later time for transmission or suggest cuts to be made or advise the channel not to broadcast the programme at all. Their decision requires unanimity and they have to lay down their reasons in a report.

The reports are then sent to the channels and, on request, to the Committee and the *Landesmedienanstalten*. The decision can be appealed against to an Appeal Committee (*Berufungsausschuß*) that is composed of 7 particularly experienced examiners. The Appeal Committee decides by simple majority. The Committee or the regulatory bodies can call on the Appeal Committee if a decision is to be revised.

In special cases, the FSF committee can be directly called on to revise the Appeal Committee's decision. Examinations take place almost every day. An examining board decides on about approximately 3 films per day. In the case of a broadcaster's request for an exception to the watershed, FSF recommendations are communicated to the competent regulatory authority, which can refuse them. However, the authorities have to take them into account in their decision as stipulated by the Agreement on Broadcasting.

In addition, members of the FSF Committee and the regional regulatory bodies are entitled to submit programmes for review. The FSF is required to pass on complaints that it receives from the public about any programmes on the air to the Committee for review. The FSF monitors programmes on television every three months to check whether any films or series should have been submitted to them.

The recommendations of the FSF are not binding. Nonetheless, the FSF has two sanctions at its disposal in the case of non-application of their decision. The first one is the ability to oblige the broadcaster to broadcast their findings. This is considered as a most efficient threat, as private broadcasters fear bad publicity. However, the sanction is never enforced in practice.

The second sanction is exclusion from the FSF. This sanction is not really practicable, especially when it concerns an important broadcaster that is paying a considerable membership fee to the FSF. As to the enforcement of FSF decisions, there is no specific institutional structure to check whether they are followed or not by broadcasters. However, in practice, the FSF operates an internal control of the application of their decisions by broadcasters.

The FSF is composed of three organs. The first organ is the *Vorstand* (Executive board). Members of the executive board are representatives of private television channels. They are responsible for the rules and finances of the FSF but do not have any influence on the examinations. The second organ is the *Prüfungsausschuß* (Examining boards), which assess programmes on a voluntary basis prior to their transmission in order to establish whether they are potentially harmful to minors. More precisely, an examining committee composed of three persons examines broadcasts. At the moment, there are about 70 examiners who work in various areas of media education. They do not work full time for the FSF. About half of the examiners also belong to the committees of the FSK and the BPjS.[15]

The third organ is the *Kuratorium* (Committee), which is composed of media scientists; media critics; people working in the field of protection of minors; the

---

[15] If either the cinema or video version of a film submitted to the FSF is on the 'index', and if it is to be decided whether the film can be broadcast after 11:00 p.m. or 12:00 p.m. or not at all, then a member of the BPjS has to be on the examining board.

standing representative of the Supreme Federal Youth Authorities at the FSK; the chairperson of the national examination board for publications potentially harmful to minors (BPjS); 11 neutral persons; and 4 representatives from the television channels. The regional regulatory authorities have chosen not to be represented within the Committee even if they were able. The tasks of the Committee are wide-ranging. The Committee has developed the FSF examination regulations, which regulate almost all the examination procedures, as well as criteria for assessing programmes. The Committee is also responsible for selecting examiners.

In 3 years (from April 94 to 31 March 1997) an average of 55 cases per month were dealt with. Since its creation in 1993 and till 1997, 1975 programmes have been examined, mainly series, TV-films, and fiction. 762 requests were refused. Since members of examining boards do not work full time for the FSF, their availability to examine programmes depends on their respective employers. Consequently, flexibility is a necessary requirement when considering possible appointments for the examining boards. The FSF does not examine advertisements.

Greece

Greece has no history of ratings or warnings concerning content on television. It therefore has no more detailed or stricter rules than those of European Commission Law concerning content harmful to minors do.

Following viewers' complaints, some private TV channels (that is, Sky TV and Star TV) have in recent years introduced an acoustic warning for programmes containing violent or pornographic scenes which are shown during peak times. The acoustic warning is not accompanied by a visual indication of ratings before the programme is broadcast. The acoustic warning is not the norm and has certainly not established a pattern in the Greek broadcasting scene.

In line with Article 22 of the *Television Without Frontiers Directive*, Law 2328/95 provides for programmes that could harm to a limited extent (and not seriously) the physical, mental, or moral development of minors to be allowed after 9:30 p.m. (less harmful) and after 12:00 a.m. (more harmful).

Ireland

At present the 2 main bodies responsible for the regulation of content in Ireland on TV are the RTE Authority, established in 1960, and the Independent Radio and Television Commission (IRTC), established in 1988. The IRTC is to be restructured and its role expanded under new legislation currently being drafted.

Although there is a range of statutory obligations, which broadcasters must respect, the ratings system (to the extent that it exists) could be described as voluntary. Statute and codes of practice govern advertising, all of which is vetted beforehand. Advertising which would be likely to breach either statute law or provisions of the code of practice is not accepted.

For example, the refusal of RTE and the IRTC to broadcast, in accordance with legislation, an advertisement for a religious event, was upheld by the Supreme Court earlier this year. Outside of television controls, advertising generally is governed by the Advertising Standards Authority of Ireland (ASAI), which monitors and regulates advertising in all media. Its members are the advertising agencies, and an annual levy is imposed, as are sanctions for breach of standards.

The system most used by the national public service broadcaster (the first national commercial television station only began broadcasting in September 1998) is simply not to select offensive or objectionable material in the first place. The requirements and responsibilities imposed in broadcasting legislation, along with its references to the national culture, demand that this be so.

Films and soaps, for example, are vetted well in advance. Where films or programmes contain violent or explicit sexual scenes or strong language verbal warnings are given beforehand or the strong language is bleeped out. Generally, however, the national public service broadcaster and, thus far, also the commercial sector simply choose suitable programming, conscious of the national psyche and moral and religious feelings.

The ratings system could be said to be descriptive and nondeterministic. It is simply indicated at the beginning of a programme that it contains explicit sexual scenes, sometimes harrowing scenes that some people might find upsetting, or that it contains strong language. It may be stated that it is not suitable for children but no age category is indicated.

Italy

In Italy, until 1990, the law did not provide for any content-related regulation directed at \—broadcasters, and the only specific provision was Article 13 of Law 161/1962, establishing the prohibition of broadcasting films which were denied a certificate or which were certified as unsuitable for minors under the age of 18. Law 223/1990 was the first to introduce a set of rules to be implemented by all broadcasters in compliance with the EC Directive 89/552/EEC. The law, in particular, provided a system of watersheds to protect minors from harmful or unsuitable films and programmes.

Section 10 of Article 15 of the Law 223/1990 deals with general programming and reads that broadcasters must not show programmes 'which harm the psychological and moral development of children, contain gratuitous violence or pornography, or induce racial, sexual, religious, or national intolerance'. Commentators argued that this provision is more strict than the one formulated in the European Commission Directive. Sections 11, 12, and 13 of the same Article deal with minors and the broadcasting of motion pictures. Section 11 reads that 'it is prohibited to broadcast any motion pictures, which have been denied a certificate or have been certified as unsuitable for minors under the age of 18'. Section 13 states that films that have been certified by the censorship committee as unsuitable for minors under the age of 14 can be broadcast only within a strict time period (between 10:30 p.m. and 7:00 a.m.).

Law 327/1991 implements in Italy the European Convention on Transfrontier Television. It states that the latter's provisions have to be applied to every programme broadcast or re-broadcast either by a terrestrial, cable, or satellite broadcaster. Article 5 sets forth that every transmitting party has to ensure that all programmes are compatible with the Convention's provisions. In particular, Article 7 reads that all programmes must be respectful of human dignity and fundamental rights. Moreover, these programmes cannot: (1) be against decency; (2) have a pornographic content; or (3) excite violence or promote racial hatred.

Furthermore, any programmes likely to prejudice children and adolescents' physical, psychological, and moral development cannot be broadcast when, given the time of performance, children are likely to watch them. Finally, with Law 451/1997, the Parliament instituted several authorities to safeguard children: a Parliamentary Commission for Minors, a National Centre for Minors, and The Fininvest—Mediaset Group.

The Parliamentary Commission's responsibility is to monitor and control the implementation of existing regulations concerning minors' protection. In particular, the Commission is entitled to request any information, data, or documents from any person or entity dealing with minors' rights or development. On the basis of the material collected, the Commission refers to the Parliament, at least once a year, the results of its activity, advising on and proposing supplementary provisions and modifications to the regulations in force, if necessary.

The National Centre for Minors operates within the Prime Minister's Office. Its responsibility is to prepare a plan concerning any measures necessary to protect minors' rights and development.

The Fininvest—Mediaset Group, in compliance with the Federation of Radio Television Commercial Broadcasters (FRT) code of conduct, introduced a labelling system with icons on its networks to guide parents in the monitoring of programmes suitable for minors. It is difficult to assess whether the icons are followed by viewers or not—particularly given the limited audience information available so far. However, their presence at the beginning of programmes offers parents additional content information and may draw needed attention.

The Code also states that the members of FRT are committed to broadcasting programmes inspired by positive civil and human values, respecting individual dignity, guaranteeing that these programmes do not contain scenes which might be disturbing to children and avoiding television or cinema trailers and promotional sequences unsuitable for children. Members are also committed to a ban on advertising of any products whose use might be harmful or dangerous for minors, such as drugs or tobacco products, during a protected slot (from 4 p.m. to 7:00 p.m.) or during any programme for children. Advertisements or trailers shown in the protected slot must, in all cases be free from any scenes which might be disturbing for children and young teenagers. Members are also committed to preventing the showing of any content, which contradicts the values of respect for human dignity, during the 15 minutes immediately before and after programmes dedicated to younger viewers.

Observance of the Code is guaranteed by a committee, set up by the signatory broadcasters and associations, and made up of six representatives from each group. The Committee examines any reported infringements of the Code, and promotes and organises outreach programmes aimed at raising critical awareness of the television message on the part of parents, teachers, and educationalists.

In addition, in January 1994, Canale Cinque implemented a colour coding system. Since 16 February 1997, Italiana Uno and Retequattro have joined in Canale Cinque's colour coding scheme, using the same classification criteria and the same graphic symbols.

The so-called 'traffic light' system is represented by 3 symbols as displayed in Table 10. As far as broadcasting of films is concerned, the rating granted for cinema viewing applies. Television films and fictional programmes that, given the violent or sexual content, may significantly impair minors are subject to Law 203 of 30 May 1995, which states that producers, distributors, and broadcasters who intend to transmit them during the daytime must apply to the censorship committee in order to obtain a certificate to do so.

TABLE 10
Canale Cinque Visual Icon System (icons approximated)

Rating	Indicator	
Not suitable for children		(A child is represented in a red circle)
Parental Guidance Advisable		(A child and an adult are represented in a yellow circle)
Suitable for all		(A child is represented in a green circle)

It is worth noting that, to date, this provision has not yet entered into force, because of the delay in appointing the competent sections that will operate within the censorship committee. These sections will have the same composition and duties as the censorship sections that review films for cinema presentation.

Law 249/1997 entrusts the Authority of Communications with powers (a) to monitor compliance with laws relating to advertising, including the enactment of specific regulations governing subject matter; (b) to guarantee that provisions concerning minors' protection are observed (in this case, the Authority must consider the provisions set forth by the existing self-regulatory codes and the opinion held by the parliamentary commission entrusted to monitor broadcasting services); and (c) to consider advice and initiatives from the new *Consiglio Nazionale degli Utenti* (CNU), a committee operating within the Communications Authority. The latter is composed of experts appointed by associations representative of different consumer categories. According to the law, these experts have to be specifically qualified in the legal, sociological, psychological or educational field and should be distinguished in the field of promotion of rights and dignity of individuals and needs of minors. It is worth noting that this Consiglio is entitled not only to advise but also to propose initiatives related to broadcasting.

The Code of Conduct adopted in 1997 sets forth an evaluative and mainly nondeterministic rating system. It states that although broadcasting of fictional programmes and films has to comply with all existing laws and regulations, it must also comply with self-rating guidelines established by each broadcaster in order to evaluate whether a film or a programme is deemed suitable for the physical and psychological safety of minors. According to the Code, each broadcaster must entrust a supervisory committee to operate within its networks. Each committee will guarantee the broadcaster's implementation of all existing rules and will provide the broadcaster with a set of guidelines necessary to carry out the required evaluation of films and programmes. To date, however, the signatories have not appointed their internal committees. The delay is partly due to concerns about the guidelines' content, which each broadcaster will have to adopt in order to comply with the Code's provisions.

In general, bills on rating systems make reference exclusively to terrestrial operators, broadcasting general programmes.

Several proposals exist. According to the 'Proposal in favour of friendship between children and TV', a self-regulatory Committee should be instituted, the tasks of which should be the following: (1) to advise the Communications Authority with reference to the implementation of a set of guidelines concerning visual symbols to be enacted by any broadcaster; (2) to monitor broadcasters' activity; (3) to apply appropriate penalties to broadcasters; and (4) to publicly disclose the applied penalties. As far as monitoring of broadcasters is concerned, the Committee should be entitled to carry out investigation of them when: (1) they do not use visual symbols concerning the suitability of the programmes broadcast; (2) symbols are utilised irregularly or not sufficiently; (3) television advertisements do not comply with standards concerning their suitability for minors; or (4) programs not suitable for minors are broadcast during a prohibited time period.

According to a Bill drafted in 1996 by Senator Salvato, a committee of Guarantors should be instituted, operating within the Office of the Prime Minister. The committee should be competent in the following matters: (1) verify that TV programs do not prejudice moral or physical development of minors, suggesting or inducing them to intolerance and discrimination based on race, sex, religion, or nationality; (2) promote studies and research; (3) identify time period suitable for minors under the age of 16; (4) prohibit during that time period broadcasting of unsuitable programs; and (5) apply penalties to broadcasters that infringe orders.

Bill 115 of 21 April 1994 concerning programs suitable for minors, stated that prior content censorship should be applied to broadcasters in order to protect minors from images, messages, and language inducing or suggesting violent conduct.

Luxembourg

In Luxembourg, the public authorities are in favour of a self-regulatory regime. Regulatory measures may invite broadcasters to adopt a visual icons system without mandating what this obligation may contain.

Provisions of the new *Television Without Frontiers Directive* have not yet been incorporated into domestic law. Debate, at this stage, seems to favour a flexible formula, which would aim to take up the provisions of Article 22. The actual trend is to allow broadcasters to organise their own signalling system. The choice between an acoustic warning and visual icons is left to the discretion of the broadcasters. Nevertheless, the *Conseil national des programmes* (CNP), in the case of *'Die heilige Hure'* (Cf. point V for the Opinion of the CNP) has expressed its preference for the French system.

In addition, the CNP salutes 'the fact that in France trailers for the works must not contain scenes likely to harm the sensitivity of the youth audience', whereas on RTL these kind of films are 'publicised throughout the day by means of advertising slots, which awaken the curiosity of a child and youth audience to whom they are not directed'.

The Netherlands

In 1983, the following was added to Article 7 of the Dutch Constitution: 'Rules concerning radio and television shall be laid down by Act of Parliament. There shall be no prior supervision of the content of a radio or television broadcast'.

In 1985, a proposition was made for a Media Act, which was implemented in 1987. The *Commissariaat voor de Media* (CvdM) became the executive institution responsible for monitoring compliance with the Act by the public and commercial broadcasters of television or radio. In 1989 the European directive, 'Television without Frontiers' appeared, and in 1991 the Media Act was amended. In a press release of 13 February 1998, the Dutch Ministry of Education, Culture, and Sports announced that the European directive would be incorporated into Dutch legislation.

The CvdM's other tasks are to stimulate discussion, coordination and cooperation between those organisations, which the Media Act has made responsible for the programmes of national broadcasters and business (Article 9a), to provide the responsible Minister with relevant information (Article 9b), as well as with an annual report (Article 9c).

The CvdM consists of 1 president and 2 to 4 other members, who are appointed and discharged by Royal Decree and by nomination of the responsible Minister. The appointment is for a period of five years and it is not possible to be reappointed. All decisions are made by a majority of votes. The Minister approves the budget and the annual financial balance.

The Media Act provides the formal regulatory framework within which the CvdM regulates the content of Dutch radio and television. The Act does not address the issue of human dignity, and there are only two Articles concerning the protection of minors. The first, Article 52a, paragraph 2b, states that the broadcasting of programmes for children younger than 13 years of age may not be sponsored. The second, Article 53, applies to all licensed television broadcasters, and deals with the time of broadcasting of films (or parts of films). The Article states that films that have been rated by the NF—Dutch Board of Film Classification (See Cinema section)—for an audience over 12 years of age may not be shown before 8:00 p.m. and that films which have been classified '16 and over' may not be broadcast before 10:00 p.m. Furthermore, the age classification must be announced before broadcasting. A classification given by the NFK is binding.

The CvdM takes the view that, where there are unclassified parts of a film that has been rated by the NFK, the overall rating should apply. Should a broadcaster wish to show these parts at an earlier time than the classification permits, it should have them classified by the NFK. The CvdM holds that it will be possible for broadcasters to have unclassified parts rated or old films re-classified.

Though it has been suggested that Article 53 could be interpreted as permitting an unclassified violent part of a film, which has an overall classification, to be broadcast at an earlier time than allowed by the Article for the whole picture, this is contrary to the intention of the legislator. Such an interpretation is also not in accordance with the NFK's understanding: that classification of a film applies to the whole film and individual scenes must be seen in the context of the film. In addition, the CvdM takes the view that the provisions of Article 53, with regard to broadcasting times, leave no leeway to make exceptions for other programmes, such as news programmes or even film review programmes showing extracts from films.

The question is raised, when monitoring compliance with the Article by these kinds of programmes, as to whether the object of protecting minors is more important than freedom of the press (*Commissariaat voor de Media* 1996: 3). In fact, the Article may be viewed as contradicting Article 7, paragraph 2 of the Constitution, which concerns freedom of speech, and which forbids prior inspection of radio and television programmes. There has not been a legal review of this conflict, probably because it has not yet been enforced.

Article 53 applies in the same way for films, film clips, or other programme parts (for example, film quizzes, and television advertising), which are not rated by the Board and which the broadcasting organisation thinks are not appropriate for viewers younger than 12 or 16 respectively. The broadcasters themselves may decide whether the rest of their programmes are appropriate or not. Every year the Media Authority examines the broadcasting times of unclassified parts of films and other programmes and reports on them in the Annual Report (*Commissariaat voor de Media* 1996: 4).

Although the broadcast organisations are not obliged to, they are requested by the CvdM to announce the age classification before broadcasting a film, whether classified by the NFK or the broadcast organisation itself. The public broadcasters comply with this request.

Article 53 of the Media Act is part of a section that applies to the public broadcasters, but its requirements are extended to commercial broadcasters by Article 71g, paragraph 1. Article 73, paragraph 2 states that if a pay-TV programme shows films or parts of films classified as '12 and over' or '16 and over', the broadcaster must announce the classification before the showing (*Commissariaat voor de Media* 1996: 2).

In letters of 21 December 1995, the CvdM called on all Dutch broadcasting stations to comply with Article 53 of the Media Act. The letters stated that the CvdM would take 'appropriate measures', should broadcasters not comply with the regulation. Article 135, paragraph 1 of the Media Law states that the CvdM can impose an administrative sanction (a fine of up to 50,000 guilders) if a broadcaster does not comply (*Raad voor het Jeugdbeleid* 1996).

The CvdM have examined how the public and commercial broadcasters comply with their responsibilities for rating films and other programmes, as well as the decision on broadcasting times, and reported its findings. In its conclusions, the Authority stated that most Dutch public broadcasters comply correctly with their responsibilities. However, they found that, as far as the Dutch commercial broadcast organisations were concerned, there is not sufficient compliance. Furthermore, the report indicated that 2 commercial broadcasters and a Dutch Music Channel needed serious interference with their programming policy to comply with their responsibility (*Commissariaat voor de Media* 1997: 13).

In May 1995, the Under-Secretary for Culture wrote a letter asking a representative of the public broadcasters, the *Nederlandse Omroepstichting* (NOS), to reflect on measures to prevent harmful effects from violent programmes. The overriding opinion is that parents/guardians are responsible for the protection of their children against television violence; however, the Under-Secretary suggested the addition of programme guides containing information on the violent content of programmes. In its response, the NOS stated that public broadcasters are well aware that violent programmes may damage children, but they took the view that the increase of violent programmes is due to the commercialisation of television. The NOS reject the proposal for information about violence in programme guides, due to the subjective nature of such information, but promise to keep the issue constantly in mind (*Raad voor het Jeugdbeleid* 1996). In the meantime according to the CvdM, the public broadcasters are prepared to publicise the film's classification in the programme guides and on teletext services (*Commissariaat voor de Media* 1996: 5).

The blueprint, '*Niet voor alle Leeftijden*', prepared by the Ministry of Public Health, Welfare, and Sports, states that the State Secretary of Education, Culture, and Science is deliberating with the NOS and the Vereniging voor Satelliet, Televisie, radio programma Aanbieders (VESTRA), the organisation representing commercial broadcasters, on a self-regulatory system to enable the implementation of the European Directive (Notitie 1997: 23). It is probable that *Nederlands Instituut Classificatie Audiovisule Media* (NICAM), the Dutch Institute for Classification of Audiovisual Media, will be set up. The Act on Film Exhibition would then be substituted by a system of self-regulation.

As far as advertising is concerned there is no specific legal framework but a self-regulatory system provides some rules. The *Stichting Reclame Code* (SRC) (Foundation Advertising Code) is an organisation representing all parties involved: broadcasters, newspaper organisations, advertising agencies, and so on. It is the SRC's objective to ensure responsible advertising, and to achieve this it has drawn up an Advertising Code. This Code, together with a number of special codes for particular product types sets out the conditions to which advertising must adhere (*Raad voor het Jeugdbeleid* 1996).

If an individual is of the opinion that a certain advertisement does not comply with the code, he or she can report a complaint by writing to the SRC. If it finds that the complaint is justified, the SRC will recommend that the advertisement in question not be used again. Because all organisations involved in any way in advertising are represented in the SRC, and most of them adhere to the Code, an advertisement or campaign will effectively be banned as a result of such a recommendation.

The sections in the Code concerning the protection of human dignity and minors are Sections 2, 3, 4, 13.1, and 13,2 Idem. Section 2 states, 'Advertising must be in accordance with the law, truth, good taste, and decency.' Section 3 states, 'Advertising may not be contrary to the public interest, public order, or good manners.' Section 4 states, 'Advertising may not be gratuitously offensive, or entail a threat to mental and/or physical public health.' Section 13.1 states, 'Advertising that is evidently aimed (partly or totally) at minors, should not contain elements in word, sound, or image, that may harm minors in any way, or by which advantage is taken of their inexperience or naivety.' Section 13.2 states,

> Television advertising may not cause minors moral or physical damage and must, for their protection, therefore meet the following conditions: (a) it may not directly stimulate minors to purchase a certain product by taking advantage of their inexperience or naivety; (b) it may not directly stimulate minors to persuade their parents or others to purchase advertised products; (c) it may not take advantage of the special trust that minors have in parents, teachers or others; and (d) it may not, without good reason, show minors in dangerous situations.

Portugal

Prior to the 1974 revolution in Portugal, there was no need for a rating system since the sole broadcasting operator, RTP, had its own in-house censors who decided what could and could not be broadcast. The growth of more diverse programming after 1974 brought about the introduction of a simple warning symbol, '0', and a verbal warning before the showing of violent, shocking, or pornographic programmes. There was also an understanding that 'daring' material could be broadcast late at night with a permanent warning symbol.

RTP had sole responsibility for the use of these warnings and the watershed. Even the official cinema classification did not enforce a warning, but operated as a guideline. However, as RTP remained under the close scrutiny of the government there was no need for detailed external rules or legislation regarding content.

Legislation introduced in 1990 and 1998 placed restrictions on the broadcasting of violent, shocking, or pornographic material, but has not attempted so far to define these concepts and no regulatory body has had the will or resources to enforce the legislation.[16] The entry of private operators into the market increased the violent and shocking content of overall television output as all broadcasting companies fiercely fought for audiences.

Having no means to diminish the levels of violent material in the broadcasting system, the regulatory body, *Alta Autoridade para a Comunicação Social, Direcção Geral da Comunicação Socialólater Instituto da Comunicação Social* decided to promote an agreement between the 3 operators about the representation of violence on television. The agreement, signed on 9 July 1997, states that in view of their social role, constitutional and legal obligations, television operators have decided to take certain measures concerning the representation of violence.

They decided that broadcasters shall identify programmes that are not suitable for sensitive elements of the public with a common symbol to enable the public to make informed choices. Broadcasters shall inform viewers about the common symbol in the press releases they provide to television magazines as well as in advertisements/announcements about the forthcoming programmes requiring such a symbol. Broadcasters shall prepare 2 promotional slots for violent series or films—one with no violent images to promote the film or series before 10:00 p.m. and another one with material acceptable for the period after 10:00 p.m. Both slots should include the symbol identifying its characteristics.

In addition, they decided that, broadcasters should declare they will pay particular attention to promoting, on the air or by other means, programmes for children and young people in order to keep parents and educators adequately informed. Apart from fiction and entertainment, the agreement looks at factual programmes. At this level, broadcasters state that the journalistic representation of violence will follow ethical rules and will not explore pain, morbid feelings, or sensationalism

The presence of a visual symbol '0' throughout the duration of a programme denotes violent/shocking content. Such material should be broadcast after 10:00 p.m., and is accompanied by verbal warnings.

---

[16] The first Television Act (Law 58/90), Article 17 deals with forbidden programmes. It states that pornographic and obscene programmes are prohibited. It is also forbidden to broadcast programmes which may encourage violence, crime, or which generally violate the fundamental rights, freedoms and civil rights provided by the Portuguese Constitution. Under the same Article, any programme that might shock sensitive individuals and minors must be broadcast after 10:00 p.m.. All violent/shocking content must be accompanied by verbal warnings and a '0' symbol. The current television law (31-A/98 which revokes law 58/90) has not introduced important changes at this level.

Spain

In Spain, though TVE, the national public service broadcaster, applied an age-based rating system from 1963 until the mid-1980s for sexually explicit films, it was considered to be too strict, and a product of old values and the spirit of censorship prevalent during the Franco regime. For this reason some Spanish broadcasters are resistant to the idea of rating, anticipating negative public reaction.

However, others, such as *Antena Tres*, and consumer associations, such as *Confederación Española de Asociaciones de Amas de Casa, consumidores y Usuarios* (CEACCU [Spanish Alliance of Housewife Associations, Consumers, and Users]), *Agrupación de Telespectadores y Radioyentes* (ATR [Television Watchers and Radio Listeners Group]) and *Asociación Usuarios de Comunicación* (AUC [Association of Users of Mass Communications]) consider that many parents would welcome some kind of guidance as to whether programmes are suitable for their children. They argue that visual warnings are not censorship following these warnings is not compulsory for the parents, but just a useful tool.

Article 17.2 of Law 25/1994 states that programmes that may be harmful to the physical, mental, or moral development of minors and any that include pornographic scenes or gratuitous violence, shall include both visual and acoustic warnings about their contents. Broadcasters may simply provide a warning, but they can also provide ratings, which give parents more information about the kind of programme broadcast. However, in practice only a few broadcasters provide warnings or ratings, and no sanction proceedings have been brought against television broadcasters for the infringement of legal provisions related to warnings. The broadcasters that do provide any warnings or ratings are mainly TVE, *Canal Plus*, and the digital satellite television platforms, *Vía Digital* and *Canal Satélite Digital*. *Antena Tres* is currently studying the implementation of a warning and rating system that will soon come into operation.

The same Article states that the slots dedicated to trailers of programmes that may be harmful to the physical, mental, or moral development of minors or, in any case, all those that include pornographic scenes or gratuitous violence, must include both visual and acoustic warnings about their content. However, in practice neither warnings nor rating systems used by broadcasters have been applied to advertisements.

TVE classifies some of its programmes (mainly films, but sometimes also television series, sitcoms, and so on) according to an evaluative, nondeterministic rating system, based on age groups that are very similar to those used for the rating of films. There are only some minor changes: for example, instead of using a '-13' age group, TVE uses '-12'. The ratings appear at the beginning of the programme, and after the advertising breaks.

Canal Plus uses an evaluative, nondeterministic rating system to rate its films, based on the same age groups used by the CCPC. The age groups are identified by means of coloured keys: green key=for the public in general; blue key=13; orange key=18; and violet key='X' rated films. These keys appear before films are broadcast, as well as on *Canal Plus* teletext and in the magazine sent by Canal Plus to its subscribers.

Vía Digital classifies all the programmes provided by this satellite digital TV platform. It uses a nondeterministic rating system, based on 2 rating criteria: an evaluative criterion, based on age groups: (all members of public, -14, -18) and a descriptive criterion (documentaries, sports, series, sex, and so on). The rating information appears at any time by pressing one of the remote control buttons. The rating information is also included in the printed TV guide sent to customers.

Canal Satélite Digital uses a descriptive, nondeterministic system, which differentiates between different content categories: documentaries, films, series, information, sport, and so on. In each of these categories, there are subcategories. For example. in films there are subcategories such as drama, comedy, horror, musical, science fiction, or 'X' rated films. There is a category called 'various', which is used for programmes that do not fall easily into a specific group, and also for programmes which have not been specifically classified. The rating information available, as well as some explanation of the programme's content, can be made to appear on the screen at any time by pressing one of the remote control buttons. The ratings are also included in the printed TV guide sent to customers.

According to Article 6 of Catalan Decree 265/1997, Catalan Cable TV operators must use visual warnings (a red triangle for programmes which may harm the sensitivity of minors due to their physical or psychological violence or eroticism; 2 red triangles for programmes which may harm the sensitivity of minors, due to their pornographic nature or gratuitous violence). The warnings must be shown during the first five minutes of those programmes that include violent or sexually explicit scenes. Cable TV operators will start to provide their services in Catalonia soon.

It is relatively easy to classify programmes according to the most commonly used rating system (age groups), especially when taking into account the fact that films and videos have already been rated by the CCPC. However, there has been a dramatic increase in the production of television programmes, and it is difficult to foresee how this system may be applied to the volume of future production. The feasibility of applying this system (or more complex and useful ones, such as those used by digital platforms, which also include a description of the content of the labelled programme) will depend on the determination of whoever is responsible for rating the programmes: digital platform operators or the producers of the programmes broadcast by the platform.

Sweden

In Sweden, the legislation for television was developed in a similar way to that for radio; that is, in a contract with the state the public service broadcaster *Sveriges Television* (SVT), was mandated to meet certain standards for the content of programmes. The major principle applied to the relationship between the company and the state then, and to a certain extent today, is called 'regulated independence'.

During the period 1986–1996, Swedish legislation was amended to accommodate satellite and commercial private television in addition to public broadcasting services. The amended legislation enabled cable networks to distribute different television channels transmitted by satellite. Commercial broadcasters were allowed to relay terrestrial-based transmissions on condition that they agreed to satisfy certain standards relating to content.

The Radio and Television Law, which came into force at the beginning of 1997, replaces several previous laws, which regulated terrestrial, cable, and satellite broadcasting. The Radio and Television Law contains regulations on, *inter alia*, permits and registration, certain general standards relating to content for different forms of broadcasting, advertisements and sponsoring, as well as examination and supervision. The law also regulates the standards applying to companies broadcasting by permission of the Government.

All terrestrial channels require a permit from the Government to broadcast; currently only 2 companies (SVT and TV4) have such a permit. SVT broadcasts on 2 channels and TV4 on 1 channel. The conditions for receiving a permit stipulate that the company must exercise their broadcasting rights in an impartial and objective manner. Furthermore, the broad principles of freedom of expression and freedom of information shall apply to television. In addition, the company shall take into account the specific influence of television in making decisions on the subjects and type of programmes it broadcasts, as well as in determining the times of broadcast. This refers, *inter alia,* to the need for caution in the production of programmes as regards violence, sex, and drugs or subject-matter, which appears to be discriminatory against people of a certain gender or ethnic background. These conditions for a permit are obligatory.

The regulations of the Radio and Television Law also apply to television companies based in, and broadcasting to, Sweden from satellite. In addition, these companies must register their activities with the *Radio och TV-verket*, the Department of Radio and Television. Television companies and cable network operators make their own decisions as to the programmes they broadcast and the broadcast times. They do so on the basis of the Radio and Television Law, the regulations in the conditions for permits (where applicable), as well as the practice of the *Granskningsnämnden*, the Swedish Broadcasting Commission.

Chapter 6, paragraph 2 of the Radio and Television Law states: 'Programmes with protracted and realistic depictions of violence or with pornographic pictures may not be broadcast on television at such a time or in such a manner that entails a significant risk that children will see the programmes, unless this is justified in view of the particular circumstances.' In practice, the rules oblige companies to schedule programmes after 9:00 p.m., when the content might frighten or agitate children. A warning may also be given directly before the programme is broadcast. In certain cases, companies use the age categorisation, which *Statens biografbyrå* applies to films shown in cinemas in Sweden.

When the content of television programmes might be seen as violent or in any other way objectionable to the public or certain portions of the public, in general an oral warning is given at the same time as programme announcements. This system has been used since the early days of Swedish television.

The Granskningsnämnd also regulates television stations in retrospect. If they violate the aforementioned law, the *Granskningsnämnd* publicises its ruling. It can also, in certain cases, oblige the companies to publicise its decision. as well as apply to the court for a judgement on a particular fine or penalty.

At present, changes to the existing control and regulation system for television broadcasts are not being widely discussed, although some attention is being given to the question of the Swedish prohibition on advertising directed at children under the age of 12. The current discussion regarding digital TV focuses mainly on questions of terrestrial versus satellite broadcasting, access to frequencies, the distribution of permits and technical standards. No special juridical treatment of digital TV has so far been developed.

It is likely, however, that the Swedish public would not approve of a visual symbol being displayed on screen during the entire broadcast of a film. On the other hand, the Swedish public might accept an acoustic warning followed by a notice about, for example, an age limit.

United Kingdom

Statutory control resides with the Independent Television Commission (ITC), and each programme licensee has to comply with its code requirements. Under its powers, derived from the Broadcasting Acts of 1990 and 1996, the ITC issues licences that allow commercial television companies to broadcast in and from the United Kingdom—whether conventional aerials, cable, or satellite receive the services; and whether it is delivered by analogue or digital means. These licences vary according to the type of service, but they all set out conditions on matters such as standards of programmes and advertising.

The ITC also regulates these services by monitoring broadcasters' performance against the requirements of the ITC's published licences and codes and guidelines on programme content, advertising and sponsorship, and technical performance. There is a range of penalties for failure to comply with them.

The ITC also has a duty to ensure that a wide range of television services is available throughout the United Kingdom and that, taken as a whole, these are of a high quality and appeal to a range of tastes and interests; it has a duty to ensure fair and effective competition in the provision of these services; and it investigates complaints and regularly publishes its findings.

The Board of Governors of the BBC is responsible for ensuring that BBC programme makers observe the Producers' Guidelines. The Governors review the content of the Producers' Guidelines annually and revise them as necessary. In addition, they regularly monitor the BBC's compliance with the Guidelines, with a formal review taking place twice a year.

Furthermore, the Broadcasting Standards Commission (BSC) members (appointed by the Secretary of State for Culture, Media, and Sport) will consider complaints about violence, sexual conduct, or a matter of taste and decency. In reaching a decision, the Commission's code of practice and research into public attitudes are considered with the material and its context. Complaints must be made in writing and need to be made within 2 months of a television broadcast.

The watershed has been in use in the United Kingdom by terrestrial broadcasters for nearly 30 years. It is set between 9:00 p.m. and 5:30 a.m., and within that period there are progressive gradations in programme content. Most cable and licensed satellite services operate with the standard 9:00 p.m.–5:30 a.m. watershed, with the exception of specially encrypted services with restricted availability to children, which have 2 watersheds: 1 at 8:00 p.m. (equivalent to the 9:00 p.m. change on other channels) and another at 10:00 p.m. when material of a more adult nature may be shown. Other cable and licensed satellite services are expected to follow similar standards to the terrestrial channels.

However, although British TV has a 'watershed' hour of 9:00 p.m. for material not considered suitable for children, almost all children over 11 watch after that time. 60 percent of those over 5 watch after 9:00 p.m. during the week, and 80 percent do so at weekends. Almost 83 percent of 13 and 14 year-olds (and 60 percent of all children) have TVs in their bedrooms. 62 percent watch TV before school every day. One in 4 children owns a VCR and uses it to tape late-night 'X-rated' programmes (in 1994, only 14 percent owned VCRs.). Boys aged 7 and 8 are the most likely to engage in illicit taping (ChildWise Monitor 1998).

The ITC believes pay-per-view services give subscribers greater choice over what is available to view in the home. Given their stricter security systems (PIN Code), the watershed is not so necessary. Provided that a suitable protective system exists, '18' rated films are permitted to be broadcast at 8:00 p.m., and '12' and '15' rated films may be shown at any time. Similar arrangements will apply to variations of the pay-per-view system, such as (Near) Video on Demand.

The Joint Working Party on Violence on Television, established in 1996 by the BBC, the ITC, and the BSC, following a meeting with the then Secretary of State for National Heritage, examined measures for protecting viewers from harmful content. It concluded that, 'Though mindful of the risk that too frequent advisory information can diminish its impact', it urges the broadcasters to continue to improve the amount and quality of advice they give to viewers. For example, it found that the wording of some warnings was unnecessarily elliptical. Descriptions applied to programmes such as 'hard-hitting', 'candid,' and 'uncompromising' were too vague. Broadcasters must increase the transparency of wording to ensure that viewers clearly recognise warnings about material, which may upset or concern them. Viewers need specific information on which they can act. Broadcasters have to find ways of delivering this, while avoiding forms that turn information into an inducement to younger viewers (Violence and Viewer 1998).

Concerning the use of symbols the Working Party did 'not wish to discourage the adoption of these techniques if broadcasters judge that they are helpful to their viewers', but they believe that they have certain drawbacks. Symbols are a very basic and limited mechanism, which may not be as effective as a specific description of problematic content.[17]

Pretransmission clearance and rating of commercials is handled by an organisation set up and funded by the broadcasters themselves, the Broadcast Advertising Clearance Centre (BACC). With the exception of some categories of local advertisements, representatives of the BACC must view every television commercial before approval for transmission can be given. Approval may be subject to conditions regarding transmission times, for example, the watershed. The BACC works closely with the ITC and is constantly taking decisions based on the requirements of the ITC Codes. The resulting 'case law' is reflected in its Notes of Guidance, which offer detailed explanation of how the principles set out in the ITC Codes are interpreted, based on practical day-to-day experience. They also contain a statement of the broadcasters' own principles in areas where these go beyond the basic requirements of the Codes. The final arbiter of acceptability remains however the ITC.

---

[17] The debate about parental control, and especially visual sign posting, is dominated within the United Kingdom by the so-called 'Red Triangle' paradigm. In 1986, Channel 4 showed a series of films known unofficially as the 'Red Triangle' series. These were all 18-rated films, which would previously have not been shown on television due to their explicit content. A red triangle appeared in the left-hand corner of the screen throughout its duration. Rather than deter those that were easily offended, it attracted viewers, and the series became something of a cult. The National Viewers and Listeners Association was appalled, and lobbied MPs. As a result a Home Affairs Parliamentary Committee hearing took place on the matter, in which the Committee was said to be appalled by graphic scenes of buggery in one of the films. The 'Red Triangle' series was never reprised after that controversy, and it has left a strong reluctance to introduce visual symbols in the United Kingdom.

INTERNET RATING SYSTEMS

Austria

In Austria, there is no code of practice that deals specifically with online services. However, general rules of civil law, copyright law, criminal law, media law, telecommunications law, trade law, and other areas of law are mandatory and apply to all online services. There is no Austrian institution which systematically rates content available online with a view to protecting minors.[18]

Though filtering software is easily available via the Internet at places such as Cyber Patrol, Net Nanny, SurfWatch, and others, it does not play an important role in Austria. One reason may be that filtering software which blocks webpages with offensive words is of limited use when it only recognises English. However, the main reason seems to be that at present, the percentage of Austrian households with Internet access is still not very high, and children who surf the Internet without an adult present are not as common as in other countries, either at school or at home.[19] Those parents whose children do surf the web on their own do not seem to be aware of what children may come across on the Internet—or they simply do not care. There is much discussion about illegal content (mainly child pornography) but very little discussion about harmful content.

As early as 1997, the *Bundesministerium für Inneres* (Federal Ministry of the Interior) established a central office to which 'netizens' could report Web or news group content, which they deemed illegal (*Meldestelle Internet*). Nowadays, there are 2 such offices: 1 fighting children pornography (*Meldestelle Kinderpornographie*) and the other fighting neo-nazi activities (*Meldestelle NS-Wiederbetätigung*). As well as traditional means of communication, these organisations can be notified by e-mail of texts or pictures thought to be illegal.

Only recently the Internet Service Providers Austria (ISPA) established a hotline for the same kinds of illegal material.[20] According to a statement on the ISPA website, notifications concerning other kinds of illegal content will not even be processed, let alone harmful but legal content.

---

[18] In the United States there are such sites, such as, http://www.cyberangels.org. Cyberangels is the name of a volunteer Internet watchdog organisation that maintains lists of kid-friendly sites.

[19] For up-to-date figures see Austria Internet Monitor at http://www.integral.co.at/aim.

[20] Tel. 07110/900121, E-mail hotline@ispa.at. More information can be found at http://hotline.ispa.at.

Belgium

In Belgium, the code of ethics for telecommunication services established a rating system based on prefixes, whereby, for example, the prefix *077* is automatically applied to adult services. Moreover, Article 20 specifies that the 'content of the services dedicated to minors must be adapted to their age and must respect their rights and interests'. In addition, 'services dedicated to minors and the promotion of these services must not contain any information that may harm or exploit their credulity, their lack of experience, or discernment'.

Belgacom has also proposed a free blocking system for services with the 077 prefix to the population of Belgium. The labelling system is judged to be too complex for the Internet, and a global solution is preferred.

Denmark

.So far the discussions in Denmark have mainly been inspired by the approach of other countries. There is a prevalent fear that the censorship practised in other countries may also be the route taken in Denmark, which would run contrary to the Danish way of thinking.

The abuse of time spent on school computers by children who use it for chatting or to find 'forbidden' home pages causes problems for teachers. According to a number of interviews with teachers, they are of the opinion that all they can do is appeal to children to use the Internet for 'reasonable' purposes only, as the Internet has so much potential for learning that it is of no use to impose particular prohibitions. The same is true of libraries. There are no common rules for libraries vis-à-vis controlling children's use of computers, but the librarians appeal to the children's sense of responsibility. Some libraries are conducting experiments to find out how they may use filters or other control devices.

For family use, some computer experts have publicly suggested that—even if there are several computers in the family—it should only be possible to use the Internet on 1 common family computer. In this way parents will have a degree of control.

Finland

No content legislation for online services has been completed in Finland, but such services are dependent on the requirements of law and order. Normal sanctions may be applied if criminal activities emerge on the Internet. The Constitution, the Penal Law, and the Civil Law can all be used to prosecute crimes on the Internet. For instance, a young man was charged in Finland for offering paedophilic materials via the Internet.

The majority of pornography, however, is not free of charge, and is therefore only accessible by registering and giving a credit card number, which generally prevents children from accessing those sites.

In the proposal for law prepared by the Committee on Freedom of Speech at the Ministry of Justice (3/1997) a liberal attitude and horizontal treatment of all media is suggested. The proposal has however several problematic points, which have been widely criticised, particularly by information technology professionals. For example, the committee proposes that network publications should have editors of full legal age, and that online programmes should be recorded for 3 months. The proposal leads to interpretation problems as well as problems of unequal treatment of different users of the Internet according to their age.

In 1997, the working group TIVEKE, at the Ministry of Transport and Communications published a report concerning public communication on information networks. In this report two new concepts were adopted to clarify the handling of public communication on information networks: public personal network communication. and content distribution (mass communication). However, public personal network communication cannot be totally excluded from the sphere of rules on electronic mass communication. According to the working group, more efficient control would be directed towards communication that is large-scale, professional, and regular.

The TIVEKE working group maintains that the self-regulation of information networks (Internet) signifies cooperation between parties involved on information networks to prevent the publication and spreading of harmful and criminal content. The objective is for the Internet as a community to restrict the spreading of harmful and criminal materials within the network. The working group suggests that content regulation should be realised solely by bodies that have the right to carry on such measures. Such bodies are content producers, final service providers, users, and authorities. Those who technically transmit data have no right to restrict the transmission of data. Unauthorised restriction may qualify as a disturbance offence in the field of electronic communication.

Measures relating to regulation of content recommended by the TIVEKE working group are as follows. Content producers and final service producers shall prepare common rules on what kind of content is not acceptable to produce and publish. As regards users and minors, the opportunities of parents and teachers to have influence on the content being received will be increased. Courts will be given authorisation to impose the exclusion of criminal contents from publicity or to have content distribution interrupted. Cooperation between the authorities of different countries shall be encouraged to prevent distribution of criminal content. Establishing hotline services can support the activities of authorities.

The development of an effective control system has so far been discouraging. Realising a coding system covering different Internet contents is very difficult.

No national entity is responsible for the rating system for online services. The vital questions at present are, Who should provide the ratings needed for technical devices? What is unsuitable for children? Who should supervise coders? Under what circumstances would it be possible to shut down a site? The Finnish Internet Association maintains that it is up to content producers to provide the ratings. However, producers' self-regulation is ineffective. Online service experts maintain that a preliminary screening is not possible.

France

In France, general laws, such as the Criminal Code, apply to protection of minors on the Internet, particularly Article 227-24, which states in its first line that 'To manufacture, transmit, or disseminate, by any means and whatever the medium, a message depicting violence or pornography or likely seriously to damage human dignity, or to trade with such message, is punishable by a 3 year prison sentence and a F500,000 fine, where this message is likely to be viewed or seen by a minor.'

However, apart from child pornography, addressed in Article 227-23 introduced by the law n° 98-468 of 17 June 1998 and published in the *Official Journal* of 18 June 1998, there are no specific provisions regarding regulation of the Internet for the purposes of protecting minors from harmful content.

Nevertheless, the so-called 'Loi fillon' of 26 July 1996 or Law n° 96-659 of 26 July 1996 art. 15 published in the *Official Journal* of 27 July 1996, establishing a legal framework for the telecommunications field, introduced, *inter alia*, the obligation for anyone, whose business is to provide connections to one or more audiovisual communication services, to offer its clients technical means, which permit them to either restrict access to certain services or to select them. This provision was integrated into the Law of September 1986 relating to freedom of communication, and constitutes its new Article 43-1.

Recently, the *Conseil d'Etat*, the supreme French administrative jurisdiction, published a report dedicated to the Internet and digital networks. (1998). It noted that existing texts, the Criminal code, or specific laws were sufficient to punish infringements relating to civil rights, data, or consumer protection. It noted also that the first case law had transposed traditional rules to the network.

In France, self-regulation by Internet operators has been the subject of several proposals and initiatives, but no concrete solutions in the matter of content deontology have been reached. There was an attempt within the Law of 26 July 1996 to create a *Conseil Supérieur de la Télématique*, Council overseeing the telematics, and to make the deontology framework more precise, but the Constitutional Council's Judgement of 23 July 1996 invalidated these provisions.

In March 1997, the so-called 'Beaussant report', from an association of online publishers called, *Groupement des Editeurs de Services en Ligne* (GESTE), introduced an Internet Charter, the main aim of which is to set up an Internet Council ([online] available: http://www.planete.net/code-internet/ccode2.html). It contains a section dedicated to illegal content and another relating to harmful content.

According to the Charter, the Internet Council would be the recipient claims relating to illegal content from users and providers and could even act on its own initiative. In the event that the Council judged the content to be illegal, it would inform the author or the person responsible for the site concerned, recommending them to modify or suppress it. If the offender did not comply with the recommendation, the Council might request technical providers to suppress or block access to the contentious content.

As for harmful content, the Charter states that providers should make a commitment to permit users to select information according to their own wishes. To this purpose, providers should promote both filtering mechanisms and rating regimes, and apply certain principles, such as respect of human dignity, the rejection of any discrimination against opinions, race, sex, and so on, and the rejection of any exploitation of minors, especially of a sexual nature. However, this project did not receive significant support from operators and users.

A new text called 'Le Manifeste' was published in July 1997. It is a short document, which defines founding principles for self-regulation and recommends the implementation of a flexible, consultative, and pluralistic self-regulatory organisation.

Finally, some professional associations, such as the *Association des Fournisseurs d'Accès et de Services Internet* (AFA) and GESTE, undertook their own initiatives.[21] AFA wrote a code of conduct while GESTE confirmed its proposal to create a supervisory body (codes of conduct online, available at http://www.afa-france.com/html/actualites/index.htm).

The AFA code of conduct contains a specific provision relating to the protection of minors, which states that subscription is refused to minors unless with express authorisation from a person exercising parental authority. On the other hand, as in the Internet Charter, AFA members must offer means for filtering content to their users. The code of conduct also states that when a user is made aware of illicit or harmful content they should refer it to the access provider concerned. The access provider should request the client to modify the content if it contravenes the contract signed by the client. If the client does not comply, the access provider may suppress the content or terminate the contract.

---

[21] AFA is composed of the following Internet Access/online services Providers: AOL Berstelmann France, Cegetel, CompuServe, FranceNet, France Pratique, France Telecom Interactive, Grolier Interactive, Imaginet, Infonie, Internet Way.

Since 1996, several reports have been published, which mention, *inter alia*, the need to promote self-regulation among operators and to involve State authorities in the creation of either a self-regulatory body, a hotline and an Observatory, or, under private law, an agency regulating the Internet (Patrice Martin-Lalande 1997). However, no proposals have yet been concretised, and discussion of how to classify Internet sites has not yet begun.

However, as in the other Member States, filtering software is available for users, though it is largely impractical as it is intended for English language sites. One exception is Cyber Patrol, which is currently preparing a French-speaking version of its filtering software. In addition, a report by the *Conseil d'Etat* noted that only few Internet operators apply the new Article 43.1 of the Law of September 1986, which requests them to provide their clients with the technical means to filter content. Finally, no hotline mechanism has been created and there are no concrete initiatives for information campaigns, warning and informing users about safe uses of the Internet.

Germany

In Germany, the only rating/labelling system is the one developed by the USK. Other organisations such as the *Freiwillige Selbstkontrolle Multimedia Dienstanbieter e.V.* (FSM) or the BPjS do not grant ratings but control the acceptability of the service pursuant to the relevant legal provisions. Services are illegal if they present an obvious moral danger to children or youth. However, these provisions include a range of undetermined legal concepts. As a consequence, the question of whether a service presents an obvious moral danger to children or youth might be interpreted in a different way by the different controlling bodies. The assessment decides merely whether the service is legally acceptable or not. In the latter case, there is no further classification of the service, but the service provider is told not to offer the contents in question any longer.

The agreement between Federal States on media services states that legal acceptability is not determined by the judgement of the controlling body, but based on objective criteria (deterministic). It leaves room, however, for interpretation, which necessarily includes subjective components. Case law offers common guidelines, but it is hardly developed in the online field.

Service providers are legally obliged to respect the provisions concerning the protection of minors in their services (mandatory). However, they have the choice whether to appoint a commissioner for the protection of minors or to allow a voluntary organisation such as the FSM to take over this task for them.

The FSM is financed by its members, which are media associations and firms such as Deutsche Telekom, the Microsoft network, or Pro Sieben Media AG.

Since mid-November 1997, 200 media companies have declared that they will follow the code of conduct developed by the FSM. Members of the FSM must apply the code of conduct and its rules regarding complaints.

Users address complaints concerning illegal content to the Complaints Committee of the FSM. Complaints can only be addressed electronically by completing an electronic complaint form on the website of the association further to §3 II of the FSM rules. This rule thus conforms to point 2d of the 'indicative guidelines for the implementation at national level of a self-regulation framework for the protection of minors and human dignity in online audiovisual and information services', included in the Recommendation of the Council of 28.05.1998, which requires that complaints should be sent and received without difficulties (telephone, e-mail, or fax).

The FSM's procedures for dealing with complaints are also in accordance with the guidelines. §4 of the FSM rules requires a preexamination of the complaint. If the complaint is admissible, the decision procedure takes place after hearing the position of the content provider, further to §5. The author of the complaint is informed of the outcome of the procedure, further to §6 VI. If the content provider does not conform to the sanction, the service provider is informed, §7 I. If the Committee concludes that the service is acceptable, this conclusion is not binding for the competent authorities. However, if the FSM concludes that a service is a violation of the legal provisions then they initiate the procedure described later.

According to the guidelines, providing for dissuasive measures proportionate to the nature of the violations should strengthen the credibility of the code of conduct. Further to §6 of the FSM rules, the following measures may be taken, according to the gravity of the violations: comment with a request to remedy the situation; expression of disapproval; or reprimand (this reprimand must be published by the service within 1 month). If the member does not comply with the sanction or, if, despite repeated requests, it does not remedy the situation, it may be excluded from the FSM. Serious instances of child pornography are to be reported to the police (epd medien [Nr. 57] 1998, 21).

Considering the ever-increasing number of documents on the Internet as well as its international character, it is impossible to have complete control of this media. The FSM staff is also small (1 lawyer who judges the acceptability of the complaints, 3 ordinary members, and 3 alternate members who form the Examining Board). The Executing Board is composed of a President and 5 other people. The success of the FSM depends considerably on the number of its members who support its work and thus wish to fulfil in this manner their legal obligations in the field of the protection of the minors. In addition to this, though the FSM may act against a member on its own initiative, it mostly acts on the basis of complaints.

It is therefore also important that users, who can contact the body if they chance on webpages likely to be harmful to minors, accept it. Since its creation, the FSM has received 185 complaints. In 35 cases, the service providers or the service supplier deleted the text or images in question or locked Internet access to them. Similar results have occurred in other countries after the FSM contacted the service providers. It receives approximately 30 to 40 complaints per month.

The FSM controls advertising on the Internet but in a rather superficial way. Rather than taking over this role from the Werberat, the body responsible for advertising, they coordinate with it to supervise advertising.

According to §7 GjSM, information and communication service providers are members of the USK if they submit their contents to it for rating and if they install a link on their website which refers to the USK. However, this is not common practice so far. The USK has supervised network contents and online games since 22 August 1997, using the same procedure as for video games. It provides a classification by age groups and a report. It charges a fee for examining websites of: 300 DM for a maximum of 25 pages; 500 DM for a maximum of 75 pages; 750 DM for a maximum of 100 pages; 1000 DM for a number of pages exceeding the limit of 100.

In addition to the voluntary bodies the Ministries for Youth and Family supervise the application of provisions concerning the protection of minors according to §18 I of the Mediendienste-Staatsvertrag (the Agreement between Federal States on media services, which came into force on 1 August 1997). This system is not based on classification of the content, but on a legal evaluation, and these authorities are not obliged to perform a general and minute supervision. They act usually on the basis of complaints or other indices. They are entitled to control content and to prohibit it partly or completely, but do not have the powers to demand content changes. Violations can lead to the imposition of a fine amounting to 500.000 DM.

The Jugendschutz.net was created in Wiesbaden in October 1997 as a Joint Office for the protection of minors in online media. The central office cooperates closely with the respective competent offices in each Federal State. Jugendschutz.net tries to locate content that might be dangerous for the minors on the Internet with the help of a browser, the so-called 'software for the protection of minors' developed specially for this purpose. When such pages are located, Jugendschutz.net contacts the respective provider, so that the latter can modify or delete the content within a determined period of time. This organisation operates as a representative central office, or national contact office, as suggested by the recommendation of the Council.

At Federal level, since the implementation of the Informations und Kommunikationsdienstegesetz (IuKDG) (the Federal Act establishing the general conditions for information and communication services, which came into force on 1 August 1997), the BPjS is responsible for the examining and 'indexing' of Internet content which is likely to harm minors. The BPjS works in cooperation with the highest authorities of the Federal States, which have created an office for the protection of minors in online services on the basis of the Agreement between the Federal States on media services. The BPjS can only act on the basis of a request emanating from the Ministries of Youth of the Federation and of the Federal States and the authorities responsible for young people (Jugend- and Landesjundendämter).

The Agreement states that a publication put on the 'index' may not be transmitted or made available through electronic information or communication services. This interdiction does not apply if technical measures have been taken to ensure that access within Germany is restricted to users of legal age. It is still unclear as to which technical measures should be taken, given the quasi-absence of case law. The BPjS considers that the so-called 'Adult-sex system' according to which the user must give a credit card number to have access to content, is enough for commercial providers of pornographic content. The BPjS has already made use of its new authority.

The BPjS is financed by the Federation, pursuant to §8III of the GjSM. Two BPjS examiners specialise in the online field, but the organisation has a limited number of computers with Internet access. §5 GjSM states certain restrictions and prohibitions in the field of advertising. A provider may not advertise the fact that its service has been put on the 'index' or is about to be inserted in the list. This provision exists to avoid the inclusion of the service in the 'index' being used for the purpose of positive advertising.

Greece

The body responsible for rating online services in Greece is the National Telecommunications Commission (NTC), which is an independent body, administratively and financially self-contained, under the supervision of the Minister of Transport and Communications. It was set up by the Telecommunications Act— Law 2246/94 of October 1994. In the case of VOD, it is also the responsibility of the Ministry of the Press and the Mass Media to introduce a rating system. Among its principal tasks is the supervision of the telecommunications and online markets, the assignment of numbers to service providers, and the delivery of opinions to the Minister of Transport and Communications regarding the granting, renewal, modification, suspension, extension, and revocation of licenses.

The NTC has not identified any rating system. It took some steps to initiate policy in June 1997. It appointed a Steering Committee to take a closer look at this issue and proposed the setting-up of a group that would be responsible for pursuing self-regulation. It also published an Internal Report on 'Illegal and Harmful Content in the Internet Globally'.

Ireland

Regulation of online services in Ireland has now been vested in the office of an independent telecommunications regulator, who recently has produced a number of reports governing various aspects of telecommunications, including the provision of broadcast services. The only legislative development has been the promise of a Bill to deal with defamation on the Internet, which has not yet been published, and the enactment of Child Trafficking and Pornography Act 1998. The Act contains a definition of child pornography. In the Act, child pornography means:

> Any visual representation that (a) shows or, in the case of a document, relates to a person who is or is depicted as being a child and who is engaged in or is depicted as being engaged in explicit sexual activity, (b) shows or, in the case of a document, relates to a person who is or is depicted as being a child and who is or is depicted as witnessing any such activity by any person or persons, or (c) whose dominant characteristic is the depiction, for a sexual purpose, of the genital or anal region of a child.

> Any audio representation of a person who is or is represented as being a child and who is engaged in or is represented as being engaged in explicit sexual activity,

> Any visual or audio representation that advocates, encourages or counsels any sexual activity with children which is an offence under any enactment, or

> Any visual representation or description of, or information relating to, a child that indicates or implies that the child is available to be used for the purpose of sexual exploitation within the meaning of *section 3*, irrespective of how or through what medium the representation, description or information has been produced, transmitted or conveyed and, without prejudice to the generality of the foregoing, includes any representation, description or information produced by or from computer graphics or by any other electronic or mechanical means but does not include (a) any book or periodical publication which has been examined by the Censorship of Publications Board and in respect of which a prohibition order under the Censorship of Publications Acts, 1929 to 1967, is not for the time being in

force; (b) any film in respect of which a general certificate or a limited certificate under the Censorship of Films Acts, 1923–1992, is in force, or (c) any video work in respect of which a supply certificate under the Video Recordings Acts, 1989 and 1992, is in force.

However, the Act does not deal specifically with the control of access by children to pornography. An amendment to the Bill, which would have dealt specifically with this issue, was defeated by a large majority at committee stage. Similarly, suggestions that the issue might be dealt with in a Children Bill were also rejected. Concern was expressed about the placing of child pornography on the Internet using websites, associated with cartoon characters, regularly accessed by children, and also about the exemption of video games from the Video Recordings Acts, particularly in light of the violence depicted in some of them.

Nonetheless, the general view of the legislature appeared to be that possible legislative control was not an immediate priority. It is expected that the matter will be addressed in the Report of the Working Group on the Illegal and Harmful Use of the Internet, which is due to be published in the near future. It has been suggested that the term 'video' be defined in sufficiently wide terms in the Video Recordings Act 1989 to apply to computer disks (Kelleher and Murray 1997). It is possible that that Act could, therefore, be used to combat pornography in the same way as the corresponding Act in England has been used in such cases as *Meechie v Multi-Media Marketing* in 1995.

Italy

The Italian Ministerial Self-regulating Code is presently in a state of '*impasse*'. As a result all connected or collateral projects, such as the implementation of a content rating system, are on hold for the time being. It is worth mentioning that at a different and non-institutional level, the collaboration between the Information Science Degree Course of the University of Cesena (who prepared the operating environment) and the *Association Città Invisibile* (who defined the rating system) has recently given birth to a pilot Italian rating agency: IT-RA.

The IT-RA rating system is evaluative and voluntary and uses the PICS system. It grants PICS labels to content providers who autonomously rate their documents, by completing a form online. Based on the level at which the content rated by the content providers, IT-RA issues the relevant PICS label (metadata), which is then associated with the Internet content. When access to the document is sought the software browser reads the level of each category and blocks access when the level is higher than that chosen by the user. The IT-RA applies to advertising as well. IT-RA Rating system is thoroughly laid out in Table 11.

TABLE 11
IT-RA Rating System

	Level 0	Level 1	Level 2	Level 3	Level 4
V	No express or implied violence	Materials denouncing violation of human rights — not harmful to minors	Implicitly violent	Expressly violent	Inducing or inciting to violence
S	No references to sex	Scientific material on sex and sexuality — not harmful to minors	Alluding or relating to erotica	Moderately sexual and non explicit	Sexually explicit and pornographic
L	No vulgarity	Materials on the use and diffusion of dialects — not harmful to minors	From time to time vulgar or dirty	Vulgar and/or blasphemous	Verbally violent
A	No advertising	Advertising but not harmful to minors	Also advertising products for minors	Subliminal advertising contents	Prevailing and express advertising contents
R	No references to religion	Material on religion	References to a particular religion	Proselitical religious references	Religious or non religious intolerance
P	Not political	Material on politics — not harmful to minors	Generic political references	References to political associations	References to political parties
R	No racial references	Racial material – not harmful to minors	Subliminal racial references	Explicit racial references	Inciting to racial hatred
D	Highly didactic and based on accurate scientific materials appropriate for minors	Highly didactic and based on accurate scientific materials appropriate for adults	Medium didactic with good scientific basis	Low didactic with poor scientific basis	Non didactic

V=Violence; S=Sex; L=Language; A=Advertising; Rel=Religion; P=Politics;
R=Racism; D=Didactic

Luxembourg

For online services in Luxembourg, Common Law is mostly applicable, though the Criminal Code may apply. The trend is to favour a self-regulatory system. However, the CNP has intervened with new media such as Internet online services. In its opinion of June 1998, it justified its intervention by commenting that 'neither the Ministry of Communications, nor the post and telecommunications companies, nor any other State organ feels responsible for nor concerned by content on the Internet and online services'. However, the CNP recognises that 'the Internet phenomenon' does not fall within its authority from a legal point of view, as it is neither a radio nor television programme, nor a programme distributed via cable.

Self-regulation and international solutions are considered essential to render a control system really efficient. According to the CNP, the success of filtering systems, such as PICS, will mainly depend on support provided by parents and educators, the local, national, and international authorities.

The Netherlands

In The Netherlands there are no formal provisions for the control of online services other than the Penal Code. Where necessary Articles 240a and 240b of the Penal Code may apply, but since the principle of freedom of speech is seen as one of the most important pillars of the Dutch Constitutional State, prior censoring of opinions by the Government is not desirable. Interference on constitutional grounds is possible only in the case of the abuse of freedom of speech. The Constitution thus does not have official rules concerning its applicability to different online services (*Raad voor het Jeugdbeleid* 1996).

As yet, no licence is required for Internet providers and the legal liability of illegal content is not clear. The President of the District Court of The Hague ruled in a copyright case that Internet access providers are not in principle responsible for the content or information offered through their infrastructure. Action against service providers would only be possible where the provider is perfectly aware of the illegal activity. As far as penal liability is concerned the Minister of Justice stated that, as well as action to prevent illegal material, self-regulation should play an important role. The Government principally takes the view those citizens, users, and educators have responsibility for themselves.

The Minister of Justice is considering a limitation of the penal liability of the provider. Through a change to Articles 53 and 54 of the Penal Code, she hopes to ensure that the same liability will exist for providers as for publishers and printers. If the Internet provider can point out from whom the illegal content originates, the provider will not be prosecuted (Meldpunt website).

Self-regulation does already exist regarding illegal information on the Internet. The *Nederlandse Vereniging van Internet Providers* (NLIP) (Dutch Federation of Internet Providers) coordinates the industry and represents most of the Internet providers in the Netherlands. The NLIP's policy towards illegal content on the Internet is published on their website and is as follows:

1. Dutch Internet providers, represented by the NLIP, will try hard (in cooperation with the police, judiciary, and European and international institutions) to eliminate illegal information from the Internet, as far as possible and as soon as possible within the legal framework. Illegal information is information that has been prohibited by Dutch law.

2. Illegal information put on the Internet cannot be totally prevented, either by Government or by Internet providers, who have even less authority. One reason for this is the Constitution's rules forbidding prior censorship and defending freedom of expression. The other is the international character of the Internet. As most of the illegal information is from abroad it is impossible to control.

3. In order to take action, different reporting points have been established by Internet providers and individuals.

4. Action may only be taken against information providers operating within the borders of the Netherlands, as the Dutch Constitution applies. Reports implicating foreign information providers will be forwarded to reporting points existing in the country from which the material originates.

A working group was set up in which the Internet providers, the *Divisie Centrale Recherche Informatie* (CRI) (Central Division of Research Information) and Internet users were represented. This group created the framework of procedures and criteria, which were used for the foundation of the first Reporting Point for Child Pornography in Europe on 20 June 1996.

According to Meldpunt.org the reporting point procedures are:

1. An Internet user reports the dissemination of child pornography on the Internet to the reporting point: meldpunt@meldpunt.org·

2. The reporting point receives the message and responds (automatically) to the reporter.

3. The reporting point checks the report.

4. If the report meets certain criteria (see the following) a warning is sent to the creator of the illegal content. This Internet user will be requested to stop transmitting the content.

5. If the Internet user disputes the warning, a second letter follows, which explains that the reporting point is not the place for discussion nor responsible for providing an explanation.

6. If the Internet user does not reply, or does not stop sending the messages/illegal content within a period of 24 hours, the report will be sent to the local police.

Before sending a warning to the Internet user, a report must fulfil three criteria. It must concern child pornography, as stated in Article 240 of the Penal Code. It must concern distribution from Dutch territory, and it must concern public distribution on the Internet.

On 21 March 1997, a second Reporting Point became operational, intended to deal with and prevent racial discrimination, anti-Semitism and revisionism within the Dutch borders of the Internet. As far as racism is concerned, Article 137d of the Penal Code could apply. A third Reporting Point for consultation on illegal material on the Internet has been set up.

The Minister announced that reports of the Reporting Point for Child Pornography received by the CRI would be investigated sooner. The national bureau of the Public Prosecutor will play a coordinating role. After a first examination by the CRI, reports may be handed over to the national bureau of the Public Prosecutor for the purposes of opening an investigation. When, in the course of the investigation, the location of the suspect in the Netherlands becomes known, the judicial hearing can be handed over to the appropriate district court of the Public Prosecutor.

Finally, the Minister takes the view that expertise from outside the police and judiciary is also important. Therefore, well coordinated cooperation is needed between the Internet Service Providers, the Internet Reporting Points, and other organisations concerned with child protection on the one hand, and the responsible Ministries, police, and the Public Prosecutor on the other.

Portugal

No national group or entity is responsible for the rating system for this medium in Portugal, and no systems of content control (for example, ratings, bans, watersheds, and so on) are in use. Some Internet users might be using blocking systems such as the Platform for Internet Content Selection (PICS), but no studies have been done to ascertain their number.[22] Among dozens of informal enquiries made to Internet users in Portuguese academia, no one was aware of PICS or indeed any other system to control content on the Internet.

---

[22] A set of technical standards whose goal is to establish a common label, readable by any software, and that can be used to convey any kind of rating. PICS is being developed by the World Wide Web Consortium, an independent American consortium, and has already been accepted by most players in the online service markets.

Spain

There are no provisions in Spain related to a rating system for audiovisual contents distributed via Internet. The draft of the *Convenio de autorregulación para el buen uso de Internet en España* proposed by the Ministry for Education and the Asociación de Usuarios de Internet (AUI) merely states that if there are many complaints about the content of the website of one of the subscribers to the code of conduct, the person in charge of that website will indicate in the homepage that the website in question contains material that might harm the sensibility of its users.

The AUI, in its website, says that it favours the use of PICS. As for labelling, AUI simply indicates that content providers may voluntarily rate their websites according to the criteria (age groups, kind of content, and so on) established by some companies, such as Netshepherd, RSAC or SafeSurf. None of these systems is specifically aimed at the Spanish public, and none of them has gained support among online services or content providers.

Sweden

There is no legislation, which limits or hinders the use of online services by children and adolescents in Sweden. The service providers are not obliged to obey any legal limitations than those in the general law. When the first type of automatic data processing was discussed in the 1960s, no need for legislation was suggested other than the protection of rights relating to authorship.

The new Act on Electronic Billboards makes Internet providers responsible for the prevention of further dissemination of criminal material on their servers. The law does not apply to providers of networks or other connections for the transmission of messages or other devices needed to use the connections, transmission of messages within an agency or between agencies or within an enterprise or a legal group of enterprises, services protected by the Freedom of Press Act or the Freedom of Expression Act or messages intended only for a certain receiver or a fixed group of receivers (electronic mail).

Providers are also obliged to remove or otherwise prevent continued dissemination of certain categories of messages from their services. This is the case if an incoming message obviously falls under the provisions of the Criminal Code that deals with instigation to crime, agitation against groups of people, child pornography, or unlawful depiction of violence.

It is established that the service supplier, in order to be able to fulfil his obligation to prevent dissemination, should have reasonable supervision over his service, taking into consideration its scale and purpose. As a general rule, providers of electronic notice-boards are not obliged to screen all incoming messages, but if a provider is informed that he is assisting dissemination of criminal material, he must act to prevent further dissemination.

If the provider, either intentionally or through gross negligence, does not prevent further dissemination of a message belonging to these categories, he shall be sentenced to a fine or to imprisonment for not more than six months or, if the crime is serious, not more than 2 years. This does not apply if the provider can be sentenced according to the Criminal Code or the Copyright Law.

In Sweden, censorship before publication is not allowed and the proposed law will not introduce such a practice. Actions concerning criminal material in electronic notice-boards will only be prosecuted after publication, as is the case with books, films, and other traditional media.

The State Computer Inspection Authority, *Datainspektionen,* is responsible for monitoring violations of personal integrity, and for implementing the computer law by authorities, companies, organisations, and private persons. The law took effect in 1973; however, it is the police who are responsible for criminal investigation in cases of computer hacking of a homepage or child pornography on the Internet or another open network.

United Kingdom

The Internet Service Providers Association (ISPA) in the United Kingdom was formed in 1995 and established a Code of Practice after a meeting with the Home Office in January 1996. The former Science and Technology Minister stated at this meeting that the United Kingdom Government's 'position is that we would want to encourage the industry to develop a system of self-regulation which might address these areas of concern, rather than considering statutory options.' They continued, saying, 'United Kingdom Internet Service Providers must devise a Code of Practice to control access to illegal and unsuitable material or face increasing political pressure for curbing legislation.' Moreover, on 14 August 1996, the Department of Trade and Industry (DTI) issued a press release (P/96/636), in which it was suggested that ISPA should 'cooperate in developing services' that are able to make use of features such as PICS, which makes it possible to rate every webpage according to its content.

Some organisations, such as universities, already had 'acceptable use' policies in place, and Demon Internet, a major United Kingdom Service Provider, had (as a reaction to a newspaper Article) developed its own self-censorship policy using the new PICS standard. Finally, following a seminar organised by the Internet Developers Association, the Internet Watch Foundation (IWF) was created. This is an independent organisation set up to implement the proposals jointly agreed by the government, the police and the two major United Kingdom service provider trade associations, ISPA and LINX. It aims to enhance the enormous potential of the Internet 'to inform, educate, entertain, and conduct business' by hindering the use of the Internet to transmit illegal material, particularly child pornography, and encouraging the classification of legal material on the Internet, in order to enable users to use it according to their own requirements. Since April 1997, the IWF has been funded by the United Kingdom industry on a subscription basis, and is controlled by a Management Board drawn from the subscribers and a Policy Board drawn from a wide range of stakeholders in the Internet, including industry, child and education, consumer, libertarian, and other media organisations.

The IWF's initial role was to operate a hotline service for users to report illegal material on the Internet. However, their experience of combating illegal material has exposed two aspects of user needs, which a hotline service alone cannot satisfy. It is not possible to quickly remove all illegal material, particularly that which originates from outside the organisation's home country and there is a lot of material that must be classified as legal, which is offensive to many users and considered unsuitable or harmful for their children.

In order to begin to tackle these problems, the IWF set up an Advisory Board early in 1997, with a brief to develop a rating system for the use of United Kingdom Internet user, but which takes the Internet's global nature into account ([online, 2001] available: http://www.iwf.org.uk/label/index.htm). The system is intended to use the PICS system, which will enable users to set parameters for the material they wish to be accessible by their terminal. All other material will be filtered out. This system will permit parents to allow their children unsupervised access to the Internet, having already set limitations on accessible material.

The Advisory Board published its Rating Report in March 1998, with the following recommendations:

IWF recommends that a world-wide rating system is developed which is based on a global approach for the description of content in objective terms, free from any particular cultural values and voluntarily applied to content by its providers. For Internet users there should be an easy-to-use filtering system built into their browser software that allows them to choose if and how to apply filtering, and their own criteria for the blocking of unwanted material. To assist users in their choice, we also recommend that 'off-the-shelf' profiles be introduced so that a familiar classification of content, such as the equivalent of a film certificate rating, can be chosen. IWF recognises that such a system will need to be attractive to content providers as well as equipment suppliers, service providers and browser producers in order to get it developed and implemented.

From a United Kingdom perspective, the categories of material that are described in the content label (and hence can be filtered) should include nudity, sex, violence and language, as in the present Recreational Software Advisory Council (RSACi) system, but with some amendments to the detailed definitions. We suggest that there should be additional categories covering exposure of personal details; making financial commitments; various forms of intolerance; potentially dangerous subjects (including, for example, promotion of tobacco, alcohol or drug misuse) and other adult themes. We also pose the possibility of users being able to choose to override their selected limits for factual news and documentary, science or art ([online, 2001] available: http://www.iwf.org.uk/label/rating_r.htm).

In parallel with the work of the Advisory Board, and with its support, IWF has been involved in establishing a European consortium of organisations, Internet Content Rating for Europe (INCORE), to promote aspects of self-regulation and rating in support of European Commission policies and plans. Following the positive support to rating and filtering from the Global Information Networks Conference in Bonn in July 1997, IWF helped found an International Working Group on Content Rating (IWGCR).

HORIZONTAL TREATMENT OF MEDIA

Of all the Member States, only the Dutch have examined seriously the potential for horizontal treatment of the 4 media—film, video, television, and online services. An interdepartmental working group was set up by the Ministries of Home Affairs and Justice, the Secretaries of Public Health, Welfare, and Sports and of Education, Culture and Science to discuss the protection of minors from harmful content in audiovisual media. Its policy was formulated in a blueprint document entitled '*Niet voor alle leeftijden; Audiovisuele Media en de Bescherming van Jeugdigen*' ('Not for all ages; Audiovisual Media and the protection of minors', 1997).

As far as horizontal treatment is concerned, the working group proposed that, for better protection, the existing system of age rating should apply to the audiovisual industry as a whole. In addition, the system needed improving, with the development of rating values, rating criteria and age limits, augmentation of expertise and information about (the application of) classification methods, product information, and so on. The working group recommended that an independent private institution should be responsible for these activities on behalf of the whole industry.

Such an institution could operate as a national support centre, consult producers and providers of audiovisual media products, report and evaluate every year compliance with the agreements made for each industry and recommend improvements. The recommendations of the working group mean that a central self-regulatory system encompassing each industry in the audiovisual media sector may be introduced *(Notitie* 1997: 16).

The industries must be encouraged to take responsibility for setting up an institution. However, because of the importance of improving the age classification system, the working group suggests subsidising a separate, possibly independent institution for this purpose.

In early 1997, the RvtV, took the initiative by implementing a discussion with the public broadcasters, represented at first by a delegation of the Audiovisual Platform (AVP); VESTRA (Association for Satellite, Television and Radio Programme Providers) representing the commercial broadcasters; NVPI Interactive and NVPI Film *(Nederlandse Vereniging van Producenten en Importeurs van beeld- en geluidsdragers* [Dutch Federation of Producers and Importers of Image- and Sound Carriers]); and the *Nederlandse Federatie Cinematografie* (NFC) (Dutch Federation for Cinematography).

The discussion was about the propositions of the RvtV and the blueprint document '*Niet voor alle leeftijden*' *(Raad van Toezicht Videovoorlichting* 1997: 3). One of its propositions was that the independent support institution to be founded should exist of three departments: one Supervisory Board, an executive bureau, and an examining committee for classification.

When approached, the *Nederlandse Omroepstichting* (NOS), the Dutch Broadcasting Foundation, and the NVPI said that this institution should be a foundation called the *Nederlands Instituut voor Classificatie van Audiovisuele Media* (NICAM), the Dutch Institution for Classification of Audiovisual Media. It could become operational in a short time. According to the blueprint, the institution should have expertise in the area of values, criteria, classification methods, and information. In its Annual Report of 1997 the NVPI proposed setting up a database, which would contain all classification data to enable keeping track of updated decisions. The first rating given would be the normative one, but it would not necessarily preclude discussions about alternative classifications.

As regards the film, video, and multi-media industries the self-regulatory-system proposed by the interdepartmental working group will leave no place for the *Nederlandse Filmkeuring* (NFK), the Dutch Board of Film Classification, and the *Wet op Filmvertoningen* (WOF), the Act on Film Exhibition. Instead of classification being made according to the grounds established by the Act, the film industry itself would be responsible for rating and ratifying agreements on classification. The Government will discuss with the organisations represented in the RvtV a broadening of the agreements in the *Convenant en Reglement Videovoorlichting* (Covenant on Video Information), to date covering only video film, multi-media, and computer games, to include an agreement on film. This seems logical because the NFC is already represented in the RvtV and because the importers/distributors of cinema films and video films are in most cases the same (*Notitie* 1997: 16–17).

As far as the television industry is concerned, the Secretary of Education, Culture, and Science is deliberating with the NOS and the VESTRA about a self-regulatory system for the protection of minors from harmful content on television. In the end, this is likely to lead to the implementation of the agreements and the European Directive. The criteria of the international broadcasting unions, the EBU, and the ACT are taken very seriously *(Notitie* 1997: 17).

According to the RvtV's Annual Report of 1997, NVPI Interactive (which represents about 13 multi-media publishers) proposed extending the current age rating, as stated in the Regulations on Video Information, to other media.

The blueprint document does not say much about the online services industry. It mentions that the NVPI and the NLIP (Dutch Federation of Internet Providers) will discuss a system of self-regulation, including a code of conduct in cooperation with the other parties. When asked, the NLIP stated that, as yet, no serious discussions between the Internet Providers and the NLIP had taken place.

Annex 2
Methodology

TEMPLATE: PARENTAL CONTROL
OF FILM, BROADCASTING, AUDIOVISUAL,
AND ONLINE SERVICES
IN THE EUROPEAN UNION

Background Overview for the Study

The European Commission Directorate-General X (Information, Communication, Culture, and Audiovisual Media) has commissioned the Programme in Comparative Media Law and Policy (PCMLP) of the University of Oxford to conduct a study on the parental control of television broadcasting in the European Union. This study is mandated by Article 22b of the *Television Without Frontiers Directive* (97/36/EC) of the European Parliament and Council of 30 June 1997. This study will provide a horizontal examination of the television broadcasting, film, video, and online services in the European Union in consonance with the Council Recommendation on the Protection of Minors and Human Dignity in the Audiovisual and Information Services (adopted 28 May 1998).

Objectives and Main Aims of the Study

The main objective of the study is to present an assessment of the advantages and disadvantages of introducing different measures at European Union level in order to enhance the control parents or guardians may exercise over the programmes that minors view.

Starting with the devices, rating systems, and family viewing policies currently in use in the Member States of the European Union the study focuses on three possible regulatory steps to be taken by the European Union: (1) requiring new television sets and/or computers to be equipped with technical devices for parental control (such as the V-chip); (2) setting up appropriate rating systems for

239

film, video, television, and online services; and (3) encouraging family television viewing and online services policies as well as other educational and awareness measures.[1]

The study will also examine the prospects for establishing voluntary national frameworks for self-regulation and assessment methodologies coordinated at European level and as a complement to the ultimate regulatory framework.

Devices, Ratings, Impact, and Harmonisation

The main elements of the study are:

1. An analysis of the different technical devices to assist in parental control of television broadcasting services and online services.[2] This will include descriptions of different devices, their cost, availability, and infrastructure needed to introduce each device.

2. A corresponding analysis of potential ratings or labelling systems to work in conjunction with or in the place of technical devices. This analysis of television and online services will be joined with a comparative analysis of rating systems used in film and video.

3. An assessment of the efficacy of each of the actual and/or foreseeable protective measure regimes of technical devices and rating systems. This assessment shall consider questions of cost, availability, compatibility, introduction, and European harmonisation.

4. An assessment of the economic impact of each of the different protective measures.

5. A comparison of the regulatory contexts for film, video, television and online services concerning the protection of minors from harmful content. This comparison will comport with the European Commission-mandated 'horizontal treatment' of the protection issue, contributing to the establishment of shared definitions and applications for classification systems for programmes and content in each of the four media sectors concerned.

The study will take into account the experience gained in this field in Europe and elsewhere (particularly Canada, United States, and Japan), as well as the views of broadcasters, producers, educationalists, media specialists, and associations.

---

[1] The terms 'rating system' and 'labelling system' are interchangeable for the purposes of this template.

[2] 'Online services' encompasses computer networks.

Country Reports

In order to assess the advantages and disadvantages of introducing new control measures throughout the European Union, the PCMLP is conducting a comparative study of the regulatory frameworks, technological capabilities, cultural contexts and relevant policy concerns within each of the 15 Member States of the European Union. The following is a brief outline of the information and issues that shall be contained in each country report.

Existing Context and Framework for Control of Film, Video, Television, and Online Services. Each report will provide a description of the existing regulatory structures for film, video, television (terrestrial, cable, satellite, and digital) and online services. The report will examine the implementation of Article 22 of the *Television Without Frontiers Directive* in the respective Member State.

The report will also discuss the cultural context, expectations, and legal provisions concerning ratings and warnings. It also will provide the country's history regarding the protection of minors from harmful content (for example, ratings or warnings concerning content). The report will address preexisting norms of presentation for warnings or ratings on broadcasting in the Member State.

Rating Systems. For each of the four media, the report will provide a specific identification of the type of ratings provider (producer self-rating, industry, nongovernmental third party or government). The report will characterise, *inter alia*, the constitution, structure, area of competence, efficiency and capacity of the given ratings providers and rating systems.

Technical Devices. The report will discuss the technical considerations of implementation for each type of technical device for television and online services. The report will discuss the effectiveness, (in both quantitative, for example, technical reliability, frequency of breakdowns and qualitative, for example, rate of utilisation and satisfaction of parents and children, ease and comfort of utilisation , terms) of both available and potentially available technical devices.

Educational and Awareness-Raising Policies. The report will examine existing and proposed educational policies and policies to encourage family viewing. They will discuss how these policies may both function (a) as an alternative to more intrusive policies and technologies and (b) as a complement to the deployment of technological devices. This discussion will contribute to the development of a typology and methodology of family viewing policies in a horizontal way across film, video, television and online services.

Costs Analysis and Economic Impact. The report will assess the associated costs for implementation of each possible technical device. They will also assess the economic impact relating to the deployment of such technical devices. This assessment will contemplate these impacts in terms of the deployment of regulatory regimes as well as in terms of regulatory obligations on manufacturers to install particular devices.

Template

The Template shall be informed by the preceding background overview. All aspects of the template shall be understood in light of the overview and any uncertainty or ambiguity shall be clarified by reference to the overview. Any remaining questions shall be clarified via direct inquiries made to the Programme in Comparative Media Law and Policy (PCMLP).

All researchers participating in any Country Report shall make themselves readily available to the PCMLP for clarification and discussion of the related research for a period of three months after the submission of the given Report.

Film Industry

Legal System.

1. Setting aside questions specifically concerning rating systems for the section immediately following, provide a background overview of the legal framework regarding the film industry.

2. Discuss relevant legal, historical, and cultural considerations concerning content regulation.

3. Identify formal provisions that control the film industry (for example, legislation, regulations, administrative provisions, and case law), describe the scope of coverage of the regulatory scheme (that is, does it apply to all cinema available in the country; is it mandatory or optional?), and identify current proposals for change to the existing regulatory structures and system for the film industry.

4. Discuss the social, economic or policy issues that appear to be driving the reform effort(s).

Rating System.

1. Identify the group or entity responsible for the rating system for this medium.

2. Describe and evaluate this ratings provider.

3. Apply Annex I and only the relevant Annex from among the following subsections of Annex I: Annex I-A: Producer Self-rating, Annex I-B: Industry, Annex I-C: Third Party, or Annex I-D: Government.

Video Industry

Legal System.

1. Given the diverse nature of the video industry identify any distinctions in legal or regulatory treatment within the industry as a whole.[3] In the case of such a distinction, apply separately the following analysis to each distinct element.

2. Discuss relevant legal, historical and cultural considerations concerning content regulation. Identify the formal provisions that control the video industry (for example, legislation, regulations, administrative provisions, case law); identify the scope of coverage of the regulatory scheme (that is, does it apply to all video industry products; is it mandatory or optional?); identify what systems are used (for example, ratings, bans, and so on) and describe how they operate; identify any current proposals for change to the existing regulatory structures and system for the video industry. Discuss the social, economic, or policy issues driving the reform effort(s).

Rating System.

1. Identify the group or entity responsible for the rating system for this medium. Describe and evaluate this ratings provider.

2. Apply Annex I and only the relevant Annex from among the following subsections of Annex I: Annex I-A: Producer Self-rating, Annex I-B: Industry, Annex I-C: Third Party, or Annex I-D: Government.

Television

Legal System.

1. Provide a background overview of the regulation of this medium. Discuss relevant legal, historical and cultural considerations.

2. Account for differences between digital and analogue, narrowcasting and broadcasting, public and private broadcasters in the following three categories: Terrestrial, Cable, and Satellite. For each of these three categories, identify the formal provisions that control television broadcasting (for example, legislation, regulations, administrative provisions, and case law). Identify the scope of coverage of the regulatory scheme (that is, does it apply to all television broadcasting; is it mandatory or optional?).

3. For each of the three categories (Terrestrial, Cable, and Satellite), setting aside questions specifically concerning rating systems for the section immediately below, identify what systems are used (for example, ratings, bans, watersheds, filtering, channelling, locking, and so on) and describe how they operate.

---

[3] Video industry refers to videocassettes as well as offline newer services such as laser-video disks, DVD, and games software or leisure software, and so on.

4. For each of the three categories (Terrestrial, Cable, and Satellite), identify any current proposals for change to the existing regulatory structures and system for television broadcasting. Discuss the social, economic or policy issues driving the reform effort(s). Please devote adequate attention to the regulation of digital television, identifying current and foreseeable developments as well as distinctions between the legal treatment of digital as opposed to analogue television.

Rating System.
1. Cultural expectations regarding ratings, acoustic warnings and symbols.

2. Identify whether the Member State has a history of ratings or warnings concerning content. Refer to this history in anticipating the cultural expectations that will likely follow from the deployment of Article 22.3.

3. Discuss any preexisting broadcasting norms in the Member State concerning the presentation of warnings or ratings.

4. Anticipate and explain the level of acceptance in the Member State to the 'presence of a visual symbol throughout [the] duration' of a programme as stated in Article 22.3.

5. Anticipate whether an 'acoustic warning' as the alternative in Article 22.3 to an omnipresent visual symbol will prompt a desire to also provide a visual indication of ratings before and after the presentation of content.

Ratings Provider.
1. Identify the group or entity responsible for the rating system for this medium. Describe and evaluate this ratings provider. Apply Annex I and only the relevant Annex from among the following subsections of Annex I: Annex I-A: Producer Self-rating, Annex I-B: Industry, Annex I-C: Third Party, or Annex I-D: Government.

Technical Devices.
1. Identify all technical devices to assist in parental control of television broadcasting currently used in the Member State.

2. Provide technical specifications for each of these devices. Explain how they are fitted to televisions or computers. Identify any other modalities (for example, ratings, software, and so on) necessary in order to properly use a given technical device.

3. For each of these devices and their required complements (for example, ratings, software, and so on) identify the cost in the Member State for installation and deployment of the technical device. In this treatment, appreciate the differences between mandatory and voluntary deployment.

4. Assess the effectiveness in quantitative (for example, technical reliability, frequency of breakdowns) and qualitative (for example, rate of utilisation and

satisfaction of parents and children, ease, and comfort of utilisation) terms of the given technical device as experienced in the Member State. Discuss what technological devices would be best suited for this country.

Introduction Scenarios for Technical Devices.

1. Discuss the possible scenarios for introduction of the technical device in conjunction with existing or proposed: (a) labelling systems, (b) regulatory structures, and (c) frameworks for self-regulation.

2. Present this discussion with an appreciation of the Member State's context within the European Union. Provide this discussion by addressing the European Commission's newly adopted horizontal approach across media to the protection of children from harmful content.

3. Account for the anticipated costs attached to each of the possible scenarios contemplated in the above question.

4. Discuss the possible development of new technical devices and their anticipated consequences.

Alternatives to Technologies.

1. Discuss the range of potentially available educational and awareness-raising measures to assist parental control in media use. Identify which strategies, if any, have gained substantial support popularly or among policymakers.

2. To the extent possible, determine the significance of the aid such alternatives provide parents in exercising control over what programmes their children view.

3. Assess the likelihood of adequately providing parents the use of these measures. Discuss the anticipated impediments to providing parents this access.

Online Services

Legal System.

1. Setting aside questions specifically concerning rating systems for the section immediately below, provide a background overview of the regulation of this medium. Discuss relevant legal, historical, and cultural considerations. Identify the formal provisions that control online services (for example, legislation, regulations, administrative provisions, and case law).

2. What is the scope of coverage of the regulatory scheme (that is, does it apply to all online services; is it mandatory or optional?).

3. Identify what systems are used (for example, ratings, bans, watersheds, filtering, channelling, locking, and so on) and describe how they operate.

4. Identify any current proposals for change to the existing regulatory structures and system for online services. Discuss the social, economic, or policy issues driving the reform effort(s).

Rating System.

1. Identify the group or entity responsible for the rating system for this medium. Describe and evaluate this ratings provider. Apply Annex I and only the relevant Annex from among the following subsections of Annex I.: Annex I-A: Producer Self-rating, Annex I-B: Industry, Annex I-C: Third Party, or Annex I-D: Government.

Technical Devices.

1. Identify all technical devices to assist in parental control of online services environments currently used in the Member State.

2. Provide technical specifications for each of these devices. Explain how they are fitted to televisions or computers.

3. Identify any other modalities (for example, ratings, software, and so on) necessary in order to properly use a given technical device.

4. For each of these devices and their required complements (for example, ratings, software, and so on) identify the cost in the Member State for installation and deployment of the technical device. In this treatment, appreciate the differences between mandatory and voluntary deployment.

5. Assess the effectiveness in both quantitative (for example, technical reliability, frequency of breakdowns) and qualitative (for example, rate of utilisation and satisfaction of parents and children, ease and comfort of utilisation) terms of the given technical device as experienced in the Member State. Effectiveness shall be measured with reference to the objectives pursued by manufacturers and promoters of the technical measures. Divergent positions concerning these objectives shall also be presented in this discussion. Where available, base this assessment on existing studies or research.

Introduction Scenarios for Technical Devices.

1. Discuss the possible scenarios for introduction of the technical device in conjunction with existing or proposed: (a) labelling systems, (b) regulatory structures, and (c) frameworks for self-regulation.

2. Present this discussion with an appreciation of the Member State's context within the European Union. Provide this discussion by addressing the European Commission's newly adopted horizontal approach across media to the protection of children from harmful content.

3. Account for the anticipated costs attached to each of the possible scenarios contemplated in the above question.

4. Discuss the possible development of new technical devices and their ramifications.

Alternatives to Technologies.

1. Discuss the range of potentially available educational and awareness-raising measures to assist parental control in use of online services. Identify which strategies, if any, have gained substantial support among policymakers or popularly.

2. To the extent possible, determine the significance of the aid these alternatives provide parents in exercising control over what content their children view.

3. Assess the likelihood of adequately providing parents access to these measures. Discuss the anticipated impediments to providing parents this access.

Prospects for Horizontal Treatment of the Protection of Minors across Media

1. Identify and discuss the system of technical devices, ratings and regulation that is most likely to be able to cover all four of the designated media. If you do not view any system as having this capacity, explain the fundamental limitations of these systems in this regard.

2. While addressing the questions in this section, please refer to Article 22 of *The Television Without Frontiers Directive* (97/36/EC).

3. State the Member State's standards pursuant to Article 22.1. Identify how these have been articulated (case law, legislation, administrative measures, and so on). Identify whether prior decency standards in the Member State bear on the formulation of this standard.

4. State the Member State's standards pursuant to Article 22.2. Identify how these have been articulated (case law, legislation, administrative measures, and so on) Identify whether prior decency standards in the Member State bear on the formulation of this standard.

5. Identify whether the Member State uses 'watersheds' or 'harbours' —designated time periods, for example from midnight to 6:00 am, when harmful content (pursuant to Article 22.2) may be aired. State the times of any such periods throughout the Member State.

6. If the Member State has not established standards clearly pursuant to either Article 22.1 or 22.2, then provide the Member State's preexisting standards regarding decency on television and for film and video. Identify how these have been articulated (case law, legislation, administrative measures, and so on).

7. Identify whether the Member State has 'more detailed or stricter rules' (Article 3.1, 97/36/EC) concerning content harmful to minors.

8. Identify whether comparable standards exist within the Member State for illegal and harmful content on online services. If so, identify whether rules exist within the Member State to prevent illegal and harmful content on online services.

Parental Obligations, Children's Rights, Rules, and Norms

1. Provide an essential overview of relevant elements of family law in the Member State, identifying children's rights and parental obligations as transcribed into law. Discuss the cultural norms regarding parental obligations and children's rights in the Member State. Compare legal rules with cultural norms.

2. Characterise the range of cultural norms within the Member State concerning the exposure of children to gratuitous violence and pornography in the media. In this characterisation, discuss the common or popular constructions of the terms 'gratuitous violence' and 'pornography' or their equivalents as well as 'physical, mental and moral development of minors'. Include in this discussion whether these terms have been transcribed into law or articulated at another governmental or administrative level.

Review of Existing Studies

1. The Country Reports should synthesise any existing research concerning harmful content, the use of technologies to assist parental control, and encouraging family viewing policies. Provide citations and bibliographic information for each study or research effort mentioned. Provide as attachments the pertinent elements of all studies examined in the Country Report that would not be readily accessible from an online source.

2. Identify any relevant studies in the Member State concerning the (a) availability of parental control technologies or rating systems, (b) rate of use, ease of use, or parent satisfaction of parental control technologies, and (c) cost associated with deployment of the technologies.

3. Identify and discuss any relevant studies in the Member State concerning the affects on children of gratuitous violence or pornography.

4. Identify any studies in the Member State concerning the use and efficacy of educational or awareness-raising measures to be used in replacement of, or in conjunction with, parental control technologies.

General Overview

The following section requires the researcher to provide her observations and assessments. This section seeks a more global or comprehensive evaluation of the issue of parental control of harmful content and thus requires the researcher to broadly apply her expertise and familiarity with the related questions.

1. Provide your perception of what developments concerning parental control are foreseeable in the Member State.

2. Provide your assessments of the following elements of the parental control issue: (a) prospects for enhancing parental control via measures taken at European level, and (b) deployment of a horizontal approach to the question of harmful content.

3. Provide your analysis of the following spheres of discourse concerning parental control of harmful content. In your analyses, identify the leaders of these discussions: (a) Policy circles (for example, government, regulators, administrative agencies), (b) Civil sphere (for example, popular discourse, interest groups), (c) Media (for example, press, television), and (d) Industry (for example, producers of film, of television, broadcasters, online service providers).

Template: Annex I: Rating Systems

Prior to applying the applicable subsection of this Annex, (Annex I-A, Annex I-B, Annex I-C, or Annex I-D) provide the following three distinctions for the given rating system.

1. Determine and explain whether the rating system is descriptive or evaluative. A descriptive system is one that provides a description of the content of the labelled media and can provide a set of indicators about different content categories.[4] An evaluative system is one that makes a judgement about content using a standard of harmfulness and typically provides a single rating indicator, usually based on age.[5] Keeping in mind that no system is purely descriptive, please provide a detailed explanation of the basis for your determination.

2. Determine and explain whether the rating system applies a deterministic or a nondeterministic rating process. A deterministic rating process is based on some objective methodology in which the final rating is the result of following the methodology. A nondeterministic rating process is based on the opinions of a rating body. Keeping in mind that no system is purely deterministic, please provide a detailed explanation of the basis for your determination.

3. Determine and explain whether the rating system is voluntary or mandatory. A system is voluntary if the content producer is free to choose to rate or have product rated. A system is mandatory if the content producer is required to rate or to have product rated by some other agency.

---

[4] The Recreational Software Advisory Council (RSAC) rating system is an example of a descriptive system. Content producers answer a detailed questionnaire about their content with respect to violence, nudity, sex, and language.

[5] The Motion Picture Association of America (MPAA) rating system is an example of an evaluative system. The ratings ascribed by the MPAA do not describe the content of the film, but what age group may see the film.

Annex I-A: Producer Self-rating

1. Identify the producers and describe their capacity[6] to provide ratings for the content they produce.

2. Characterise the structure, rationale and efficiency of any of this industry's existing rating system(s).

3. Discuss the feasibility of this system providing ratings for the volume of existing and future production in this medium.

4. Identify the volume of programming this system can be anticipated to accommodate for this medium.

5. Identify and discuss whether this rating system is applied to advertisements. If a separate rating system exists for advertisements, apply Annex I and the applicable subsection.

Annex I-B: Industry

1. Identify the industry board(s) for this medium.

2. For each industry board, (a) characterise the board's express purpose and its competence[7] (b) state the age and size; (c) characterise its capacity to provide ratings; (d) characterise the structure, substance, and define the content of this rating system; (e) assess the feasibility of this system providing ratings for the volume of existing and future programming and content; and (f) identify the maximum volume of programming and content this system can be anticipated to accommodate and explain the answers.

3. Identify whether there is an international industry board with a presence in the Member State.

4. If so, (a) characterise this presence and corresponding function of the board; (b) identify whom exactly the industry board represents; (c) identify the express purpose and function of the industry board, (d) state the board's age, size, and date of first presence in the Member State; (e) characterise the industry board's capacity to provide ratings; (f) characterise the structure, substance, and define the content of this rating system; (g) assess the feasibility of this system providing ratings for the volume of existing and future programming and content; and (h) identify the maximum volume of programming and content this system can be anticipated to accommodate. Explain.

---

[6] Capacity, for the purpose of this template, refers to the (a) legal capacity and (b) organisational and economic capacity to manage the ratings responsibility for the volume of output.

[7] Identify the addressees of decisions, the legal nature of the ratings provider's decisions vis-à-vis the addressees, and characterise the compulsory level of this decision. Determine whether ratings decisions are binding or not binding instruments. In the case of binding instruments, identify the available enforcement methods to ensure proper application and/or to punish addressees that fail to comply with a given decision.

5. Identify and discuss whether this rating system is applied to advertisements. If a separate rating system exists for advertisements, apply Annex I and the applicable subsection.

Annex I-C: Third Party (Commercial or Noncommercial)

1. Identify whether any third party rating entity exists in the Member State for this medium.

2. Describe their function and competencies.

3. State how long the rating entity has performed this function.

4. Identify and explain the rating systems under consideration in the Member State. Determine if these systems are State-specific or designed to provide classification at European level.

5. Characterise the current capacity for this rating system. Assess the feasibility of this system of providing ratings for the volume of existing and future content.

6. Provide the reasonable expectations for expansion of this system in order to accommodate greater volume.

7. Assess the maximum volume of programming that this system can be anticipated to accommodate.

8. Identify and discuss whether this rating system is applied to advertisements. If a separate rating system exists for advertisements, apply Annex I and the applicable subsection.

Annex I-D: Government

1. Identify whether any governmental rating entities for this medium exist in the Member State.

2. Describe their function and competencies.

3. State how long the rating entity has performed this function.

4. Identify and explain the rating systems under consideration in the Member State. Determine if these systems are State-specific or designed to provide classification at the European level.

5. Characterise the current capacity for this rating system. Assess the feasibility of this system of providing ratings for the volume of existing and future television programming.

6. If presently there are no such entities in the Member State, assess the likelihood for formation of such entities.

7. Assess the maximum volume of programming this system can be anticipated to accommodate.

8. Identify and discuss whether this rating system is applied to advertisements. If a separate rating system exists for advertisements, apply Annex I and the applicable subsection.

Template: Annex II

Taken from Directive 97/36/EC of the European Parliament and of the Council of 30 June 1997 Amending Council Directive 89/552/EEC on the Coordination of Certain Provisions Laid Down by Law, Regulation or Administrative Action in Member States concerning the Pursuit of Television Broadcasting Activities

CHAPTER V: Protection of Minors and Public Order

Article 22

1. Member States shall take appropriate measures to ensure that television broadcasts by broadcasters under their jurisdiction do not include any programmes which might seriously impair the physical, mental or moral development of minors, in particular programmes that involve pornography or gratuitous violence.

2. The measures provided for in paragraph 1 shall also extend to other programmes which are likely to impair the physical, mental or moral development of minors, except where it is ensured, by selecting the time of the broadcast or by any technical measure, that minors in the area of transmission will not normally hear or see such broadcasts.

3. Furthermore, when such programmes are broadcast in unencoded form Member States shall ensure that they are preceded by an acoustic warning or are identified by the presence of a visual symbol throughout their duration.

Article 22a

Member States shall ensure that broadcasts do not contain any incitement to hatred on grounds of race, sex, religion, or nationality.

Article 22b

1. The Commission shall attach particular importance to application of this Chapter in the report provided for in Article 26.

2. The Commission shall within one year from the date of publication of this directive, in liaison with the competent Member State authorities, carry out an investigation of the possible advantages and drawbacks of further measures with a view to facilitating the control exercised by parents or guardians over the programmes that minors may watch.

This study shall consider, *inter alia*, the desirability of:

• The requirement for new television sets to be equipped with a technical device enabling parents or guardians to filter out certain programmes;
• The setting up of appropriate rating systems,
• Encouraging family viewing policies and other educational and awareness measures,
• Taking into account experience gained in this field in Europe and elsewhere as well as the views of interested parties such as broadcasters, producers, educationalists, media specialists and relevant associations.

COUNTRY REPORTS: LIST OF EXPERTS

Austria

Dr Albrecht Haller. Dr Haller works as an associate in the Vienna office of the international law firm, 'Bruckhaus Westrick Heller Loeber'. He also lectures in copyright law at the University of Vienna. Dr Haller received a Master of Law and Doctor of Law Degree from the University of Vienna and a Master of Arts Degree from the University of Music and Dramatic Arts in Vienna. He has produced numerous publications on copyright and media law, including notes on relevant developments in Austria for IRIS.

Belgium and Luxembourg

Mr Serge Robillard. Serge Robillard is a legal expert based in Brussels. He joined the Research Department of the European Institute for the Media in November 1991. In 1997, he published a study on 'Television and Culture: Policies and Regulation in Europe' with Emmanuelle Machet. A study on Convergence, including analysis of the protection of minors within the Information Society, will be soon published. He has made several evaluations of programming aspects for broadcasters and media authorities. He has also made several presentations on legal/regulatory issues and was involved in the European Platform of Regulatory Authorities (EPRA). He has published a study on regulatory bodies (London 1995) and contributed to several research projects. From 1990 to 1991 he worked as a legal expert at the Ministry of the French Speaking Community of Belgium where he was in charge of media expertise. He was also an Associate to the Belgium delegation within the Council of the European Union.

Denmark

Dr Brigitte Tufte. Brigitte Tufte is Associate Professor, Dr.ped. at the Royal Danish School of Educational Studies. She has conducted research since the early 1980s, taught and published extensively within the field of children *and* media, media education and youth culture. She is currently Section President of the International Association of Mass Communication Research's Section on Media Education and project leader on a 5-year research project on girls' and boys' everyday life and media culture.

Dr Thomas Tufte (son of Dr. Brigitte Tufte). Dr. Tufte is Assistant Research Professor, PhD at the Department of Film and Media Studies, University of Copenhagen. He gained his PhD in a media ethnographical analysis of TV fiction in Brazil. He provided the Danish country report for the European research project, 'Proximity Television and the Information Society in Europe', and is currently finalising a 3-year research project on globalisation and new technology. He is also an associate member of the ORBICOM communication network and co-editor of the Danish Journal of Communication (Medienkultur).

Finland

Dr Anu Mustonen. Dr Mustonen is currently Head of PR and Information at the University of Jyväskylä, Finland. With a degree in journalism and a PhD in Psychology, she has been engaged as a reporter for the national papers, 'Karjalan Maa' and 'Outokummun Seutu' since 1987, and is a researcher for the Finnish Broadcasting Company and a researcher/lecturer in the Department of Psychology at the University of Jyväskylä. She has produced numerous publications investigating the relationship between the issues of violence in the media, children and psychology and has since 1995 been the reviewer for the *Journal of Broadcasting and Electronic Media*.

France

Mr Frederic Pinard. Mr Pinard is a lawyer specialising in Media, Public, and European Law. In 1995 he obtained a post-graduate diploma in Economic and Communication law, focusing on Media law and Economics, encompassing traditional media and new media and, more generally the information society. In a professional capacity he has worked as a consultant, legal adviser, editor of a newsletter and researcher/writer. He has worked for the Council of Europe, the Eurimages Fund and the European Audiovisual Observatory.

Germany

Dr Runar Woldt. Dr Runar Woldt started his professional career as a researcher and lecturer at the University of Stuttgart-Hohenheim, Department of Journalism. He was then an editor of 'Media Perspektiven', a German media journal published by the public broadcasting organisation ARD (1986–91). Since December 1991, he has been Head of Research at the European Institute for the Media (EIM), based in Düsseldorf. Runar Woldt's main research interests include the socioeconomic developments of the media in Europe, European media policies, and the impact of regulation and market structures on media performance. He has produced numerous publications on a variety of related subjects.

Emanuelle Machet. Emmanuelle Machet is a researcher at the European Institute for the Media (EIM) based in Düsseldorf. She has a degree in media law from the University of Poitiers and has carried out post-graduate work in European studies at the University of Aachen. She is the secretary of the European Platform of Regulatory Authorities (EPRA) and has recently published together with Serge Robillard 'Television and Culture: Policies and Regulations in Europe'.

Greece

Dr Petros Iosifides. Dr Ioifides is currently lecturer in Mass Communications at the University of North London, with responsibilities including the design and teaching of MA courses, 'Principles in Mass Communications' and 'Communications and New Technologies'. His research duties include production of papers and proposals in the areas of media market structure, technological convergence and audiovisual content regulation, with a particular interest in the protection of minors. He has participated in the EC project examining the European Union multimedia market in the past.

Ireland

Dr Marie McGonagle. Marie McGonagle is a lecturer in law at the National University of Ireland, Galway, where she specialises in Media and Entertainment Law, and teaches Family Law. She has lectured and published widely on Media Law issues, has been involved in training print and audiovisual journalists, has acted as consultant to media and journalists' organisations on legal issues and matters of law reform. In 1996, she was appointed to the Irish Government's Commission on the Future of the Newspaper Industry. She has also participated in a number of seminars and projects for Article 19, the Council of Europe, and other national and international organisations.

Italy

Ms Cristina Cabella. Cristina Cabella received a degree from the University of Milan School of Law in 1988 and a LL.M from the University of London, Queen Mary and Westfield College in 1990. Thereafter she was Associate Researcher in Intellectual Property at the University of London, Queen Mary and Westfield College from 1990 to 1991. She has practised in the Intellectual Property department of two major London City firms: Lovell White Durrant (1990–1991) and Freshfields (1998). Her practice areas are intellectual property and information technology, Internet, and digital media. She advises among others a number of US software firms including Seagate, Aim-Tech, Security Dynamics Technologies, NETg, Engineering Animation, on Shrink-wrap Click-wrap software license agreements, software translation agreements, and software escrow agreements.

Netherlands

Dr Jo Groebel. Dr Groebel is chairman of the Communications Psychology Department at the University of Utrecht. He is also the founder and director of the Post-Graduate School of Media Management and Development— University of Utrecht and Visiting Professor at the University of California Los Angeles (UCLA). He is a member of the German UNESCO-Commission, the Media Commission of the German BundesPräsident and the 'Mediaraad', advisory committee to the Dutch Government.

Portugal

Dr Helena Sousa. Dr Sousa is currently Deputy Head of the Department of Communications Science at the University of Minho, where she lectures on 'International Information and Media Sociology'. She has previously worked as a journalist for the national newspaper, 'Jornal de Notícias', on national and international political issues.

Dr Manuel Pinto. Dr. Pinto is Vice-President of the Institute of Child Studies. He wrote his thesis about 'Television in Children's Everyday Life'. As former head of the Education and Culture Section of 'Jornal de Notícias', he has extensive experience as a journalist in educational issues.

Spain

Dr Alberto Perez Gomez Dr Perez Gomez is a Lecturer in European and Constitutional Law at the University of Alcala (Madrid). His main field of research is Communications Law and he has published several articles in this area. He is the Spanish correspondent for IRIS, the European Audiovisual Observatory's monthly magazine, the Institute für Europäisches Medienrecht de Amsterdam (EMR) and the Institute for Information Law of Amsterdam. He has participated in several research projects related to the media, and is also a practising lawyer. He previously researched the legal protection of minors in Spain when preparing a joint publication about Information Law in Spain.

Sweden

Dr Jonas Wall. Jonas Wall is a lecturer at the University College of Gävle. In 1979, he initiated one of the first Swedish university courses in the field of mass communication. He has conducted extensive research on the role of the mass media in the development of adolescents and wrote one of the first Swedish books in this field. In 1992 the Swedish government appointed him as a film censor, and since 1996 he has taught courses in mass communication theory and methodology at the University College of Gävle, Sweden. He has published several books on theme of children and the mass media.

United Kingdom

Mr Stefaan Verhulst. Stefaan G. Verhulst is the Programme Director of the Programme in Comparative Media Law and Policy at the Centre for Socio-Legal Studies, Wolfson College, Oxford University. He was previously senior researcher for IMPS at the School of Law, University of Glasgow. In addition, Mr. Verhulst serves as an Expert Consultant for the Council of Europe, a Legal Correspondent for the European Audiovisual Observatory and is the co-editor of the *International Journal of Communications Law and Policy*.

QUESTIONNAIRE FOR BROADCASTERS

1. Have you implemented a parental control system(s)?

NO

If no, please answer Section 1C of the Questionnaire and skip to question 2.

YES

Is it your own system? Yes No

If so, please answer Section 1A of the Questionnaire and skip to question 2.

Is it a system determined by a third party? Yes No

If so, please answer Section 1B of the Questionnaire and continue to question 2.

2. All respondents should answer Sections 2, 3, and 4 of the Questionnaire.

3. Please fill in the section below so that we can send you the final report of the study.

Title:
Name:
Company:
Address:

Telephone:
Fax:
E-mail:

4. Which industry/group of interested parties do you represent?

    a)   Digital/analogue broadcasting entity
    b)   Film/video distributor
    c)   Internet service provider
    d)   Trade association
    e)   Other (please specify)

Please return this form with your questionnaire. Thank you.

Section 1A: Broadcasters Who Have Implemented Own Parental Control System

Implementation

1. When did you implement the parental control system(s) currently in use?

2. Is it a voluntary or mandatory system? If the system is mandatory, please describe the nature of the legal instrument mandating it, its issuing body, and discuss its specific requirements.

3. Which parties were involved in the conception and implementation of the actual system(s) (viewers' and family associations, producers, authors, other broadcasters, government authorities, and so on)?

4. Which cultural, legal, and technical considerations have been taken into account?

Description—Functioning—Evaluation

1. To which content (for example, programs, films, news, advertisements, chat room, multimedia content, and so on) do you apply your rating/labelling system?

2. How is your system represented (for example, acoustic warning, visual symbol, and so on)?

3. What is the qualitative nature of the system? Identify whether the system is (a) evaluative or descriptive,[8] and (b) deterministic or nondeterministic.[9] State the criteria used.

4. Is a specific body responsible for the classification? Is it an internal or external body? What is the composition of this body? Do any legal instruments bind this body? If so, identify the kind of instruments as well as the corresponding competence of this body.

5. Do you exercise control over the classification decisions issued by the body?

6. Apart from these systems, what other measures have you provided in order to facilitate parental control?

7. How do you evaluate the effectiveness of the parental control systems (when, how, by whom, and so on)? How do you adapt the systems to the change of practises?

---

[8] A *descriptive* system is one that provides a description of the content of the labelled media and can provide a set of indicators about different content categories. (The 'Recreational Software Advisory Council'—RSAC–USA) provides an example of a descriptive system. Content producers answer a detailed questionnaire about their content with respect to violence, nudity, sex and language.)

An *evaluative* system is one that makes a judgement about content using a standard of harmfulness and typically provides a single rating indicator, usually based on age. (The 'Motion Picture Association of America'—MPAA–USA) provides an example of an evaluative system. The ratings ascribed by the MPAA do not describe the content of the film, but what age group may see the film. The 'Entertainment Software Rating Board' (ESRB–USA) provides a combination of content descriptors and age classification.)

[9] A *deterministic* rating process is based on some objective methodology in which the final rating is the result of following the methodology. A *nondeterministic* rating process is based on the opinions of a rating body. Keeping in mind that no system is purely deterministic, please provide a detailed explanation of the basis for your determination.

Appreciation

1. What specific technical difficulties have you met in implementing your rating/labelling system?

2. What is the cost imposed by this system? Who bears this cost? What is the impact of the rating/labelling system on your budget?

3. Has this rating/labelling system had an appreciable impact on the value of your existing catalogue of works?

4. Has this rating/labelling system had an impact on the audience and thereby on your programming strategy? Discuss any studies you have conducted on this issue.

5. Has this rating/labelling system had an impact on sponsors, advertisers, and thereby on your programming strategy? Discuss any studies you have conducted on this issue. What is your marketing strategy concerning the ratings? Where are the rating/labelling systems published (specialised magazines, general newspaper, hotlines, and so on)?

6. Has this rating/labelling system had an impact on your image vis-à-vis viewers either as individuals or as parents? Discuss any studies you have conducted on this issue.

7. Has this rating/labelling system created any tension with producers and authors of the work labelled? How has this tension been resolved?

Section 1B: Broadcasters Applying Parental Control Systems Decided by a Third Party

Implementation

1. When was the parental control system(s) currently in use implemented?

2. Which body issued the current system? (Broadcaster, Regulatory Body...)

3. Is it a voluntary or mandatory system? If the system is mandatory, please describe the nature of the legal instrument mandating it, and discuss its specific requirements.

4. Which parties were involved in the conception and implementation of the actual system(s)? (viewers' and family associations, producers, authors, other broadcasters, government authorities, and so on)

5. Which cultural, legal, and technical considerations have been taken into account?

Description—Functioning—Evaluation

1. To which content (for example, programs, films, news, advertisements, chat rooms, multimedia content, and so on) do you apply the rating/labelling system?

2. How is the system represented (for example, acoustic warning, visual symbol, and so on)?

3. What is the qualitative nature of the system? Identify whether the system is (a) evaluative or descriptive,[10] and (b) deterministic or nondeterministic.[11] State the criteria used.

4. Are you responsible for the classification of the programs you broadcast?

5. If not, which entity decides the classification? How? If yes, how do you proceed? Is a specific body responsible for the classification? Is it an internal or external body? What is the composition of this body? Do any legal instruments bind this body? If so, identify the kind of instruments as well as the corresponding competence of this body?

6. Do you exercise control over the classification decisions issued by the body?

7. Apart from these systems, what other measures have you provided in order to facilitate parental control?

8. How do you make the evaluation of the parental control systems (when, how, by who)? How do you adapt the systems to the change of practises?

Appreciation

1. What specific technical difficulties have you met in complying with the rating/labelling system?

---

[10] A *descriptive* system is one that provides a description of the content of the labelled media and can provide a set of indicators about different content categories. (The 'Recreational Software Advisory Council'—RSAC) provides an example of a descriptive system. Content producers answer a detailed questionnaire about their content with respect to violence, nudity, sex and language.)

An *evaluative* system is one that makes a judgement about content using a standard of harmfulness and typically provides a single rating indicator, usually based on age. (The 'Motion Picture Association of America'—MPAA provides an example of an evaluative system. The ratings ascribed by the MPAA do not describe the content of the film, but what age group may see the film. The 'Entertainment Software Rating Board'—ESRB–USA—provides a combination of content descriptors and age classification.)

[11] A *deterministic* rating process is based on some objective methodology in which the final rating is the result of following the methodology. A *nondeterministic* rating process is based on the opinions of a rating body. Keeping in mind that no system is purely deterministic, please provide a detailed explanation of the basis for your determination.

2. What is the cost imposed by this system? Who bears this cost? What is the impact of the rating/labelling system on your budget?

3. Has this rating/labelling system had an appreciable impact on the value of your existing catalogue of works?

4. Has this rating/labelling system had an impact on the audience and thereby on your programming strategy? Discuss any studies you have conducted on this issue.

5. Has this rating/labelling system had an impact on sponsors, advertisers and thereby on your programming strategy? Discuss any studies you have conducted on this issue. What is your marketing strategy concerning the ratings? Where are the rating/labelling systems published (specialised magazines, general newspaper, hotlines, and so on).

6. Has this rating/labelling system had an impact on your image vis-à-vis viewers either as individuals or as parents? Discuss any studies you have conducted on this issue.

7. Has this rating/labelling system created any tension with producers and authors of the work labelled? How has this tension been resolved?

8. What is your assessment of the role of the Regulatory Body/Industry Board?

Section 1C: Broadcasters Who Have Not Implemented a Parental Control System

Please give your reasons for not having implemented a parental control system to date.

Sections 2, 3, and 4: All Broadcasters

New Technologies

1. What is your evaluation of the recent technical devices (V-chip, EPG, PICS, blocking, filtering systems)? Are there any technical, financial or cultural obstacles to the implementation of such devices or further parental control measures generally? What would be the foreseeable consequences for your company in both financial and technical terms?

2. Would you voluntarily implement a technical device regime for your programming? What do you believe is the proper role of the regulatory body in this context?

3. If you are a film or video distributor, or a broadcaster, have you developed any systems specifically in response to the development of digital technologies for the television environment? If you are an online content provider, have you

developed any systems specifically in response to recent technological developments in the online environment? If so, please discuss.

4. If you have not developed any systems specifically for these technological developments, what are your views concerning facilitating parental control in the context of these new technologies? Do you anticipate these new modes permitting you to improve information either for parents or for the protection of minors? Through what types of measures and/or devices may this be achieved?

Horizontal and European Approach

1. If a horizontal approach is not already in place, do you consider a horizontal approach as appropriate, feasible, or efficient?[12]

2. In your view is there a need for European cooperation or harmonisation on this issue? What kind of commonalties at European Union level is needed (age classification, and so on)?

Conclusions

1. Is there any discussion concerning the improvement of the actual system, the implementation of a new system or further measures such as the V-chip? In what environments? Who are the parties involved? Is the actual stage of these discussions preliminary, intermediate or advanced?

2. Do you think that your industry is culturally, structurally, technically, or economically prepared to make this new step? Do you think that your industry is capable of collaborating on a high level with the whole industry to implement necessary accompanying measures for these new devices such as a common rating/labelling system? Do you think that your actual rating/labelling system would be adaptable to these new requirements?

Please feel free to add any information that seems relevant for our understanding and the aim of the study.

---

[12] This idea of horizontal treatment concerning parental control is derived from the Council Recommendation on the Protection of Minors and Human Dignity in the Audiovisual and Information Services (adopted 28 May 1998). Here, the term horizontal encompasses any rating or labelling system capable of covering content in the four media sectors designated in this Recommendation (for example, film, video, TV, and online services), as well as a device employing such a system in television and personal computer environments.

CONTACT LIST

Regulatory Bodies

Austria

- Dr Woflgang Jedlicka, Kommission zur Wahrung des Rundfunkgesetzes (Rundfunkkommission)
- Hofrat Dr Ernst Marker, Kommission zur Wahrung des Regionalradiogesetzes
- Prof. Dr. Elmar A. Peterlunger, Fachverband der Audiovisions- und Filmindustrie Österreichs [Association of the Audiovisual and Film Industry]
- Mr Martin Schweighofern Film Comission
- Mag. Gerhard Schedl, Österreichisches Filminstitut
- Dr. Hans Peter Lehofer, Telekom-Control GmbH
- Herr Mendel, Meldestelle Kinderpornographie

Belgium

- Ms Fadila Laanan, CSA
- Ms Monica Glineur, Cabinet de la Ministre-Présidente
- Ms Myriam Lenoble, Service général de l'audiovisuel et du multimédia
- Mr Robert Van Moeseke, Flemish Community
- Mr Paul Vandevelde, Flemish Community
- M. Claude Lelievre, WTC Tour 1
- M. Jean Luc Paternoster, Cabinet due Vice Premier Ministre et Ministre de L'Economie et des Telecommunications

Denmark

- Ms Susanne Boe, The Media Council for Children and Youth
- Ms Margit Andersen, Forbrugerstyrelsen
- Ms Liselotte Widing, The Nordic Council of Ministers
- Mr Litten Hansen, COPY DAN

Finland

- Ms Ulla Lång, Valtion elokuvalautakunta
- Mr Antti Alanen, Valtion elokuvatarkastamo

France

- Mme. Sophie Jehel, Conseil Supérieur de l'Audiovisuel (CSA)
- M. Jean-Claude Debray, Centre National de la Cinématographie (CNC)

Germany

- Herr Joachim von Gottberg, Freiwillige Selbstkontrolle Fernsehen e.v. (FSF)
- Frau Inge Kempenich, Freiwillige Selbstkontrolle der Filmwirtschaft (FSK)
- Dr. Detlev Müller-Using, Freiwillige Selbst-kontrolle Multimedia Dienstanbieter e.v. (FSM)
- Herr Susanne Grams, Medienanstalt Berlin Brandenburg (MABB)
- Dr. Thomas Voß, Hamburgische Anstalt für neue Medien (HAM)
- Frau Katja Kirste, Unabhängige Landesanstalt für das Rundfunkwesen Schleswig-Holstein (ULR)
- Frau Jutta Klepper, Bremische Landesmedienanstalt
- Frau Sabine Mosler, Niedersächsische Landesmedienanstalt für privaten Rundfunk (NLM)
- Frau Annette Schriefers, Landesanstalt für privaten Rundfunk - LPR Hessen
- Herr Werner Röhrig, Landesanstalt für das Rundfunkwesen (LAR)
- Frau Ulrike Handel, Landesanstalt für Kommunikation (LfK Baden-Württemberg)
- Frau Verena Weignandt, Bayerische Landeszentrale für neue Medien (BLM)
- Frau Susanne Rieger, Landesrundfunkzentrale (LRZ Mecklenburg/Vorpommern)
- Herr Walter Demski, Landesrundfunkausschuß für Sachsen - Anhalt (LRA)
- Frau Angelika Heyen, Thüringer Landesmedienanstalt (TLM)
- Frau Cosima Stracke-Nawka, Sächsische Landesanstalt für privaten Rundfunk und neue Medien (SLM)
- Herr Peter Beherns, Landeszentrale für private Rundfunkveranstalter (LPR Rheinland Pfalz)
- Herr Kurt-Henning Schober, Landesanstalt für Rundfunk (LfR Nordrhein-Westfalen)

Greece

- Mr Nikos Kaimakis, National Broadcasting Council
- Mr Mouzourakis, 'National Telecommunications Commission' (EET)
- Mr Andreas Takis, Ministry of Press and the Mass Media

Ireland

- Mr Sheamus Smith
- Ms Celene Craig, The Independent Radio and Television Commission
- Ms Etain Doyle
- Mr Francesco Ventura, Commissioni Speciali del Dipartimento dello Spettacolo and
- Commissione per i lungometraggi, cartometraggi ed i film per ragazzi c/o Presidenza del Consiglio
- Mr Gabriele Malinconico, Commissione Parlamentare di indirizzo e vigilanza RAI
- Mr Francesco Tonucci, Comitato TV e minori c/o Dipartimento per l'informazione e l'editoria della Presidenza del Consiglio
- Mr Paolo Luigi Galassi, Consiglio Consultivo Utenti c/o Garante per la Radiodiffusione e l'Editoria
- Mr Antonio Amendola, Commissione Prodotti e Servizi c/o Autorità per le Garanzie nelle Comunicazioni
- Mr Piero Fattori, Ufficio Pubblicità Ingannevole c/o Garante della Concorrenza e Mercato

Luxembourg

- Mr Pierre Goerens, Ministère d'Etat Service des médias et de l'Audiovisuel
- Mr Joy Hoffmann, Centre National de l'Audiovisuel
- Mr Jean Paul Zens, Prime Minister's Office
- Mr Kugener, Conseil National des Programmes

Netherlands

- Sir/Madam , Ministerie van Verkeer en Waterstaat
- Mr. A.G.M. Driedonks, Ministerie van Verkeer en Waterstaat
- Mr. Jan van Dijk, Ministerie van Justitie
- Mr. Harry Kramer, Ministerie van Onderwijs, Cultuur en Wetenschappen
- Mr. H. Koetje, Commissariaat voor de Media
- Mr. Cor Crans, Nederlandse Filmstichting

Portugal

- Juiz Conselheiro José Maria Gonçalves Pereira, Alta Autoridade para a Comunicação Social
- Mr. Rui Assis Ferreira, Instituto da Comunicação Social
- Mr. Carlos Pedro Fernandes, Inspecção Geral das Actividades Culturais
- Mr Luis Filipe Nazaré, Instituto das Comunicaç'es de Portugal

- Mr. Augusto Vitor Coelho, Comissão Nacional de Protecção de Dados Pessoais Informatizados

Spain

- Mr Jose Antonio Muñoz Ruiz, Ministerio de Fomento
- Mr Angel García Castillejo, Comisión del Mercado de las Telecomunicaciones
- Mr Jordi Conde, Consell Audiovisual de Catalunya
- Mr Juan Martín García, ICAA
- Ms Ana Mato, Partido Popular
- Mr J. Gómez Castallo, Asociación de Autocontrol de la Publicidad
- Mr Esteban González Pons, Partido Popular - Senado
- Ms Beatriz De Armas, Instituto deCinematografía y Artes Audiovisuales- ICAA
- Mr Antonio Alvarado, Ministerio de Fomento
- Ms Maria Teresa Varela, Ministerio de Fomento
- Ms Elena Alvarez, ICAA

Sweden

- Mrs Anita Bondestam, Datainspektionen
- Mr Greger Lindberg, Granskningsnamnden
- Mr Gunnel Arrback, Statens Biografbyra

United Kingdom

- Ms Margaret Ford, British Board of Film Classification
- Ms Matti Alderson, Advertising Standards Authority
- Ms Andrea Millwood-Hargrave, Broadcasting Standards Commission
- Mr Anthony Smith, ICSTIS
- Mr Michael Redley, Independent Television Commission
- Ms Sarah Tane, Independent Television Commission
- Ms Laurie Hall, Video Standards Council (VSC)

Broadcasters

Austria

- Dr. Rainer Fischer-See, Österreichischer Rundfunk (ORF) [Austrian Broadcasting Corporation]
- Mag. Perle, Telesystem Tirol Kabelfernsehen
- Mag. Friedrich Spandl, W1

- Mr Hermann Hobodides, Columbia TriStar Filmverleih Ges.m.b.H.
- Ing. Christian Langhammer, Constantin-Film Verleih-,Vertriebs-and Produktionsges.m.b.H.
- Mr Hans König, Polyfilm Verleih
- Herr Michael Eisenriegler, Black*Box*Systems
- Herr Herbert Herdlicka, EUnet
- Herr Klaus Matzka, magnet

Belgium

- M. Jean-Charles De Keyser, RTL-Tvi
- M. Pol Heyse, RTL Tvi
- M. Gérard Loverius, RTBF
- M. Jean-Frédéric Laignoux, RTBF
- M. Pierre Maes, Canal Plus
- Mme. Michèle Legros, Canal Plus
- M. Lut Vercruysse, VRT
- M. Jan Vandenhoutte, VTM

Denmark

- Mr Anders Krarup, TV2
- Mr Niels J. Langkilde, TV3
- Mr Mogens Vemmer, The Danish Broadcasting Corporation
- Children and Youth Department

Finland

- Mr Martti Soramäki, Finnish Broadcasting Company
- Mr Tauno Aijala, MTV
- Mr. Arto Kivinen, Nelonen
- Ms. Anne Lallo, Cable tv
- Suomen kaapelitelevisioliitto
- Mr Jouko Jämsä, Columbia TriStar Egmont Film Filmdistributors
- Ms Juha Mäkelä, Buena Vista Int. Finland
- Ms Aune Turja, Warner Bros. Finland Oy
- Mr Markku Koistinen, United International Pictures Oy
- Mr Timo Manty, Finnkino
- Mr Freddy Kamras, Kamras Film Group

France

- M. Edouard Boccon-Giboud, TF1
- M. François Tron 2

- Mme. Bibiane Godfroid, Canal +
- M. Henri L'Hostis, ARTE
- M. Thomas Valentin, M6
- Mme. Eve Baron, Canal J
- M. Michel Thoulouze, Ellipse Cable
- M. Jean-Baptiste Jouy, Paris Premiere
- M. Patrice Besombes, Serie club
- M. Richard Pezet, AMLF
- M. Jean Labadie, BAC Films
- M. Michel Saint Jean, Diaphana Distribution
- M. Bertrand Cocteau, UGC Distribution
- M. Gilles Boulanger, E.D. Distribution
- M. Jean-François Davy, New video agency
- M. Pierre Brossard, TF1 Vidéo
- M. Marc Bonduel Television Distribution
- M. Fabrice Sergent, Club-Internet
- M. Jean-Frederic Farny, Planete.net
- Wanadoo—France Telecom Interactive

Germany

- Dr. Albrecht Hesse, Bayerischer Rundfunk (BR)
- Dr. Hans-Werner Conrad, Hessischer Rundfunk (hr)
- Herr Helfried Spitra, Mitteldeutscher Rundfunk (mdr)
- Dr. Reinhart Binder, Norddeutscher Rundfunk (NDR)
- Herr Stephan Abarbanell, Ostdeutscher Rund-funk Brandenburg (ORB)
- Dr. Peter Dany, Radio Bremen (RB)
- Herr Hans-Dieter Metz, Saarländischer Rundfunk (SR)
- Frau Inge Mohr, Sender Freies Berlin (SFB)
- Dr. Norbert Waldmann, Südwestrundfunk (SWR)
- Herr Rolf Marx, Westdeutscher Rundfunk (WDR)
- Dr. Dieter Landmann, Zweites Deutsches Fernsehen (ZDF)
- Herr Dieter Czaja, RTL plus Deutsch-land Fernsehen GmbH and Co. KG
- Dr. Hans-Henning Arnold, VOX Film- und Fernsehen GmbH and Co. KG
- Herr Berthold Brüne, SAT.1 Satelliten Fernsehen GmbH
- Frau Andrea Weller, RTL 2 Fernsehen GmbH and Co. KG
- Herr Michael Groh, Pro Sieben Media AG
- Frau Elke Gohs, n-tv Nachrichten-fernsehen GmbH and Co. KG
- Frau Ulrike Beckmann, Premiere Medien GmbH and Co. KG
- Herr Claude Schmit, SuperRTL RTL Disney Fernsehen GmbH and Co. KG
- Frau Sylvia Schultz, VIVA Fernsehen GmbH and Co. KG
- Dr. Dirk Stötzel, MTV Networks GmbH / VH-1 Television GmbH and

Co. KG
- Frau Karin Rüdinger, TM 3 Fernsehen GmbH and Co. KG
- Frau Annette Rohn, DSF Deutsches Sportfernsehen GmbH
- Herr Martin Rabius, Kabel 1 K1 Fernsehen GmbH
- Frau Anja Humberg, DF 1 Gesellschaft für Digitales Fernsehen GmbH and Co. KG

Greece

- Mrs Errika Valianou, Antenna TV
- Mr Tasos Konstantinidis, Mega Channel
- Press Office, Star TV
- Press Office, Sky TV
- Mr Nikos Papageorgiu, ERT-1
- Mrs Margarita Vardaki, Odeon
- Mrs Zamouzaki, Prooptiki A.E.
- Mr Maravellas, OTEnet S.A.
- Mr Pantelis Tzortzakis, FORTHnet S.A.
- Mr Alexandros Psirakis, Hellas on Line S.A.
- Mrs Loukia Taliadorou, Compulink Network S.A.

Ireland

- Mr Andrew Burns, RTE

Italy

- Ms Maria Rosaria Monaco, RAI - Radio Televisione Italiana
- Mr Mario Brugola, MEDIASET
- Mr Stefano Buccafussa, Gruppo TMC Telemontecarlo
- Mr Alberto Peruzzo, Rete A
- Mr Giuliano Morello, Elefante TV Telemarket
- Mr Claudio Federico, Rete Capri
- Mr Claudio Scotto Di Carlo, Gruppo TELEPIU'
- Mr Manfredi Traxler, UNIDIM - Unione Nazionale delle Imprese Industriali di distribuzione Multimediale
- Mr Andrea Marcotulli, ANICA -Associazione Nazionale Industrie Cinematografiche Audiovisive e Multimediali
- Mr Stefano Lamborghini, AIIP -Associazione Italiana Internet Provider

Luxembourg

- Mr Gerard Lommel, CLT-UFA

Netherlands

- Mr. B. Klap, AVRO
- Mr. H. Lubberding, AVRO
- Mr. R. Kraan, EO
- Mr. A.C.G. Verlind, KRO
- Mr. H.J. Hemink, NCRV
- Mr. G. Baars, TROS
- Mr. J. Nagel, VARA
- Mr. F. de Jonge, VARA
- Mr. B. Gersing, NOS
- Mr. R. Oosterman, HMG
- Mr. U. Glorie, Veronica
- Mr. B. Soepnel, SBS6
- Mr. Vacant, TMF
- Mr. K. Bisseuil, Canal+
- Mr. Ruud Lamers, Warner Home Video
- Mr. W.M. van Miltenburg, NVDO

Portugal

- Mr Manuel Roque, Rádiotelevisão Portuguesa (RTP
- Mr Francisco Pinto Balsemão, Sociedade Independente de Comunicação (SIC)
- Eng. Carlos Moreira da Silva, Televisão Independente
- Mr. Luis Augusto Silva, Lusomundo
- Mr José Manuel Castelo Lopes, Castelo Lopes
- Mr António Avelar Gomes, Columbia Warner
- Mr António da Cunha Teles, Animatógrafo
- Eng. Carlos Sousa Alves, Telepac
- Eng. Pedros Ramalho Carlos, IP Global
- Mr. João Luis Traça, Esotérica

Spain

- Rosa and Iván , TVE
- Ms Ana Estebaranz, Telecinco
- Mr Javier Albert, Antena 3
- Mr Javier Carrillo, Canal Plus andCanal Satélite Digital
- Ms Isabel Rodriguez, Canal 9
- Mr Reyes, Telemadrid
- Ms Carmen Segovia, Via Digital
- Ms Mari Carmen Millán, Asociación Fonográfica y VideográficaEspañola
- Información , RedesTB

- Información, Servicom
- Mr Jose Manuel Fernández Bilbao, Sarenet
- Información, Arrakis
- Información, Euskaltel
- Mr Jose Antonio Félez, Asociación de Distribudiores y Editores de Software de Entretenimiento (ADESE)
- Mr Gilberto Sánchez, Anaya Interactiva
- Información, Zeta Multimedia
- Mr Juan Diaz Bustamante, Friendware

Sweden

- Mrs Rauni Kaukonen, Sveriges Television SVT1, SVT2
- Mr Jan Scherman, TV4 AB
- Mr Svante Stockselius, TV3
- Mr Mats Orbrink, Kanal 5 AB
- Mr Stig Goran, TV1000 Sverige AB
- Mr Stefane Pierre France, Canal+ Television AB
- Mrs Erik Lenschooten, TV6 Broadcsting AB
- Mr Jacob Lyth, ZTV AB
- Mr Jonas Hultkvist, TV8
- Mr Jan Olof Svensson, Bestseller Filmdistribution AB
- Mr Eric Broberg, Buena Vista International
- Mr Mats Caneman, Buena Vista Home Entertainment
- Mr Ulf Rennstam, CIC Video AB
- Mr Zoran Slavic, Columbia Tri-Star Films AB
- Mr Klas Hansson, Egmont Entertainment AB
- Mr Guy Scott, Fox Film AB
- Managing Director , Max Films AB
- Mr Berth Milton, Milcap Publishing Group AB
- Mr Mikael Midigh, Scanbox Sweden AB
- Mr Peter Possne, Sonet Film AB
- Mr Robert Enmark, Svensk Filmindustri AB
- Mr John Mirisch, United International Pictures AB
- Mr Peter Jansson, Warner Bros Sweden AB
- Mr Lars Hakansson, Warner Home Video Sweden AB
- Mr Joakim Hedin, DHE Distribution Home Entertainment
- Mr Bettan von Horn, Folkets Bio
- Mr Ulf Berggren, Polyfilm
- Managing Director , Polygram AB
- Mr Matthias Nohrburg, Triangelfilm AB
- Mr Christer Hagstrom, Wendros Cartoon AB
- Mrs Ola Johansson, Telia Telecom AB

- Mr Robert Hultmann, Tele 2 AB
- Mrs Madelen Forsberg, Telenordia Internet

United Kingdom

- Mr Phil Harding, BBC
- Ms Emma Somerville, British Interactive Broadcasting
- Ms Deanna Bates, BSkyB
- Ms Sarah Andrew, Channel 5 Broadcasting
- Mr John Willis, Channel Four Television Corporation
- Ms Karen Brown, Channel Four Television Corporation
- Mr Brent Harman, Flextech
- Ms Susan Woodward, Granada Television Ltd
- Mr Mark Gallagher, Independent Television Association
- Mr Marcus Ezekiel, OnDigital
- Mr Melanie Quirk, Yorkshire Television Ltd
- Ms Camille de Stempel, AOL
- Mr Mark Cook, UUNet UK
- Mr Paul Edge, Cable and Wireless
- Ms Charon Wood, LineOne—Springboard Internet Services Ltd.
- Ms Janet Henderson, British Telecommunications plc
- Mr Keith Mitchell, LINX (London Internet Exchange
- Mr David Kennedy, ISPA Secretariat
- Mr Trevor Smale, The Cable Communications Association
- Mr Andrew Brown, The Advertising Association

Producers

Austria

- Herr Peter A. Mayer, Adi Mayer Film KG
- Herr Kurt Mrkwicka, MR-Film
- Herr Reinhard Schwabenitzky, Star-Film
- Ms Golli Marboe, Sternstunden
- Herr Veit Geidschuka, Wega-Film
- Mag. Katharina Wagenhofer, ORF-Teletext ProduktionsgmbH

Beligum

- M. Henri Benkoski, CITY FILMS
- M. Frédéric Young, SACD
- Mr. Marcel Heymans, Belgian Video Federation

Denmark

- Mrs Susanne Teilmann, Danske Filmproducenter I/S
- Mr Henrik Kristensen, Dansk Reklame Film A/S
- Mr Klaus Hansen, International Television Entertainment
- Ms Eva Loekkegaard, LEGO System
- Mr Henrik Madsen, NovaVision
- Ms Malene Paulli, Egmont Imagination
- Ms AnneMette Madelung, Egmont Entertainment
- Mr Ole Ivanoff, IVANOFF
- Mr Preben Soerensen, Arbejdernes Radio- og Fjernsynsforbund
- Mr Per Holst, Per Holst Film A/S
- Ms Susanne Wad, The Danish Film Institute

Finland

- Mr Kari Sara, Fennada Filmi Oy
- Mr Claes Olson, KinoProduction
- Mr Lasse Saarinen, Kinotar Oy
- Mr Pekka Kosonen, WSOY/New Media
- Ms Maarit Heino, Helsinki Media
- Mr Jan Blomqvist, Toptronics

France

- M. Philippe de Chaisemartin, Gaumont
- M. Paulo Branco, Gemini Films
- Mme. Carole Scotta, Haut et Court
- M. Daniel Marquet, Le Studio Canal +
- M. Marin Karmitz, MK2
- M. Renaud Delourme, Editions Montparnasse
- M. Nicolas Moulin, Cabotages
- M. Stéphane Dykman, Globe Trotter Network SA
- M. Denys Wissler, La tête dans les nuages (MMP
- Mme. Marion Capecchi, OH ! Net communications
- M. Thierry Desmichelle, M6 Interactions

Germany
- Dr. Dieter Frank, Bavaria Film GmbH
- Herr Sauer, Ufa Film und Fernseh- GmbH
- Herr Otto Meissner, novafilm- Ferseh-produktion; Otto Meissner KG
- Herr Jan Krämer, Studio Hamburg
- Herr Christian Rottmann, ENDEMOL Entertainment Productions

- Herr Claus Schmitt-Holldack, Polyphon Film- und Fernsehgesellschaft mbH
- Herr Michael Burghoff, VIDEAL Gesell-schaft zur Herstel-lung von audiovisuel-len Produkten

Greece

- Mrs Lazari, Greek Cinematography Centre
- Mrs Margarita Iliopoulou, Mythos Production of Culture
- Mr Panagiotis Christodoulidis, MLS
- Mrs M. Papageorgiou, Papasotiriou S.A

Ireland

- Ms Trish Moran, Little Bird Productions
- Ms Maria Collins, Health Kitchen
- Ms Lorna Colborn, Merlin
- Mr Alan Moloney, Parallel Films
- Mr Sean Walsh, Millbrook Studios

Italy

- Mr Adriano Ariè, APT - Associazione Produttori Televisivi
- Mr Martin Treu, UNIVIDEO -Unione Produttori Distributori Importatori Italiani di Opere e Supporti Audiovisivi e Multimediali
- Mr Enzo Porcelli, API - AutoriProduttori Indipendenti
- Mr Massimo Cristaldi, APC - Associazione Produttori Cinematografici
- Mr Gianni Massaro, UNPF - Unione Nazionale Produttori Film
- Mr Francesco Carlà, Multi Simul Mondo
- Mr Roberto Liscia, ANEE -Associazione Nazionale Editori Elettronica

Luxembourg

- Mr Frank Elstner, Frank Elstner Productions

Netherlands

- Mr. Nassenstein, Endemol Entertainment TV
- Mr. P. Erkelens, Idtv Film and Video Productions
- Mr. B. de Jung, Nintendo Europe
- Mr. J. van Zigl, columbia TriStar
- Mr Paul Solleveld, NVPI

Portugal

- Mr Manuel Roque, Rádiotelevisão Portuguesa (RTP
- Mr Francisco Pinto Balsemão, Sociedade Independente de Comunicação (SIC)
- Eng. Carlos Moreira da Silva, Televisão Independente
- Mr Nicolau Breyner, Nicolau Breyner Produção (NBC
- Mr Carlos Cruz, Carlos Cruz Audiovisual
- Ms Teresa Guilherme, Teresa Guilherme
- Ms Ana Delfino, Endemol
- Mr Rui Pacheco, Porto Editora
- Professor Rui Soares, Instituto de Comunicação Multimedia
- Mr Rui Marques, Forum Multimedia
- Eng. Pedro Portela, Sensoria

Spain

- Mr Arqué Ferrari, Federación de Asociaciones deProductores Audiovisuales Españoles (FAPAE)
- Ms Nathalie Garcia, Columbia-TriStar
- Enrique , Globomedia
- Mr Alberto Azcona, Asociación Española de Fabricantes de Juguetes
- Oficina principal, Ubi Soft
- Mr Ibón Celaya, Zeppelin TV
- Información, Dinamic Multimedia

Sweden

- Mr Christer Abrahamsson, Cinema Art Productions AB
- Mr Christer Nilsson, Gotafilm AB
- Mr Johan Skogh, Mekano Film and Television
- Mr Tobias Bringholm, Meter Film and TV AB
- Mr Lasse Lundberg, Moviemakers AB
- Mr Klas Olofsson, Sandrew Metronome AB
- Mr Goran Bagge, Sonet Film AB
- Mr Johan Sundberg, Strix Television AB
- Mr Jan Edholm, Svensk Filmindustri AB
- Mr Hans Ottosson, Svenska Filminstitutet
- Mrs Maria Curman, SVT Drama
- Mr Marten Ass, Wegelius TV AB
- Mr Peter Levin, Bonnier Multimedia AB
- Mr Stefan Magnusson, Egmont Entertainment AB
- Mr Stefan Lampinen, Electronic Arts Nordic AB
- Mr Per Tornell, Levande Bocker

- Mr Peder Hegerstrom, Liber AB
- Mr Thomas Bruhl, Vision Park Entertainment
- Mr David Philipson, Bitos

United Kingdom

- Ms Anna Home, Children's Film and Television Foundation
- Ms Amanda Churchill, Diverse Production
- Ms Claudia Milne, Twenty Twenty Television
- Ms Zoe Black, AMXstudios Ltd.
- Mr Jonny Bradley, Automatic Television
- Mr Richard Holmes, P.A.C.T (Producers Alliance for Cinema and Television
- Mr Bernard Clark, P.A.C.T (Producers Alliance for Cinema and Television

Interest Groups

Austria

- Mag. Irene Rautner, Katholisches Jugendwerk
- Mag Sonja Brauner, Kinderfreunde
- Prof. Wolfgang Glück, Film Academy Vienna
- Mag. Gerlinde Seitner, Österreichisches Filminstitut
- Hofrat Dr. Matzenauer, Hörer- und Sehervertretung
- Mr Werner Raff, Tele-Zeitschriftenverlag

Beligum

- Professor Boris Libois, Laboratoire Etudes sur transformation de l'Etat social,
- M. Pierre Gordinne, La Médiathèque
- Professor Marc Minon, LENTIC
- Professor Alain Strowel, Faculté Universitaires Saint-Louis
- Mr Christian Bontinckk, Centre coopératif de la consommation
- Mr Benoit Goosens, Association des Téléspectateurs actifs
- Mr Marcel Colin, Conseil de l'Education aux Medias

Denmark

- President Peter Zinkernagel, Multimediabranchen. DK
- Secretariat , Foreningen af Danske Videogramdistributoerer
- Rektor Soeren K. Lauridsen, Danske Boernefilmklubber
- Mr Peter Danelund, Dansk BiblioteksCenter A/S

• President Johan Schluter, Multimediaforeningen
• Ms Bente Buchhave, Children and Culture
• Mr Per Schulz Joergensen, The National Council for Children's Rights

Finland

• Ms Helena Molander, Mannerheimin lastensuojeluliitto, The Mannerheim League for Child Welfare
• Mr Teuvo Peltoniemi, A-klinikkasaatio
• Mr Kalle Kinnunen, Dark Fantasy Ry.
• M. Guillaume Soulez

France

• M. Jean-Philippe Calmus, Association des jeunes téléspectateurs/Les pieds dans le PAF
• M. Françoise Meauzé, MTT (Média, télévision et téléspectateurs)
• M. Pierre Campmas
• M Christian Gauttelier, Enjeu télé (Association Enfance, Jeunesse et Télévision)
• M. Patrice Laume, Union Syndicale des Producteurs Audiovisuels (USPA)
• M. Pascal Rogard, Société civile Auteurs des Réalisateurs Producteurs (ARP)
• M. Christophe Sapet, Ass. Des fournisseurs d'accès à des services en ligne et à Internet
• M. Patrick Robin, Ass. Des fournisseurs d'accès à des services en ligne et à Internet
• M. Francois-Noel Robinet, Ass. Des fournisseurs d'accès à des services en ligne et à Internet
• M. Jérôme Lecat, AFPI (Association Française des Professionnels de l'Internet) association de fournisseurs d'accès

Germany

• Frau Ingrid Hillebrandt, Bundesarbeitsge-meinschaft Kinder- und Jugendschutz (BAJ)
• Frau Mirjam Jaquemoth, Verbraucherzentrale NRW
• Herr Stefen, Deutsche Gesell-schaft für Jugend-schutz e.V. (DGJ) / Redaktion Jugend Medien Schutz-Report
• Dr. Helga Theunert, Institut Jugend Film Fernsehen
• Dipl. Päd. Theodor Spiering, Päd. Hochschule Freiburg, Arbeitsbe-reich Medienpädagogik
• Dr. phil. Dieter Baacke, Uni Bielefeld Experte Medienpädagogik
• Prof. Dr. Ulrike Six, Universität Koblenz-Landau

Greece

- Professor Stylianos Papathanassopoulos, National and Kapodistrian University of Athens
- Mrs Athina Parlika, EKPIZO
- Mr Giannis Inglezakis, Centre for Consumer Protection (KEPKA)
- Mr Haralampos Kouris, Consumer Institute (INKA)
- Mr Mpampis Antholpoulos, General Secretary of New Generation

Ireland

- Dr Eamonn Hall, Telecom Eirann
- Ms Cian O'Tiarnaigh, ISPCC
- Senator Joe O'Toole, Irish National Teachers' Association
- Professor Farrell Corcoran

Italy

- Mr Giuliano Sacchi, Associazione Spettatori
- Mr Paolo Bafile, Associazione Italiana Ascoltatori Radio TV
- Ms Elena Del Bo, Telefono Azzurro
- Mr Flavio Manieri, CODACONS
- Ms Clelia Pallotta, Media Evo
- Ms Marina Migliorato, Movimento Difesa del Cittadino
- Ms Mara Colla, Confederazione dei Consumatori
- Mr Gustavo Ghidini, Movimento Consumatori
- Mr Mario Quinto, Unione Nazionale Consumatori
- Mr Domenico Volpi, Gruppo di servizio per la letteratura giovanile
- Mr Emilio Mayer, Associazione Cattolica Esercenti Cinema
- Mr Franco Passuello, Associazione Cattolica Lavoratori Italiani
- Mr Bruno Forte, Associazione Italiana Maestri Cattolici
- Mr Emilio Mayer, Associazione Nazionale Circoli Cinematografici Italiani -ANCCI
- Mr Giuseppe Richiedei, Associazione Genitori -AGE /
- Mr Stefano Versari, Associazione Genitori Scuole Cattoliche
- Mr Sergio Tavassi, Coordinamento Genitori Democratici

Luxembourg

- Mr Nicholas Estgen, Action familiale et populaire
- Mrs Lily Gansen, Foyer de la Femme
- Mr Fernand Weides, Association pour la Multimedia
- Mr Ed Kohl, Office due Film Scolaire
- Union Luxembourgeoise des Consommateurs

Netherlands

- Mr. Tony Holtrust, Raad voor Cultuur
- Mr. Asselbergs, Raad voor Cultuur
- Mr. Peter Nikken, Stichting Kinderkast
- Mr. Olaf Vlaar, NVPI

Portugal

- Prof. Manuel Lopes da Silva, Associação Portuguesa de Telespectadores
- Mr. Rui Teixeira da Mota, Associação de Espectadores de Televisão
- Mr. Carlos Alberto Pereira, Confederação Nacional das Associaç'es de Pais
- Ms. Maria Teresa, Confederação das Associaç'es de Família
- Dr. Maria Emília Brederode dos Santos, Instituto de Invovação Educacional
- Dr. Manuel Pinto, Instituto de Estudos da Criança
- Mr António Santos, Projecto Público na Escola
- Ms. Manuela Eanes, Instituto de Apoio à Criança

Spain

- Mr Jesús Busto Salgado, MEC
- Mr Alvaro Fernández de Miranda, Defensor del Pueblo
- Mr Javier Urra Portillo, Defensor del Monor de Madrid
- Consejería de Educación , Comunidad de Valencia
- Información , Centro Reina Sofia para el estudio de la violencia
- Mr Alejandro Perales Albert, Asociación Usuarios de Comunicación (AUC)
- Ms Juana María González, Confederación Española de Asociaciones de Amas de Casa, Consumidores y Usuarios (CEACCU)
- Ms Engracia Asenjo, Agrupación de Telespectadores y Radiooyentes (ATR)
- Mr Miguel Pérez Subias, Asociacion de Usuarios de Internet (AUI)
- Mr Xavier Ribas, Asociacion de Usuarios de Internet (AUI)
- Mr Joan Ferrés, Universidad de Barcelona
- Ms Carmen Candeotti, Ministerio de Educación y Cultura (MEC)

Sweden

- Mr Ted Weissberg, Sambandnet
- Mr Lars H Gustafsson, Riksforb. Hem and Skola
- Mrs Suzanne Askelof, Radda Barnen

United Kingdom

- Mr Roger Blamire, British Educational Communications and Technology Agency
- Professor Clive Walker, Centre for Criminal Justice Studies
- Mr Nigel Williams, Childnet International
- Ms Rosalind Benn, Christian Action Research and Education
- Ms Annie Mullins, NCH Action For Children
- Mr John Beyer, National Viewers and Listeners Association
- Mr Jocelyn Hay, Voice of the Listener and Viewer
- Ms Diana Whitworth, National Consumer Council
- Mr David Kerr, Internet Watch Association
- Mr Mark Stephens, Liberty

European Organisations

Broadcasters

- Mr Daniel Zimmermann, ACT
- Mr Peter Kokken , ECCA
- Mr Paolo Baldi , UER/EBU, Switzerland
- Mr Michael Wagner, DVB Project Office C/O EBU, Switzerland
- Mr David Wood, I.T.U./R, Switzerland

Interest Groups

- Mr Pascal Rogard , CICCE
- Mr Gérard Nauwelaerts , EACEM
- Ms Florence Ranson , EAT
- Mr Philippe Probst , FEITIS, Switzerland
- Mr Gilbert Gregoire , FIAD
- Mr André Chaubeau , FIAPF
- Ms Katrin Schweren, Bureau Européen des Unions des Consommateurs (BEUC)
- Ms Ursula Pachl, Bureau Européen des Unions des Consommateurs
- Ms Margaretha Mazura, European Multimedia Forum

Producers

- Mr Jorge Arque Ferrari, CEPI
- Mr Robert Strasser , CEPI
- Mr Gérard Gabella , SPA (Software Publishers Association), USA
- Mr Jean-Paul Commin , IVF

References

GENERAL

Action Group on Violence on Television. (1997, 30 April). Report to the Canadian Radio-Television and Telecommunications Commission.

Andersen, N. & Ventura, G. (no date). Television and violence lesson plan. YTV Canada, Inc. [online] (2001). Available http://inclass.ytv.com/inclass-lessons.asp.

Aufderheide, P. (1992). Media Literacy: A report of the national leadership conference on media literacy. Washington, D.C.: The Aspen Institute.

Balkin, J. M. (1998). Media filters and the V-chip. In M. Price (Ed.), *The V-chip debate: Content filtering from television to the Internet* (pp. 59–90). Mahwah, New Jersey: Lawrence Erlbaum Associates.

BBC says digital televisions must guarantee viewers access to all services. (1998, 14 October). *BBC Press Release.*

Buckingham, D. (1990). *Watching media learning: Making sense of media education.* England: The Falmer Press.

Collins, R. (1994). *Broadcasting and audiovisual policy in the European single market.* London: John Libbey.

Craufurd Smith, R. (1998). Sex and violence in the internal market: The impact of European Community law on television programme standards. *Contemporary Issues in Law, 3*(2), 135–153.

Digital TV: C&W launches digital cable TV: Bad news for BSkyB?. (1999, 26 June). *Hack Watch News.*

Digital Video Broadcasting (DVB). (1997). Implementation Guidelines for the use of MPEG-2 Systems, Video and Audio in Satellite, Cable and Terrestrial Broadcasting Applications. DVB Standards and Bluebooks, version 1.1,DVB Document A001 rev 4 July.

Digital Video Broadcasting (DVB). (1998). Specification for service information (SI) in digital video broadcasting (DVB) systems. DVB Standards and Bluebooks, version 1.1, DVB Document A038 March.

The DVB interactive TV debacle. (1998, 14 December). *Inside Digital TV*, sec. no. 8.

Dyson, R.A., (1998, April). Media literacy: Who needs it and what does it mean? *In; Gazette, 60*(2).

EACEM, General Secretariat. (1998). Possible methods for implementing parental control signalling in analogue TV systems. Brussels, European Association of Consumer Electronics Manufacturers.

Federal Communications Commission (FCC). (1998, 10 July). In the matter of carriage of the transmissions of digital television broadcast stations. CS Docket No. 98–120.

Federman, J. (1993). Film and television ratings: An international assessment. Unpublished report. Studio City, CA: Mediascope.

Federman, J. (1996). *Media ratings, design, us,e and consequences*, Studio City, CA: Mediascope, Inc.

Federman, J. (1998). Media rating systems: A comparative review. In M. Price (Ed.), *The V-Chip debate: Content filtering from television to the Internet* (pp. 99–132). Mahwah, New Jersey: Lawrence Erlbaum Associates.

Field report. (1998, March). *Broadcast Engineering*.

Goldberg, D. Prosser, T. & Verhulst, S. (1998). *EC media law and policy*, Essex: Longman.

Hamilton, J. (1994). Marketing violence: The impact of labelling violent television content. Paper presented at the International Conference on Violence in the Media. New York, St John's University.

The Henry J. Kaiser Family Foundation. (1998, September 24). Major new study of the V-Chip TV rating system: TV rating system doesn't flag most sex and violence for parents, but most who use it assume it does. Press release for Rating the TV ratings: One year out: An assessment of the television industry's use of V-Chip ratings. California. [online] (2001) available: http://www.kff.org/content/archive/1434/ratings.html.

Herman, G., & Leyens, J. P. (1977). Rating films on television. *Journal of Communication, 27*(4).

High Level Group on Audiovisual Policy (Chaired by Commissioner Marcelino Oreja). (1998, October 26). The digital age: European audiovisual policy. Report.

Hobbs, R (1998). Media literacy and citizenship education. In M. Salvador & P. Sias (Eds.), *The public voice in a democracy at risk*. Westport, CT: Praeger Press. [online] available: http://interact.uoregon.edu/MediaLit/FA/mlhobbs/democracy.html.

Hobbs, R. (2001). Taking charge of your TV: A guide to critical viewing for parents and children. [Online] (2001). available: http://www.cyfc.umn.edu/Documents/C/C/CC1024.html.

Hobbs, R. (n. d.) The uses (and misuses) of mass media resources in secondary schools. [online] (2001). Available: http://interact.uoregon.edu/MediaLit/FA/mlhobbs/uses.html.

Kinghorn, J. R. (1997, 21 January). Laboratory report: TACS: A proposal for a TV access control system based on Teletext. Philips Semiconductors Systems Laboratory Southampton, England.

Martin, C.D. & Reagle, J.M. (1997). An alternative to government regulation and censorship: Content advisory systems for the Internet. *Cardozo Arts and Entertainment Law Journal, 15*(2).

Philips Consumer Electronics. (1997, August). NexTView electronic program guide gives more information at the touch of a button. Philips Consumer Electronics Press Releases.

Resnick, P. (1996). PICS: Internet access controls without censorship. *Communications of the ACM, 39*(10).

Roberts, D. F. (1998). Media content labelling systems: Informational advisories or judgemental restrictions?. In M. Price (Ed.), *The V-Chip debate: Content filtering from television to the Internet* (pp. 157–177). Mahwah, New Jersey: Lawrence Erlbaum Associates.

Special survey of technology and entertainment: Wheel of Fortune. (1998, 21 November). *The Economist*.

Sweden digital television network rollout decided. (1998, 23 March). *FT Asia Intelligence Wire*, Business section.

Theunert, H. (1998). Jugendschutz im digitalen Fernsehen: eine Untersuchung der Technik und ihrer Nutzung durch Eltern. Publications of Die Landesmedienanstalten, no. 11, Berlin: VISTAS.

United Kingdom: Consultant's report points to digital confusion ITC to resolve Sky/BDB dispute. (1998, 6 May). *Interspace*.

Voorhoof, D. (1995). Critical perspectives on the scope of Article 10 of the European Convention on Human Rights. Strasbourg: Council of Europe Press, 66 p. (Analyse critique de la portée et de l'application de l'article 10 de la Convention européenne des Droits de l'Homme, Strasbourg, Les éditions du Conseil de l'Europe, 1995, 70 p.)

Wiseman, A. (2000, September 1). PDC (programme delivery control) explained. 625 Andrew Wiseman's Television Room [online] (2001). Available: http://625.uk.com/pdc/.

Wurtzel, A., and Surlin, S., (1978). Viewer attitudes towards television advisory warnings. *Journal of Broadcasting, 22*.

Yoshida, J. (1998, 23 November). Microsoft, Sun duel hits new turf—In WinCE end run, Europe seeks new Java subset for digital TVs, set-top boxes, *Electronic Engineering Times*.

Yoshida, J. (1999, 18 January). Consumer crowd cozies up to Java, *Electronic Engineering Times*.

MEDIA & CHILDREN: THEORIES

Bandura, A. (1973). *Aggression: A social learning analysis*. Englewood Cliffs, NJ, Prentice-Hall.

Berkowitz, L. (1986). Situational influences on reactions to observed violence. *Journal of Social Issues, 42*, 93–106.

Berkowitz, L. (1989). The frustration-aggression hypothesis: Examination and reformulation. *Psychological Bulletin, 106*, 59–73.

British Broadcasting Corporation. (1972). *Violence on Television: Programme Content and Viewer Perceptions*. London: BBC.

British Broadcasting Corporation (BBC), Broadcasting Standards Commission, & Independent Television Commission (ITC). (1998). Violence and the viewer: Report of the joint working party on violence on television, 1998. London: BBC/BSC/ITC.

Browne, K. & Pennell, A. (1998). The effects of video violence on young offenders: Research findings No. 65. Home Office Research and Statistics Directorate. [online] (2001). Available pdf: http://www.homeoffice.gov.uk/rds/pdfs/r65.pdf.

Buckingham, D. (1996). *Moving Images—Understanding Children's Emotional Responses to Television*, Manchester: Manchester University Press.

Drotner, K. et al. (eds.). (1997). *Tankestreger. Nye medier, andre unge*. Copenhagen: Borgens Forlag.

Fridberg, T. et al. (eds.) (1997). *Fridberg, T. et al. (eds.) (1997). Mønstre i mangfoldigheden: De 15–18 åriges mediebrug i Danmark*. Copenhagen: Borgens Forlag.

European Association of Consumer Electronics Manufacturers (EACEM), General Secretariat. (1998). Possible methods for implementing parental control signalling in analogue TV systems.

Eron, L.D. (1971). *Learning of aggression in children*. Boston: Little Brown.

Eron, L. D. & Huesmann, L. R. (1986). The role of television in the development of pro-social and antisocial behavior. In D. Olweus, J. Block, & M. Radke-Yarrow (Eds.). *The development of antisocial and pro-social behaviour: Research, theories, and issues*. New York: Academic.

Feshbach, S. (1984). The catharsis hypothesis, aggressive drive, and the reduction of aggression. *Aggressive Behaviour, 10*, 91–101.

Gerbner, G. (1990). Violence profile 1967 through 1988–89: Enduring patterns, The Annenberg School for Communication, University of Pennsylvania, Department of Communication, University of Delaware. January. [online] (2001) Available: Children Youth and Family Consortium Electronic Clearinghouse: http://www.cyfc.umn.edu/Documents/C/B/CB1029.html.

Gerbner, G., & Signorielli, N. (1988). *Violence and terror in the mass media*. Paris: UNESCO.

Gerbner, G., Gross, L., Morgan, M. & Signorielli, N. (1986). Living with tele-
vision: The dynamics of the cultivation process. In Bryant, J. & Zillmann,
D. (Eds.), *Perspectives on media effects*. Hillsdale, NJ, Lawrence Erlbaum
Associates.

Gunter, B. (1998). The importance of studying viewers' perceptions of television violence. *Current Psychology, 7*, 26–43.

Gunter, B. & Furnham, A. (1984). Perceptions of television violence: Effects of
programmes genre and the physical form of violence. *British Journal of
Social Psychology, 23*, 155–164.

Gunter, B. & Wober M. (1988). *Violence on Television: What the Viewers
Think*. London: John Libbey.

Huesmann, L. R., (1986). Psychological processes promoting the relation
between exposure to media violence and aggressive behaviour by the viewer. *Journal of Social Issues, 42*, 125–140.

Huesmann, L. R. (1988). An information processing model for the development
of aggression, *Aggressive Behaviour, 14*, 13–24.

Hucsmann, L. R., & Eron, L. (Eds.). (1986). *Television and the aggressive
child: A cross-national comparison*, New Jersey: Lawrence Erlbaum
Associates.

Huesmann, L. R., Eron, L.D., Lefkowitz, M.M. & Walder, L.O. (1973).
Television violence and aggression: The causal effect remains. *American
Psychologist, 28*(7), 617–620.

Johnston, J. & Ettema, J.S. (1982). *Positive images: Breaking stereotypes with
children's television*. California: Sage.

Linz, D.G. & Donnerstein, E. (1989). The effects of violent messages in the
mass media. In Bradac, J.J., (Ed.), *Message Effects in Communication
Science*. Newbury Park: Sage.

Linz, D.G., Donnerstein, E. & Penrod, S. (1988). Effects of long-term exposure
to violent and sexually degrading depictions of women. *Journal of
Personality and Social Psychology. 55*, 758–768.

Livingstone, Sonia M. & Bovill, Moira. (Eds.). (2001). *Children and their
changing media environment: A European comparative study*. New Jersey:
Lawrence Erlbaum Associates.

Livingston, S., Holden, K. J., & Bovill, M. (1998). Children's changing media
environment: Overview of a European comparative study. Media Research
Group, Department of Social Physchology, London School of Economics
and Political Science.

Morrison, D. E. (1992). *Television and the Gulf War*. London: John Libbey.

Morrison, D. & MacGregor, B. (1993). Detailed findings from the editing
groups. In Hargrave, A. M. (Ed.), *Violence in factual television*. London:
John Libbey.

National Television Violence Study: Executive Summary, (1998). (Vol. 3).
California: Sage Publications, Inc.

UNESCO clearinghouse on children and violence on the screen. (1998). *Children and media violence*. Yearbook.

Valkenburg, P. (1997). *Vierkante ogen: opgroeien met TV & PC*. Amsterdam: Balans.

Van der Voort, T. H. A. (1988). *Television violence: A child's eye view*. Amsterdam: Elsevier Science Publishers.

Violence on television in Britain: A content analysis—1995–96. (1996, December) Report to the Broadcasting Standards Council, British Broadcasting Corporation, British Sky Broadcasting, Channel Four Television, ITV Association, and Independent Television Commission.

Wiegman, O. (1995, April). De agressieve Nintendo-generatie. In *SEC, Tijdschrift over samenleving en criminaliteitspreventie. jaargang 9*, nr. 2. Den haag: Ministerie van Justitie, interne uitgave.

Wiegman, O. & Van schie, E. (1997, April). De schadelijke gevolgen van computerspellen; Nederlands onderzoekers pleiten voor keurmerk. In *SEC, Tijdschrift over samenleving en criminaliteitspreventie, jaargang 11*, nr. 2. Den haag: Ministerie van Justitie, interne uitgave.

Zillman, D. (1971). Excitation transfer in communication-mediated aggressive behavior. *Journal of Experimental Social Psychology, 7*, 419–434.

WEBSITES

Broadcast Advertising Clearance Centre (BACC). [online] (2001) Available: http://www.bacc.org.uk.

The British Board of Film Classification (BBFC) [online] (2001) Available: http://www.bbfc.co.uk/.

Bundesministerium für Inneres (Federal Ministry of the Interior, Austria). [online] Available: http://www.bmi.gv.at.

Canadian Association of Media Education Organisations (CAMEO). [online] (2001) Available: http://interact.uoregon.edu/MediaLit/CAMEO/index.html.

The Center for Media Literacy [online] (2001) Available: http://www.medialit.org.

The Commissariaat voor de Media, The Netherlands. [online] (2001). Available: http://www.cvdm.nl.

Cyber Angels. [online] (2001). Available: http://www.cyberangels.org.

Cyber Patrol [online] (2001) available: http://www.cyberpatrol.com.

European Association for Audio-visual Media Education. [online] (2001). Available: http://www.datanet.be/aeema/.

Education Information Network in Europe (EURYDICE). [online] (2001). Available: http://www.eurydice.org/.

Finnish Board of Film Classification. [online] (2001). Available: http://www.vet.fi.

Internet Service Providers Austria (ISPA). [online] (2001). Available: http://www.ispa.at.

Internet Watch Foundation. [online] (2001). Available: http://www.iwf.org.uk/.

Just Think Foundation [online] (2001). Available: http://www.justthink.org.

Kein Mord Am Bildschirm ('No Murder on Screen' [anti-violence campaign in Austria]) [online] (2001) Available: http://www.kinderfreunde.at/aktionen/kmordabs.html.

Media Literacy Online Project. [online] (2001) Available: http://interact.uoregon.edu/MediaLit/HomePage.

The Media and Communication Studies Site. [online] (2001) Available: http://users.aber.ac.uk/dgc/plaudits.html.

Meldpunt Kinderporno. [online] (2001) Available: http://www.meldpunt.org.

Movie Mom [online] (2001). Available: http://www.moviemom.com/.

Nederlandse Vereniging van Internet Providers (NLIP) (Dutch Federation of Internet Providers. [online] Available: http://www.nlip.nl.

Net Nanny [online] (2001) Available: http://www.netnanny.com.

Pacific Mountain Network. (1991). Creating Critical Viewers [online] (2001). Available: http://www.cyfc.umn.edu/Documents/C/C/CC1026.html

Recreational Software on the Internet. (RSACi). [online] (2001). Available: http://www.rsac.org.

Screen It! Entertainment Reviews for Parents [online] (2001). available: http://www.screenit.com.

SurfWatch [online] (2001) available: http://www.surfwatch.com.

Sky Digital [online] (2001). available: http://www.sky.com/skydigital/.

The Television Project. [online] (2001). Available: http://www.tvp.org/

United Kingdom Film Education. [online] (2001). Available: http://www.filmeducation.org.

Word Wide Web Consortium (W3C). [online] (2001). Available: http://www.w3.org.

TV Parental Guide. [online] (2001). Available: http://www.tvguidelines.org.

INTERNATIONAL INSTRUMENTS

Universal Declaration of Human Rights, Paris, 10 December 1948.

European Convention for the Protection of Human Rights and Fundamental Freedoms, Rome, 4 November 1950.

UN Covenant on Civil and Political Rights, 1966.

U N General Assembly, *Convention on the Rights of the Child*, 12 December 1989, A/RES/44/25.

Bratislava Resolution, November 1994.

The Children's Television Charter, March 1995.

Children's charter on electronic media, 13 March 1998.

EUROPEAN UNION
(CHRONOLOGICAL ORDER)

Directive 86/529/EEC of 3 November 1986 on the adoption of common technical specifications of the MAC/packet family of standards for direct satellite
television broadcasting.

Council Directive 89/552/EEC on the coordination of certain provisions laid
down by law, regulation or administrative action in Member States concerning the pursuit of television broadcasting activities. *OJEC* No. L 298, 17
October 1989, p. 23. [*Television Without Frontiers*].

Directive 92/38/EEC of 11 May 1992 on the adoption of standards for satellite
broadcasting of television signals.

Directive 95/47/EC of the European Parliament and of the Council of 24
October 1995 on the use of standards for the transmission of television signals, *OJEC* No. L 281 of 23 November 1995, p. 51.

Commission of the European Communities. (1996, 16 October). European
Commission, Illegal and harmful content on the Internet, Communication to
the European Parliament, the Council, the Economic, and Social Committee
and the Committee of the Regions, 16 October 1996

Commission of the European Communities, (1996). Green Paper on the
Protection of Minors and Human Dignity in Audiovisual and Information
Services, COM(96) 483 final.

Television Without Frontiers. Directive 97/36/EC of the European Parliament
and of the Council of 19 June 1997 amending Council Directive
89/552/EEC on the coordination of certain provisions laid down by law, regulation or administrative action in Member States concerning the pursuit of
television broadcasting activities. *OJEC* No. L 202 of 30 July 1997, p. 60.

Treaty establishing the European Community. *Official Journal*. (10.11.1997) C
340, pp. 173–308; As amended by the Treaty on European Union and the
Treaty of Amsterdam.

Multiannual Community action plan on a safer use of the Internet by combating illegal and harmful content on global networks. *OJEC* No. C 48 of 13
February 1998, p. 8.

Council Recommendation of 24 September 1998 on the development of the
competitiveness of the European audiovisual and information services
industry by promoting national frameworks aimed at achieving a comparable and effective level of protection of minors and human dignity.
(98/560/EC), *OJEC* No. L 270 of 7 October 1998, p. 48.

Decision No /98/EC of the European Parliament and of the Council for adopting a Multiannual Community Action Plan on promoting safer use of the Internet by combating illegal and harmful content on global networks. Adopted on 21 December 1998.

European Commission, 19 July 1999. Communication on the Study on Parental Control of Television Broadcasting to the Council, European Parliament and Economic and Social Committee. COM/99/371 FINAL

COUNCIL OF EUROPE
(CHRONOLOGICAL ORDER)

Resolution (67) 13 on Press and the protection of youth, adopted by the Ministers' Deputies on 29 June 1967.

Resolution (69) 6 on Cinema and the protection of youth, adopted by the Ministers' Deputies on 7 March 1969.

Recommendation No. R (84) 3 on Principles on television advertising, adopted by the Committee of Ministers on 23 February 1984.

Recommendation No. 1067 (1987) of the Parliamentary Assembly of the Council of Europe on Cultural dimension of broadcasting in Europe, adopted by the Assembly on 8 October 1987.

Recommendation No. R (89) 7 on Distribution of videograms having a violent, brutal or pornographic content of 22 April 1989.

European Convention on Transfrontier Television (ETS No. 132), Strasbourg, 5 May 1989.

Recommendation No. R (90) 10 on Cinema for children and adolescents.

Recommendation No. R (92) 19 on Video games with a racist content, adopted by the Committee of Ministers on 19 October 1992.

Resolution 1011 (1993). On the situation of women and children in the former Yugoslavia, adopted by the Assembly on 28 September 1993.

Recommendation 1286 (1996). of the Parliamentary Assembly of the Council of Europe on a European strategy for children, adopted by the Assembly on 24 January 1996.

Recommendation No. R (97)19 On the portrayal of violence in the electronic media, adopted by the Committee of Ministers on 30 October 1997.

European Council Recommendation. (1998). On the development of the competitiveness of the European audio-visual and information services industry by promoting national frameworks aimed at achieving a comparable and effective level of protection of minors and human dignity, of 24 September, *Official Journal* L 270, 07.10.

NATIONAL REFERENCES[1]

Austria

Bundesgesetz über die Aufgaben und die Einrichtung des Österreichischen Rundfunks (Broadcasting Act) (1999). As amended by Bundesgesetz, mit dem das Rundfunkgesetz und die Rundfunkgesetz-Novelle 1993 geändert werden (Federal Act to Amend the Broadcasting Act and the 1993 Amendment to the Broadcasting Act), *Federal Law Gazette* I 1.

Gesetz betreffend die Regelung des Kinowesens (Wiener Kinogesetz 1955) of October 21, 1955, [Act concerning the Regulation of Cinemas (Vienna Cinema Act 1995)] *Vienna Law Gazette* 18, 1955, as amended July 31, 1998.

Gesetz zum Schutz der Jugend (Wiener Jugendschutzgesetz 1985) of April 26, 1985 [Vienna Minors Protection Act of 1985], *Vienna Law Gazette* 34, 1985.

Belgium

Communauté française de Belgique (French Community of Belgium) en collaboration avec la RTBF et le Vif/L'Express. (1997, Octobre) *La violence à la télévision*, disponible auprès du service de l'audiovisuel et des multimédias du Ministère de la Communauté française de Belgique.

Frydman, M. (1993). *Télévision et violence*, Bilan et réponses aux questions des parents et éducateurs, Grands dossiers du 21ème siècle, EMPC/EMIS, Charleroi.

Mouvement Anti-Pédophile sur Internet. (1996). *La pornographie infantile sur Internet*. Facultés Universitaires Notre-Dame de la Paix de Namur, Namue.

Denmark

Andersen, D. (1995). *Skolebørns fritid*. København. Socialforskningsinstituttet.

Bekendtgørelse nr. 30 af (16. januar 1998) om Medierådet for Børn og Unge.

Bekendtgørelse nr. 2 af (5. januar 1998) om et Børneråd. Statsministeriets bekendtgørelse.

Bekendtgørelse nr. 69 af (30. januar 1998) om lokal radio—og fjernsynsvirksomhed. BEK. LBK Nr. 138 af 19/02/1998.

Bekendtgørelse af lov nr. 435 af (1. juni 1995) om mærkning af videogrammer.

---

[1] For some of the countries no relevant studies were published.

BEK nr. 491. 11.6.1997—LBK nr. 138. 19.2.1998.

Betalingskortloven. Lov nr. 811 af (12. september 1994).

Betænkning nr. 1347 1997 om Bibliotekerne i informationssamfundet. Kulturministeriet.

Betænkning om Bibliotekerne i Informationssamfundet. (1997). Afgivet af Udvalget om Bibliotekerne i Informationssamfundet. Kbh.: Kulutrministeriet. Betænkning nr. 1347. 1 bind samt 1 bilagsbind.

Betænkning om Børn og unges brug af massemedier. (1966). Kbh.:Medieudvalget. Statsministeriet, (betænkning nr. 1311).

Billeder i bevægelse—en udfordring for skolen. (1996). Undervisningsministeriet.

Børnerådet. Årsberetning. (1996–97).

Christensen O. & Tufte, B. (1998, August). Pigers og drenges mediebrug og hverdagsliv. Danmarks Lærerhøjskole.

Drotner, K. (1995). Mediedannelse: Bro eller barriere? – om børn og unges mediebrug. Kbh.: Medieudvalget Statsministeriet.

Drotner, K., et al. (Eds.). (1996, 5 januar). Tankestreger. Nye medier, andre unge. Copenhagen. Borgens Forlag. Filmlov. Lovbekendtgørelse nr. 342.

Fridberg, T. et al. (Eds.). (1997). Mønstre i mangfoldigheden: De 15-18 åriges mediebrug i Danmark. Copenhagen. Borgens Forlag.

Guidelines for the Department for Children and Young People in The Danish Broadcasting Corporation. (1998, november). Hvem ? Hvad ? Hvor ? og Hvorfor ? i B&U.

Grünbaum, P. (1997). Børn og computere. En håndbog for voksne. Kbh.: Gyldendal.

Kort og Godt. (1988, August). Børn, unge og markedsføring. Forbrugerstyrelsen.

Kulturministeriets bekendtgørelse om reklame og sponsorering i radio og fjernsyn. § 16–23.

Markedsføringsloven. Lov nr. 428 af (1. juni 1994).

Massemedier. Lovbekendtgørelse (29 januar 1997) nr. 75 om radio og fjernsynsvirksomhed.

Medieansvarslov. Lov (6 juni 1991) nr. 348.

Medievold—børn og unge/Udvalg vedrørende film-, tv- og videovold. (1995, marts). Kbh.: Kulturministeriet.

Finland

Act on the Classification of Video and Other Audiovisual Programmes (1987).

Alasuutari, P. Armstrong, K. & Kytömäki, J. (1991). Reality and fiction in Finnish TV viewing. research report 3. Helsinki: Yleisradio. 63–93.

Huesmann, L.R. (1988). An information processing model for the development of aggression. *Aggressive Behavior*, 14, 13–24.

Huesmann, L.R., & Miller, L.S. (1994). Long-term effects of repeated exposure to media violence in childhood. In L.R. Huesmann (Ed.), *Aggressive behavior: Current perspectives*. New York: Plenum, pp. 153–186.

Huesmann, L.R., & Eron, L.D. (Eds.). (1986). *Television and the aggressive child: a cross-national comparison*. Hillsdale, NJ: Lawrence Erlbaum Associates.

Kainulainen, K., Metsistö, M.-L., & Tervomaa, R. (1994). *Viestintäksvatus peruskoulun ala-asteelle* [Media Education for Elementary School]. Helsinki: Painatuskeskus.

Kytömäki, J. (1991). They probably have some internal system which tells them what's good and what isn't. Parental control and mediation of TV viewing in families with schoolchildren. In Alasuutari, P. Armstrong, K. & Kytömäki, J. (1991). *Reality and fiction in Finnish TV viewing*. (pp. 63–93). Translation from Finnish by David Kivinen. Series: Research report/Yleisradio, Research & Development; 3. Yleisradio, Helsinki.

Kytömäki, J. & Paananen, S. (Eds.) (1988). *Televisio ja väkivalta. Suomalaisia näkökulmia*. Oy Yleisradio Ab. Sarja B 5. Helsinki: Hakapaino.

Lagerspetz, K. & Viemerö, V. (1986). Television and aggressive behavior among Finnish children. In Huesmann, L.R., & L.D. Eron (Eds.), *Television and the aggressive child: a cross-national comparison* (pp. 81–110). Hillsdale, NJ: Lawrence Erlbaum.

Lagerspetz, K.M.J., Wahlroos, C. & Wendelin, C. (1978). Facial expressions of pre-school children while watching televised violence. *Scandinavian Journal of Psychology*, 20, 43–53.

Huesmann, L.R., Lagerspetz, K., & Eron, L.D. (1984). Intervening variables in the TV violence-aggression relation: Evidence from two countries. *Developmental Psychology*, 20, 746–775.

Mustonen, A. (1991). Aggressio Suomen televisiossa. Oy Yleisradio Ab. Tutkimus- ja kehitysosasto. *Tutkimusraportti*. Helsinki: Hakapaino..

Mustonen, A. (1997). Nature of screen violence and its relation to program popularity. Aggressive Behavior, 23, 281–292.

Mustonen, A. & Pulkkinen, L. (1993). Aggression in television programs in Finland. *Aggressive Behavior*, 19, 175–183.

Mustonen, A. & Pulkkinen, L. (1997). Television violence: The development of a coding scheme. *Journal of Broadcasting and Electronic Media*, 41, 168–189.

Mustonen, A. & Pulkkinen, L. (in press). *Psychological roots of media use*.

Mustonen, A. & Pulkkinen, L. (submitted). *Adults as viewers of media violence*.

Sini-Härkönen, R. (1994). *Viestintäkasvatuksen ulottuvuudet*. Helsingin yliopiston opettajankoulutuslaitos, tutkimuksia 125. Helsinki: Yliopistopaino.

Suoninen, A. (1993). *Televisio lasten elämässä*. Nykykulttuurin tutkimusyksikön julkaisuja 41, Jyväskylä: Jyväskylän yliopisto.

Toivonen, K. (1991). *Persianlahden sota, joukkotiedotus ja peruskoululaisten ahdistuneisuus.* Mindstorm-projekti 1. Lapin yliopiston kasvatustieteellisiä julkaisuja B 17. Rovaniemi: Lapin yliopisto.

Toivonen, K. (1992). *Tunteiden myrsky. Sotauutiset silmin kuultuna ja korvin katseltuna.* Mindstorm-projekti 2. Lapin yliopiston täydennyskoulutuskeskuksen julkaisuja 34. Rovaniemi: Lapin yliopisto.

Viemerö, V. (1986). Relationships between filmed violence and aggression. Turku, Finland: *Reports from the Department of Psychology,* Åbo Akademi, Monograph Supplement Nr. 3.

Viemerö, V. (1996). Factors in childhood that predict later criminal behavior. *Aggressive Behavior,* 22, 87–97.

Viemerö, V. & Paajanen, S. (1992). The role of fantasies and dreams in the TV viewing-aggression relationship. *Aggressive Behavior,* 18, 109–116.

Werner, A. (1996). *Lapset ja televisio* [Children and television] Finnish edition, Suoninen, A. (Ed.). Tampere: Gaudeamus.

Ireland

Kelleher, D. and Murray, K. (1997). *Information Technology Law in Ireland,* Dublin.

France

Bellemare, C. Caron-Bouchard, M. & Gruau, M. (1995). *L'intelligence audiovisuelle des 12-17 ans,* Communauté des Télévisions Européennes, Nathan.

Bertrand, G. Corset, P. (1997). Pratiques télévisuelles dans la famille, Institut National de l'Audiovisuel, janvier.

Bertrand, G. Dereze, G. Grevisse, B. & Mercier, P. (1994). *Temporalités de la télévision, temporalités domestiques,* contrat CNRS.

Centre International de l'enfance. (1991). *Les synthèses bibliographiques, La relation enfant-télévision.*

Chaillet, M. (1993). Apprendre par les images de la television. *Ressources 95* n° 3, 2e trimestre.

Chaillet, M. (1995). Apprendre par la télévision, apprendre à l'école, *Réseaux* n° 74, CNET.

Chalvon, M. Corset, P. Souchon, M. (1991). *L'enfant devant la television des annees 90,* Casterman.

Conseil d'Etat. (1998, July 2) *Rapport du Conseil d'Etat: 'Internet et les réseaux numériques'*—adopted by the General Assembly of the Conseil d'Etat. [online] (2001) available: http://www.internet.gouv.fr/francais/index.html

Conseil Supérieur de l'Audiovisuel. (1997, 15 décembre). Médias et protection de l'enfance, Colloque du 15 décembre. Les rapports du CSA.

Conseil Supérieur de l'Audiovisuel. (1998, mai). Signalétique anti-violence: les résultats d'une étude quanlitative. Lettre du CSA, n°104, 1–5.

Conseil Supérieur de l'Audiovisuel. (1997, avril). La protection de l'enfance et de l'adolescence à la television. les brochures du CSA.

Conseil Supérieur de l'Audiovisuel. (1995, septembre). Enquête sur la représentation de la violence dans la fiction à la télévision en France / Une semaine de programmes de fiction examinés à la loupe. réalisé par Jehel-Cathelineau Sophie, CSA.

Décret du 1990, 23 February pris pour l'application des articles 19 à 22 du code de l'industrie cinématographique et relatif à la classification des œuvres cinématographiques.

Duru-Bellat, M. (1995). Aspirations et pratiques educatives des familles des familles, face a leurs enfants, garcons ou filles. Rapport IREDU, Université de Bourgogne/CNRS.

GRREM. (1997). Les jeunes et les médias, demain—Problématiques et perspectives, Forum international organisé par le Groupe de recherche sur la relation enfants/médias sous l'égide de l'UNESCO. Actes du colloque publiés par le GRREM.

GRREM. (1996, Avril). L'écran et les apprentissages. Actes du séminaire du GRREM 25 et 26 septembre 1995, Documentation de l'Institut National de la Jeunesse et de l'Education Populaire n° 24.

Patrice Martin-Lalande. (1997, avril). 'L'Internet : un vrai défi pour la France' Report to the Prime Minister—avril 1997.

Livingstone & Lunt. (1994). Les théories de la reception. Réseaux n° 68, CNET.

Lurcat, L. (1995). Le temps prisonnier. Des enfances volées par la television, Desclée de Brouwer.

Melh, D. (1996). La télévision de l'intimité, Seuil.

Neveu, E. (1990). Television pour les enfants : état des lieux. Communications n° 51, Seuil.

Official Journal (1998a, 21 February). no. 44.

Official Journal (1889b, 1 December). no. 278.

Proulx, Serge. Laberge, Marie-France. (1995). Vie quotidienne, culture télévisuelle et construction de l'identité familiale. Reseaux n° 70, CNET.

Télévision et apprentissage. Dossier Réseaux n° 74.

Germany

Agreement between the Federal States on Broadcasting in United Germany. (1991, 31 August). Last amended on 25 November 1997

(Rundfunkstaatsvertrag - RStV).

Aufenanger, S. (Hg.) (1991). *Neue Medien - neue Pädagogik? Ein Lese- und Arbeitsbuch zur Medienerziehung in Kindergarten und Grundschule.* Bundeszentrale für politische Bildung, Schriftenreihe Bd.301. Bonn.

Bachmair, B. (1995, March). Spiel mit der Gewalt. Zur Bedeutung von Wrestling-Sendungen für Kinder und Jugendliche. In: *Medien Praktisch*, (p. 23–27).

Bayerische Landeszentrale für neue Medien. (Ed.). (1996). *Medienkompetenz im Informationszeitalter. 1. Fachtagung des Forums Medienpädagogik derBLM.* München.

Brosius, H.-B. (1987). Auswirkungen der Rezeption von Horror-Videos auf die Legitimation von aggressiven Handlungen. In *Rundfunk und Fernsehen*, p. 71.

Emnid. (1998). *Nutzung der d-box bei Abonnenten von Premiere Digital,* Telefonische Umfrage.

Fehr, W. & Fritz, J. (1997, February). Zum Problem virtueller Gewalt. Von der Wirkungsforschung zur Normen- und Werteentscheidung. In: *Medien Praktisch*, S. 39–41.

31 GjSM-Gesetz über die Verbreitung Jugendgefährdender Schriften und Medieninhalte, Promulgated on 12 July 1985 (*Federal Law Gazette* I: 1502), last amended by Article 6 of the Information and Communication Services Act of 22.7.1997 (*Federal Law Gazette* I: 1870). [online] (2001). available in English: http://iecl.iuscomp.org/gla/statutes/GjSM.htm.

Glogauer, W. (1991). Kriminalisierung von Kindern und Jugendlichen durch Medien. Wirkungen gewalttätiger, sexueller, pornographischer und satanischer Darstellungen. Baden-Baden.

Glogauer, W. (1996). Auswirkungen von Gewalt, sexuellen Darstellungen und Pornographie in den Medien auf Kinder und Jugendliche. In: *Bundesministerium des Innern (Hg.): Medien und Gewalt.* Bonn.

Grimm, Jürgen. (1996). Das Verhältnis von Medien und Gewalt oder welchen Einfluß hat das Fernsehen auf Jugendliche und Erwachsene? In: *Bundesministerium des Innern (Hg.): Medien und Gewalt.* Bonn.

Grobel, J. (2/1993). Worauf wirken Gewaltdarstellungen? Woher kommt reale Gewalt? In: medien praktisch, pp. 23–24.

Grobel, J. (9/1997/3). Medienkompetenz und Kommunikationsbildung. Anmerkung zur Rolle von Politik, Produzenten, Pädagogik und Prosumenten. In *Medien-psychologie*, p. 235.

Halefeldt, E. (1998). Medienpädagogische Aktivitäten auf Bundes- und Länderebene. Schriftenreihe Bd. 3, Hrsg.: Medienpädagogischer Forschungsverband Südwest. Baden-Baden: Nomos Verlag.

Kunczik, M. (1993, January). Audiovisuelle Gewalt und ihre Auswirkungen auf Kinder und jugendliche. Eine schriftliche Befragung klinischer Psychologen und Psychiater. In: *Medienpsychologie*. pp. 3–19.

Lukesch, H. (1988). Medienkonsum von Kindern und Jugendlichen unter besonderer Berücksichtigung sexueller Inhalte. In Kluge, N. (1988). *Medien als Sexualaufklärer*. Frankfurt.

Maier, R. (Hg.). (1997). *Medienerziehung in Kindergarten und Grundschule*. München.

Mohr, Inge. (1998). *Jugendschutz im Fernsehen*, edia Perspektiven, 1.

Schorb, B. & Theunert, H. (1998). *Jugendschutz im digitalen Fernsehen. Wie er technisch funktioniert und wie Familien damit umgehen*, Berlin.

Six, U. (1995). *Konzepte für medienpädagogische Elternarbeit*. Hrsg.: Unabhängige Landesanstalt für das Rundfunkwesen. Kiel.

Sobiech, D. (1997). *Theorie und Praxis der Medienerziehung im Vergleich. Eine Analyse von Konzepten, Strukturen und Bedingungen.* München.

Strafgesetzbuch-StGB (Criminal Code). As promulgated 10 March 1987 (*Federal Law Gazette* I: 945, p. 1160), last amended by Article 7 of the Act of 31.8.1998 (*Federal Law Gazette* I: 2600)

Theunert, H. (1992). *Zwischen Vergnügen und Angst - Fernsehen im Alltag von Kindern: eine Untersuchung zur Wahrnehmung und Verarbeitung von Fernsehinhalten durch Kinder aus unterschiedlichen soziokulturellen Milieus in Hamburg.* Berlin.

Theunert, H. (1996). *Gewalt in den Medien - Gewalt in der Realität. Gesellschaftliche Zusammenhänge und pädagogisches Handeln.* München.

Theunert, H. (1998). Jugendschutz im digitalen Fernsehen: eine Untersuchung der Technik und ihrer Nutzung durch Eltern. Publications of *Die Landesmedienanstalten*, no. 11 Berlin: VISTAS.

Theunert, H. & Schorb, B. (1995). *"Mordsbilder": Kinder und Fernsehinformation. Eine Untersuchung zum Umgang von Kindern mit realen Gewaltdarstellungen in Nachrichten und Reality-TV.* Berlin.

Winterhoff-Spurk, P. (1997, October). Medienkompetenz: Schlüsselqualifikation der Informationsgesellschaft? In *Medienpsychologie*, p. 182.

Italy

Deputies Melandri, Griffagnini & Giulietti. (1997, June). Study connected to the so-called Proposal in favour of friendship between children and TV.

Eurispes. (1996). Rapporto Italia. A report concerning statistics on media and minors.

Menduni, E. (September 1996). Un esperimento di riduzione contrattata del consumo televisivo infantile. (Experiment concerning reduction of children's TV viewing), promoted by University of Siena, in *Problemi dell'informazione*, XXI, n.3.

The Netherlands

Buwalda, W. (1997), *Leeftijdsclassificatie en productvoorlichting; de audiovisuele branche in Nederland. Justitiële verkenningen: Film- en videogeweld.* 3. Deventer: Gouda Quint BV.

Commissariaat voor de Media (1996), *Beleidslijn Televisie en Jeugd.* Hilversum.

Commissariaat voor de Media (1997), *De Omroep Gekeurd, bijlage.* Hilversum.

Groebel, J., & Smit, L. (1996). *Media en Geweld.* Rapport in opdracht van het Ministerie van Onderwijs, Cultuur en Wetenschappen, OCenW. Utrecht, Universiteit Utrecht. Vakgroep Massacommunicatie.

Groebel, J., & Smit, L. (1997). *Gewalt im Internet* [Violence on the Internet]. Report for the German Parliament. Bonn: Deutscher Bundestag.

Letter of the Secretary of Justice and the Secretary of Culture to Parliament; 'Notitie Jeugd en Video: een kwestie vaan voorlichting'; Tweede Kamer 1985–1986, 19519, nrs. 1–2.

Nikken, P. de Leede, N. & Rijkse, C. (in press). *Game-Boys en Game-Girls: opvattingen van jongens en meisjes over computerspelletjes.* Utrecht: Stichting Jeugdinformatie Nederland.

Nederlandse Filmkeuring, Jaarverslag 1997 (in press). Den Haag.

Notitie (1997), *Niet voor alle Leeftijden: Audiovisuale Media en de Bescherming van Jeugdigen*, Rijswijk: Ministry of Public health, Welfare and Sports, directie Jeugdbeleid.

Raad van Toezicht Videovoorlichting, Jaarverslag, (1997) Oudekerk a/d Amstel: Aeroprint/J.K. Smit & Zonen.

Raad voor het Jeugdbeleid (Council for Youth Policy). (1996) Prepared for the Green paper on Minors, The Protection of Minors and Human Dignity in the Information Society. Unpublished report.

Valkenburg, P. (1997). *Vierkante ogen: opgroeien met TV & PC.* Amsterdam: Balan.

Van der Voort, T.H.A. (1990). *De invloed van televisiegeweld.* Amsterdam: Swets en Zeitlinger, tweede druk.

Wiegman, O. (1995, 2 April). De agressieve Nintendo-generatie, in: *SEC, Tijdschrift over samenleving en criminaliteitspreventie.* jaargang 9, nr. Den haag: Ministerie van Justitie, interne uitgave.

Wiegman, O. en Van schie, E. (1997, April). De schadelijke gevolgen van computerspellen; Nederlands onderzoekers pleiten voor keurmerk. In: *SEC, Tijdschrift over samenleving en criminaliteitspreventie*, jaargang 11, nr. 2.

Portugal

Almeida, Ana Nunes. (1995). Wall Karin A Família in Portugal Hoje, Oeiras, Instituto Nacional de Administração.

Alta Autoridade para a Comunicação Social. (1995). A Violência nos meios de comunicação social, Colóquio Internacional. International Conference, Lisboa: AACS.

Brederode, S. & Emília, M. (1991). *Aprender com a televisão—O segredo da rua sésamo*. Lisbon: TV Guia Editora.

Conselho Nacional da Educação. (1994). A Educação e os meios de comunicação. Actas do Seminário, 2–3 December 1993, Lisbon: CNE.

Fonseca, Teresa. (1996). A Televisão e a multiculturalidade: Apropriação das mensagens televisivas por crianças de diferentes etnias. Tese de Mestrado (MA thesis), Lisbon: ISCTE.

Mesquita, M. J. (1991). O Impacto da Televiolência no Processo Socialização da Criança—O Exemplo da Guerra do Golfo. Dissertação de Mestrado em Psicologia do Desenvolvimento (MA Thesis). Porto, Faculdade de Psicologia e Ciências da Educação.

Monteiro, M. B. (1984). La Construction Sociale de la Violence—Approche Cognitive et Dévelopementale. These présentée en vue de l'obtention du grade de Docteur en Psychologie (Ph.D. thesis) Université Catholique de Louvain, Faculté de Psychologie et des Sciences de L'Éducation.

Paixão, Rui. (1995, 1 November). Que Alternativas Oferecemos à Televisão? In *Público*.

Pereda, M. Visitación. (1997). Audiovisualización, Escuela y Tiempo Libre: la Recepción Televisiva del Preadolescente, un proceso de Mediación Múltiple. Tese de doutoramento em fase de finalização (unfinished Ph.D. thesis), Faculdade de Psicologia e Ciências da Educação, Universidade do Porto.

Pereira, S. (1993). A Televisão no Jardim de Infância—Práticas se Atitudes dos Educadores da Rede Pública do Distrito de Braga e Contributos para o Uso Criterioso da Televisão. Braga: CEFOPE, Universidade do Minho.

Pinto, Manuel. (1995). A Televisão no Quotidiano das Crianças. Tese de Doutoramento em Ciências da Comunicação (Ph.D. thesis), Braga: Instituto de Ciências Sociais, Universidade do Minho.

Pinto, M. Baleiras, A. Santos, A. & Pereira, S. (1993). Escola e Comunicação Social-Desafios e Propostas de Acção. Braga, CEFOPE, UM.

Ponte, C. (1994). Programação e Produção Televisiva para Crianças.: Um Estudo de Ofertas RTP 1957-1991. Tese de Mestrado em Ciências da Comunicação (MA thesis), Lisbon, Faculdade de Ciências Socias e Humanas, Universidade Nova.

Soares, A. (1984). Pre-adolescents preferences about heroes and plots in books and mass-media. Boston: Boston University, School of Education.

Vilhena, M. da C. (1984). A pilot study of a unit of television critical viewing for portuguese children. Boston: Boston University: School of Education.

Spain

Alonso, M. (1995). Teleniños públicos, teleniños privados, AKAL.

Aparici, R. García Matilla, A. García Matilla, García Matilla, E. Gutiérrez Martín, L. A. & Monsváis Flores, R. (1995). Television, curriculum y familia—Concurso Nacional de Proyectos de Investigación sobre Educación y Televisión.

Aragó Mitjans, J. M. (1981). La violencia en televisión: Su impacto en niños y adolescentes: Psicología evolutiva.

Area Moreira, M. (1995). La educación audiovisual como tema trasversal del curriculum—Concurso Nacional de Proyectos de Investigación sobre Educación y Televisión.

Calatayud, D. (1994). Violencia en pantalla: Protección de los derechos de los menores.

Campuzano, A. (1993). *Tecnologías audiovisuales y educación*, Madrid, AKAL.

Consell de l'Audiovisual de Catalunya. (1997). La representació de la Violència a la televisió.

Consell de l'Audiovisual de Catalunya. *How to watch TV*. (Book I: News; Book II: Fiction; Book III: Advertising) (These books were originally written in Catalan but the State Ministry for Education and Culture is now translating them into Spanish, and has the intention of distributing them directly to schools and among parents by means of parents associations.)

Defensor del Menor de la Comunidad de Madrid. (1997). *Investigación de contenidos violentos emitidos por Telemadrid y Onda Madrid susceptibles de afectar a los menores.*

Defensor del Pueblo. (1997). *La protección de la juventud y de la infancia y los medios de comunicación—Informe del Defensor del Pueblo.*

Díaz, C. (1995). *Violencia y televisión*, Madrid.

Erausquin, M. A. (1991). *Los teleniños*, Barcelona.

Gallego Arrufat, M. J. (1995). El profesor (Educador, Enseñante y Televidente) y la programación televisiva—Concurso Nacional de Proyectos de Investigación sobre Educación y Televisión.

García Muñoz, N. (1997). *Comportamientos y hábitos de consumo televisivo del niño en el contexto familiar.*

García Cortazar Nebreda, M. L. (1997). *La influencia de la familia y los educadores en la percepción y asunción de los mandatos sobre la television.*

Ferrés i Prats, J. (1997). *Estrategias para el uso de la television*—Biblioteca Virtual de Tecnología Educativa.

Ferrés i Prats, J. (1995). *Televisión y educación*, Barcelona, Paidos.

Independent Television Commission. (1998). Overview of 27 years of annual surveys. Unpublished Report. London: ITC.

López García, (1993). *Sexo, television, y niños.*

Lurçat, L. (1995). Els efectes violents de la televisió. *In-fàn-ci-a*, No. 84, 29–34.

Marinas Herreras, J.M. (1995). *Ver la televisión con los niños*—Concurso Nacional de Proyectos de Investigación sobre Educación y Televisión.

Ponce, R. Teleniños y violencia: la discusión que no cesa. In Radio Televisión Valencia (Ed.), *Televisión. Niños y jóvenes*. Valencia.

Revista Galega de Educación (Dossier). (1994). Os efectos da television. *Revista Galega de Educación*, No. 20, 43–58.

Sadurnì, M. (1994). La percepción de la realidad a través de las imágenes televisivas: un estudio sobre la huella de la violencia televisiva en la mente infantil", *In-fàn-ci-a* No. 26, 24–29.

Sanmartín, J. Grisolía J.S. y Grisolía, S. (Eds.) (1998). *Violencia, televisión y cine.*

Seijas Candelas, L.R. *La violencia en televisión,* Madrid.

Senado. (1995). Informe de la Comisión Especial sobre contenidos televisivos, Madrid.

Tojo, R. et al. (1994). Nenos, adolescentes e televisión: riscos biopsicosociais. *Revista Galega do Ensino*, No. 2, 9–20.

United Kingdom

Akdeniz, Y. (1996). Computer pornography: A comparative study of the US and UK obscenity laws and child pornography laws in relation to the Internet. *International Review of Law Computers & Technology,* 10(2), 235–261.

Akdeniz, Y. (1997). The regulation of pornography and child pornography on the Internet. *Journal of Information, Law and Technology* (JILT).

Bannister, A.D. (1996). *Telecommunication regulation and the Internet.* London: Denton Hall.

Barendt, E. (1995). *Broadcasting law*, Oxford: Clarendon Press.

Barendt, E. et al, (1998). *The Yearbook of Media and Entertainment Law*, Vol. 3, 1997–98, Oxford: Clarendon Press.

Bazalgette, C. and Buckingham, D. (1995). *In front of the children: Screen entertainment and young audiences.* Indiana: Indiana University Press.

Beesley, M. E. (Ed.). (1996). *Markets and the media. Competition, regulation and the interests of consumers.* London: IEA.

Broadcasting Act 1996, 24 July. United Kingdom, Parliament.

Browne, K. & Pennell, A. (1998). *The effects of video violence on young offenders: Research findings* No. 65. Home Office Research and Statistics Directorate. [online] (2001). Available pdf: http://www.homeoffice.gov.uk/rds/pdfs/r65.pdf.

Buckingham, David. (1990). *Watching media learning: Making sense of media education*. England: The Falmer Press.

Buckingham, D. (1993). *Children talking television*. London: The Falmer Press.

Buckingham, D. Davies, H. Jones, K. & Kelley, P. (1999). *Children's Television in Britain*, London: BFI.

Carey, P. and Verow, R. (1998). *Media and entertainment law*, London: Jordans.

Cave, M. (1995). *Traffic management on the superhighway: Reforming communications regulation*. In: R. Collins & J. Purnell (Ed.), Managing the information society. London: IPPR.

ChildWise Monitor. (1998, April 3). Annual survey by ChildWise Monitor, (a youth survey group). Reported in *The Ottawa Citizen*.

Hoffmann-Riem, W. (1996). *Regulating media*, London, NY: Guildford Press.

Livingstone, S. (1998). *Making sense of television*, London: Routledge.

Millwood-Hargrave, A. (1995). *The scheduling game*. London: John Libbey and Broadcasting Standards Council.

Millwood-Hargrave, A. (1998). The V-Chip and television ratings: British and European perspectives. In M. Price (Ed.), *The V-Chip debate: Content filtering from television to the Internet* (pp. 91–98). Mahwah, New Jersey: Lawrence Erlbaum Associates.

Pace report (1998). Pace Micro Technology plc, Unpublished Report.

Regulating for changing values. (1997). A report for the Broadcasting Standards Commission, Broadcasting Standards Commission, London: British Standards Commission.

Robertson, G. & Nicol, A. (1992). *Media law*, London: Penguin Books.

Smith, G. J. H. (1996). *Internet law and regulation*. London: FT Law & Tax.

Tunstall, J. (1997). The United Kingdom. In: *The media in Western Europe: The euromedia handbook*. London: Sage.

Violence and the viewer. (1998). Report of the Joint Working Party on Violence on Television, ITC, BSC and BBC.

Violence on television in Britain. (1998). ITC.

United Kingdom: Consultant's report points to digital confusion ITC to resolve Sky/BDB dispute. (1998, 6 May). *Interspace*.

Williamson, P. (1995). The regulation of British broadcasting. In: M. Bishop, J. Kay & C. Mayer, (Ed.), *The regulatory challenge*. (pp. 160–190) Oxford: Oxford UP.

GLOSSARY OF ACRONYMS

GEIE	Groupement Européen d'Interêt Economique
GjSM	Gesetz für die Verbreitung jugendgefährdender Schriften und Medieninhalte
ICAA	Instituto de Cinematografia y Artes Audiovisuales
IDL	Independent Data Lines
INCORE	Internet Content Rating for Europe
IRD	Integrated Receiver Coder
A.G.E.	Associazione Genitori
ANICA	Associazione Nazionale Industrie Cinematografiche Audiovisive e Multimediali
API	Application Programme Interface
ASAI	Advertising Standards Authority of Ireland
ATSC	Advanced Television Systems Committee
ATR	Agrupación de Telespectadores y Radioyentes
AUC	Asociación Usuarios de Comunicación
AUI	Asociación de Usuarios de Internet
AVP	Audiovisual Platform
BACC	Broadcast Advertising Clearing Centre
BBFC	British Board of Film Classification
BPjS	Bundesprüfstelle für jugendgefährdende Schriften
BSC	Broadcasting Standards Commission (formerly the Broadcasting Standards Council)
CCE	Comissão de Classificação de Espectáculos
CCE	Comissão de Classificação de Espectáculos
CCPC	Comisión de Calificación de Películas Cinematográficas
CEACCU	Confederación Española de Asociaciones de Amas de Casa consumidores y Usuarios
CICF	Commission intercommunautaire de contrôle des films
CNC	Centre National de la Cinématographie
CNP	Conseil national des programmes
CNU	Consiglio Nazionale degli Utenti
CRI	Divisie Centrale Recherche Informatie
CSA	Conseil supérieur de l'audiovisuel
DAVIC	Digital Audio-Visual Council
CvdM	Commissariaat voor de Media
DPR	Decreto Presidente della Repubblica
DR	Danmarks Radio
DTI	Department of Trade and Industry

DVB	Digital Video Broadcasting
EACEM	European Asociation of Consumer Electronics Manufacturers
EBU	European Broadcasting Union
ECHR	European Court of Human Rights
ECJ	European Court of Justice
EFTA	European Free Trade Association
EPG	Eletronic Programme Guide
ETS	Enhances Teletext Specification
FSF	Freiwillige Selbstkontrolle Fernsehen
FSK	Freiwillige Selbstkontrolle der Filmwirtschaft
FSM	Freiwillige Selbstkontrolle Multimedia Dienstanbieter e.V.
IRTC	Independent Radio and Television Commission
ISPA	Internet Service Providers Association
ISPA	Internet Service Providers Austria
ITC	Independent Television Commission
IuKDG	Informations- und Kommunikationsdienstegesetz
IWF	Internet Watch Foundation
IWGCR	International Working Group on Content Rating
JÖSCHG	Fesetz zum Schutz der Jugend in der Öffentlichkeit
MCCY	Media Council for Children and Young People
MPAA	Motion Picture Association of America
NFC	Nederlandse Federatie Cinematografie
NFK	Nederlandse Filmkeuring
NICAM	Nederlandse Instituut Classificatie Audiovisule Media
NLIP	Nederlandse Vereniging van Internet Providers
NORDICOM	Nordic Information Centre for Media and Communication Research
NOS	Nederlandse Omreopstichting
NTC	National Telecommunications Commission
NVDO	Nederlandse Video Detaillisten Organisatie
NVGD	Nederlandse Vereniging Grammafoonplaten Detailhandelaren
NVPI	Nederlandse Vereniging van Producenten en Importeurs van beeld- en geluidsdragers
ORF	Österreichischer Rundfunk
PDC	Programme Delivery Control
PICS	Platform for Internet Content Selection
RAI	Radiotelevisione Italiana
RSACi	Recreational Software Advisory Council
RTE	Radio Telefís Éireann
RvtV	Raad van Toezicht Videovoorlichting
SCA	Secretariado do Cinema e do Audivisual

SRC	Stichting Reclame Code
TIVEKE	TIetoVErkkojen Kehittämishanke
TUPS	Testo Unico di Pubblica Sicurezza
TVI	Televisisão Independente
UNESCO	United Nations Educational, Scientific, and Cultural Organisation
USK	Unterhaltungssoftware Selbstkontrolle
VBI	Vertical Blanking Interval
VESTRA	Vereniging voor Satelliet, Televisie, radio programma Aanbieders
VSC	Video Standards Council
VUD	Verband der Unterhaltungssoftware Deutschland e.V.
WOF	Wet op Filmvertoningen
WSS	Wide Screen Signalling
YLE	Yleisradio

Author Index

A–C

Andersen, N., 124
Aufdeheide, 120
Balkin, J., 46
Bovill, M., 11
Buckingham, D., 123
Collins, R., 22

D–F

Dyson, R.A., 120
Federman, J., 43, 48, 52, 53, 116

G–K

Goldberg, D., 22
Hamilton, J., 116
Herman, G., 111
Hobbs, R., 120, 122, 123
Kinghorn, J.R., 6

L–M

Leyens, J.P., 111

Livingstone, S., 11
Martin, C.D., 50
Millwood-Hargrave, A., 115

P–R

Prosser, T., 22
Reagle, J.M., 50
Resnick, P., 34
Roberts, D.F., 49

S–V

Surlin, S., 116
Theunert, H., 26
Ventura, G., 124
Verhulst, S., 22

W–Y

Wiseman, A., 15
Wurtzel, A., 116
Yoshida, J., 34

Subject Index

Alta Autoridad para a Comunicaçao, 78
Application Program Interface (API), xix, 23, 32–34, 38
Association for Media Education in Scotland, 130
Audioband, 13
Austria
  cinema rating systems, 60, 61, 63
  digital television, 26
  media education, 125
  television rating systems, 77, 79
  video rating systems, 69, 70
  visual icons, 82, 86, 92

B

BBC, 30, 114, 121
Belgium
  cable and satellite penetration, 18, 26
  cinema rating systems, 61
  Flemish Community, 78, 82, 89, 91
  French Community, 92, 78
  German Community, 78
  social efficiency of rating, 111
  television rating systems, 78, 79, 81
  video rating systems, 70
  visual icons, 92, 84, 86, 87, 91, 92
Blocking see also Filtering and Screening, 17
  activity, 3
  approach, 95, 96
  capacity, xii, xiii
  device, 5, 120
  environment, 30, 93
  functions, 8, 10
  kit, 14
  mechanism, xii, xvii, 22, 24
  programme (s), 12, 26, 27, 31, 41, 109
  regimes, xii
  videocassettes, 46
British Board of Film Classification, 30, 59
British Film Institute (BFI), 126
Broadcaster
  accountability, xv
  carry governmental rating, xxii
  carry third party rating, xvii, xxii, 45, 47
  independence, 47
  rating, xvii, xxii, 39, 47, 77–90
  responsibility, xiii, xiv, xviii, xxiii, xxiv, 2, 35, 56, 93, 94
  self-censor, 78
  self-rate, xxii, 37
  self-regulation, xxiv
Broadcasting see also Television
  analogue, 21, xiv, xviii, 5, 8
  Interoperability, 7, 31–35
  digital, xv, xvi, 5, 8, 27, 47, 93–105
  enhanced broadcasting, 33
  European market, 3, 52
  labelling systems, 78
  media literacy efforts, 121
  public broadcasting, 12, 43
  pay-per-view, 19, 20, 21, 30, 36, 81, 93, 94
  standards adoption, 22, 30, 33
  transfrontier or cross border, 44, 45, 91
Broadcasting Standards Commission, 114

C

Canada, xi, xiii–xvii, 2
Canadian Association of Media Education Organisations (CAMEO), 120
Canadian Radio and Telecommunications Committee, 3
Catholic Communications Centre (Ireland), 129
Censor, 69, 115
Censorship, 48, 43, 59, 80, 87
  niche-filtering, xxi
  self-, 78
  upstream, xii
Center for Media Literacy, 120
Centre de Liaison de l'Enseignement et des Moyens d'Information, 128
Centre National de la Cinématographie, 60
Centre Régional de Documentation Pédagogique (CRDP), 127
Cine-Clubs, France, 127
Cinema, see also Film, 18, 19, 71, 74
  rating/regulatory approaches, 2, 3, 43–48, 51, 53, 58–68

warning systems, 55–57
Cinematograph Commission, 60
Channel-hopping, 39–42, 121
Comissão de Classificação de Espectáculos, 60
Commission de surveillance, 60
Commission intercommunautaire de contrôle des films, 60
Communidades Autónomas (Catalonia), 60
Conseil Supérieur de l'audiovisuel (CSA), 69, 78
Consumer Electronics Manufacturers, Association (USA), 26
Convergence, 36, 37
Creating Critical Viewers, 124

D

Denmark
    cable and satellite penetration, 18
    cinema rating systems, 63, 64
    media literacy, 125
    television rating systems, 76, 79, 81
    video rating systems, 68, 70
Digital Application Programme Interface, xix, 23, 32–35, 38
Digital Audio-Visual Council (DAVIC), xix, 7, 23, 25, 32, 33, 38
Digital Video Broadcasting (DVB), xix, 6, 23, 25, 30–34, 38
Directives
    86/529/EEC, 22
    92/38/EEC, 22
    Advanced Standards Television, 30
    Television Without Frontiers, xiii, 3, 91

E

Education Department of Sveriges Radio, 131
Electronic Programme Guides, xiii, xviii, xix, xxii, 7, 26, 27, 30, 32, 36, 38, 42, 45, 56, 98, 104
    analogue, 14–22
    digital, 22–24
    NexTView, xv, xix, 14–18, 22, 30, 34, 47
    Programme Delivery Control, 15
    whitelist, xvii, 15, 39, 41, 42,121
Encryption, 45, 80
    encrypted channels, 2, 79
    encrypted services, 81, 93
    unencrypted channels, 79, 80
England, see also United Kingdom
    media education, 125–126

European Association for Audio-visual Media Education AEEMA/EAAME, 124
European Association of Consumers (EACEM), xix, 9, 22,
European Commission, xi, xvi, xix, xx, 34, 44, 65, 105, 124
European Parliament, 124, xvi

F

Film, see also Cinema
    media education
        Denmark, 125
        England, 125
        Finland, 126
        France, 127
        Germany, 128–129
        Scotland, 130
        Sweden, 131
        United Kingdom, 121
    rating systems, 1, 2, 46–47, 58–68
    social efficiency of ratings, 111–118
Filtering, see also Blocking and Screening
    administration, 47–49
    advisory information trigger, 1, 3, 5
    content assessment, 50–52
    digital, 30–32, 36, 55, 94–105
    EPG, 15, 24, 27, 36
    mechanisms, xvii, xviii
    pluralistic, xx–xxiii
    programme delivery control (PDC), 15
    programmes filtered in, 14
    regulatory control, 109
    technologies, xvi
    voluntary, xix
Finland
    acoustic warnings, 81
    cable and satellite penetration, 18
    digital setting, 95
    media education, 126–127
    television rating systems, 77, 79
    video rating systems, 68–70
    visual icons, 82, 86, 92
Finnish Broadcasting Company, 127
Finnish Newspaper Publisher's Association, 126
Federal Communications Commission (FCC), 23
Freiwillige Selbstkontrolle der Filmwirtschaft (FSK), 59, 68

Freedom
  content providers, 90
  of expression, xi, xii
  of speech, 107
  viewer, 68

              G

Gateways
  analogue, 7
  converged, 18, 22
  d-box, 23
  EPG, 22–24, 26, 27, 30–32, 36, 38, 40,
      42, 45, 56, 88, 104, 121
  set-top box, xiv, xix, 7, 16
Germany
  analogue shut-off, 21
  cable and satellite penetration, 18
  cinema rating systems, 59–64
  media education, 123, 128, 129
  online rating, 53, 72–74
  rating administration, 47
  rating classification, 51
  television, 78, 87, 89, 90
    digital satellite, 26
    encrypted services, 81
  video rating systems, 68
  visual icons, 82, 86, 91
  watershed, 80
Greece
  cable and satellite penetration, 18
  cinema rating systems, 61, 62, 68
  informational content assessment, 52
  rating administration, 48
  television rating systems, 78
  video rating systems, 69
  visual icons, 86, 91
  watershed, 80

              I

Information Transmission
  direct, 5
  indirect, 5
Institute du Language Total,127
Institut Für Publizistik der Universitat Mainz,
      128
Institut Jugend Film Fernsehen,129
Instituto de Cinematografía y Artes
      Audiovisuales, 60
Internet, see also Online Services
  children with, 11
  convergence, 36, 37

  media education,120–122
  metadata, xviii
  PICS, xxii, 34
  self-rating, 47, 48, 100, 101
  third party rating, 36, 102, 103
Internet Watch Foundation, 36, 76
Ireland
  acoustic warnings, 81
  cable and satellite penetration, 18
  cinema rating systems, 63
  conversion system, 95
  media education, 129
  providing programming related informa-
      tion, 40
  television rating systems, 78
  video rating systems, 68
  visual icons, 82, 91
  watershed, 80
Italy
  cable and satellite penetration, 18, 21
  cinema rating systems, 61, 63–65
  media education, 129
  online services, 72, 74
  rating administration, 47
  social efficiency of ratings, 111, 113–114
  television rating systems, 77
  video rating systems, 71
  visual icons, 82, 86, 87, 92
  watershed, 80
ITC, 114
IT-RA, 51, 74–76

              J

Jugendfilmkommission, 61
Just Think Foundation, 124

              K

Kaiser Family Foundation, 118–119

              L

Labelling, see also Rating
  bit capacity, 8
  cinema rating systems, 1, 2, 58–68
  economic efficiency, 72–77
  information-poor, 27
  judgement, 52–55
  media education, 1, 119
  nongovernmental labelling groups, xxiv
  North American labelling schemes, xvi
  online services, 72–77

programme information, xiv, xxi
standardized programme information
    syntax, 34, 35
social efficiency, 110–118
television rating systems, 2, 77–90
third party, xxii, 36
transition to digital, 5, 36–37
V-chip, 3–5
video, 68–72
LEONARDO DA VINCI, 124
Luxembourg
    cable and satellite penetration, 18
    cinema rating systems, 63, 69
    television rating systems, 77
    video rating systems, 71
    visual icons, 86, 92
    watershed, 80

M

Maastricht Treaty, 124
Mass Media Entertainment Project, 126
Media Literacy, xiv, xvi, xix, xx, xxiii, xxiv, 1,
    119
    media education
        Austria, 125
        Denmark, 125
        England, 125–126
        Finland, 126
        France, 127
        Germany, 128–129
        Ireland, 129
        Italy, 130
        Netherlands, 130
        Scotland, 130
        Spain, 131
        Sweden, 131
    recommendations, 120–124
Media Literacy Online Project, 120
Motion Picture Association (MPAA), 117, 118
The Movie Mom, 122

N

National Board of General Education, Finland,
    126
National Institut Für Film Und Bild im
    Wissenschaft und Unterricht, 129
National Media Research Association
    (Denmark), 125
Nederlandse Filmkeuring (NRK), 60
Netherlands
    acoustic warnings, 81
    cable and satellite penetratrion, 18

cinema rating systems, 60, 61, 63, 65
media education, 130
television rating systems, 77
video rating systems, 71
visual icons, 82, 86, 92
watershed, 80

O

Online (Services), see also Internet
    information about television content, 40,
        121
    media education, 119–131
    rating administration, 47–49
    rating classification, 51, 53
    rating solutions, 72–77
    visual warnings, 56

P

Parent(al)
    choice, xi–xxv
        digital environment, 22–32
        convergence, 36, 37
        EPG, 14–24
        gateways, 7
        information transmission, 56
        need for a pipe or pathway, 6, 7
        positive approaches, xvii, xviii, 38
        transition from analogue to digital, 5
    education, xix, xxiv, xxv, 119–131
    responsibility, xxiii, 95
    social efficiency of ratings
        Belgium, 111
        France, 111–113
        Italy, 113–114
        United Kingdom, 114–116
        United States, 116–118
    supervision, xi, xiii, 109
Philips Semiconductors, 6
Platform for Internet Content Selection (PICS),
    xxii, 34, 37, 74
Portugal
    acoustic warnings, 81
    cable and satellite penetration, 18
    cinema rating systems, 60, 61, 63, 68
    rating administration, 47, 48
    television, 78
    video, 68
    visual icons, 82, 83, 86, 87, 92
    watershed, 80
Province Advisory Board, 60

R

Rating(s)
  classification, 50–55
  compulsory, 24, 38, 69, 102
  descriptive, xiii, xxi, xxiii, 46, 52–57, 72,
    76, 92–98, 100, 102, 103
  criteria, xix, 24, 34, 42, 74, 96, 98,
    101, 103
  deterministic, 50–52, 57, 63, 103
  digital transition, xv
  evaluative, xiii, xx, xxi, 13, 46, 51,
    52–55, 57, 61, 72–74, 91, 92, 94–97
  informational, xviii, 52–55
  information-poor, 27
  information-rich, 27
  information syntax, 34, 42
  judgemental, xi, 3, 8, 13, 53, 54, 96
  nondeterministic, 50–52, 57, 63, 87, 90
  pluralistic, xiii, xvii, xxiv, 44, 52, 55,
    101–103
  self- see also self-regulation, xx, xxii,
    xxiii, xxiv
  self-disclosure, 48–49
  semideterministic, 50–52, 57, 63, 72, 90
  third party, xvi, xvii, xx–xxiii, 7, 16, 24,
    36, 37, 39, 42, 45, 47–49, 52,
    100–103, 121, 122
  video, 68–71
  vocabulary, xix, 30, 55, 59, 61, 69, 72,
    74, 86, 89
  voluntary, xix, 30, 55, 59, 61, 69, 72, 74,
    86, 89
Recreational Software Advisory Council
    (RSAC), 48, 51, 76
Regulation see also Rating and Labelling
  cinema, 45, 48, 68
  content, xiv
  digital setting, 94
  economic efficiency, 108–110
  online, 72
  self-, xvi, xxiv, 36, 46, 59, 72, 73, 76,
    104, 108
  social efficiency, 110–118
  television, 45, 78, 81, 86
  video, 45, 48

S

Scotland
  media literacy, 123, 130
Scottish Council for Education Technology, 130
Scottish Film Council, 130

Screen It! Entertainment Reviews for Parents,
    122
Screening, see also Filtering, Blocking
  digital, 30, 36
  pluralist(ic), xviii–xxi, 30
  pre-, 55
Secretariado do Cinema e do Audiovisual
    (SCA), 61, 64
Self-regulation, xvi, xxiv, 36, 46, 59, 72, 73,
    76, 104, 108
Set-top box, xiii–xvii, xix, 7, 16, 18, 23, 26, 27,
    32
  d-box, 26
SOCRATES, 124
SORGEM, 112
Spain
  acoustic warnings, 81
  analogue shut-off, 21
  cable and satellite penetration, 18
  cinema rating systems, 60–63, 68
  European ratings conversion, 95, 96
  media education, 131
  online services ratings systems, 74
  preselection EPG, 57
  television
    classification system, 45
    rating systems, 77, 78
    visual icons, 82, 84, 86, 87, 90, 91, 94
  third party, 101
  video rating systems, 68, 71
  watershed, 80
Standards
  DAVIC, 25, 30
  DVB, 25, 30
  DVB-SI Digital Video Broadcasting
    Service, 31–32
  MPEG-2, 30, 31
  MPEG-5, 33
Statens biografbyrå, 60
Sweden
  acoustic warnings, 81
  analogue shut-off, 21
  cable and satellite penetration, 18, 26
  cinema rating systems, 63–65
  digital broadcasting, 27
  media education, 131
  television rating systems, 77
  video rating systems, 68, 69, 71
  visual icons, 82, 86, 89
  watershed, 80

T

Teletext, 9–13
    bit capacity, 7–8
    Enhanced Teletext Specifications (ETS),
        9
    Independent Data Lines, 12
    packet 8/30, format 9, 6
    packet 6, 9, 12
    VPS, 6
    Wide Screen Signalling (WSS), 6, 12–13
Television, *see also* Broadcasting
    analogue, xiii, xv, 7, 16
    cable, xv
    channel allegiance, xxiii
    digital, xv, xvi, xvii, 7, 16, 18, 25–30, 34,
        36, 37, 100
    pay-per-view, 19, 20, 21, 30, 36, 81, 93,
        94
    replacement, 16, 17
    rating effectiveness
        France, 111–113
        United Kingdom, 114–116
        United States, 116–118
    rating systems, 18, 60, 93–106
    satellite, 21
The Television Project, 123
Third Party
    entities, 36, 100–103
    labellers, 37
    programme packages, 16
    providers, xvii, xx, xxii, xxiii, 24, 42, 45
    rating, xxi, xxii, 7, 37, 39, 48, 49, 52,
        100–102
    rating systems, xvi
Time-shifting, 8, 10, 12
    set-shifting, 12
Transparency, xx, xxi, 44, 49, 52, 64, 96
Treaty of Amsterdam, xix

U

United Kingdom
    cinema rating systems, 59, 63–65
    digital terrestrial television, 27, 37

    evaluative ratings, 53–55
    media literacy, 120
    online rating classifications, 51
    online rating systems, 72, 76
    satellite, 26
    social efficiency of rating systems, 111,
        114–116
    television rating systems, 80–82
    television replacement, 16–17
    transfrontier rating systems, 45
    V-chip, xiv
    video rating systems, 68
    visual icons, 82, 86, 91
United Kingdom Film Education, 121
United States, xi, xiii, xiv, xv, xvi, xvii, xx, 2,
        3, 23, 25, 49, 51, 53, 74, 110, 111
    media education, 122
    rating social efficiency, 116–118
Unterhaltungssofware Sebstkontrolle (USK)
        72–74

V

Valtion elokuvatarkastamo, 80
V-chip, xiii, xiv, xv, xvi, xxii, 3, 4, 6, 9, 13, 25,
        117, 118
Vertical Blanking Interval (VBI), xiv, xv, 4, 6,
        12

W

Warning(s)
    acoustical, xii, xviii, 45, 55, 56, 78, 81,
        89, 91, 111, 112
    text, xviii, 71
    visual, 43, 45, 55–57, 69, 78, 81–84, 86,
        91–93, 111–113
Watershed, xxiii, xxiv, 2, 36, 43, 45, 56,
        79–81, 89, 114–116

Y

YTV Canada, Inc., 136